The Cristal Experiment

The Cristal Experiment

A Chicano Struggle for Community Control

Armando Navarro

THE UNIVERSITY OF WISCONSIN PRESS

The University of Wisconsin Press
2537 Daniels Street
Madison, Wisconsin 53718

3 Henrietta Street
London WC2E 8LU, England

Printed in the United States of America

Library of Congress Cataloging-in-Publication Data
Navarro, Armando, 1941–
    The Cristal experiment : a Chicano struggle for community control
/ Armando Navarro.
    456 pp.   cm.
    Includes bibliographical references and index.
    ISBN 0-299-15820-9 (cloth: alk. paper).
ISBN 0-299-15824-1 (pbk. alk. paper)
    1. Mexican Americans—Texas—Crystal City—Politics and
History—20th century. 3. Crystal City (Tex.)—Politics and
government. 4. Crystal City (Tex.)—Ethnic relations. I. Title.
F394.C83N37   1998
976.4'437—dc21   98–17431

This book is dedicated to the memory of
César Chávez,
a friend, a nonviolent warrior,
who inspired me and others to become involved
in the struggle for social justice

Contents

Preface

This book is a case study of two electoral revolts that occurred in 1963 and 1970 in the small, dusty, and rural community of Crystal City, Texas, or Cristal, as it is known in Spanish by Mexicanos.[1] These political takeovers were experiments in what I call the *politics of community control*, meaning control over the local government structures and public policy process. Both are of historical significance to the study of Chicano and local politics for different reasons, which this book will examine. At the core, however, is that in both revolts Mexicanos wrested political control from the local gringo power holders.[2]

The revolts occurred during the tumultuous "epoch of protest" (1955–1974). They were products of exogenous and endogenous antagonisms, which by 1965 gave rise to the Chicano Movement. The pervasiveness of political activism, conventional and unconventional, and the concomitant calls for change, impelled all the movements—civil rights, New Left, antiwar, Black Power—of the 1960s.[3] This was a time of protest, militancy, and social unrest. For Mexicanos the Chicano Movement was a repudiation of accommodation- and assimilation-oriented politics. It fostered a political and cultural renaissance that was predicated on *Chicanismo*.[4] To some Mexicano activists references to *El Movimiento* and *La Causa* were calls for self-determination, for a Chicano nation, *Aztlán*, whereas others regarded such language as a call for reformation of the existing social order.[5]

At the heart of the Cristal experiment was self-determination, Mexicanos' having control over their political destiny. After decades of political subordination and powerlessness, Mexicanos in Cristal shook up the gringo power holders of Texas in 1963 by winning control of the town's city council and holding it for two years. But it was not until the second revolt, in 1970, that the subordination and powerlessness of the Mexicano community really began to change. The differences between the two experiments were partly a reflection of a changing political climate. Whereas the 1963 revolt occurred at the height of the civil rights movement, the 1970 revolt coincided with the apex of social

★ Austin

Del Rio   Nueces River   • San Antonio

• Uvalde

Eagle
Piedras • • Pass   • Crystal City
Negras
Carrizo   • Cotulla
Springs

Corpus
Christi

Nuevo • • Laredo
Laredo

Brownsville

Matamoros •

Map of South Texas

protest and radicalism. The two political takeovers differed in leadership, ideology, organization, and strategy and tactics. Specifically, the first revolt was much more spontaneous, ephemeral, and accommodationist in its struggle for change, whereas the second revolt lasted longer and was the product of a the Mexican American Youth Organization's Winter Garden Project, a well-calculated plan of action oriented toward decolonization of Mexicanos in south Texas.

This book comes at a propitious time. Latinos, especially Mexicanos, are fast becoming the majority population in numerous local communities throughout Aztlán and the nation. Latinos have reached a level of political sophistication that makes the existence of a plethora of

Cristals inevitable. This demographic "browning of America" is engendering the "re-Mexicanization" of Aztlán. Hence, this book is partly inspired by this new historical reality, that Latinos in the twenty-first century will be able to multiply the Cristals many hundredfold.

I believe this book provides the most comprehensive analysis of community control and the Cristal experiment to date. It goes beyond John Shockley's *Chicano Revolt in a Texas Town* (1974), which provides a well-written account of Cristal's politics from 1963 to 1973. This book is an expansion of my dissertation, a bifurcated in-depth case study of the Mexican American Youth Organization (1967–1972), the Raza Unida Party's second revolt, and its peaceful revolution (1970–1973). In 1973 my family and I spent four months in Cristal while I conducted my research. It was exciting and satisfying to witness and examine what I believe was one of the most important political struggles produced by the Chicano Movement. I was able to observe and interview the Raza Unida Party's leadership, supporters, and adversaries and participate in its activities. In short, I experienced the dynamism of a community control experiment that sought to empower people and bring about massive change.

While at the University of Utah I conducted additional research trips to Cristal in 1974 and I was there again in 1975, at the apogee of the political fractiousness. I had planned to produce a case study of the Raza Unida Party's peaceful revolution. However, because of the growing schisms that led to its political breakdown in 1975, I decided to suspend my research. I felt that the study would be counterproductive and would add to the growing controversies and conflict. After fifteen years (1977–1992) as a community organizer, I returned to academia full time and resumed my research on the Mexican American Youth Organization and the Raza Unida Party. I revisited Cristal in 1995 and spent two weeks working in archives and interviewing former Raza Unida Party leaders and adversaries.

This book is long overdue. I have tried to be as objective as possible and to put aside my biases and prejudices. I say this because I am a product of the Chicano Movement. Like José Angel Gutiérrez and other Mexicano scholars today, my scholarship and activism have always been intertwined and inseparable. I make no apology that my analysis is hypercritical of the gringo power holders and the liberal capitalist system.[6] Concomitantly, however, because of my commitment to scholarship I have developed an analysis that comes to grips with the good and the bad of both community control experiments. My findings provide various lessons that I believe bring new thought to the theory and practice of community control. Thus, although I believe this book is a comprehensive examination of the Cristal experiment and community control, much more research needs to be done.

This book is part of a four-volume series that I have committed to finish before the year 2000. The volumes are interrelated and complement each other. My first book, entitled *Mexican American Youth Organization: Avant-Garde of the Chicano Movement in Texas* (1995), is an in-depth case study of the Mexican American Youth Organization from 1967 to 1972. This is my second work. *The Cristal Experiment: A Chicano Struggle for Community Control* picks up where the first book left off. The third book is to be called *Third-Party Movements in the United States: The Rise and Fall of the Raza Unida Party*. It will provide an in-depth case study of third-party movements, especially the Raza Unida Party (RUP), and will examine the prospects for a new Latino or multiethnic-multiracial party in the twenty-first century. The fourth book is to be entitled *What Is to Be Done? The Building of a New Movement* and will provide a comprehensive analysis of the mechanics of building a new mass movement that is oriented toward the reformation of the liberal capitalist system.

Research Methodology

My research methodology relies on primary and secondary sources. I used three research methods: in-depth interviews; content analysis of numerous primary and secondary sources (diaries, letters, minutes, newspapers, magazines, journal articles); and participation-observation of participants. From 1973 to 1993 I conducted fifty-nine in-depth interviews with Mexican American Youth Organization and Raza Unida Party leaders. In particular, during the twenty years I interviewed José Angel Gutiérrez, the driving force behind the second revolt, for more than twenty hours on a myriad of related topics. During my two-week stay in Cristal in 1995 I did thirty more in-depth interviews with key RUP leaders, influential community members, and adversaries. By early 1996 I had conducted six more interviews, bringing the total to ninety-five. In addition, while in Cristal in 1973 and 1995 I conducted extensive research in RUP's archives at the local library. In 1993 I spent a week in the library at the University of Texas at Austin where I examined more than forty boxes of the personal papers of José Angel Gutiérrez. Among the documents I analyzed were his diary, letters, personal position papers, legal briefs, and a plethora of newspaper, magazine, and journal articles. I also reviewed back copies of Cristal's only newspaper, the *Zavala County Sentinel*, on microfilm for 1970–1981. Moreover, as a participant-observer during my visits to Cristal in 1973, 1974, and 1975, I gained insight into the dynamics and interworkings of RUP's politics of community control and peaceful revolution. This contributed significantly to the development of my analysis.

Acknowledgments

First and foremost, I am indebted to the people of Cristal for their support in conducting the research for this study. Without their cooperation and willingness to participate in the numerous interviews and "platicas" that I conducted on various aspects of the Cristal Experiment, there would have been no book. My appreciation and thanks go to the numerous Raza Unida Party leaders and supporters, city, county, and school officials for their cooperation and inspiration. Their sincerity and commitment to the Raza Unida Party's struggle for social change, empowerment, and community control were exemplary. I salute them, for they inspired the building of a stronger Chicano Movement. Through their actions they demonstrated that Mexicanos in the United States have the capacity, courage, and will to control their political destiny.

I would like to specifically thank José Angel Gutiérrez and his former wife, Luz, for the hospitality and support they exhibited to my family during our four-month stay in Cristal in 1973. Moreover, I want to acknowledge their cooperation, along with that of Viviana Santiago, in allowing me to interview and have access to them in subsequently answering innumerable questions on various aspects of the Cristal Experiment. José Angel alone was interviewed several times during the course of my research. My gratitude goes to the various city, county, and school officials who cooperated during my subsequent visits to Cristal in 1974, 1976, and 1994. I would be remiss if I did not also thank the publisher and editor of the *Zavala County Sentinel*, Dale Barker, as well as those who opposed the Raza Unida Party for their assistance.

Beyond the people of Cristal, there are numerous other people to whom I am indebted. My appreciation goes to my family, grandchildren, brother and sisters, and nieces and nephews, who have always been a source of support and inspiration. Moreover, I would like to recognize those who through their scholarly input assisted me in this intellectual endeavor. I want to express my gratitude to scholars Rodolfo Acuña and Ignacio Garcia, who reviewed the initial manuscript and advised me on how to improve it. I am appreciative of the superb final editing done by Polly Kummel.

At the University of California, Riverside, I want to recognize the intellectual and moral support given to me by Carlos Vélez-Ibáñez, Dean of the College of Humanities, Arts, & Social Sciences, and political scientist Max Neiman for his suggestions on developing the study's conceptual framework on community control. I especially want to thank and recognize Maria Anna Gonzales for her incisive suggestions, which greatly improved the quality of the manuscript, and for her invaluable editing. My appreciation also goes to Marcella Ruiz for having transcribed the numerous interviews, Pamela Norman for having typed and assisted in the editing of the manuscript, and Felix Martel for his assistance in conducting the research during our two week stay in Cristal in 1994. I would also like to acknowledge the support of my colleagues, particularly that of Professor Cliff Trafzer, in the Department of Ethnic Studies. This acknowledgment would not be complete if I did not recognize the generosity of UC Mexus, under the leadership of Director Juan-Vicente Palerm, for giving me the grant that allowed me to complete my research.

Lastly, I want to extend my appreciation to all those whom I have met and worked with in the struggle for the betterment and empowerment of our people. I cannot forget to thank my friends and fellow activists who have also been a source of encouragement and motivation. To them, I want to say muchismas gracias por todo el apoyo que me han dado atravez de los años. Que siga la lucha por nuestro pueblo.

The Cristal Experiment

Introduction: Community Control as a Conceptual Framework

During the epoch of protest (1955–1974) Mexicanos in Crystal City, Texas, in 1963 and again in 1970 experimented with the concept of community control. After decades of internal colonialism they rejected their political subordination and powerlessness.[1] The two historically unprecedented political takeovers form the basis of what I describe in this book as the Cristal experiment. Before community control became popular in the mid- and late 1960s, Mexicanos in Crystal City (hereafter Cristal, as used by Mexicanos) took control of the city council by winning all five seats that were in contention in 1963. Although this council's term of office was short-lived (1963–1965), many have perceived it as setting a political precedent, the first electoral revolt by Mexicanos in south Texas (or Aztlán, for that matter).

In 1970 the Mexicanos of Cristal once again opted for what they believed was community control. This time they won control of both the city council and school board. This political takeover was different from the first in that Mexicanos in Cristal used a third party, La Raza Unida [A United People] to execute their community control strategy. Thus the Raza Unida Party in Cristal initiated the peaceful revolution grounded in the pursuit of community control. One consequence of the second revolt was that the Chicano Movement incorporated the idea of community control in its lexicon and agenda.

Far too many works written about the Chicano Movement are essentially descriptive and omit exploration of its theoretical underpinnings. I hope to remedy that oversight.

Community Control: Nurtured by the Fury of Protest

The 1960s, known as the epoch of protest, were a product of both exogenous and endogenous forces. This turbulent era produced several protest movements that shook the nation's political institutions and structures. Activists of various ideological persuasions and from ethnic

3

and racial groups sought to change—through reform or radical transformation—the political, economic, social, and even cultural fabric of
the United States. Critical of the capitalist system and often divided
on questions of ends and means, especially from 1962 to 1974, radical
as well as reform-minded activists were instrumental in putting the
development of community control on their change-oriented agendas.
The viability of community control as a political mechanism was facili-
tated by the emergence of the civil rights movement and the New Left
during the late 1950s.

The New Left, defiant of the "Old Left," was one of the great political surprises of the mid-twentieth century. It arose suddenly, in the
wake of the conformism that permeated what scholar John P. Diggins
describes as the "politically silent generation of the fifties." Diggins
characterizes the New Left as "something of a historical mutation" that
defied the Old Left.[2] The New Left was a group of young, essentially
middle-class, activists who were often jaded by affluence and disillusioned by the contradictions of a capitalist system. They became
involved in the civil rights movement and began to identify their
struggle with that of the working class. New Left activists claimed to
be chained to neither doctrine nor history. They unequivocally rejected
the old Marxist leftists as sellouts and dogmatically ideological. Initially, the New Left was primarily a nonideological, reformist, and de-
centralized movement. But by the late 1960s it came to embrace Marxist doctrine and was increasingly radical and structured.

During the reformist formative years of the New Left, participatory
democracy was at the top of its agenda, although it got there gradually.[3] The New Left's involvement in the struggle to desegregate the
South was instrumental in developing its antiestablishment posture.
The New Left believed that the two-party system in the United States
was a sham designed to protect the power monopoly of the corporate
rulers, that "bourgeois democracy" was merely an instrument of class
oppression, that the task of the activist was to tear the liberal mask
from the tyrant's face, and that the New Left's mission was to lead a
gullible citizenry out of the polling places and into the streets to reform
so-called democratic institutions.[4] Moreover, its involvement with such
civil rights organizations as the Congress of Racial Equality (CORE)
and the Student Nonviolent Coordinating Committee (SNCC) and
their protest and organizing activities—Greensboro in 1960 and the
Freedom Riders of 1961—helped create the political climate that gave
rise to the New Left's commitment to community control.[5]

The emergence of the New Left organization Students for a Democratic Society (SDS) and its call for participatory democracy helped
propel the use of community control as a political tool.[6] In its efforts

to define its direction SDS met at Port Huron, New York, in 1962. Tom Hayden was the principal intellectual architect of the Port Huron Statement. The manifesto, which was critical of the nation's liberal capitalist system, impelled and shaped the New Left's incipient student activism. The document included a social analysis and program for radical change and suggested strategy and tactics for achieving the goals of SDS. The Port Huron Statement described participatory democracy this way: "As a social system we seek the establishment of a democracy of individual participation, governed by two central aims: that the individual share in those decisions determining the quality and direction of his life; that society be organized to encourage independence in men and provide the media for their common participation."[7]

However, the Port Huron Statement was open to interpretation by SDS leaders. To Robert Alan Haber, national secretary for SDS, participatory democracy meant a model, another way of organizing society. To him the statement was, above all, a charge to action, not an ideology or theory. Hayden, who became president of SDS, saw participatory democracy as a way to break the chains of the nation's apathy via action. Bob Ross, an early SDS leader, equated the idea of participatory democracy with embryonic socialism. Steve Max, another SDS leader, thought it was a fine idea but one that could not be achieved under the existing economic structure of the United States. To Max participatory democracy without socialism was impossible.[8]

Regardless, to most activists who identified with the New Left participatory democracy meant that all people (women, ethnic and racial communities, the poor) would have the right to participate. Alienated and disillusioned with traditional electoral politics, the New Left postulated that representative democracy could legitimately serve the interests of all people only if they, the citizenry, participated directly in what political scientist David Easton describes as the "authoritative allocation of values."[9] In their classic work, *The Civic Culture: Democracy in Five Nations* (1963), political scientists Gabriel Almond and Sidney Verba write of the worldwide demand for participatory democracy: "If there is a political revolution going on throughout the world, it is what might be called the participation explosion."[10] If taken literally, participatory democracy means the end of representative government.

By the late 1960s participatory democracy had been embraced by the civil rights, antiwar, Black Power, Chicano, and Native American movements. The idea of involving the masses in making public policy and governing was manifested in bold slogans such as "People Power," "Black Power," "Chicano Power," and "Red Power." Some activists sought inclusion in the existing system, whereas others advocated taking control of local government structures. In 1968 the Kerner Commission excoriated the exclusion of ghetto residents from the decision-making process that affected their lives and community.[11] Martin Luther King Jr., seconding the commission's findings in the wake of the Watts riot in Los Angeles, said, "It is the desperate cry of one who is so fed up with the powerlessness of his existence . . . he would rather be dead than ignored." Through his Industrial Areas Foundation social reformer Saul Alinsky was trying to address just these problems by creating poor peoples' organizations that sought to empower people in the struggle to effect social change.[12]

Meanwhile, Stokely Carmichael and Charles V. Hamilton, as described in their classic *Black Power* (1967), had recognized that gaining increased participation in existing institutions and political structures was not enough. They called for a search for new forms and, if necessary, the creation of parallel community institutions controlled by blacks. The interest in parallel institutions was linked to the idea of community control.[13] By 1966 the civil rights movement had fallen into decline, and the call for community control was becoming louder as black politics became more radicalized.

The federal government, through its promotion of citizen participation, also contributed to the movement toward community control. The federal role dates to the passage of the Housing Act of 1954. This legislation required municipalities, as a condition for receiving federal funds for urban renewal, to show proof of citizen participation. During the mid-1960s the urban policies of the Johnson administration also encouraged citizen participation. But it was with the passage of the Economic Opportunity Act (EOA) of 1964 that the federal government's attitude toward citizen participation changed drastically. The act sought to free about thirty-five million people from poverty in the United States. It was a major weapon in the arsenal of Lyndon Johnson's war on poverty. He believed that by mobilizing all levels of government the United States could eradicate poverty within its borders. His administration created an independent agency, the Office of Economic Opportunity (OEO), to administer the various war on poverty programs.

Among the measures created under the EOA was the Community Action Program (CAP), to be administered by the nonprofit Community Development Corporation (CDC). CAP had essentially three basic objectives in serving poor communities: to provide and improve public services for the poor; mobilize both public and private resources to cope with the problems of poverty; and engage the maximum feasible participation of the poor in carrying out the antipoverty program.[14] According to Bryan T. Downes,

The maximum feasible participation clause mandated by the Economic Opportunity Act fostered a new role for the poor. Citizen involvement in the Community Action Program, it was believed, would bring a new perspective to local problem solving efforts. Public service bureaucracies controlled by middle-class white professionals would be humanized and the poor would have the opportunity to help themselves. . . . It was felt that federal funds could ensure the creation of effective new political organizations of the poor, because of the likely opposition of local elites to the creation of alternative service delivery systems and countervailing power centers.[15]

Complementing the mission of CAP was the establishment of local Community Action Agencies (CAAs). They were the controversial cornerstone at the local level of the war on poverty. The CAAs' governing boards included representatives of the poor, public officials, and private organizations. CAAs could choose from a variety of programs authorized by the Equal Opportunity Commission.

Initially, CAAs were independent of city governments. Their boards of directors were comprised primarily of individuals from impoverished neighborhoods. However, this method of empowering people ultimately fostered conflict between the agencies and city governments. In response, Congress in 1967 passed the Green Amendment to the Economic Opportunity Act. The amendment limited the authority of CAAs and guaranteed city governments one-third representation on the boards of directors. CAAs became more oriented toward improving the delivery of services than to mobilizing citizen participation. Eventually, the Nixon administration dismantled the OEO and transferred the antipoverty programs to other federal agencies. Consequently, by 1974 the CAAs were totally dependent on local governments for their survival.[16]

Nonetheless, CAAs acted as accelerators for the politicization and participation of the poor and disadvantaged. According to Mario Fantini, Marilyn Gittell, and Richard Magut, "The underlying strategy in these efforts was that the poor could best define their own needs and direct the policies of institutions established to serve them."[17] CAAs were aimed not only at increasing goods, income, and education for the poor but also at effecting some redistribution of decision-making power. Thus the war on poverty programs served to further and foster the emerging movement of community control.

However, the idea of directly involving the poor in the decision-making process was not without its vociferous critics. One such scholar was Daniel Patrick Moynihan, who in his book *Maximum Feasible Participation* (1969) argued that placing poor people in control of schools or other government structures simply weighed them down with yet another obligation they were not competent to meet. He was adamant that giving the poor control of institutions would not solve the problem of poverty.

The Quest for Community

The pursuit of participatory democracy did not emanate exclusively from the idealistic New Left, Mexicanos, black activists, or federal government antipoverty programs. It was also impelled by an intellectual renaissance of inquiry, ideas, and theories in the 1960s. Scholars of various disciplines joined in protesting not only the Vietnam War but the validity of this country's political and economic institutions and policies. Debate permeated this nation's universities and colleges, with academics publishing furiously on these and other related issues. The literature of urban politics during the '60s and early '70s reflected a profound interest in community control, what it should mean, and what it meant within the context of U.S. society. Although community control was very much a product of the radicalism of the time, its historical genesis precedes the formation of the United States as a nation-state.

The quest for community control is as old as Western civilization. In Athens during the fifth century B.C. people began to debate the issues associated with majority rule, a community of citizens who directly participated in governing by listening, discussing, and finally voting on issues of public policy. It was at this time that the word *dëmokratia* (democracy) was coined. It came from *dëmos*, meaning "people," and *kratos*, meaning "authority or power."[18]

However, even Athenian democracy fell short of allowing total participation. Only the adult male citizen had the right to attend the general assembly that met ten times a year to enact all laws and elect the state's officers. Women, resident immigrants, and slaves were prohibited from participating in the political process because they were perceived as less capable than the adult male citizen. Control belonged to an elite. Until the eighteenth century, democracy carried unfavorable connotations because the Athenians' example of direct democracy was for many years interpreted to mean unrestrained mob rule.[19]

This view was evident in the writings of the first great political theorist, Aristotle (384–322 B.C.), in his classic *Politics*, which treated democracy as a coherent system of government. Although not opposed to popular sovereignty, Aristotle vehemently objected to extreme direct democracy. To him it lacked the legal structure that protected the rights and interests of the women, resident immigrants, and slaves who comprised the majority. He classified governments into three types: government by the one, government by the few, and government by the many. For each, he postulated, there was a right and/or wrong form. The right form of government was one that served the common interests of the people, whereas the wrong form of government served the personal interests of the ruler. He used the word *polity* to describe government by many to serve the common interests of the people, whereas he used *democracy* to describe government of many to serve their personal interests. He feared democracy because he believed that the pursuit of self-interest would result if governing power were turned over to the "rabble in the streets." Aristotle equated democracy with mobocracy, or rule by the mob.[20]

During the Ages of Reason and Enlightenment of the seventeenth and eighteenth centuries and with the emergence of liberalism, democracy was redefined as a republic, or representative democracy. Writings such as John Locke's *Second Treatise of Civil Government* (1690); Jean-Jacques Rousseau's *Social Contract* (1762); Charles Louis Montesquieu's *The Spirit of the Laws* (1748); and James Madison, Alexander Hamilton, and John Jay's *Federalist Papers* (1777–1788) gave form to representative democracy. Those who framed the Constitution of the United States did not believe that government should be directly in the hands of the people. Instead, they opted for a republic, or representative form of democracy, in which the people govern indirectly by electing representatives who make public policy. In theory these representatives would serve the people's interests.

In the nineteenth century utopian socialists challenged Western political thought on democracy. The writings of socialists such as Robert Owen, Henri Saint-Simon, and François Fourier sought to reconstitute society on a more egalitarian basis. Owen, considered the father of British socialism, was the first to use the concept. All opposed capitalism and opted for some form of cooperativism. They blamed capitalism for the evils of the time—the abuses of the industrial revolution and the restrictions on the ownership of private property. They sought to ameliorate the people's suffering by advocating the equalization of wealth and power. The Marxist theorists and revolutionaries who followed propounded that capitalism suffered certain insoluble contradictions that could only lead to growing pauperization and the eventual collapse of capitalist governments and revolution. The work of these theorists indirectly contributed to the popularization of the concepts of participatory democracy and community control because they emphasized the people—the proletariat in control of the means of production.

The concept of community has historically been a subject of debate and controversy in Western social and political thought; its root traces to Greek idealism, the Athenian *polis*. Like so many other concepts in the social sciences and humanities, *community* has no settled definition. Scholars David W. Minar and Scott Greer, among others, would concur that it is both empirically descriptive of a social structure and normatively toned. They write, "Community is indivisible from human actions, purposes, and values. It expresses our vague yearnings for a commonality of desire, a communion with those around us, an extension of the bonds of kin and friend to all those who share a common fate."[21] To scholar Harold W. PFautz, "Its unique status stems from its anchored position in space, typically connoting an autonomous, inclusive, self-sustaining social system . . . a society." Sociologists generally emphasize one of two approaches to studying community. The first distinguishes community as an ecological order, a product of functional relationships among human groups and institutions that evolve from sharing a common living space. The second distinguishes community as a social order that is the smallest territorial system encompassing the major features of society, that is, a society in miniature.[22] Sociologists draw a distinction between *Gemeinschaft* [community] and *Gesellschaft* [society]. Every society to some degree is a form of community, yet not every community is a functioning society.

What then is community? Simply defined, a community is a collection of people who occupy a given space and share a common social relationship or interest. PFautz writes, "Members of a human community not only reside and act together, they feel and think together."[23] Thus community infers a sense of common identity of feeling, of *we* rather than *I*.

Equally important to the understanding of community control is the concept of control and its relationship to power. Control connotes power, and power denotes control. Political scientists generally concur that the exercise of power is the driving force of politics. Most definitions of power intertwine influence and control. Hans Morganthau's classic *Politics Among Nations* (1967) refers to power as mutual relations of cَntrol among the leaders of public authority and between the leaders and the people. V. O. Key describes politics as power consisting fundamentally of relationships of superordination and subordination, of dominance and submission, of the governors and governed. According to George E. G. Catlin, politics is "the study of the act of control, or . . . the act of human or social control." With a similar view Harold Lasswell defines politics as the study of "influence and the influential." However, the definition perhaps most applicable to the study of community power is Robert Dahl's: "A has power over B to the extent that he can get B to do something that B would not other-wise do."[24]

Power comes in different forms. It can be micro or macro in scope. With micropower an individual's power is based on position, knowledge, money, reputation, specialized skill, and the like. With macropower a nation's power is measured by the size of its army and the sophistication of its weaponry, its gross national product, abundance of natural resources, size of its population, and the like. Similarly, a political organization's power is determined by the size of its membership, its financial resources, and its ability to influence policy. Nations and their government structures and policies—as well as their political parties, interest groups, and corporations (among other entities)—are products of power relationships. Thus no examination of community control as a theory would be complete without an understanding of power—control.

What Is Community Control?

The notion of community is as ill defined as the idea of community control. Many books and articles deal with these concepts yet fail to provide working definitions. Some use community control synony-mously with *decentralization, participation, power sharing, neighborhood government, neighborhood corporations, consumer representation,* and *mini-city halls.*[25] Each term makes different assumptions about the nature of urban government, and each has different ways of dealing with the problems inherent in the urban crisis, especially bureaucratic respon-siveness. What, then, is community control? In essence, as a social the-ory it is the absolute and direct transfer of power to the people. Com-munity control represents a rational problem-solving process and the advancement of the interests of all. It is a process in which everyone shares information, conducts meaningful discussion, and partakes in the decision making.

Scholars such as Alan A. Altshuler, Joseph F. Zimmerman, and Mil-ton Kotler were in the intellectual vanguard of the movement for com-munity control. All were writing in the late 1960s and early 1970s, the epoch of protest, as they sought a redefinition of governance at the local level. They attempted to foster a political reformation that would bring the poor into the decision-making process and decentralize the delivery of services. To Altshuler community control symbolized greater participation by the people in the political and economic lives of their cities. He saw the agenda of reform as including the sharing of as much authority as possible with neighborhood communities; direct

representation of such communities on city councils, boards of education, police commissions, and other significant policy bodies; representation of the formerly disenfranchised in far more than token numbers
at all levels of public service; similar representation in the labor forces
of government contractors; and various applications of public resources to help development of community-controlled businesses.
This formal agenda was accompanied by one that was informal and
sought to reorient the spirit of government with a commitment to pursue racial equality from the perspective of making policy *with* rather
than *for* the public.[26]

Other proponents of community control sought a remodeling of local government structures. Advocates of establishing a federated city
sought a redistribution of political power. Joseph F. Zimmerman proposed that the city government handle such citywide services as water
supply, sewage treatment, and refuse disposal, whereas newly created
neighborhood governments would be responsible for schools, libraries,
health services, neighborhood parks, and day-care centers.[27] Some
scholars described community control as a form of decentralization;
they believed that improving services and decentralizing local government would reduce the alienation of the public and its government.

A principal supporter of neighborhood government was Kotler,
who embraced the idea of self-rule. He believed that the inner-city
slums of the United States were not governed by consent but were
controlled and administered by outside forces. He argued that some
residents of poor neighborhoods saw their communities as "occupied
territories." Kotler, like others, believed that the creation of neighborhood governments would help dissipate the discontent that periodically erupted into civil disorder. With a sense of revolutionary zeal he
said, "We must accept the neighborhood as the source of revolutionary
power and local liberty as its modest cause."[28]

The idea of community control was given further clarity by various
federal government commissions and their public reports. In 1967 the
prestigious Advisory Commission on Intergovernmental Relations, a
panel of federal, state, and local officials, recommended

the enactment of State legislation authorizing large cities and county governments in metropolitan areas to establish neighborhood subunits of government with limited powers of taxation and a local self-government with respect
to specified and restricted functions, including the administration of specified
portions of Federal, State and local programs. Such subunits would be dissolu-
ble by the city or county governing board at any time.[29]

The 1968 report of the Kerner Commission proposed that local governments develop neighborhood action task forces as joint community-

government efforts to achieve more effective communication and improve the delivery of city services to ghetto residents. The commission also urged local government to establish neighborhood outlets for local, state, and federal administrative and public service agencies.[30]

Adherents of neighborhood government supported the establishment of neighborhood city halls. In 1968 the National Commission on Urban Problems (Douglas Commission) had two recommendations for reviving inner-city neighborhoods: accelerate improvement in poor neighborhoods by providing adequate city services, and decentralize municipal services to neighborhood city halls.[31] By 1970 these ideas were becoming reality. A survey released that year by the Center for Governmental Studies and the International City Management Association identified seventy-two cities that had reported the existence of "little city halls" or neighborhood multipurpose centers operating under municipal auspices.

Advocates of community control advance the belief that if people are adequately involved, local institutions and community problem solving will be effective.[32] The idea of community control is predicated on the notion that citizens in a democratic society can and ought to seek redress from bureaucratic tyranny, institutional obsolescence, and the insensitivity of indifferent and self-serving politicians. This was very much the case with the first electoral revolt initiated by Mexicanos in Cristal in 1963.

Part One

The Genesis of the
Cristal Experiment

1

The Electoral Revolt of 1963

The Cristal experiment in community control began in 1963 in the small south Texas town of Crystal City, or Cristal, as it is called by Mexicanos. After years of living under internal colonialism, Mexicanos—who accounted for about 80 percent of the town's population of ninety-one hundred—rebelled politically against the gringo power holders. The revolt was nonviolent, and its weapons were not guns but ballots. This revolt represents the first phase of what I call the Cristal experiment in community control. For the first time in the history of south Texas, five Mexicanos, who became known as "Los Cinco," ran for city council seats and won control of that body. As a result of their unprecedented victory, Cristal became the first community to put in effect the notion of community control. Although the revolt was short-lived, it was instrumental in fostering the dialectical antagonisms that by 1970 yielded a much more powerful Mexicano takeover—the second revolt, which is the focus of the study. This chapter examines the politics of the first revolt and the six years that followed.

Cristal: An Overview

Cristal is located in south Texas between the Nueces and Rio Grande rivers, 120 miles southwest of the city of San Antonio, and about 45 miles from the United States–Mexico border. It is at the heart of a multimillion-dollar agribusiness area called the Winter Garden area.

Rich in soil and watered by the Nueces River, the Winter Garden area is comprised of seven counties—Zavala, Dimmit, Uvalde, Maverick, Val Verde, Kinney, and La Salle. Cristal grows various winter vegetables, but it is best known for its spinach crops. In fact, it calls itself the Spinach Capital of the World—a six-foot statue of Popeye stands in front of city hall.

Cristal's history is crucial to the analysis of the Cristal experiment. Unlike numerous other communities throughout Aztlán, Cristal was not a product of either Spanish or Mexican colonization.[1] Following the independence of Texas from Mexico in 1850, the area where Cristal sits today was incorporated into the municipality of San Antonio de Bexar. It was not until 1858 that the Texas Legislature carved Zavala County from Maverick and Uvalde counties. The first small settlements after the Civil War were Muerlo, Batesville, and Loma Vista. In 1884 the legislature established Zavala County's government infrastructure and named Batesville the county seat.[2]

Large-scale farming developed in the area in the late nineteenth and early twentieth centuries. Pressured by the need for inexpensive labor, local gringo landholders encouraged immigration into the area, which brought an initial influx of mostly white immigrants. In 1907 the Cross S Ranch, a spread of about 110,000 acres, was divided into plots of ten acres each, and land was appropriated for the establishment of a new settlement in 1907. The settlement was named Crystal City, after the clear artesian water in the area. On April 12, 1910, with a population of 530, Cristal was incorporated as a municipality and adopted the city council form of government.[3]

Even in the 1920s Cristal appeared to be a thriving small rural town. It had telephone and electrical services, a bank, hotel, various other businesses, and a volunteer fire department. In 1928 Cristal became Zavala's new county seat, and the mayor-council form of local government was changed to the city manager form. The first city manager was A. P. Hancock, under whose administrative leadership Cristal's infrastructure experienced its greatest growth.[4]

From 1910 to 1929 the demand for inexpensive labor grew. The increase in the Mexicano population was dramatic. Agriculture in south Texas reluctantly became dependent on Mexicanos.[5] Instead of relying on white immigration—which required much more time, effort, and money, gringos opted to use the Mexicano population, which was in greater supply because of "push" and "pull" factors. Mexico's chronic political instability and immense poverty pushed Mexicano migration into the area. From 1920 to 1929 the Mexicano population, located mostly in south Texas, nearly tripled—from 251,827 to 683,681.[6] Thus south Texas agriculture, dependent on the Mexicano labor force, "pulled"—embraced—an open border position. By the 1930s Mexicanos were Cristal's new majority. According to U.S. Census figures, the city had a population 7,760 Mexicanos, 2,269 whites, and 19 African Americans.[7]

Despite their numbers, the status of Mexicanos in Cristal from the time of their arrival was that of a segregated internal colony dominated by the minority gringo power holders. The Great Depression of 1929 exacerbated Mexicanos' status with a specter of nativism. All of a sudden, their labor was not in demand. Instead, Mexicanos became scapegoats, perceived as taking jobs away from local white workers. Historian Paul D. Taylor describes the prevalence of this racist mind-set: "Belief in the inferiority of [Mexicanos] was general, and was assumed by many to be axiomatic, although whether the inferiority was biological or social . . . Color and class differences were emphasized, and especially the fact that the [Mexicanos] . . . were predominantly laborers."[8]

Deportation and repatriation drives became commonplace throughout south Texas during the depression. Between 1929 and 1939 about 250,000 Mexicano adults and children, many of them U.S. citizens, were repatriated to Mexico. Victimized by massive unemployment and poverty, Mexicanos in the area endured deplorable living and health conditions.[9] Their unemployment was further exacerbated by technological advancements in the mechanization of agriculture. This created the beginning of the "migrant stream"—Mexicanos who sought relief to their squalor by traveling to the midwest in search of seasonal work.

The presence of a segregated educational system perpetuated Mexicanos' subordinate status. By the late 1930s Cristal had ten elementary schools, one for whites, eight for Mexicanos, and one for African Americans. The Mexicano and African American schools violated the U.S. Supreme Court's "separate but equal" doctrine (*Plessy v. Ferguson*, 1896). They were grossly unequal.[10] In 1942 the eight Mexicano schools were consolidated into three. Few Mexicanos were allowed to attend the high school, supposedly because they were unqualified.

Despite this history of oppression and exploitation, Mexicanos from Cristal and the surrounding areas volunteered for active duty in the armed forces during World War II, fighting gallantly in Europe and the South Pacific in defense of democracy. The same occurred in the 1950s with the Korean War. Yet upon their return to Cristal, Mexicano veterans were once again confronted by the stark reality of being denied full access to democracy. In 1950 nine Mexicanos were graduated from high school, an increase of six graduates since 1940.[11] Politically, although Mexicanos represented more than 70 percent of the population by the late 1950s, Cristal's city council, school board, and the Zavala County Court of Commissioners were all made up of gringos. Segregation continued in public and private facilities. Mexicanos were segregated in the use of the local theater, swimming pool, restaurants, and neighborhoods. As a result, Cristal had four barrios: Mexico Chico, Quizpero, Switche, and Mexico Grande.[12]

Despite the impoverished state of most Mexicanos, Cristal as a city underwent some economic growth in the 1940s and 1950s. During World War II a Japanese and German internment camp that housed about three thousand war prisoners was built in Cristal. It produced some jobs for local Mexicanos.[13] During these year Mexicanos continued to be part of the growing migrant stream. In 1945 the California Packing Corporation—which later became Del Monte—built a plant, cultivated about thirty-two hundred acres for winter vegetables, and dug wells for irrigation. The plant employed hundreds of Mexicanos during the spring and fall months, allowing some to escape the drudgery of farmworker life. In 1956 the workers organized and formed a Teamsters' local.

During these years a small Mexicano middle class began to emerge, boosted also by the Supreme Court decision in *Brown v. Board of Education* (1954) and the GI Bill of Rights. Because of *Brown* the quality of the education offered Mexicanos by Cristal's schools gradually improved, and the GI Bill helped veterans further their education and secure low-interest home loans. As a result, Mexicano entrepreneurs established restaurants, grocery stores, bakeries, gas stations, taverns, and fruit stands in various parts of the city's four barrios.

But the overwhelming majority of Mexicanos in Cristal still lived under the yoke of internal colonialism. The gringo and Anglo minority still controlled all important aspects of economic and political life. The omnipresence of their power, coupled with their use of the poll tax and political, economic, and physical intimidation, maintained the oppressive status quo.

Preconditions to the Revolt

Reform or revolutionary social movements do not occur in historical vacuums. Revolutionary movements are shaped dialectically and are products of historical antagonisms. They are rooted in human reaction to political, economic, social, or cultural conditions in the environment.[14] Theorist Chalmers Johnson refers to these antagonisms, or preconditions, as "accelerators" or "dysfunctions" that contribute to throwing the system out of equilibrium. Harry Eckstein adds to the analysis by alluding to preconditions and precipitants. He denotes a precondition as the circumstances that create the precipitant. Whereas the preconditions create the circumstances or climate of change, the precipitant is the match that ignites the flame of revolution.[15]

The Mexicanos' internal colonial status in Texas, and particularly in Cristal, was the exogenous precondition that helped bring about a climate of change. Before the early 1960s Mexicanos in Cristal seldom questioned their marginalized status. They seemed almost resigned to their oppression. For them life was characterized by debilitating poverty, few educational opportunities, limited economic opportunity, and no political choice.[16] Sociologist Julian Zamora and colleagues describe their powerlessness:

The political power of the community—school board, school system, city and county offices, and law enforcement—was firmly entrenched among a handful of Anglos, elected by the 14.5 percent Anglo population of Cristal. In 1959 and preceding years, Mexican Americans only accounted for 10 to 15 percent of the voters registered in Cristal, although they comprised 85 percent of the town's population. The political decision-making by the long-term Anglo office holders (until 1963 the mayor of Cristal had served continuously for thirty-eight years; each of the five city council members had served for over thirty-eight years) was more akin to the "divine right of kings" than to a democratic electoral process. Through the complaisant predominant Mexican-American population the idea was perpetuated that only Anglos were fit to hold office or other responsible positions in the community.[17]

Another scholar, John Staples Shockley, explains that before 1963 Mexicanos in Cristal tended to be politically apathetic and abased. He writes, "The Mexicans did not think of themselves as people able to challenge the Anglos over issues, run for office, and in general partake of the running of a democratic society."[18] Yet by the late 1950s and early 1960s the emergence of the civil rights movement was acting as an exogenous precondition. It helped create the gradual political awakening of Mexicanos, both locally and regionally.

An examination of Cristal's history from the mid-1950s to 1962 reveals several endogenous preconditions that collectively produced a climate of change. The circumstances fostered the people's desire for change, their politicization, and ultimately their political participation. These preconditions included the veterans' land scandal, urban renewal controversy, candidacy of E. C. Muñoz, López elementary school incident, and rising expectations of Mexicanos.

During the mid-1950s allegations of corruption surfaced that involved several Texas state government as well as some Cristal officials. The furor was the result of what the press labeled the veterans' land scandal. It involved several high-ranking officials in the administration of Governor Allan Shivers. Land speculators had jumped on a state program to help veterans buy land at low prices. The speculators would buy land intended for veterans, then turn around and sell it to the veterans at grossly inflated prices. During the course of the investigation rumors circulated of wrong-doing by state officials, especially state land commissioner Bascom Giles and Shivers. Both served on the Veterans Land Board, which had been created in 1950 to purchase land that was later to be resold to veterans over a forty-year period at low interest rates.

Robert A. Calvert and Arnoldo De León describe how the scam worked:

Once a veteran had chosen the land and notified the board of willingness to purchase the property, an official inspector checked its value and authorized the board to purchase the land for resale to the veteran. Giles bypassed these checks on the board by picking corrupt appraisers to evaluate the land and by having all purchases of large tracts of land subdivided for sale to veterans sent directly to his office for approval rather than to the board. He later added the notice of large tract purchases to the board's minutes. In collusion with real estate dealers, Giles authorized inflated prices for land for sale to either nonexistent or defrauded veterans.[19]

The program provided long-term low-interest loans to veterans to reimburse the state for the purchase of the land. It was not uncommon, however, for veterans to default on their loans because they usually were unaware that they had purchased the property. A major repercussion was that the state was left with a surplus of land for which it had paid exorbitant prices. Shivers's approval ratings in the polls dropped dramatically as a result. The scandal passed when Giles pleaded guilty to fraud and was sentenced to six years in prison.[20]

The scandal stimulated Mexicanos' interest in local politics for the first time. In Cristal speculators who appeared to have a good working relationship with city and county officials had used Mexicano veterans to obtain either more land or money for the speculators. The scandal awoke Mexicanos to the abuse of power by local government leaders.

At about the same time (1957–1958) gringo power holders in Cristal adopted an urban renewal program that became another precondition of the revolt. Cristal had virtually no paved streets in the barrios and less than half the town had sewerage. But the decision to apply for urban renewal funds and float bonds was not motivated by the deplor-

Table 1.1. 1960 Cristal School Board Elections (Four Open Seats)

Candidate	Number of Votes
S. S. Peters	730
R. E. Boyer	725
B. R. Guyler	722
H. M. Addison	731
E. C. Muñoz	311

Source: *Zavala County Sentinel*, April 18, 1960.

able condition of Cristal's infrastructure; rather, the city fathers wanted to make sure that the infrastructure of the business segment of the city was well developed. This was obvious: by 1963 only the white-owned business section of the city had received the improvements. The issue of urban renewal contributed to the Mexicanos' politicization. Some Mexicanos viewed urban renewal with skepticism and animosity because of the likelihood that their homes would be condemned and they would be forced to relocate.[21] In increasing numbers they began to openly criticize the urban renewal plan.

Mexicanos were becoming more politically aware on other fronts too. Three years earlier, in the spring of 1960, E. C. Muñoz, an insurance agent, had run for the school board, which had always been made up of only whites. Although Muñoz lost, the campaign was instructive. Only one other Mexicano had ever sought election to the seven-member school board. Mexicano voter turnout increased in those two elections, in part because the campaigns increased their awareness of issues affecting them.[22] But whites usually ran unopposed.

Because voter turnout citywide was always low for school board elections, Muñoz felt that he had an excellent chance to win. He couldn't have been more wrong. "His candidacy," writes Shockley, "spurred the four Anglo incumbents, all seeking re-election, into making sure the Anglos turned out to vote."[23] The gringo power holders campaigned hard against Muñoz, who lacked a campaign organization, had limited resources, and was up against the white elite. The citizens of Cristal cast 1,034 votes, a record turnout, in the April election (see Table 1.1 for a breakdown).

With about seven hundred whites and six hundred Mexicanos registered to vote in the district, only a few Mexicanos could have voted for the four white incumbents. In a typical election Muñoz's 300 votes would have been more than enough to get him elected to one of the four open seats. (Cristal holds separate election days for city council and school board because the voting populations are different. The school district encompasses an area larger than Cristal itself.) To Mexicanos the unwillingness of whites to share power was clearly wrong—most of the district's students were Mexicano.

Adding to Cristal's changing political climate was an incident involving the Baptist minister, Arnold López, that occurred immediately after Muñoz lost the school board race. The mostly white elementary school denied Reverend López's son admission to the first grade. Mexicanos at this time were still victims of de facto segregation, and only a few had been enrolled at the school because of the practice of testing Mexicano children on their English comprehension. Only Mexicanos who scored high were admitted. Yet Reverend López's son had scored extremely high.

López reacted by organizing Cristal's first major protest of de facto segregation. Helped by Gerald Saldaña, a mail carrier, López mobilized so many people for the protest that the gringos' stereotype of the passive and politically inept Mexicano disappeared. The protest, coupled with the possibility of legal action (this was nearly ten years after *Brown v. Board of Education*), forced the white-controlled board to reluctantly agree to break up the segregated primary schools. Unfortunately, once they gained victory, the Mexicanos quickly disbanded.

Still, the Mexicanos' political restlessness was growing and led to their involvement in the surplus commodities issue during the winter of 1962. That winter was particularly severe. A freeze destroyed most of the area's vegetable crops, creating massive unemployment. With some people going hungry, about 125 Mexicanos marched to a meeting of the Zavala County Court of Commissioners, as the elected governing board is called, to request a surplus commodities program for an emergency period of thirty days. Bowing to the pressure, the commissioners agreed to provide emergency assistance. However, the commissioners later voted against extending the program beyond the thirty days, even though many people were still unemployed. According to Shockley, "The majority of the board feared continuing the program might lessen the Mexicanos' desire to work."[24]

Thus the various endogenous preconditions—the veterans' land scandal, Muñoz candidacy, López elementary school incident, and the ruined crop—served as catalysts for Mexicanos' politicization. These events occurred against a backdrop of other exogenous events that had given Mexicanos some reasons for optimism since the end of World War II. Among the more salient were the GI Bill; the *Brown* decision; the federal civil rights acts of 1957 and 1960, as well as Texas antidiscrimination laws; increased job opportunities in both the private and public sectors, a result of the booming postwar economy; and the activism of the growing civil rights movement. Also important was the unprecedented political involvement of Mexicanos in the 1960 presidential election in support of John F. Kennedy via the Viva Kennedy Clubs.[25]

Muñoz's candidacy for the school board was among the issues that alarmed the local governing elite. In 1961 whites sought to mitigate Mexicanos' discontent by running two Mexicanos for city council, Salvador Galván and Ed Ritchie, who represented white political and economic interests. But the Mexicanos were not impressed—they knew that Galván and Ritchie were nothing more than strawmen. In 1962 José (Cleto) López became the first Mexicano to run for county commissioner, although he was defeated in his bid for the seat from Precinct 2.[26] (Zavala County had four commissioners, each elected from a single district, or precinct.)

Nor were Mexicanos in Cristal merely reacting to local and national events. Endogenously, more Mexicanos were being graduated from high school, having received an education of higher quality than had been available to their parents; more jobs were open to Mexicanos at the Del Monte plant, where workers had unionized; and urban renewal programs had begun. Thus, despite continued hardships, in the early 1960s some Mexicanos were better off socioeconomically. These gains also served to heighten their expectations.

The First Electoral Revolt

By late 1962 all these events meant that Mexicanos were less willing to tolerate gringo control. That November they began planning a poll-tax drive for early 1963. As was the case throughout Texas, all citizens who wanted to vote were required to pay a poll tax of $1.75. Historically, gringos had used the poll tax as a powerful political tool to impede the electoral participation of Mexicanos and African Americans—poor people in general. In early 1963 a young Mexicano from Cristal told a reporter, "I always called Crystal City home, but I didn't pay attention to elections. It was the Anglos' town, so I let them run it."[27]

The poll-tax drive was spearheaded by the Teamsters' local at the Del Monte plant and in January 1963 was joined by the newly organized Cristal chapter of the Political Association of Spanish-Speaking Organizations (PASSO), under the leadership of Juan Cornejo. The sense of political disassociation that the young man expressed to the reporter did not deter PASSO's leadership. In fact, PASSO leaders believed that political conditions were propitious for a successful poll-tax drive among Mexicanos.

But the first discussion of a poll-tax drive occurred in 1962, started by a disgruntled local businessman, Andrew Dickens. (Shockley credits Dickens with starting the revolt: "The spark that set off the explosion in Cristal was in fact an Anglo."[28]) Dickens had had a serious disagreement with the white-controlled city council over a property lease. He had sought help from city and county officials, and they had refused. Dickens, vowing to defeat what he described as the gringo political machine, sought a coalition with Mexicanos to build a movement that would win community control of the city council. Dickens had approached Cornejo about this.

That month Cornejo and Dickens traveled to San Antonio to meet with Ray Shafer, president and business manager of the powerful Teamsters' Local 657, based in San Antonio. Cornejo and Dickens were seeking political and financial support from the Teamsters at the state level because the two men had limited resources and lacked experience in organizing campaigns. They convinced Shafer that Mexicanos could gain a majority on the Cristal city council, and that winning control of the council would strengthen the Teamsters at the Del Monte plant, and enhance Teamster organizing efforts in other parts of south Texas. The Teamsters agreed to provide the outside organizational expertise and the bookkeeping that allowed some Mexicanos to pay the $1.75 poll tax in installments.

Del Monte's management, which enjoyed an amicable and collaborative relationship with the local white elite, discouraged all employees from participating in the drive, and most refused. This left the poll-tax drive temporarily in limbo.[29] Cornejo, now the main leader of the poll-tax drive, sought to remedy the problem by organizing a chapter of the Political Association of Spanish-Speaking Organizations (PASSO). Organized in 1961, PASSO was the first statewide Mexicano political action organization in Texas. It sought the political empowerment of Mexicanos and other Latinos. As an umbrella organization or confederation, its goal was to bring other Mexicano and Latino groups and their sympathizers together in a powerful multistate organization that would be active in electoral politics and lobbying. According to Roberto A. Cuellar,

The leaders of the newly-formed political front expressed in a constitution that all persons interested in the plight of the Spanish-speaking population would unite and, through political action, find solutions to problems of an economic, educational, and cultural nature that afflicted the Mexican-American community. In addition, these leaders aimed to encourage direct involvement of their people in politics, hoping to achieve the election and appointment to local, state, and national office persons sympathetic to the goals of PASSO.[30]

Cornejo recognized the value of forming a local PASSO chapter and convinced several local Mexicanos to do so. Cornejo wanted to finish the poll-tax drive and leave it well organized for the upcoming 1963 local elections. In late 1962 he met with Alberto Fuentes Jr., PASSO's state secretary, and other officials, to talk about forming a PASSO chapter in Cristal.

In fact, Cornejo was approaching them at an auspicious moment. PASSO leaders had had trouble mobilizing Mexicanos statewide. PASSO's state chairperson, Albert A. Peña, who was also a Bexar County commissioner, believed that Mexicanos in Texas were politically passive because they feared losing their jobs if they participated politically, and they believed they could not win against gringos.[31] But Fuentes understood well the potential effect of Texas's changing demographics, and he believed that political conditions were perfect for a successful poll-tax drive. He asserted that PASSO's paramount mission was to "awaken the sleeping giant."[32] PASSO agreed to form a chapter in Cristal.

The rather unholy alliance between PASSO and the Teamsters was grounded on mutual interest, expedience, and anticipated gains. The Teamsters took care of the financial, organizing, and administrative aspects of the poll-tax drive, and PASSO took care of getting the word out because it had access to the Mexicano community. The Cristal takeover was important to PASSO leaders because they felt that a victory in Cristal would enhance their statewide consolidation, political clout, and growth.

The Teamster-PASSO coalition (hereafter referred to as the alliance) believed that surprise was an imperative element in making the poll-tax drive, and the subsequent election campaign, successful. After several weeks of intensive work a record number of Mexicanos paid their poll tax. The alliance went so far as to subsidize some who did not have the money. Others borrowed the money for the poll tax from the alliance and were allowed to pay it back in installments.

The drive was an unprecedented success. In 1960, 683 Anglos and 646 Mexicanos had paid their poll taxes. In 1962 white registration dropped to 538, whereas 795 Mexicanos were registered. With the poll-tax drive of 1963, Mexicanos became an overwhelming majority of the voting population—1,139 of 1,681 registered voters.[33]

The poll-tax drive was only the beginning of the alliance's fight to win control of the Cristal city council. PASSO's leadership had assigned Martin Garcia of Kingsville, Texas, the organization's district director for the Corpus Christi area and a part-time law student, to provide technical assistance to Cornejo and others for the poll-tax drive. Garcia lived in Cristal for the duration of the campaign and worked closely with Cornejo's newly formed PASSO chapter to register voters.[34]

Upon completion of the poll-tax drive the alliance's effort accelerated. The Teamsters' Shafer sent Carlos Moore, a labor union director, and Henry Muñoz, who was proficient in various aspects of electioneering, to Cristal to help Cornejo and Garcia. Shafer felt that the foursome could produce the votes to gain a majority on the city council, provided that Mexicanos could maintain their faith in the campaign, refuse to be intimidated, and refrain from selling out, as had often been the case.[35] Moore and Muñoz would concentrate on these problems.

After they arrived in Cristal in February, the alliance accelerated its efforts to form a campaign organization for the April city council elections. According to political scientist José Angel Gutiérrez, a former resident of Cristal who became the driving force behind the second revolt, "These individuals provided election law expertise, technical campaign assistance, and leadership to our fledgling local PASSO chapter."[36] On February 8 Garcia, Moore, and Cornejo held a community meeting attended by only twenty-three people. The alliance leaders decided to form the Citizens Committee for Better Government, an innocuous-sounding entity designed to help PASSO and the Teamsters play down their image as outside agitators.[37] A local Teamster member, Moses Falcón, chaired the committee. Twenty-two Mexicanos and one Anglo (Dickens) became directors of the committee. They decided to run a slate of five candidates in the April city council elections.

Cuellar describes how the several organizations coordinated the campaign:

> While Garcia and Moore worked in Cristal, the state leaders of PASSO and the Teamsters supervised the affair from their headquarters in San Antonio. Fuentes directed the election campaign by calling in instructions to the civic workers in Cristal and making several personal appearances. Ray Shafer, Teamsters Union director and business agent, helped the campaign by making himself easily accessible for advice and assistance.[38]

Moore proved to be indispensable. His thorough knowledge of legal procedure and election codes made him the ideal technical adviser. He was the perfect person to deal with the opposition at city hall: "Moore drove a Cadillac in Cristal, wore expensive suits, smoked big cigars, and always carried an election code book under his arm."[39] For weeks the opposition thought he was a lawyer.

Selecting the five candidates became one of the most difficult tasks the citizens committee faced. The committee discussed whether it would be smart to have a slate that included both Mexicanos and Anglos. The members concluded that Dickens—who was ineligible to run because he lived outside the city limits—was the only Anglo who would dare run on an alliance-sponsored slate. The only option was to form a slate of qualified Mexicanos. But in searching for candidates they ran up against fear. Garcia later told sociologist Julian Samora and colleagues, "I was depressed by the small number [at citizens committee meetings], considering Juan Cornejo was a business agent for the Teamsters, I thought for sure he would bring his membership. But there were others watching through the windows of the meeting hall and listening outside the door, all afraid to participate. Even though they brought their poll taxes, the election process was strange to them."[40]

Several Mexicanos were approached to run but declined, saying they were afraid they would lose their jobs or that they were worried about the safety of their families. Some middle-income Mexicanos showed no interest in running and made it clear that they wanted nothing to do with the citizens committee or the alliance. They believed that the Teamsters' involvement meant that the campaign would focus on the interests of only the lower-income cannery and migrant workers.[41]

Recruiting five viable Mexicano candidates began to seem almost impossible. The citizens committee had to follow the election codes, which stipulated candidate eligibility requirements. In addition, it sought potential Mexicano candidates who strongly supported its efforts. Complicating the candidate recruitment endeavors was the low level of education. Mexicanos in Zavala County who were older than twenty-five had a median of 2.3 years of schooling. Therefore the organizers felt that it was important to recruit people who were more educated and knowledgeable of the workings of local government.

Still, the number of Mexicanos who attended citizens committee meetings was increasing steadily. By the fourth meeting the committee had sixteen prospective candidates. To make the first cut, the committee decided, individuals had to have paid their poll tax, own property, and be free of debt to the city. Only nine aspirants remained, and all pledged to support the five who would be chosen. At the next meeting attendees were invited to address the field of nine, and after some deliberation the committee chose Juan Cornejo, business agent for the Teamsters; Manuel Maldonado, clerk at the local Economart store; Antonio Cárdenas, truck driver; Reynáldo Mendoza, operator of a small photography shop; and Mario Hernández, real estate salesman.[42] They became known as Los Cinco [The Five]. The *Dallas Morning News* summarized their backgrounds: "The candidates represented the plight of their group. Their average education was about the seventh grade. They dressed in workmen's clothes. They had little knowledge of city economics and government. They deeply resented the Anglos."[43] Years later, discussing the process used to select the final slate, Cornejo recalled, "I was not at that particular meeting nor was I part of the selection process, but after the meeting one of those who did attend came by to tell me that my name was one of the five on the slate."[44]

While the citizens committee focused on the city council election, two politically independent Mexicanos, Jesús Maldonado and Lorenzo Olivares, had filed their candidacy for the school board. To the citizens committee the school board elections were not as important because only two of the seven seats were to be contested. Therefore the two campaigns were purposely kept separate. The two Mexicano school board candidates made it clear in their campaigning that they were not interested in gaining control of the school board. Furthermore, they were not trying to disrupt the board, and they were not accusing the board of discrimination against Mexicanos. They said in an apologetic way that they were not running because of grudges against whites but because they felt Mexicanos needed representation on the school board. They saw their role as interpreters for Mexicanos who were unable to speak English well.[45]

The city council campaign by the citizens committee relied on building a strong grassroots organization. Its strategy was to polarize the city's Mexicano and white communities. The committee used Saul Alinsky's tactic of heightening the level of conflict to the point that no one could doubt the identity of the enemy.[46] The enemy was the gringo elite that controlled the politics, economics, and education of the region. Public rallies were essential to the organizing strategy. Gutiérrez explained their importance:

The election campaigns centered around public rallies. Days before the rally, the local sound truck that advertised the Mexican movies at *el teatro* Luna, would give notice of the upcoming event. The day of the rally, the sound truck would remind the folks of the meeting and give names of the featured speakers. People gathered around the speaker's area to hear the speeches. Our rallies were held in *La Placita* in the Mexico Chico neighborhood.[47]

To target Mexicano voters the citizens committee took precinct maps and developed block-by-block drives to get out the vote.[48] It also used many other conventional campaign techniques: "Posters displaying unpaved streets were posted and meetings were held at which state PASSO leaders and liberal politicians from San Antonio gave speeches. An intensive house-to-house campaign was launched aimed at educating people in how to mark their ballots. 'Palm cards' which could be taken secretly into the voting booth were provided to remind the voter of the names of Los Cinco candidatos."[49]

As the citizens committee intensified its organizing efforts, Cristal's politics became increasingly polarized. Initially, whites and their supporters were overconfident, failing to consider the Mexicano organizing efforts significant enough to present a serious challenge. Their reaction to the poll-tax drive was moderate. In part, this was attributable to the new city manager, James Dill, hired the year before, who made the mistake of not monitoring poll-tax payments.[50] In this case the stereotype of politically inept and apathetic Mexicanos worked in their favor.

The polarization and political insecurity of whites did not become evident until immediately after the selection of Los Cinco. Concerned about the growing momentum of Los Cinco, some white power holders, who were not part of the city administration, sought to divide the Mexicano vote by convincing Reverend Arnold López, a local Baptist minister, to run as an independent. They convinced him to run by arguing that Los Cinco were an embarrassment to the Mexicano community because of their lack of education. However, the people who approached him did not promise him any substantial support. In fact, they were ardently supporting the five incumbents: Ed Ritchie, W. P. Brennan, Bruce Holsomback, J. C. Bookout, and S. G. Galván. But when López began to aggressively attack Los Cinco, and some whites began to show some interest in supporting the minister, the whites asked him to withdraw and he refused. The weakening of white control became still more evident with the entry to the race of yet another independent candidate, Dr. Henry Daly. He too was asked to withdraw, and he too refused.[51] Realizing that the traditional power structure was in trouble, "Mrs. Zimmerman and Mrs. Charles Huffman organized a telephone committee to solicit every one of the 542 Anglo names on their list of poll tax holders," one newspaper reported.[52]

Assertions that Los Cinco were unqualified and inexperienced hovered over the campaign. In addition to character assassination, whites used obstructionism, harassment, and intimidation to discourage the Mexicanos' candidacy. For example, at the beginning of the campaign Los Cinco went together to city hall to file their candidacy papers. The city clerk informed them that there were no more filing forms. One candidate secured an old form from a Mexicana who worked in the courthouse. Copies were made for the other four and photos were taken. They filled out the forms, had them notarized, and filed them with the surprised clerk.[53] Meanwhile, gringo businesses and finance companies were pressing for immediate payment from Mexicanos who owed them money and happened to be active in the Los Cinco campaign.

Gutiérrez, then a student at a community college in nearby Uvalde, told an interviewer about this incident involving the Texas Rangers:

After speaking at a rally I got a ride home with friends, and they dropped me off at the house on the corner of Edwards and Eighth Avenue. As my friends turned the corner, the Rangers stopped them and blocked their car with a car in front and one in the back. The officers had been following us. The Rangers pulled my friends out of the car as I ran across the street to help them. I got slapped immediately by [Captain A. Y.] Allee. I didn't know the names of the other Rangers. One car was full of deputies, though, and the other car had Rangers in it. Allee was the one who slapped me. I fell down and he kicked me once. That was all I was willing to take, so I ran back to my house. The other boys also ran, but the Rangers managed to get two boys into one car and took them to jail, where they held them without filing charges. The Rangers just scared them, telling them that they weren't supposed to be at these political rallies and that the rallies were Communist-inspired. The Rangers told them it was no place for kids and that they ought to stay home and get to school early.[54]

Such intimidation by the Texas Rangers was commonplace, especially as the citizens committee meetings became too large to be held inside and were moved outdoors. Whenever Allee came into Cristal, all local and county law enforcement agencies came under his command, as stipulated by state law. Samora and colleagues further explain the intimidation by the rangers:

In effect, Allee put the town under martial law. If there was a traffic violation, Allee wrote the ticket. An unofficial curfew was established and Mexican Americans walking alone at night were subject to verbal and physical abuse, as well as to arrest on a variety of false charges. Favorite sites for harassment were the Chicano owned or patronized bars. Whenever Allee saw more than ten persons gathered in a bar, he would shut it down. . . . The Veteran's Bar was a favorite target. Although other bars were also closed, they weren't closed because . . . [Mexicanos] were noisy or abusive, but because Allee felt that the . . . [Mexicanos] were stirring up trouble. He would just shut the bars, and there was no argument.[55]

Mexicanos regarded Texas Rangers, who were infamous for perpetrating violence against Mexicanos, as close kin of Hitler's storm troopers.

Another serious incident occurred two weeks before the April election. Several Mexicano employees of the Del Monte plant were dismissed for wearing Los Cinco campaign buttons. The Teamsters intervened and were able to have them reinstated. This strengthened the campaign organizing efforts of the citizens committee and helped the workers feel confident and secure in openly supporting Los Cinco. The campaign organizers used all the incidents to charge gringos with blatant discrimination and to stir Mexicanos' discontent.[56]

During the closing weeks of the campaign the citizens committee conducted many rallies and meetings and did a lot of door-to-door canvassing. The committee also relied on two emotional incidents to gain greater Mexicano participation. The first was the announcement by the local Lions Club of its support for an all-white Boy Scout troop.[57] The second involved Teamster organizer Martin Garcia, who was asked to leave a restaurant after ordering a beer. Both incidents were widely publicized and cited by Los Cinco as examples of the kind of treatment that had impelled them to run for office. The candidates reminded Mexicano voters of the inequality in city services, segregation in recreational facilities such as swimming pools, lack of paved streets in the barrios, and discrimination in the schools. In a letter addressed to the city's Mexicanos, PASSO's Peña exhorted them to vote for Los Cinco:

It is very important that you unite for the candidates of the Cristal Citizens for Better Government. In a constitutional democracy . . . it is standard procedure that majority rules. Our people are definitely in the majority in Cristal, yet we have never had adequate representation. We have many problems of discrimination. . . . The opposition brags that our people will never be united because they can be bought off. . . . I am happy to see that you and these five brave men are making a noble effort to prove to the people of Texas and the World that our people are capable of assuming responsibility of their government.[58]

The letter intensified tensions because it also declared that Los Cinco were "the only true Mexicanos" in the race.

At one point the citizens committee had filed a complaint with the Justice Department and asked that federal marshals be sent to town to protect voters on election day. Although no one ever responded, the complaint prompted the use of fourteen state law enforcement officers to patrol the city as well as the polling places. In an effort to keep Mexicanos from voting, gringo farmers offered them double wages, or $2 per hour, if they would work on election day. This was unheard of. Del Monte scheduled the Teamster workers for overtime. It took a call from Teamster president Jimmy Hoffa to Del Monte's headquarters in San Francisco to guarantee that workers would be given time off to vote.[59]

On election eve the citizens committee showed its political muscle by holding the largest rally in the history of Cristal. About three thou-

sand enthusiastic supporters attended the event. The citizens committee brought in such prominent figures as state representatives Jake
Johnson and John Alaniz, and Alberto Fuentes, PASSO's state executive
secretary, among others, who addressed the enthusiastic pro–citizens
committee crowd.

Martin Garcia told the crowd in Spanish:

> We're here tonight because deep in our hearts, we're all Mexicans and tomor-
> row we're going to go out and vote for our people. . . . You have come to matu-
> rity, as we have in San Antonio. You have shown you are first class citizens
> willing to do everything you can for your country. Your compadres in San
> Antonio have come down here on their own to help you. Now you must help
> others—in Sinton, Mathis, Baytown, Eagle Pass, and all the other towns where
> people need help. There is discrimination in Texas and the only way you can
> stop it is through your vote.

Alberto Fuentes said:

> The gringos say they are not afraid of this election. They say they never worry
> until the day before the election, then they go out and get the vote. "Give a
> Mexican a dollar and he will sell himself," they say. But this is no longer true.
> The Mexicanos' eyes are open, and the price is higher now. The man who
> wants to buy a vote must pay liberty, respect, dignity, education for the chil-
> dren, and a higher standard of living for all, and progressive government—
> that is the new price. We're going to have people there in the polling booth
> tomorrow to help you. Do not be afraid. . . . The victory we win tomorrow is
> here tonight. The Anglos know this now. More important, we know it too.

And José Angel Gutiérrez reminded the rally, "They say there is no
discrimination, but we have only to look around us to know the truth.
We look at the schools . . . the houses we live in . . . the few opportunities . . . the dirt streets . . . and we know."[60]

The citizens committee also aired a series of complaints of discrimination and harassment, including allegations of broken windshields
and punctured tires on cars displaying Los Cinco bumper stickers. The
citizens committee pointed out that all the incidents were ignored by
local law enforcement agencies.[61]

Gringos responded by alleging that the speakers and Peña's letter
proved that the citizens committee was being discriminatory, if not
racist. The local power structure hoped to gain the Mexicano vote by
announcing on radio and in flyers a decision to spend about $500,000
to pave the streets of the city's barrios.[62]

By election morning Cristal was a totally polarized community.
Gringos had constantly reminded both whites and Mexicanos that the
citizens committee was a creation of outside agitators who were stirring up Mexicanos in order to take control of city government. They

had pressed this allegation in paid advertisements in the *Zavala County Sentinel*, a weekly that was the only local newspaper. In February Andrew Dickens had dropped out of the citizens committee, charging that the Teamsters were masterminding the whole operation.[63] City attorney Jay Taylor declared, "Certainly we're resentful of this union bunch coming in here stirring up a bunch of rabble."[64]

On election day the citizens committee was busy with a major grassroots get-out-the-vote drive. It was an impressive show of organization. Poll watchers monitored the polling place, voters were provided with transportation, and volunteers went house to house, passing out sample ballots and providing instructions on election laws. Vehicles equipped with sound systems criss-crossed the city's barrios. The weeks of preparation and organizing produced confident and emotionally committed Mexicanos who were ready to vote without fear.

By evening hundreds of Mexicanos were gathered in the city square to await the results. Ranger Allee, irritated by the assembly, approached Cornejo and demanded, "Tell your people to go home." Cornejo replied that people deserved to see the election results. "It will be goddamn midnight," replied Allee.

Fuentes recalled that when the results were reported late that evening, "It could have been Times Square when World War II ended. I was standing beside the tall slender deputy sheriff, who had been chewing tobacco. His mouth fell open and the tobacco hit the ground. All he could say was 'I'll be god-dammed. They won 'em all.'"[65] Table 1.2 provides the results of the city council election.

Mexicanos in Cristal were aware that they had made political history. This was the first time in post-1848 Texas history that Mexicanos had successfully wrested political control of a city council from gringo power holders. A sense of strength replaced decades of powerlessness. The old stereotype of Mexicanos as apathetic, docile, disorganized, and incapable of coming together was dead. *Texas Observer* reporter Larry Goodwyn captured the fervor and enthusiasms: "Within seconds [of the victory announcement] there was pandemonium; the winners were hoisted upon the shoulders, so was Garcia, so was Fuentes. Handshaking, horns blowing, a couple of Mexican versions of the rebel yell, and remarkably suddenly they fled to cars and dispersed under the gazes of the Rangers."[66] The political victory resonated throughout Texas and the rest of Aztlán.

The Aftermath

The election got international coverage. All the stories described how Los Cinco had outfoxed the gringos, overcoming decades of subordi-

Table 1.2. 1963 Cristal City Council Election Results*

Candidates	Number of Votes
Citizens Committee Slate	
Manuel Maldonado	864
Juan Cornejo	818
Mario Hernández	799
Antonio Cárdenas	799
Reynaldo Mendoza	795
Incumbents	
Ed Ritchie	754
W. P. Brennan	717
Bruce Holsomback	716
J. C. Bookout	694
S. G. Galván	664
Independents	
Henry Daly	164
Arnold López	146

*1,572 votes cast; Cristal had 1,681 registered voters.

Source: Jerry Deal, "Latin Ticket Sweeps to Victory at Crystal City," *San Antonio Express*, April 3, 1963.

nation and powerlessness. Some reporters referred to the takeover as a political revolution. They wondered if this was the beginning of a larger Mexicano empowerment movement that would soon engulf south Texas. Journalists flocked to Cristal to witness the transfer of power. In an editorial the *Corpus Christi Caller-Times*, recognizing the radical implications of the revolt and that Los Cinco had won without the support of the small, emerging Mexicano middle class, wrote,

Political historians have noted that Latin Americans rarely have been able to agree among themselves on the issue of candidates. Under the patron system voters followed the wishes of their patron. As this system died, a distinctive middle class began to emerge. Ironically, this middle class identified itself with the Anglo population rather than the Latin. Instead of providing a reservoir for political candidates, the middle class tended to stand apart from the political struggle, or if they took a part they tended to side with the candidates and slates chosen by Anglos. It is apparent that the incident of Cristal represents a revolt against the "Uncle Toms" of the Latin community. The candidates who won at Cristal, with the help and financing of the Teamsters Union and PASSO . . . represent workers, not the Latin middle class.[67]

Drawn to the story in part by the election's 95 percent voter turnout, the media had discovered the Mexicano community. This also put Los Cinco, especially Juan Cornejo, whom the council members designated as mayor, in the political spotlight.

The media quickly began to focus on Cristal's political climate. Stories described the city's unprecedented political polarization and volatility. The *San Antonio Express and News* reported, "The Anglos are hurt; hurt by national publicity they feel has distorted the facts, pictured them and their town in a bad light; hurt by false charges from both sides of the political fence; hurt by defeat. Many refuse to accept it."[68]

Although the national and international press, particularly reporters from Mexico, gave Los Cinco and the revolt generally good coverage, the opposite was true of the Texas press. Stories in Texas papers were filled with skepticism and outright disbelief that the revolt had succeeded, with headline writers painting the election in terms of war. (*Houston Chronicle*, April 14: "Texas Town Split by Political War." *San Antonio Light:* "Crystal City War Denied." The *San Antonio Express* was less sensational: "Latino Ticket Sweeps to Victory at Crystal City.") The press wrote so much about the revolt that Texas newspaper editors voted it the second most newsworthy story of 1963—second only to the assassination of President Kennedy in Dallas. Cognizant of the implications of the unprecedented victory, journalists from throughout Texas, the nation, and Mexico converged to interview Los Cinco.

Los Cinco's control of the city council was challenged immediately by the former leadership and its supporters. From the beginning, governing the community proved to be much more difficult than winning the election. On election night Ranger Allee, accompanied by four other rangers, had visited the Veteran's Bar, where the Mexicanos were holding an informal victory party. Addressing the crowd, and Cornejo in particular, Allee warned that although they had won, they should watch their step.[69] The *Texas Observer's* Goodwyn reported on Allee's warning: "Allee went in there saying, 'Your god-dam people got to show some respect.' He told everyone to go home and he closed down the bar. As if the celebration was mob action on our part, as if we had no right or reason to celebrate. He spoke of 'those other people,' meaning the losers. 'How do you think they feel?' He threatened that 'they' might start an unnamed 'something' that he couldn't protect us against."[70]

Allee's words were but a preamble. The ousted white power holders struck the morning after the election. According to Shockley,

The day after the council election, Manuel Maldonado, the top vote-getter on the ticket and the man ironically most respected by the Anglos, lost his job at the Economart store. Anglo pressure had been strong enough that his employer reluctantly caved in. Another member of Los Cinco, Antonio Cardenas, found that his wages were halved from $77 to $35 a week. Within a few days a third member of Los Cinco, Mario Hernández, had turned against the other four and began echoing the charges the Anglos were levelling at the council-elect. Financial security was at the core of this difficulty as well. The Anglo leadership confronted him with a series of bad checks he had written, and told him that if he did not say just what they told him to say, he would be prosecuted to the fullest extent of the law. He immediately did what they told him to do, and his "charges" received enormous publicity.[71]

Only Cornejo, who was protected by the Teamsters, was temporarily spared the economic reprisals. Although Los Cinco had political control, they did not wield economic power. Economic power still rested with whites who controlled the land, businesses, and overall economy of the region.

Whites directed their economic resources away from Los Cinco. This pressure was calculated to disrupt, divide, and ultimately lead to the retaking of their lost power. For example, during the two-week interval between the election and the swearing-in of Los Cinco, city government was essentially reduced to chaos. In an attempt to cripple Los Cinco's ability to govern, whites launched two initiatives: to prevent the annexation of the Del Monte plant into the city in order to secure additional revenues (the white-controlled council had voted to sign a seven-year contract that exempted the Del Monte plant from being annexed for purposes of getting additional tax revenues); and to encourage the resignation of several city officials, including the city manager (this was what created havoc within the city administration).

State and local law enforcement agencies reacted to Los Cinco's victory with anger and hostility. Zavala County Sheriff C. L. Sweeten voiced his displeasure publicly. After the election the Texas Rangers continued to patrol Cristal. Their rationale was that they were merely trying to keep agitators from coming into the community. Several incidents involved Cornejo and Allee. For example, right after the election Cornejo learned that someone had given Allee the only key to the council chambers. Cornejo asked Allee to return it, and the ranger refused. As Cornejo told the *San Antonio Express,* he reminded Allee, "Wait a minute. I am the mayor, and this is the city council. We decide this." Allee told him to sit down and shut up. Cornejo replied, "I am not going to sit down and shut up. That's why I was elected." Allee grabbed him by the lapels, slapped him across the face, and pushed him repeatedly into the wall, causing him to hit his head. "You little Mexican son-of-a-bitch, don't you talk to me like that. I'm the law around here," the ranger barked. Cornejo continued, "He told me that was only a sample. If I didn't keep my mouth shut to the papers, it would get a lot worse."

After weeks of rhetorical sparring, a much more serious incident occurred. While Cornejo was at city hall signing checks, Allee asked him to come into his office. He accused Cornejo of making false statements about him. Cornejo told reporters that Allee had called him an SOB. Furthermore, he said that Allee had grabbed him and banged his head against the wall several times. Cornejo also charged that Allee had threatened him with more bodily harm if he continued to speak publicly against Allee.[72]

The incident was so serious that PASSO's Fuentes, fearing for Cornejo's life, arranged a charter flight from Cristal to San Antonio for the mayor. Cornejo's departure from Cristal became a media circus. Newspapers from all over Texas gave the incident front-page coverage, especially upon learning that Cornejo had contacted state and federal officials requesting their intervention.[73] In his complaint to the U.S. Department of Justice Cornejo accused Allee of violating his civil rights. In addition, telegrams were sent to U.S. Attorney General Robert Kennedy and U.S. Senator Ralph Yarborough, D-Texas, about the harassment by Allee.

Yarborough, who had publicly congratulated Cornejo after the election, supported Cornejo. In Dallas Yarborough denounced "men wearing pistols, who were not part of city government." Such men, Yarborough exclaimed, "are a relic of a primitive age in Texas which should have passed away with the frontier." He added, "This is the most flagrant and extraordinary usurpation of power I have heard of since the oil boom days in Borger and before that in Reconstruction."[74]

Cornejo also took his complaint to Texas governor John Connally and Attorney General Waggoner Carr. But both officials came out publicly in support of the ranger. Connally told Cornejo: "The Texas Rangers were sent to Crystal City for the sole purpose of maintaining law and order and to prevent violence. Apparently their efforts have been successful to date and they will remain as long as the situation warrants. Every effort will be made to insure that the elected officials may perform their duties. I urge your cooperation."[75] On May 6 Cornejo sued Allee, asking $15,000 in damages and seeking a restraining order. The suit was dismissed for lack of witnesses. The Zavala County commissioners voiced support for Allee and the rangers, as did a delegation of Cristal residents that met with Colonel Homer Garrison Jr., director of the Texas Department of Public Safety. The eight-person delegation, which included representatives from the Mexican Chamber of Commerce as window dressing, urged Garrison to leave the rangers in Cristal, apparently for purposes of continued intimidation and harassment.

The whites' arsenal of harassment tactics included challenging the qualifications of two members of Los Cinco on the basis of property ownership; an unsuccessful attempt to recall Los Cinco; charges of voting irregularities; instigating city patrols by Texas Rangers and ranger harassment of the city's Mexicano police force (Cristal police were Mexicano, whereas the county sheriff and deputies, as well as the rangers, were white); outright intimidation; co-opting some Mexicanos with employment and other material inducements; using divide-and-conquer tactics; and forming a white-Mexicano coalition.

In 1964, in preparation for the Zavala County elections, whites joined forces with disenchanted middle-income Mexicanos. They established a political coalition, the Citizens Association Serving All Americans (CASAA). Ed Salinas Sr. was elected president; David Darter, vice president; Clarence Harper, secretary; and John C. Spencer, treasurer. Elected to the board of directors were Luz Arcos, Carlos Avila, Dale Barker, Adolph Fohlis, and Frank Guerrero, Jr. CASAA also formed a women's auxiliary.[76]

In structuring CASAA the whites deliberately balanced the leadership roles by having nearly equal numbers of whites and Mexicanos on the board of directors.[77] Its membership base was also mixed in order to give the appearance of inclusion and participation. Whites knew that if they were to regain political control of the city council in 1965, they would have to enlist Mexicanos. They went after Mexicanos who were more middle class and willing to assimilate. CASAA's paramount purpose was to act as a countervailing power to Los Cinco; its ultimate objective was the overthrow of the Mexicano-controlled city council. The *Sentinel* reported further that the coalition was designed to "to prevent the takeover of Zavala County by outside political pressure groups, to endorse and support local candidates for public office within Zavala County and to rid the county of persons already in public office who are under domination of outside interests."[78]

CASAA proved its political capability in the county elections. Cornejo and other PASSO leaders made it clear that controlling Cristal's city council was merely the first step to gaining control of the county. However, when making this bold pronouncement, PASSO's leadership failed to take into consideration the fact that the terms for county officers were staggered. For instance, the post of county judge was not up for election nor were two of the four seats on the court of commissioners. (The titles of elected officials in Texas counties are somewhat unusual, as are some duties. As chief executive officer of the county, the judge manages the county's administration, prepares the budget, presides over the court of commissioners, and is a voting member of that board. The county judge also presides over misdemeanor and civil cases.) Only the positions of county attorney, sheriff, tax assessor–collector, and two commission seats were to be contested. Nonetheless, PASSO organized a slate of candidates, which included Antonio G. Yanas for commissioner and Santos Alcozer for constable.

CASAA maximized its political advantages. For example, the county elections were scheduled for May rather than April, which allowed CASAA to concentrate on middle-class Mexicanos rather than the migrants who left Cristal after April for seasonal work. CASAA also launched an aggressive absentee voter campaign. Mayor Cornejo was outmaneuvered politically at every turn because CASAA supporters had control of the county government and county-state elections. CASAA even went so far as to mimic PASSO's organizing tactics: CASAA held free barbeques and organized rallies that were well attended, and the organization even endorsed and actively supported Jesús Rodríguez, owner of a local grocery store, for county commissioner.[79] CASAA did this to neutralize PASSO's allegations that CASAA was racist.

The highly contested May 1964 county election required a run-off, which was held in June in conjunction with the state primary.[80] CASAA soundly defeated PASSO. The *Zavala County Sentinel* reported, "The threat of PASSO last year to take over Zavala County failed last Saturday when a record number of voters cast ballots."[81] CASAA's Rodríguez received 474 votes to the 306 votes for PASSO's Yanas and became the first Mexicano ever elected to the Zavala County Court of Commissioners. CASAA's candidate for constable, Rannie Hale, defeated Santos Alcozer by 461 to 315 votes. In all, county residents cast 1,964 votes in the election, the highest ever for a run-off. However, the number was small in comparison to the record 3,416 votes cast in the first election in May. Table 1.3 provides the results of both the May and run-off elections and dramatizes the significant loss of support for the PASSO candidates because of the absence of the migrant workers.

For PASSO the results of the June election produced only one win, Julian Salas's for justice of the peace in Precinct 3. He beat Abie Guevara.

Several factors contributed to the defeat of the PASSO candidates. Unlike the 1963 revolt, neither PASSO at the state level nor the Teamsters mobilized its resources behind Cornejo's local PASSO efforts. Both took the position that they wanted to allow local Mexicanos to organize themselves. This seemed to be in response to the acrimonious attacks by CASAA that depicted Los Cinco as puppets of PASSO and the Teamsters. As a result of the election in Cristal, PASSO split into

Table 1.3. 1964 Zavala County Election Results

Office/Candidate	May Primary	June Run-Off	Drop in Support
Constable, Precinct 3			
Santos Alcozer (PASSO)	489	315	35%
Rannie Hale (CASAA)	489	461	6%
Commissioner, Precinct 3			
Antonio Yanas (PASSO)	448	306	32%
Moses Falcón (ex-PASSO)	4		
Jesús Rodríguez (CASAA)	363	474	8%
Busey Coleman (unendorsed CASAA member)	155		

Source: John Staples Shockley, *Chicano Revolt in a Texas Town* (Notre Dame, Ind.: University of Notre Dame Press, 1974), 62.

two distinct factions.[82] The local PASSO chapter was left with a diminishing membership, poor organization, and serious infighting, which "sapped the morale of the whole campaign effort."[83]

Governing the community became more difficult for Los Cinco. Shockley writes, "The nature of the victory—the inexperience of the candidates, the dependence upon outside help, and the vulnerability of the Mexicano community in a town which had always been dominated by Anglos—came back to haunt all those who had worked for the electoral success."[84] The inexperience of Los Cinco was apparent during the early weeks of the takeover. PASSO and Teamster officials were always present during the transition phase. They were conspicuous "technical advisers" who helped in the various aspects of governance. They even advised Mayor Cornejo on parliamentary procedure.

Initially, Cornejo understood that he was to run the city. He did not understand that the city charter called for a city manager form of government, which designated the city manager as the chief administrative officer. This misperception became one of the mayor's greatest mistakes. The Los Cinco–hired city manager, George Ozuna, the first Mexicano in Texas to hold that post, and Cornejo became engaged in a drawn-out power struggle. By 1964 relations between the two had led to Ozuna's firing and subsequent reinstatement by court order. Cornejo made another move to oust Ozuna, but he was thwarted by Louise Shafer, assistant business agent for the Teamsters in Cristal and wife of the the San Antonio Teamster boss, and Arthur Gochman, the Cristal city attorney, who sought to play a mediating role.[85]

The power struggles between Cornejo and Ozuna resurfaced in August 1964. Ozuna was once again fired by a 3 to 1 vote, with Cornejo, Mendoza, and Hernández voting for his dismissal, Maldonado voting against, and Cárdenas abstaining. However, the action was again over-turned. District Judge Ross E. Doughty ruled that the council had not followed proper procedure in the firing and therefore was in violation of the city's charter. This decision also affected Ray Perez, chief of po-lice, who had also been fired by the council.[86] The discord between Cornejo and Ozuna continued until Cornejo's term ended in 1965.

In fact, the naming of Cornejo as mayor had not been without con-troversy. Los Cinco had disagreed about who would hold the post. Traditionally, the mayor was whoever had received the most votes, which meant that Maldonado should have gotten the job. However, because of Maldonado's financial difficulties stemming from the loss of his job, the post went to the second-highest vote getter, Cornejo, who also was one of the architects of the takeover.[87]

These were not the only problems. Not long after he was elected, Councilman Hernández caught his colleagues by surprise when he made statements to the press that echoed the gringo rationale for using the Texas Rangers to patrol Cristal. His colleagues figured that Her-nández was being pressured into doing so. Later, in a conversation with Fuentes, Hernández acknowledged that he was being coerced. His lack of employment had led him to pass several bad checks, which gave the city attorney the legal leverage to convince him to support-ing the former power holders. By late December 1964 three of Los Cinco—Mendoza, Hernández, and Cárdenas—had been removed from office because they had failed to pay their utility bills.[88] Mendoza was replaced by E. C. Muñoz, and Hernández by Antonio G. Yanas, but because of a "standoff"—a 2–2 vote—no one replaced Cárdenas. These difficulties made the council look ridiculous in the eyes of the public and press. The media in particular were hypercritical of Cornejo and Cárdenas, the two remaining councilmen of the original Los Cinco.

As the April 1965 city council elections approached, the fighting and divisions between the Mexicano councilmen and city's administration worsened. In January a scuffle broke out at a city council meeting be-tween Cornejo and Maldonado over Maldonado's being in arrears for his 1963 taxes; this later turned out to be an error. Cornejo vehemently attacked Maldonado, accusing him of being directed and controlled by Ozuna. Furthermore, Cornejo alleged that both Maldonado and Muñoz were unfit to be council members.[89] In an audacious move Cor-nejo called for the ousters of Maldonado and Muñoz and the firing of Ozuna. In fact, Cornejo had come to the council meeting with the names of their replacements in hand. Hilario Lozano and José de la Fuente were to replace the two city council members and José Torres the city manager. The vote produced a tie. The political impasse had to be settled in the courts. District Judge Doughty ruled the firing of Ozuna and the dismissal of Maldonado and Muñoz were illegal. The conflict between Cornejo and Ozuna continued to weaken Cornejo's reelection efforts.

Meanwhile, the citizens committee had been absent from the political scene. As stated earlier, the committee had gradually begun to assume a lower profile; by late 1964 it had disappeared. Both the Teamsters and PASSO took on extremely low profiles, each for different reasons. Statewide, PASSO was plagued by internal power struggles between its liberal and conservative wings. Led by Hector Garcia, the conservative forces persuaded some PASSO members to quit the organization for the American G. I. Forum, and the League of United Latin American Citizens. The issue of PASSO's involvement with the Teamsters created discord among PASSO members because many were strongly antilabor.[90]

Thus PASSO was falling apart organizationally and was incapable of providing any meaningful assistance to Cornejo in the 1965 city council elections. Without PASSO's experienced organizers and their vital resources, Cornejo and his local PASSO chapter did not possess the experience or the funds to rebuild the grassroots political machine of 1963.

The Teamsters also fell into difficult times statewide. The press in Texas was critical of the union for its overt role in fostering the revolt in Cristal. After the takeover CASAA continued to hammer at the idea that the enemy was not the Mexicanos but outside forces such as the Teamsters.[91] However, the local Teamsters continued to support Cornejo and Los Cinco until the Cornejo-Ozuna power struggle became relentless.

In August 1964 Cornejo and Shafer had a falling-out that proved highly damaging for Cornejo. The press by this time was eager to verify the role and level of support that the Teamsters were providing to Cornejo. That month Shafer publicly suggested that the Teamsters would provide support for the reelection of Cornejo and his slate. Simultaneously, however, Louise Shafer, in her capacity as assistant business agent for the Teamsters in Cristal, fired Cornejo as union representative. She did this shortly after Cornejo moved to dismiss City Manager Ozuna. The situation became more ridiculous when Cornejo publicly announced that the local PASSO chapter would end its affiliation with the Teamsters if he were not reinstated as union rep. Cornejo also foolishly sought Ray Shafer's removal as Teamster manager. The Teamsters wasted no time replacing Cornejo with Moses Falcón, and

Cornejo became the only mayor in Texas who was receiving unemployment compensation.[92]

Cornejo and his local PASSO chapter were left to fend for themselves against the powerful opposition of CASAA. As he prepared for his reelection, Cornejo was clearly on the defensive. Unemployed, his car repossessed, and the Mexicano community totally fractionalized, he was clearly vulnerable to CASAA's political attack.

The Electoral Overthrow of PASSO

After two turbulent years the revolt had spawned its own endogenous antagonisms that produced an opportunity for a countercoup by CASAA. Nevertheless, by February 1965 Cornejo and the local PASSO chapter were beginning to mobilize for the upcoming election that would decide who would control the city council. The Cornejo-PASSO forces did not include the citizens committee, the organizational weapon that led the revolt in 1963. Also missing were the anger and determination that had energized the Mexicano community into electoral rebellion against the gringo power holders. Whereas in 1963 the majority of the Mexicano community were unified, in 1965 the opposite was true. Mexicanos were divided and once again becoming increasingly alienated politically. The political bickering, infighting, and power struggles had rekindled the people's distrust in politics.

Cornejo's PASSO developed its slate of candidates for city council, which included José de la Fuente, Hilario Lozano, Virginia Musquiz, and Antonio Yanas. With the exception of Yanas, who was already on the council, the other PASSO candidates were people Cornejo had tried to appoint during the power struggle with Ozuna. Cornejo's PASSO was also in trouble because it lacked money as well as the people to formulate and carry out the grassroots door-to-door canvassing tactics used in the 1963 campaign. Cornejo also was without a campaign platform and resorted to relentlessly accusing CASAA of "causing all the commotion" on the council.[93]

Opposing Cornejo were CASAA and Mexicanos who were disenchanted with PASSO but not necessarily supportive of CASAA. CASAA stood ready to topple what its partisans referred to in newspaper interviews as Cornejo's "band of low-income Latins." CASAA was "supremely well organized from start to finish," according to Shockley.[94] Armed with volunteers, literature, ads, and money, CASAA conducted an effective door-to-door voter registration and absentee ballot drive. It characterized Cornejo's administration as a circus. The CASAA slate,

Table 1.4. 1965 Cristal City Council Election Results

Candidates	Absentee Ballots	Election Day Vote	Total
CASAA Slate			
Carlos Avila	505	743	1,248
Bill Leonard	508	723	1,231
Ed Stocking	496	691	1,187
Humberto Castillo	477	650	1,127
Ed Salinas	502	624	1,126
PASSO Slate			
Juan Cornejo	30	945	975
José de la Fuente	24	933	957
Hilario Lozano	29	895	924
Antonio Yanas	24	890	914
Virginia Musquiz	25	829	854
Independent Slate			
Manuel Maldonado	41	239	280
Ramón Garza	19	123	142
Joseph Varner	13	49	62

Source: John Staples Shockley, *Chicano Revolt in a Texas Town* (Notre Dame, Ind.: University of Notre Dame Press, 1974), 74–75.

the epitome of inclusion and balance, included Carlos Avila, Bill Leonard, Ed Salinas, Ed Stocking, and Humberto Castillo.

On the independent ticket was Manuel Maldonado, one of Los Cinco who had served out his full two-year term. Maldonado had become one of Cornejo's adversaries and therefore chose to run as an independent. Joining him on the independent ticket were Ramón Garza and Joséph Varner. The three independents supported Ozuna's retention as city manager. But Maldonado had little chance of winning, and the presence of the independents in the race helped to ensure that Cornejo would be beaten, because they split the Mexicano vote.[95]

On the day of the election Cornejo's PASSO slate was soundly defeated. Although PASSO's candidates took the greatest number of votes at the poll on election day, CASAA's absentee ballot drive catapulted its candidates to victory. Cornejo received only 30 votes by absentee ballot compared to more than 500 absentee votes for each of the three CASAA candidates. A record 2,377 votes were cast, 1,752 by people voting in person. CASAA's slate had received 90 percent of the absentee vote. Table 1.4 provides the results.

In an interview with the *Sentinel* Cornejo conceded, "We were beat by the absentee vote." Clarence L. La Roche, a reporter for the *Houston Chronicle*, summarized why Cornejo and his slate lost: "Massive outside help from the Teamsters and PASSO two years ago put the all-Latino ticket in office. This time around that help was unavailable for Cornejo and his ticket. The opposing CASAA out-organized, out-worked, and out-planned the local PASSO-Cornejo combine."[96]

Still, the first revolt left an historic imprint. The message was clear. No longer would Mexicanos accept being politically disenfranchised, subordinate, and powerless. "It seemed clear that Mexican Americans in the community, through both CASAA and PASSO, had solidified their role as participants and that the ancien régime could not be restored," Shockley observes. Historian David Montejano writes, "The event far outweighed the takeover of a community of 9000. It symbolized the overthrow of Jim Crow." Historians Robert A. Calvert and Arnoldo De León agree: "The victory was both symbolic and very important, because it notified Anglos that no longer could the minority population rule unchallenged. Cristal portended the passing of the order."[97]

Despite all the problems encountered and caused by the Los Cinco council, its members made some changes that improved the quality of life for Cristal's Mexicanos. Most of these changes were the result of the combined leadership of Cornejo and Ozuna. In 1965, in the middle of his conflict with Cornejo, Ozuna released a report detailing the changes the city had made since Los Cinco were sworn in in 1963. Cristal had secured about $5 million in federal funds for urban renewal. Many streets had been paved, nearly one hundred outdoor privies had been removed, construction of a new city hall was underway, a $129,000 storm drainage project had been completed, and 154 street lights had been installed.[98] Despite all the internal bickering, Los Cinco's record for making improvements in the city's infrastructure for the benefit of all surpassed that of their white predecessors. The cardinal difference was that, although Los Cinco were committed to improving the socioeconomic conditions of the Mexicano, they did not exclude the rest of the community from reaping the benefits. Their predecessors, on the other hand, did nothing to ameliorate conditions for Mexicanos.

Los Cinco also had given the emerging Chicano Movement a boost. Both gringos and Anglos in Texas were forced to face the reality that some Mexicanos were no longer willing to accept their internal colonial status. The citizens committee's goal of community control predated the plethora of literature and oratory from the New Left, Black Power, and poor people's advocates of the mid- to late 1960s. Cristal served as a political laboratory in which community control was tested empirically—PASSO's plan was to export the "Cristal Rebellion" to other

Mexicano communities in south Texas. Although short-lived, the revolt of 1963 proved dialectically successful and invaluable as a precondition in the advancement of a more radical political climate that developed in Texas and throughout Aztlán after 1965.

CASAA's counterrevolt had produced an alliance between the old white power holders, now mostly consisting of the business, ranching, and farming elite, and the Mexicanos who had opposed Los Cinco. Whites had learned that they could never again govern without allowing access or representation to some Mexicanos. This change was also the result of whites' recognition that they constituted only about 20 percent of the city's population, which would be insufficient to fend off any future political challenges from the Mexicano community. They also realized that even though the revolt ended in failure, politically it had further aroused the Mexicanos' expectations. Although whites remained economically omnipotent, their political power and control had diminished. No longer could they wield their authority arbitrarily.

The Politics of Transition (1965–1969)

Although the Cristal experiment ended essentially in failure, the notion of community control did not end with the ouster of Cornejo and company. For the next five years control of the city council would remain in the hands of Mexicanos. Whites learned that to regain control of politics in Cristal, they would have to take indirectly rather than directly, that their greatest power was economic. Thus their economic clout allowed them to reestablish political control of the city's politics. In most cases Mexicanos who were elected to city council did not dare challenge, impinge on, or threaten whites' political and economic interests, which they continued to exercise through CASAA. Consequently, Mexicano power and control was, at best, symbolic or illusionary. Mexicanos lacked an agenda for social change and empowerment. For purposes of analysis, the subsequent five years can be described transitional. It was not until the second revolt in 1970 that the politics of community control sought the decolonization of Cristal and the rest of south Texas.

Thus from 1965 to 1969 whites acquiesced to the political pragmatism of running integrated slates of candidates through CASAA, a practice applied to both city and county elections. The majority of candidates on CASAA's city electoral slates were Mexicano, clearly reflecting the demographic reality of a Mexicano majority. Even the most blatant gringo racist reluctantly supported trustworthy and responsible Mexicanos. Throughout the five years that followed the countercoup, Mexicanos were the majority on the city council. The difference was that the Mexicano community had no well-defined agenda. Whites' agenda was clear: to reestablish control and influence and to use co-optation to achieve their ends. Shockley explains:

This Anglo process of cooptation was designed not only to prevent a general Mexican-American challenge to the board, but also to develop stable, responsible and trustworthy Mexican leadership which could serve to counter the more radical Mexicans. Anglos hoped the selection of these Mexicans could be used as proof of their good intentions. It was hoped and expected that these Mexicans would serve as examples to the whole Mexican community and be proof that the establishment was indeed open to Mexicans.[99]

Whites clearly relied on CASAA as the organizational mechanism by which they could exert their influence and power. An illustration of this was the designation of Carlos Avila as mayor in 1965. Whites did not feel threatened, although three of the five Cristal council members were Mexicano. All three were middle class and very conservative. Shockley describes them as wanting to be more Anglo than Mexicano: "Many Mexicans were in CASAA because they wanted to be like Anglos and they wanted to be accepted by the Anglos." Likewise, the Mexicano council members were acceptable to the white elite because the councilmen were "properly qualified" and expressed the "correct patriotic impulses."[100]

CASAA's governance and control did not accommodate the growing expectations of the Mexicano community. The Mexicanos on the city council did not represent the sentiments, aspirations, or agendas of the still powerless majority. Working-class Mexicanos were still not part of the community's circle of power. Mexicanos continued to suffer discrimination, poverty, and injustice. The Texas Rangers' "hate Mexicanos" mentality continued. At one point in 1965 former council member Maldonado was severely beaten by a white sheriff's deputy, jailed, and subsequently hospitalized. Historically, local law enforcement agencies in Texas were run by whites who did the bidding of the local white elite.

This incident and others gave rise to economic boycotts against CASAA officials, a tactic pioneered by the civil rights movement. Selective economic boycotts proved particularly effective against the Lone Star State beer distributor in Cristal and a grocery store owned by CASAA official Jesús Rodríguez. The boycotts continued well into 1968. During this time altercations between CASAA and PASSO supporters were commonplace, especially in the town's taverns. Supporters of the old citizens committee accused Mexicanos in CASAA of being traitors and

Table 1.5. 1967 Cristal City Council Election Results

Name/Faction	Absentee Votes	Election Day Votes	Total
Paulino Mata (CASAA)	305	812	1,117
Ed Salinas* (CASAA)	313	800	1,113
Hilario Lozano (PASSO-Cornejo)	55	1,039	1,094
Roberto Cornejo (PASSO-Cornejo)	58	1,036	1,094
Moses Falcón (PASSO-Falcón)	57	1,028	1,085
Juan Cornejo (PASSO-Cornejo)	59	1,025	1,084
Charlie Crawford (CASAA)	301	778	1,079
Bill Leonard* (CASAA)	306	306	1,071
Natividad Granados (PASSO-Falcon)	53	1,015	1,068
Humberto Castillo (CASAA)	302	743	1,045

*Incumbent

Source: John Staples Shockley, *Chicano Revolt in a Texas Town* (Notre Dame, Ind.: University of Notre Dame Press, 1974), 95.

Tio Tacos (Mexicanos who supported CASAA, and very much wanted to be accepted by gringos and Anglos). CASAA's Mexicano supporters in turn alleged that PASSO's members were a disgrace in the eyes of whites.[101] At no point during this period was conflict absent from Cristal.

These were the years of coalition politics. CASAA's coalition included Mexicanos, Anglos, and gringos. Although political conflict was still commonplace, it was not at the level or intensity that characterized the first revolt. Politics does indeed make for strange bedfellows. Initially, CASAA governed fairly quietly. Although the city council had a Mexicano majority, and Avila was serving as mayor, Ozuna resigned as city manager, pressured to do so because of his connection to Los Cinco. An inept white replaced him.

In the 1967 election CASAA, weakened by the absence of a strong opposition, a sense of complacency, and internal controversies, lost its majority on the council. But PASSO was also on a course of self-destruction. Its two competing factions were led by Cornejo and Falcón. Anti-CASAA Mexicanos still functioning under the auspices of PASSO won three of the five council seats, theoretically giving them community control. The election results appear in Table 1.5.

The three losing CASAA candidates contested the results in court, claiming that votes had been cast by noncitizens or individuals with fraudulent addresses. As a result of the suit, PASSO candidate Moses Falcón lost his seat to Charlie Crawford. Cornejo also filed suit, claiming fraud after he came in sixth. He alleged that CASAA had tampered with the absentee ballots. However, he withdrew the suit with no public explanation. With CASAA regaining control after Crawford won the suit, newly elected council member Paulino Mata, well liked by whites, was elected mayor by the council.

In April 1969 Cornejo again ran for the council on a slate with incumbent council member Hilario Lozano and Ramón de la Fuente and Alfred Terán. Juan Cornejo's brother, Roberto, decided not to seek reelection, leaving Cornejo's slate with only four candidates. The results of the election were humiliating for the Cornejo-PASSO team. The slate lost nearly 2 to 1. Many Mexicanos expressed their disapproval of the election by not voting at all. By 1969 the alienation of Cristal's Mexicano voters had increased. They had seen little improvement since the ouster of Los Cinco, so they could see no reason to vote. Although Francisco Benavides was the top vote getter for the CASAA slate, Paulino Mata was again chosen as mayor by what Shockley calls the "Mata team," which subsequently replaced CASAA as the white-controlled political machine.[102] By now Cornejo, who had run twice unsuccessfully for both city council and county commissioner during this period, found himself and PASSO discredited and without much support from the working-class Mexicanos of Cristal.

With a growing sense of accommodation and apathy the Mexicano community appeared to be politically quiescent. In 1969 the city charter was changed to provide for staggered two-year terms of office—only a portion of the council seats would be vacant in any given year. According to Herbert Hirsch and Armando Gutiérrez, "Through this strategy the power-holders felt sure that a complete turn-about would never recur, since they felt that Chicanos would be unable to sustain an organizational effort for more than one year."[103] The politics of these years helped foster the political climate that would give rise to the Cristal school walkouts.

Part Two

The Politics of Community Control: RUP's Peaceful Revolution in Cristal

2

The Second Electoral Revolt (1970)

The five years that preceded Cristal's second revolt in 1970 were relatively quiet. The Chicano Movement had emerged as a political force
by 1965, but its characteristic fervent protest and militant activism had
not really reached Cristal. Although the Mexican American Youth Organization (MAYO), one of the most militant Chicano organizations,
had been in the forefront of the Chicano Movement in various parts of
Texas, it had not done much organizing in the Winter Garden area,
where Cristal is located. However, in 1969 it became the first Chicano
organization in the nation to put into effect a political plan (known as
the Winter Garden Project) oriented to community control, empowerment, and change, that targeted the Winter Garden area of Zavala,
Dimmit, and La Salle counties. From 1970 to 1975 the change brought
about by the second revolt was so extensive that I describe it as the
Raza Unida Party's "peaceful revolution."

MAYO: Catalyst of the Second Revolt

MAYO was organized in 1967 by five Mexicano students, one of whom
was José Angel Gutiérrez. With a constituency of college students and
barrio youth, MAYO's adherence to protest and militant politics made
it the most controversial and radical Mexicano advocacy organization
in Texas. It confronted and took on many issues, especially in educa-

55

tion. During its brief history before the second revolt it initiated thirty-nine school walkouts and dealt with numerous other social and political issues. MAYO's leaders became the architects and implementers of the Mexicano third party, La Raza Unida, the major player in Cristal's second revolt.

In May 1969 MAYO held its statewide board meeting at Uvalde and after much deliberation approved the plan to use the Winter Garden Project to create a movement for the decolonization of the three counties and win control of the area's city councils, school boards, and county governments. MAYO also planned to launch La Raza Unida, which would be the main political mechanism for implementing the plan.

José Angel Gutiérrez—who had grown up in Cristal, was involved in the first revolt as an undergraduate, and now was pursuing graduate studies in political science—was chosen to organize the Winter Garden Project and get it started. With his return to Cristal, the political stage was set for the Cristal school walkouts. They became the spark that ignited the fires of electoral revolt among Cristal's restive Mexicanos. This time, however, the political results were so historically significant that Cristal became the political matrix of the increasingly political Chicano Movement.

Gutiérrez: The Organic Intellectual

As with Juan Cornejo's first revolt, personality drove the second. The noticeable difference was that Gutiérrez was by far the more educated, articulate, politically experienced, and Machiavellian of the two. Whereas Cornejo had an eighth-grade education, Gutiérrez by 1970 was working on his doctoral degree in political science.

Historian Tony Castro compares Gutiérrez to the Chicano Movement's three other main leaders, César Chávez, Reies López Tijerina, and Rodolfo "Corky" Gonzales:

José Angel Gutiérrez is not like other leaders of the Chicano movement. A generation gap separates him and the older threesome, Chávez, Tijerina, and Gonzales. Young, college-educated, the son of a doctor, Gutiérrez may have the most brilliant mind of any of the civil rights leaders of his lifetime. He represents the new breed of Chicano professionals produced by the colleges and universities, but he is still a Chicano with the old dream of revolution. Yet, even in revolt, there are contrasts between him and the older leadership: Chávez is cautious, Gutiérrez self-confident; Tijerina is aggressive, Gutiérrez cunning; Gonzales is uncompromising, Gutiérrez fluid. Gutiérrez is a Chicano prodigy, a well-read intellectual by Anglo standards who can just as comfort-

ably organize barrio youth to counter the very system that taught him. Gutiérrez has two major enemies—the dreaded gringo, of course, but also himself.
Sometimes Gutiérrez is too sharp-tongued, too self-confident, and too daring,
particularly when accusing the gringo of racism and cultural genocide against
Mexican-Americans.[1]

Castro's analysis of Gutiérrez is important for understanding the
political framework of Cristal's second revolt and peaceful revolution
and how they were tied to the politics of Gutiérrez. Political movements are generally transitory. Although some succeed, most fail. More
important, great movements are products of great leaders.[2] James Mac-
Gregor Burns provides an excellent definition of leadership: "leadership over human beings is exercised when persons with certain motives and purposes mobilize, in competition or conflict with others,
institutional, political, psychological, and other resources so as to
arouse, engage, and satisfy the motives of followers." Burns differentiates between what he calls "transactional" and "transforming" leadership. Where the former accentuates the exchange of valued things and
essentially the maintenance of the status quo, the latter "occurs when
one or more persons engage with others in such a way that leaders
and followers raise one another to higher levels of motivation and
morality."[3]

It was Gutiérrez's transforming leadership qualities that impelled
RUP's politics of community control and the peaceful revolution. In
just a few months he was able to take a community that was cynical,
distrusting, and politically alienated and transform it into one that was
optimistic, unified, and participating. The peaceful revolution's political agenda during the first five years of community control was motivated and optimistic. Those who once despaired had hope. They were
motivated to change their community's political profile by the opportunity to improve the quality of their lives. This became evident in Mexicanos' determination to defeat every electoral challenge to their community control of the school district and city council.

Perhaps Gutiérrez would not agree, but he was the peaceful revolution incarnate.[4] The two were linked by his charismatic and assertive
personality, adroitness, and acumen. His role was that of organizer,
intellectual, and leader. He epitomized the mass movement leadership
triad described by sociologist Eric Hoffer. Hoffer says that mass movements require three types of ideal leaders: people of words, fanatics,
and practical people of action. People of words start the mass movement, fanatics bring about change, and practical people of action insti-
tutionalize change.[5] Gutiérrez played all three leadership roles in starting the peaceful revolution, carrying it out, and institutionalizing it.

Gutiérrez energized the people with his ideas, courage, and actions. Historian Crane Brinton alludes to the preeminent and inextricable role of intellectuals in the history of revolutions. He postulates that it is "the transfer of the allegiance of the intellectuals" from the established regime to the struggle for change that signals the approach of a revolution and reveals the pivotal role of the intellectual. Yet, as Thomas H. Greene discovered in analyzing both revolutionary and nonrevolutionary movements, "the allegiance of the intellectual, except to their own ideas, is almost always in doubt."[6] This was not the case with Gutiérrez.

Guided by MAYO's general blueprint for community control and empowerment through the Winter Garden Project, Gutiérrez became its implementer. He designed it and organized the Mexicano third party. He in turn evolved from being the organizer of the second revolt to the undisputed political boss of RUP's peaceful revolution in Cristal. This made him into one of the most notable national leaders of the Chicano Movement (CM). As various Chicano scholars have written, RUP's success in taking over Cristal catapulted Gutiérrez to national prominence within the CM. He joined Chávez, López Tijerina, and Gonzales as part of what historians Matt S. Meier and Feliciano Rivera labeled "the CM's four horsemen."[7]

In the peaceful takeover Gutiérrez operated much as what Antonio Gramsci describes as the "organic intellectual." Gramsci was convinced that intellectuals can overcome the public's false consciousness by abandoning academia's ivory tower aloofness and merging with the masses as organic intellectuals. Gutiérrez was resolved to break gringos' dominance by becoming more knowledgeable; he agreed with Gramsci's hypothesis that the organic intellectual should not await a felicitous moment to become the catalytic agent for overcoming the people's hegemonic confinement.[8] The alliance between Gutiérrez and the people became a profound cult of personality.

Gutiérrez's opponents, journalists, and academics described his followers as *Gutierristas*. The politics between the Mexicano majority and the white minority became so polarized and personalized that there was virtually no neutral ground. No one ever doubted who was guiding the peaceful revolution. Although Luz Gutiérrez, Viviana Santiago, Virginia Musquiz, José Mata, Ventura Gonzales, and others made important leadership contributions, José Angel Gutiérrez was the indisputable leader and intellectual force of the Raza Unida Party and the political, educational, social, economic, and cultural changes it sought.

Gutiérrez was born in Cristal on October 25, 1944. His father was a physician who had served as a medical officer in General Pancho Villa's army during the Mexican Revolution (1910). The senior Gutiérrez moved to Cristal during the 1920s, married, and settled down. He set up his practice to serve only Mexicanos. His son later wrote about how the family's middle-class status won the Gutiérrezes respect from both the Mexicano and white communities: "Because of his standing and role in the community, my mother and I were treated very well, with great respect and deference." Whites' respect was atypical, wrote journalist Richard Vara: "Because of Gutierrez's father's professional status, he was respected by Anglos during a period when Mexicans were not highly respected in South Texas."[9]

José Angel was twelve when his father died. Vara explains that the doctor's death was both a profound personal loss to his son and taught the boy "what it was to be a Mexican." José Angel Gutiérrez told Vara about the devastating consequences of the senior Gutiérrez's death: "From one day to the next we lost our economic base. We were no longer considered to be middle class. I became just another Mexican. The credit was cut off at the bank, the drug store, the department store." The ensuing years proved both economically and socially difficult for the boy and his mother. His mother, Concepción, who had only an eighth-grade education, could not find work. The white community shunned her and the boy. Gutiérrez writes, "They told her with their actions to return to her Mexican world or leave town if she didn't like the new treatment."[10] The traumatic rejection, coupled with the social degradation that followed, planted in Gutiérrez an anger and frustration that intensified as he matured, became more educated, and engaged actively in politics.

While José Angel was in school, his mother worked in the fields; he sometimes accompanied her. In high school he was a champion debater, maintained excellent grades, and served as president of his junior and senior classes. While a student at the junior college in Uvalde, he was initiated into community politics in 1963 with his involvement as a student activist in the first revolt. In 1966 he was graduated from Texas A&M University at Kingsville. During his undergraduate years he became involved in student politics, helping to organize a student chapter of PASSO. After a brief try at law school at the University of Houston he enrolled at Saint Mary's College, obtaining a master's degree in political science in 1968. There he and four other young student leaders organized MAYO, one of the most militant advocacy organizations of the CM. Gutiérrez's activism continued as he worked toward his doctoral degree in government at the University of Texas at Austin, which he was awarded in 1976.

In his autobiography Gutiérrez categorically rejects Thomas Carlyle's "great man" theory, yet Gutiérrez was indispensable to the success of the peaceful revolution.

RUP's Peaceful Revolution: A Framework for Change

The term *peaceful revolution* refers to the major political, educational, social, and economic changes that occurred during RUP's five years of community control, 1970–1975. It can, of course, be seen as a contradiction in terms. In most cases revolutions are violent and involve a major transformation of the social order: power is never given, it is taken. In *Political Order in Changing Societies* political scientist Samuel Huntington defines revolution as "a rapid, fundamental, and violent domestic change in the dominant values and myths of a society, in its political institutions, social structure, leadership, and government activity and policies."[11] With the exception of violence, all other aspects of Huntington's definition apply to RUP's peaceful revolution. The definition is useful for purposes of describing and understanding the breadth of change attempted by RUP in Cristal.

Although in reality the peaceful revolution was reformist, the scope of the intended changes made it revolutionary. Its design as the catalyst for the decolonization of Mexicanos in south Texas and throughout Aztlán made the Cristal experiment unique. The second revolt wrought changes that justify the term *revolution:*

- replacement of the white governing elite on the city council and school board and briefly at the county level
- empowerment of Mexicanos and successful implementation of community control, as manifested in Mexicanos' participation on many city, school, and county committees and commissions
- significant change within the educational, economic, social, and cultural sectors of the community
- dramatic changes in Mexicanos' political culture, characterized by progressive changes in the community's attitudes, values, myths, and symbols that produced high levels of political participation and unprecedented self-confidence
- repudiation of assimilation and the ardent espousal of a mixtures of cultural nationalism (Chicanismo) and a strong dose of socialist ideas and principles within the confines of the system's capitalistic structure, laws, and political culture

Cristal was the only community in the nation to undergo such a radical transformation. No other community that participated in the Winter Garden Project experienced the magnitude of change and the notoriety that went with it.

The Cristal School Walkouts

In the later winter and early spring of 1969 Gutiérrez systematically organized voters throughout the targeted three-county area, spending weeks researching the local power structures; building support for the Winter Garden Project; securing financial commitments; establishing a newspaper, *La Verdad;* and forming the community-based political organization that would run the Winter Garden Project, Ciudadanos Unidos [Citizens United]. By late November he had organized Cristal's high school students in preparation for the school walkouts.

In April 1969 a few Mexicano students had been angered by the high school's discriminatory practices in selecting its cheerleaders. Although the student body at Crystal City High School was heavily Mexicano, only one of the four young women selected as cheerleaders was Mexicana; the other three were white. Gutiérrez advised the Mexicano students to postpone any confrontation with the white-controlled administration until the fall. The rationale was twofold: maintaining the momentum of a school boycott would be impossible during summer vacation, and during the summer Cristal temporarily loses almost half its population to the migrant stream.

That fall the students protested the selection process for homecoming queen and her court. Few Mexicanas were eligible because the rules stipulated that candidates had to have at least one parent who had been graduated from the high school. By December the Mexicano community was following developments avidly. The students had approached the administration with eighteen broad, diverse demands, among them that all student elections be conducted by students and not the administration; that all administrators, teachers, and staff become bilingual and bicultural; that the district provide bilingual-bicultural education; and that the district hire a Mexicano counselor. The administration rebuffed them.

On December 9 the students initiated a full-fledged walkout. At the peak of the demonstration about sixteen hundred students were boycotting the elementary, junior high, and high schools. Their actions received national attention, and in January 1970 the school administration finally caved in, acceding to most of the students' demands. The Mexicano community was inspired, this time to gain control of the school board and city council.

The Genesis of the Raza Unida Party

Gutiérrez used the community's repoliticization in the Cristal school walkouts of 1969 to carry out both the Winter Garden Project and his plan for a Mexicano third party.[12] (From 1968 to 1970 MAYO organized thirty-nine school walkouts throughout Texas as part of its organizing crusade to effect educational change. Cristal's walkout was the thirty-ninth and MAYO's only success, attributable to Gutiérrez's adroit organizing skills and the effective student leadership of Severita Lara, Mario Treviño, and Diana Palacios.) After the Cristal school board acceded to students' demands in late January 1970, Gutiérrez accelerated his organizing efforts in regard to the Winter Garden Project and RUP. Since his return to Cristal in 1969, he had deliberately concentrated on forming RUP instead of pushing for a nonpartisan advocacy organization to lead the Mexicano struggle for empowerment.

Still, Gutiérrez recognized the importance of having a nonpartisan community-based political organization that could act as a buttress for RUP. Before he formally established the RUP in 1970, in late 1969 he organized Ciudadanos Unidos (CU). While MAYO had promulgated the Winter Garden Project, it was CU that became the local political community organization and ultimately the political machine that drove the implementation of community control. During the course of the school walkout, Gutiérrez used the many rallies, community meetings, marches, and pickets to convince people of the importance of staying organized, joining CU, registering to vote, and building a Chicano third party.

Gutiérrez used Alinsky's tactic of picking at the people's sore of discontent. Gutiérrez acknowledged the school boycott's importance and accomplishments, but instead of celebrating the victory he sought to create an insatiable hunger for more change. In January 1970 he tried to convince Cristal's Mexicanos that they had not won a major victory, that the real victories were ahead. Students and parents responded positively to Gutiérrez's assessment. "I didn't want for us to win all of our demands so that when we sobered up, we would realize that we hadn't won that much," he said not long afterward. "These feelings would carry over into the election."[13] Meanwhile, students continued to complain that teachers were harassing them and that school officials were procrastinating on the question of amnesty.[14]

To Gutiérrez, getting Mexicanos elected to office was not enough. He sought total community control of the local educational and government institutions in order to implement community control, participatory democracy, and other policy aspects of the Winter Garden Project. Historian Ignacio Garcia explains, "It was MAYO's philosophy that reforms would come when the Chicano community had not only the votes to make changes but also the strength to resist outside pressures to rescind them. Empowerment also called for a shake-up of the organizational structure and a changing of the guard."[15]

On January 17 more than 150 people attended a special meeting in Zavala County to form RUP. Their response was overwhelmingly positive, exactly as Gutiérrez had hoped. Those who attended the meeting eagerly became strong RUP supporters.[16] They elected officers and set goals. They chose Luz Gutiérrez, who was married to José Angel, as Zavala County chair, elected committee members for the county's four precincts, and approved the name of the party.

The party's name had been chosen before the meeting, the result of a telephone discussion with Warren Barnett, a lawyer who advised Gutiérrez on the legal aspects of forming a political party, as well discussions with Bill Richey, a Vista volunteer who operated out of Cotulla, and Viviana Santiago, a teacher who came to Cristal as a volunteer. (Richey, working as an organizer, assisted Gutiérrez in implementing the Winter Garden Project. Santiago, recruited by Gutiérrez at a state MAYO conference in December 1969, arrived in Cristal later that month, during the school walkouts. She quickly became one of the most important technician-leaders of the peaceful revolution and a key Gutiérrez confidant.)

Gutiérrez had wanted to call the third party the "Mexican American Democratic Party," but Texas electoral laws limit parties' names to three words. Furthermore, state election officials said the new party's name could not include the word *democratic* because it was already the name of the Democratic Party. Santiago and Richey pushed for "Raza Unida Party." Gutiérrez believed that a Spanish name would alienate people more than unite them, that people, especially the Mexicano middle class, were not ready for it. Gutiérrez finally acquiesced for strategic reasons.[17] *Raza unida* [the people united] was a term already in vogue as a rallying cry among Mexicano activists across Aztlán, and especially within MAYO, since the organization had participated in national coalitional policy conferences held under that banner in 1967 and 1968. Consequently, the recommendation was presented at the January 17 meeting in Zavala County, and it was approved.

On January 23 Gutiérrez filed the application, signed by eighty-nine people, for formal recognition of RUP in Zavala County. He announced that, as required by Texas election laws, RUP would hold a convention on May 2, 1970, to nominate candidates for the November general elections.[18] Similar applications were filed in Dimmit, La Salle, and Hidalgo counties (Hidalgo, deep within Texas's Rio Grande Valley, is outside the targeted Winter Garden area). Gutiérrez's strategy called for first establishing RUP on a multicounty basis, then statewide, and eventually throughout Aztlán.

The announcement of RUP's formation brought enthusiasm, alarm, and much debate throughout the state. The enthusiasm came generally from those who had participated in the walkouts or were involved in the party's formation. The alarmists judged RUP to be un-American, nationalistic, racist, and segregationist. Mexicanos throughout Texas argued heatedly over the merits of a Mexicano political party versus the opportunities available to them as liberals in the Democratic Party or as liberal Republicans.[19] Nonetheless, the reaction from the majority of Mexicanos in Cristal was positive.

Although RUP was not yet a certified political party, by February 1970 RUP candidates had filed for partisan county and nonpartisan local offices throughout the three-county Winter Garden area and Hidalgo County. By the filing deadline in early February RUP candidates were declared in all races for open county offices in Zavala, Dimmit, La Salle, and Hidalgo counties in preparation for the November elections. RUP's campaigns for local offices in the four counties produced sixteen candidates for the upcoming April school board and city council elections. RUP's top priority was to recruit qualified, eligible, and willing Mexicano candidates who were committed to building the party and were supportive of the Winter Garden Project.

Finding candidates proved difficult. In the past any Mexicano candidate who opposed the interests of the white community was harassed, intimidated, and coerced. A common tactic was to have defiant Mexicanos fired from their jobs. Interestingly, some Anglos favored the idea of taking power away from the gringos, but few wanted to participate in the electoral revolt as candidates. CU finally decided to back Gutiérrez, Arturo Gonzales, and Mike Pérez to fill the three vacancies on the Cristal school board. Gutiérrez, who had not planned to be a candidate himself, recalled that "by February I had switched my position, I was going to be able to stay as an organizer behind the scenes. There were going to be a lot of decisions that had to be made. It would take a lot of raw guts to break through the many barriers. So I decided then to be a candidate for office."[20]

Arturo Gonzales worked as a service station attendant through one of the local war on poverty programs. Initially, a group of students had asked him to run for the school board. Only Gutiérrez had filed his candidacy, so at a CU meeting Gonzales volunteered to do likewise. At that same meeting Mike Pérez, a local radio announcer and businessperson, was asked to run, and he too agreed. Pérez's political assets were his popularity and the possibility that he could get free political advertising from KBEN, his employer.[21]

Because of the 1969 charter change that mandated staggered terms of office in Cristal, RUP could not sweep a majority onto the city council in one election; only two of the five seats were to be contested.

Pablo Puente and Ventura Gonzalez were RUP's candidates. However, in a desperate attempt to hamper the growth of RUP, which was becoming increasingly popular, city officials affiliated with CASAA disqualified Puente a few weeks before the election because he was not a property owner (the city charter stipulated that any person wishing to run for the city council had to be a property owner). This was another technique for keeping the Mexicano majority disenfranchised. Gutiérrez, assisted by lawyers from the Mexican-American Legal Defense Fund (MALDEF), went to court to challenge Puente's disqualification.

MALDEF's intervention was an achievement in itself, because Rep. Henry B. Gonzalez, D-Texas, had attacked the group for assisting MAYO in the past. MALDEF was vulnerable because it was dependent on foundation monies, especially the Ford Foundation, which had given MALDEF a $2.2 million grant. Because of its support for groups such as MAYO, MALDEF later was pressured into moving its central office from San Antonio to San Francisco. Gutiérrez was able to recruit MALDEF by arguing that the people of Cristal, not MAYO, were seeking MALDEF's help.

Electoral Revolt in the Winter Garden Area

In March RUP and the Mexicano communities intensified their political activity throughout the targeted counties. The April elections were to be a kind of graduation for MAYO's Winter Garden Project and baptism for RUP. Their objectives were to ensure a large Mexicano voter turnout; force the opposition to make mistakes; use the election to further educate and politicize Mexicanos on the merits of both RUP and the Winter Garden Project; remind and convince Mexicanos that their enemies were the local gringos; and develop CU's organizational base and mobilizing capability. The last was to be accomplished by relying on the extended family method of organizing that Gutiérrez developed. It relied on nuclear and extended family members to recruit new members into CU and registered voters into RUP.[22] The unifying and mobilizing theme of the RUP campaigns was that the time had come for a transfer of power—from the white minority to the Mexicano majority and that Mexicanos were capable of governing.

In addition to the goal of decolonizing the Mexicano community, Cristal's second revolt differed from the first revolt in a number of other factors. The second revolt encompassed a much bigger geographic area, and it sought control of both city and school institutions. Also, the leadership of the second revolt was far more sophisticated, capable, and well versed in the game of politics. Unlike PASSO in 1963,

CU was well organized and had a powerful grassroots base of support in the Mexicano community.

In the weeks before the elections Mexicanos' enthusiasm was evident. Not since the first revolt had Mexicanos in Cristal shown so much commitment and willingness to become politically involved. Now organized through MAYO, students ran voter registration and education drives. With a rapidly expanding membership base CU was eager to demonstrate its political muscle and mobilization capability.

In the closing days of the campaigns countless rallies, meetings, and social fund-raisers were held for RUP candidates. In organizing these events Gutiérrez relied on a technique commonly used by Mexico's El Partido Revolucionario Instituciónal (PRI): free beer, food, and music. This technique helped to create a large pool of volunteers for the various campaigns. With ample volunteers and organizing bodies such as CU, MAYO, and others, RUP ran a strong grassroots mobilization campaign that included precinct canvassing, literature development and distribution, media blitzes, telephone canvassing, sound trucks in the neighborhoods, poll watching, and precinct-by-precinct get-out-the-vote drives. This formula put a well-organized political machine behind the RUP candidates. In an effort to ensure a clean election Gutiérrez requested federal observers. Within a few days he was informed by the Texas Advisory Committee to the U.S. Civil Rights Commission that federal marshals would serve as observers.[23]

Initially, local whites did not see RUP as a serious threat. However, with the success of the school boycott and RUP's visible political mobilization for the elections, whites responded, reviving their old organization, Citizens Association Serving All Americans (CASAA), which had helped to topple Los Cinco. As in 1965, CASAA chose Mexicano candidates believed to agree with white interests and who therefore were safe.[24] Because the coalition strategy had worked before, the power holders thought it would work again. They gave their candidates money and personnel. CASAA volunteers distributed literature, worked the telephones, and sought ways to stop RUP's growing groundswell of support.

CASAA's basic strategy was to attack Gutiérrez's credibility as a candidate. The organization depicted him as un-American, a dangerous radical, a communist, and an atheist. Some called him a potential murderer, in reference to a statement he had made—"Kill the Gringo"—in 1969 as the leader of MAYO. He made the statement in the course of a speech he was giving at a press conference in San Antonio right after MAYO's Del Rio march, which was called to protest the firing of VISTA (Volunteers in Service to America) workers who had collaborated with MAYO. Gutiérrez had rashly asserted that unless there was social change for Mexicanos in the barrios, it might be necessary to kill gringos in order to eliminate them.[25] CASAA also characterized RUP's candidates as unqualified to hold public office and threatened economic reprisals against Mexicanos who voted for RUP candidates.

The attacks on Gutiérrez became more intense and vitriolic as election day drew closer. The April 2 issue of the *Sentinel* reprinted a February 28 article from the *Odessa American* that contained excerpts from a speech given by Gutiérrez in Odessa before about two hundred members of MAYO. In the article, which bore the headline "MAYO Leader Wants Change, 'Eliminate' the Gringo," Gutiérrez was quoted as describing the gringo as being virtually "inhuman," "a bigot," "a racist," and "just plain animal." According to the story, Gutiérrez also told the leaders of MAYO that they had had the guts to tell "the man" that "1. We don't like you; 2. We're going to get rid of you, and 3. We are going to stand right on top of you, and you better leave while you can." In the course of the speech Gutiérrez also described the gringo as "an Acapulco jet-setter who believes that all Mexicans are ignorant."

The reprint appeared just two days before the school board election and immediately became controversial. The *Sentinel*'s publisher, Dale Barker, charged that RUP supporters had sought to buy every copy of the paper to prevent their distribution to the electorate. *San Antonio Express* reporter Sam Kindrick called Luz Gutiérrez, and she denied Barker's allegation. She told Kindrick she was aware of the story about her husband's talk but said she had not bought the papers. "We'll win the race anyway—José's speech won't make a bit of difference," she told him. But in an interview three years later she acknowledged that Barker was right. She said that RUP members bought the newspapers in a effort to provide an explanation of José Angel's comment before people read the article. She said that RUP was concerned that CASAA would use the remarks to try to win Mexicano votes by depicting José Angel as a radical, communist, and atheist bent on eliminating the gringo.[26]

In an act of desperation the day before the April 4 school board elections CASAA dropped about two thousand leaflets from an airplane over Cristal. The leaflets contained excerpts from Gutiérrez's Odessa speech. The leaflets also warned of impending economic stagnation and other problems, should RUP candidates win. CASAA's leadership claimed that RUP candidates were unqualified to serve in public office because they were either inexperienced or uncommitted. Throughout the campaign CASAA stressed the importance of supporting its responsible, business-oriented candidates who, the organization alleged, represented the interests of all the community. One political advertisement in the *Sentinel* emphasized the need for

Responsible Men for Responsible Jobs: Education and City Government are big businesses that need proper management by competent and responsible people. It is important that you vote for men who offer business and professional experience and willingness to devote their time to representing the best interests of all citizens.[27]

CASAA's anti-RUP strategy included intimidation. Gringo ranchers and farmers sought to persuade RUP supporters to vote for CASAA's candidates. If persuasion failed, gringos threatened voters with unemployment. This was not a new tactic. It had been used in the 1963, 1965, and 1967 local elections. Another was to spread word that if RUP candidates won, industry would never come to Cristal.[28] The implication was obvious: if people wanted more jobs, they had to vote for the CASAA candidates. In retrospect, CASAA's overall strategy backfired. It heightened tensions and cemented the distrust that Mexicanos had long felt for whites.[29]

Gutiérrez and RUP responded to CASAA's attacks by increasing the intensity of the campaign's organizing efforts. Shockley writes that to counter the attacks Gutiérrez brought to political rallies autographed photographs of senators Ted Kennedy and George McGovern and the invitation sent to Gutiérrez for the Nixon-Agnew inauguration. Throughout the campaign Gutiérrez warned voters of the inevitability of attacks on him and RUP.[30]

In the middle of the vitriol the state's Fourth Court of Civil Appeals ruled on March 20 that the question of putting Puente's name on the ballot was moot because absentee balloting had already begun. MALDEF carried RUP's appeal to federal court. Shockley explains the rationale used in the appeal:

Appealing to the federal court, [MALDEF] attorney [Jesse] Gamez . . . claimed that such a decision by the court opened the door to fraud. Any community, he argued, could wait until just before the start of the absentee balloting to deny a candidate a place on the ballot for any number of clearly unconstitutional practices and could do so successfully because the question would immediately become moot.[31]

Four days before the election a federal district judge in San Antonio ruled the charter provision unconstitutional. He ordered Puente's name put back on the ballot and that new ballots be printed. As a condition, Puente had to agree not to contest the 150 absentee ballots that had already been cast.[32]

In Cristal, CU carried out an unprecedented get-out-the-vote mobi-

Table 2.1. 1970 School Board and City Council Elections in Cristal

School Board		City Council	
RUP		RUP	
Mike Pérez	1,397	Ventura Gonzalez	1,341
Jose Angel Gutiérrez	1,344	Pablo Puente	1,306
Arturo Gonzales	1,344		
CASAA		CASAA	
E. W. Ritchie	1,119	Emmett Sevilla	835
Rafael Tovar	1,090	Charlie Crawford	820
Luz Arcos	1,081		

Source: *Zavala County Sentinel,* April 9, 1970.

lization. For both the school board and city council elections hundreds of student and adult volunteers canvassed Cristal's precincts door to door. In addition to making hundreds of phones calls to voters in the targeted areas, CU volunteers drove several vehicles equipped with sound systems that played Tex-Mex music and made passionate pleas to residents to vote. In order to boost people's confidence as well as influence the undecided voters to vote for RUP's candidates, Gutiérrez directed voters to remain near the polling places and staff tables decorated with posters and flags and loaded with literature about RUP candidates. The grassroots voter mobilization paid off in both elections, with RUP candidates scoring impressive victories. The voter turnout in the April 1970 local elections was considerably higher than for the 1968 presidential election.[33]

The school board election, on April 4, produced the highest voter turnout in the history of the district. Of the 3,100 people registered to vote, 2,544 went to the polls. The results showed that although CASAA had secured 227 absentee votes to RUP's 27, on election day RUP garnered 54 percent of the vote.

The results carried over into the Cristal city council elections three days later, with 2,222 voters turning out. (Only in 1967 had voter turnout been higher, when 2,280 voted.[34]) RUP candidates took an impressive 60 percent of the votes cast. See Table 2.1 for the results of both elections.

RUP also scored big in Cotulla, where Juan Ortiz, Arseno Garcia, and Raul Martinez, RUP's La Salle County chair, had done much of the political organizing, registering about two thousand Mexicano voters during January alone. Alfredo Zamora Jr., a schoolteacher, became Cotulla's first Mexicano mayor in thirty years, defeating by a vote of 587–584 incumbent Paul Cotulla whose family had founded the town. RUP candidate Enrique Jimenez received 636 votes to the 493 that went to his opponent, Claude Franklin Jr. George Carpenter Sr., the RUP candidate, got 667 votes to Ray Keck's 439 votes. The only RUP loss in Cotulla was that of Alfredo Ramirez, who garnered 530 votes to incumbent Arthur Hill's 575 votes. RUP candidates also won seats on the Cotulla school board. Reynaldo Garcia defeated incumbent Chester Bell Jr., 667 votes to 536, and Rogelio Maldonado polled 693 votes to incumbent F. D. Henrichman's 524.[35]

In Carrizo Springs two RUP-supported candidates also won. Rufino Cabello received 711 votes and Jesús Rodríguez polled 639 votes to defeat Mayor Joe Schmitt, who garnered 470 votes, and Eddie Leonard, 423 votes. Cabello and Rodríguez had started out as RUP candidates, but both switched their status to independent a week before the election. They declared that the campaigns against the RUP candidates in Cristal had become so dirty and polarizing that identifying with RUP was political suicide. Nonetheless, RUP in Carrizo Springs continued to actively support them.[36]

Only in Hidalgo County did RUP fail to produce an electoral victory. Still, RUP's electoral revolt produced unprecedented results. Of the fourteen seats the party contested, RUP won twelve. With some Mexicano candidates shifting their political allegiance to RUP, the party won community control of both Cristal's and Cotulla's city councils and Cristal's school board. With the election of Arturo Gonzales and Puente to the Cristal city council, Councilman Francisco Benavides announced his support for RUP, giving the party a 3–2 majority. Likewise, Eddie Treviño, a holdover on the school board, gave RUP a tenuous 4–3 advantage over CASAA.[37]

The Winter Garden Project had produced a record crop. Mexicanos were euphoric. Gutiérrez, who had engineered the victories, reacted by enthusiastically predicting that the RUP would create many more Cristals anywhere and everywhere Mexicanos wanted them. The victories in Cotulla and Carrizo Springs were perhaps more remarkable than the ones in Cristal because neither town had undergone the political mobilization that Cristal had. RUP's success in those towns proved that the strategies that led to the second revolt would work in other south Texas communities.[38]

RUP maintained its momentum. RUP leaders moved aggressively throughout the targeted three-county area to ensure that people understood the significance of what had happened. In an open letter to *La Verdad* (RUP's local newspaper) the party's winners committed themselves to effecting major change within the city and school institutions. The letter was written in Spanish; translated, it read, "We want to give our most expressive thanks to all the people who gave us their support and vote, because without their vote, we would not have won. You the Mexicanos elected us, and during the time we serve you, we will do everything within our power to improve the educational system and the city."[39]

Whites expressed cynicism and anger. E. F. Mayer, president of the Cristal school board, said, "Other communities better wake up or they will be facing the same thing." The second revolt soon led to an exodus of white families from the area. Barker, the *Sentinel's* publisher, told the *San Antonio News* that so many people had left Cristal that the local Rotary Club had been deactivated. Jack Kingsberry, a local rancher and businessman, claimed that two industrial firms were no longer interested in locating in Cristal because RUP candidates had won.

"Anglos," writes historian Ignacio Garcia, "soon realized after the election that the situation was different from the one in 1963. Although most of the voters were still illiterate and poor, they no longer seemed as afraid, and without doubt they were better led. The Mexicano revolt of 1963 was an uncontrolled flood of passions, but this one was a calculated barrage of blows from a wide-awake and power-hungry giant."[40]

Some Texas newspapers were even-handed in their coverage. The *Big Spring Herald's* headline on its election story read, "MAYO Leader Whips the Establishment." And the *San Antonio Light* reported, "Raza Unida Wins Major Seats in Area Election."[41] At the dawn of the peaceful revolution these and other newspapers avoided sensationalism and essentially stuck to the facts.

Historian John Chavez describes what was at the heart of whites' fear: "As the successes of Castro's Cuba promised to spread his revolution to the rest of Latin America, [whites] feared the successes of Crystal City would spread similar revolts throughout the Southwest." According to historian David Montejano, "The electoral take-over by Raza Unida of Crystal City and Zavala County in 1970—the second uprising—stunned the state, frightened Anglo residents of South Texas, and [subsequently] prompted Governor Ralph Briscoe to denounce Zavala County as a 'Little Cuba.'"[42]

Indeed, Mexicanos throughout Aztlán were watching the Winter Garden area. "As a result of Raza Unida's vitality and commitment to political action, Crystal City has become a symbol to Chicanos of strength through Unity," historians Matt S. Meier and Feliciano Rivera declared in their 1972 book. "The political apathy that formerly was noted throughout the lower Rio Grande region is disappearing. . . . From Crystal City, the spirit of La Raza Unida has already spread over the Southwest."[43] Still, not all Mexicanos agreed. In an editorial dated May 15, 1970, *La Verdad,* a Spanish-English weekly published in Nueces

County, described Gutiérrez as a "nut." The editorial continued, "The editor of *La Verdad* does not pretend to be a doctor of any sorts but he definitely knows that there is SOMETHING amiss in the man's overall conduct, in his verbal outbursts, in his profane style of attacks against the gringo philosophy of life and politics."

But to many activists across Aztlán, Crystal City became "Cristal," a symbol of better things to come. Urban and rural Mexicanos suddenly became more conscious of the importance of expanding the CM's agenda to include Mexicano community control and empowerment. (The Chicano Movement's early years were oriented toward a social and cultural agenda, especially within education. It was not until the second revolt that the Chicano Movement's focus was broadened to include electoral politics.) Thus, as a result of the second revolt, a RUP organizing contagion quickly spread throughout Texas and the rest of Aztlán and into the midwest.

RUP's Power Consolidation (1970)

Throughout 1970 Gutiérrez continued to move to consolidate RUP's governing majorities on Cristal's city council and school board.[44] The elections did not produce governing majorities in either case. Those evolved only after the elections, when incumbent school board member Treviño and council member Benavides declared their alliance with the RUP electees. Although appointed three years earlier by the white members of the school board, Treviño had evolved into what Shockley describes as "a quiet, one-man opposition."[45] He had become increasingly disenchanted with the white board members' insensitivity and indifference to the educational concerns of Mexicano students. (Chapter 8 further explores how Treviño became the swing vote that gave RUP control of the school board.)

Benavides had been elected to the city council with the support of whites in 1969; at the time he was part of Mayor Paulino Mata's team. Gutiérrez noted, "It wasn't I who convinced him [Benavides], it was group pressure." RUP supporters reminded the councilman that although he had secured the most votes in the 1969 city council election, whites had persuaded the rest of the council to offer the position of mayor to Mata, whom they felt was safer and more trustworthy.[46]

Whites had backed the 1969 charter reform that staggered city council terms in order to prevent another takeover. The Treviño and Benavides defections sent a powerful message to the white elite that they no longer had control, directly or indirectly. Shockley explains:

These defections also emphasized problems that Crystal City Anglos faced in trying to coopt Mexican Americans into their leadership. If Anglos picked Mexicans that were absolutely trustworthy, they could also be absolutely sure that such Mexicans would carry little weight in the Chicano community. If they picked men who were independent and respected in the Chicano community, then Anglos would not be able to rely on them in critical situations. This presented a strategic dilemma for the Anglos for which there was no easy solution.[47]

Throughout RUP's efforts to consolidate its power, Gutiérrez was cognizant of and concerned about white efforts to co-opt the Mexicano leadership as in 1965. To counter this Gutiérrez relied on CU and RUP to foster a mind-set of cooperation. Maintaining the loyalty of the two converts was going to be a major task. Gutiérrez figured that with Benavides, a businessperson financially independent of the white elite, it was only a matter of giving him an opportunity to get things done.[48]

Treviño, however, worked at the Del Monte plant as an inspector, a good job with a decent salary. Like Cornejo and others before him, he was vulnerable because of the relationship between Del Monte management and the white elite and Del Monte's willingness as a company to use economic pressure or intimidation against Mexicano workers who did not toe the political line. But, as Gutiérrez recalled, Treviño proved to be unyielding in his commitment to change in the Cristal schools:

They applied a lot of pressure, but Eddie had a lot of balls. He simply said he was not going to succumb, that he was going to go with his Raza, even if they fired him. We knew that just before the election they [Del Monte] had fired thirteen different people. And that after we took power again, they fired some fourteen more. We had some thirty people fired from Del Monte for being active with us. . . . We assured him. . . . I did commit that he would be taken care of in terms of getting another job and would be retrained if necessary. Eddie was solid . . . he would not be moved.[49]

Throughout 1970 CU's membership expanded to include families representing the various sectors of the Mexicano community—workers, students, teachers, administrators, and businesspeople. Prodded by Gutiérrez, they began to participate in the community as never before. Before the second revolt few Mexicanos attended city council meetings. Now Mexicanos started attending the city council and school board meetings in great numbers. Before the second revolt usually only a few people attended meetings; after the revolt some meetings attracted one hundred to two hundred people.

The bureaucratic transfer of power to Mexicanos began less than two weeks after the election. On April 16 the lame duck city council accepted the resignations of Nell Warden, chairperson of the planning commission, and James Pipes, a member of the zoning commission. On April 23 a *Sentinel* headline announced, "Taylor Resigns City Attorney Post." Taylor claimed he was much too busy to continue in the post. The new council hired a lawyer from San Antonio, Jesse (Jesús) Gámez, the MALDEF attorney who was a native of Cristal. He was also hired by the RUP-controlled school board as legal council for the Cristal school district.

Throughout April the RUP city council members pressured those administrators and staff members who were considered to be political opponents to resign. In late May the city council named Bill Richey as city manager, replacing W. W. Marlowe, whose resignation took effect May 15. Richey had been a predoctoral student with Gutiérrez at Saint Mary's University in San Antonio and at the University of Texas. Both he and his wife, Linda, had been VISTA volunteers in Cotulla in late 1969 and then worked in Cristal with MAYO's Texas Institute for Educational Development (TIED) in 1970. TIED was a nonprofit corporation formed in 1969 by MAYO for the specific purpose of securing state and federal funding so that it could continue its advocacy efforts. TIED was one of the main programs that MAYO used to provide jobs for its organizers. The Richeys became an integral part of Gutiérrez's team. The connection with Gutiérrez and his activist agenda gave Bill Richey the respect, legitimacy, and trust that won him the backing of a majority of the city council and CU for the city manager job. The Richeys were what Gutiérrez would describe as Anglos—white folks who were compassionate and supportive of the CM.

The resignations of Warden and Pipes as well as other city officials and volunteers gave Richey an opportunity to appoint Mexicanos supportive of RUP's embryonic peaceful revolution. Teresa Flores became city clerk; Juan Ramirez, city public accountant; José Garza, assistant city manager; and Ramón Garza, utilities supervisor. But they faced an administrative dilemma in recruiting committed and knowledgeable Mexicanos: "No one had expertise. No one knew how to run our schools or our city. . . . We stressed the ideological and philosophical. . . . The ideological was that we should take power and we did," Gutiérrez said. "The philosophical were that we were committed to helping the poor, the working class, the migrant, and that we must empower them. We now had to deliver to these people who had never been catered to before." [50]

The reality was that Cristal's local labor pool of qualified Mexicanos offered few individuals who had expertise in the areas the city needed. So the city was compelled to recruit outsiders for many key administrative positions, which became a destabilizing factor in RUP's peaceful revolution.

Throughout 1970 RUP also worked hard to ensure the inclusion of Mexicano RUP supporters on the city's commissions and committees. Gutiérrez said there was no purge of whites from those positions: "We didn't have to. They would threaten to resign or boycott and so off they would go."[51] They were casualties of RUP's "browning" of Cristal's administration.

RUP's second revolt and the peaceful revolution that ensued catapulted Gutiérrez to national prominence. A few days after the second revolt he set out on a national speaking tour designed to propagate the formation of RUP and the significance of RUP's emerging peaceful revolution. In San Antonio Gutiérrez addressed about eleven hundred people on the evils of the two-party system and its contribution to the colonization of Mexicanos in south Texas:

The [Mexicano] has been kept in a perpetual state of dependency. He's been pushed out of school . . . the wages, the housing, the health, the governments, the distribution of wealth, the control of the land and every institution you can think of. Colonialism is there in South Texas and it's comparable to some of the stable dictatorships of Latin America such as Haiti and the Dominican Republic and pre-Castro Cuba. . . . That's what we're trying to fight because colonialism, like communism, is the control of many by a few.[52]

Gutiérrez next traveled to Washington, D.C., where he appeared before a Senate subcommittee. In the weeks that followed he accepted speaking engagements at thirty-three academic institutions, including Stanford, Notre Dame, Wesleyan University, and Michigan State.[53]

In Cristal, RUP's monthly newspaper, *La Verdad*, expanded its circulation. RUP used its paper to counter what party members perceived as bias in a column called "The Barker," written by the publisher of the family-owned *Zavala County Sentinel*, a weekly with a circulation of about twenty-five hundred in the early 1970s. The Barker was a compendium of local doings—restaurant reviews, store openings, local gossip, and political information. The publisher often dropped political tidbits in among the other odds and ends. During election periods the column would feature political items gleaned from the news pages that were not complimentary to RUP or to Gutiérrez in particular. The publisher never had words of praise or support for RUP, and his editorial page always endorsed RUP's opposition. Although Barker made plain his antipathy to RUP, he was never blatantly partisan or overly acrimonious. He was subtle but effective in demonstrating his disapproval of RUP's politics and policies.

National coverage of the second revolt continued well into 1975—both Cristal and Gutiérrez were newsworthy. For Mexicanos Cristal became symbolic of what "Brown Power" could do—turn a backwater town into a political mecca.[54]

In 1970 Gutiérrez also organized Los Voluntarios de Aztlán. The extensive media coverage was drawing some Mexicanos and non-Mexicanos, particularly students, to Cristal to volunteer their services to La Causa (the cause). In desperate need of technicians, teachers, administrators, and other types of administrative support personnel, Gutiérrez initiated a RUP-sponsored volunteer program that resembled a domestic peace corps. Carlos Reyes, who served as a voluntario, equated Los Voluntarios de Aztlán to Cuba's Venceremos brigades, groups of young people who volunteered to go to Cuba to cut sugar cane.

The voluntarios provided internal security; wrote for *La Verdad;* prepared "La Carta Noticiera" (RUP's national newsletter); prepared correspondence, reports, and proposals; organized community and RUP activities; and even served as part-time teachers in the local schools. In some cases some voluntarios remained in Cristal and worked for the city, the schools, and programs developed by RUP. The voluntarios were paid $5 a week and were given their meals and a place to stay. "Our meals were provided by various RUP supporters who had restaurants like Pepa's Cafe, the Cross Y Restaurant, and Nano Serna's Oasis," Reyes recalled many years later.[55] For five years Los Voluntarios were quite an asset to RUP's peaceful revolution.

Women were pivotal in both the school walkouts and the second revolt but had not been allowed full membership in CU. The men claimed that women should not join because CU meetings were very political and because the men liked to drink after the meetings, an activity that lasted well into the early hours of the morning. Encouraged by Gutiérrez, the women organized an auxiliary to CU. They initially called themselves Sociedad Femenil Chicanas de Cristal [the Society of Chicana Feminists from Cristal].[56]

But after the April elections women were no longer willing to accept exclusion from CU and decided to storm a CU meeting to demand inclusion and full membership. The revolt was led by Luz Gutiérrez, Virginia Musquiz, Elena Rivera, Ninfa Moncada, Juanita Santos, and others and brought their immediate acceptance as full members in CU. Within a year CU had approximately two hundred families as members.[57]

Other Salient City Issues

The RUP-controlled city council moved on many policy issues that reflected its determination to engender a peaceful revolution. In addition to consolidating its power and purging the city administration of political enemies, the council set to work on the Del Monte annexation right after the RUP takeover. Just before the new council was sworn in in April, the old white-controlled city council had voted to extend the city's agreement with the local Del Monte Foods plant (located about a mile from city hall) that exempted it from taxation and annexation. The RUP city council was confident that it could get the agreement thrown out—the former city attorney and a city council member had been employed by Del Monte, a clear-cut conflict of interest. But to the new council's surprise the issue became entangled in a costly three-year legal battle that the city lost. The failure to annex the plant caused the city to lose $14,000 in annual revenues.

In June the city council passed a resolution preventing the Department of Public Safety (highway patrol) from patrolling within Cristal's city limits without a formal request from the city police, mayor, or city manager.[58] Citizens had been complaining to Richey that highway patrol officers were policing in the city's barrios and La Placita, a popular Cristal park, when meetings were being held. Richey told the *Sentinel* that "the highway patrol had no business out in the barrios and that their . . . business was out on the highways." He added that "the resolution was made necessary by the public antipathy to the Highway Patrol and Texas Rangers." Richey also promised to increase the size of the city's police department and to provide its officers with more training and better administration.[59] In addition, the city barred the Texas Rangers from patrolling Cristal's streets.

Colonel Wilson Speir, director of the Department of Public Safety, said he knew of no other city in Texas that had passed such a resolution. Ranger Captain A. Y. Allee wrote a letter to the editor of the *Sentinel:*

This is one of the most absurd things I ever heard of. It looks as though the highway patrol stepped on someone's toes. I am also with the Texas Department of Public Safety, and I know of a certain group that was going to run me out of town—they never did try. I am for the Texas Highway Patrol 100 per cent and laying 2-1 odds that Col. Wilson Speir will not change them or move them out of city limits. I just hope Col. Speir will send more in. People can get killed in car wrecks in the city limits of Crystal City as easily as they can on our highways.[60]

As Shockley explains, "This action by the new city government symbolized the contempt that La Raza Unida had for state police practices."[61] Given the abusive relationship law enforcement agencies had with Mexicanos in south Texas, the council's action was designed to give people confidence in their local government and RUP's leadership. Richey's actions told people they no longer had to fear police harassment or brutality.

That September the city council moved aggressively on several policy items. One priority was to increase wages and benefits for city workers. Richey proposed a 10 percent wage increase, explaining, "It is my desire to bring the city's wages up to at least the federal minimum wage of a $1.60 per hour." The council also voted to provide city employees with workers' compensation insurance. At the same time, the council rejected a request by Dr. Henry Daly to be reimbursed by the city for the $1,100 he had paid to have his trailer park paved. Richey maintained that the city had no reason to reimburse him. Richey stressed that in the past individuals would do as they pleased and then expect the city to foot the bill. He also asserted that a subdivision being developed by the former mayor of San Antonio, B. H. Holsomback, was illegal because it was never approved by the city Planning and Zoning Commission or the city council.[62] Holsomback had asked the city to pay for paving the streets of the subdivision.

The council also designated October 12–18 as "Semana de la Raza" [Week of the People] and made September 16 (Mexican Independence Day) a legal holiday. This was a manifestation of RUP's commitment to preserving Mexicano culture through cultural nationalism. That month the city supported CU's efforts to form a Mexicano union, Obreros Unidos Independientes [Independent United Workers] at the Del Monte plant.

As the year's end drew nearer, RUP escalated its struggle to consolidate its community control. CASAA retaliated politically by becoming increasingly intransigent in its efforts to block RUP's consolidation of power. At a city council meeting in late November the two political blocs clashed when Gutiérrez, who was president of the Crystal City Independent School District, and Rodolfo (Rudy) Palomo were nominated to the Urban Renewal Commission. To CASAA their appointments were an example of RUP's desire to monopolize control of the city's commissions and committees. CASAA's leadership immediately contested the appointments—the Urban Renewal Commission was the city's most powerful commission, overseeing the awarding of contracts for thousands of dollars' worth of urban renewal projects as well as the distribution of jobs. On December 2 the city council held a special session to confirm the nominations. Mayor Paulino Mata and Councilman Santos Nieto challenged the legality of the special meeting and left in protest. As a result, the RUP majority voted unanimously to oust Mata as mayor and elected Francisco Benavides as Cristal's new mayor. That done, the council confirmed the appointments of Gutiérrez and Palomo.[63]

The city administration continued to move aggressively on several fronts. The council moved to annex Camposanto, the all-Mexicano area located near the Mexicano cemetery and north of the Del Monte plant. For years residents of that barrio had tried to become annexed into the city so they could get city water. Using urban renewal monies, the council also moved to install streetlights in municipal parks, plant more trees, and extend drainage lines. Even areas not covered by urban renewal were similarly improved; playground and basketball equipment were installed at La Placita. Shockley concludes, "All these changes provided clear material and symbolic evidence that the city government of Crystal City was committed to the [Mexicano] community."[64]

By the end of the year the failure of the city to attract new industry, a criticism that arose at the beginning of RUP's peaceful revolution, had become an issue. The incredible media hype created by the takeover and the manifold changes that ensued gave Cristal a reputation of being a locus of "brown" radicalism. This image greatly contributed to the city's inability to attract job-producing new industries. The city's Industrial Foundation, set up by a previous white city administration to attract new industry to Cristal, had an unsuccessful history of essentially focusing on labor-intensive textiles. The new administration sought to attract jobs through government contracts and small business loans to Cristal's emerging Mexicano entrepreneurs.[65] RUP's struggle to create new jobs became increasingly dependent on federal and state resources as well as private foundations.

1970 Winter Garden County Elections

As RUP concentrated on consolidating its control of the city council and school board in Cristal, it began to campaign for control of the counties in the Winter Garden area. In 1970, in preparation for the November county elections, Gutiérrez sought to educate and socialize Mexicanos about why it was important for them to have their own political party. Shockley further explains:

There were ideological as well as practical reasons for forming a third party. The Raza Unida leadership had little love for the Democratic party. The party had, after all, been the dominant party throughout South Texas and thus to them had been the main instrument of repression in the area. And the Republicans had been a nearly totally Anglo party in the community from the beginning. Gutiérrez argued that by forming a third party, Raza Unida supporters could participate in their own institution, one that valued rather than exploited them.[66]

Early in 1970 Gutiérrez had formed countywide RUP organizing committees in the three targeted counties. Texas electoral law stipulated that candidates for county offices could appear on the ballot only if their party was legally on the ballot. The law provided two means by which to get RUP on the ballot: by primary or by convention. The former was more difficult and expensive, requiring costly filing fees, whereas the latter simply dictated that RUP select delegates to hold a convention at a time prescribed by electoral law.[67] On May 2, 1970, RUP held county conventions in Zavala, La Salle, and Dimmit.

RUP once again made history. For the first time in Texas history Mexicanos chose candidates of their own rather than those of another political party (the Democrats). In Zavala County RUP nominated Julian Salas for county judge; Carmen Flores for county treasurer; Isaac Juárez for county clerk; Ramón de la Fuente for county commissioner, Precinct 2; José Serna for county commissioner, Precinct 3; Esteban Nájera for county commissioner, Precinct 4; Manuel Palacios for justice of the peace, Precinct 2; and Pedro Contreras for justice of the peace, Precinct 3.

Because they believed that all was in place for the November elections, José Angel Gutiérrez and Luz Gutiérrez, an employee of the Colorado Migrant Council, traveled north to Minnesota with the departing migrant workers in the spring of 1970. After a few weeks they left for California, where he enrolled in a special course on the Chicano experience at the University of California at Berkeley, led by scholars Octavio Romano, Nick Vaca, and Rodolfo Acuña. Luz Gutiérrez recalls that they left Cristal simply because they desperately needed a break from their activism and politicking. "We figured that it was a good way to break away from the day-to-day syndrome of Cristal and the Partido Raza Unida. We were so tired."[68]

They returned to Cristal that summer in time to organize efforts to get on the November ballot. Then white county officials refused to place the RUP candidates on the ballot, forcing the party to take them to court. "We definitely had to fight this thing out in the courts to decide just what exactly we had to do to qualify for the ballot," Gutiérrez said.[69] Determining RUP's legal status became a nightmare because of the ambiguity and contradictions in the procedures required for third parties. The crux of the legal problem was how to interpret a section of the Texas Election Code (Article 13:54) that read,

Any political party without a state organization wanting to nominate candidates for county and precinct offices may only nominate such candidates therefore under the provisions of this title by primary elections or by a county convention held on the legal primary election day, which convention shall be composed of delegates from various election precincts in said county, elected therein at primary conventions held in such precincts between the hours of 8:00 a. m. and 10:00 p. m. on the date set by law. All nominations made by any such parties shall be certified to the county clerk by the chair of the county committee of such party, and after taking the same course as nominations of other parties so certified, shall be printed on the official ballot in a separate column, headed by the name of the party; provided, a written application for such printing shall have been made to the county judge, signed and sworn to by three per cent (3%) of the entire vote cast in such county at the last general election.

Gutiérrez denounced whites' efforts to keep RUP off the ballot as indicative of their unwillingness to share power with Mexicanos. RUP's tricounty leadership argued that it had followed Article 13:54 to the letter. RUP's leadership pointed out that in January RUP had secured the required signatures in all three counties. That same month temporary party officers had been elected; its candidates had filed in February, and the party held its conventions in May. Whites countered with a laundry list of technical errors that they claimed disqualified RUP, among them giving the year as 1969 instead of 1970 on a Zavala County form, holding the La Salle County precinct conventions in improper locations and at the wrong time of day, and allowing people who had voted as Democrats in the Dimmit County primary to sign RUP's petition to be on the ballot.

Attorneys for RUP asked the Fourth Court of Civil Appeals and subsequently the Texas Supreme Court to order RUP placed on the ballot. Both courts ruled against RUP. Associate Justice Fred Klingman, explaining the ruling of the state's highest court, said, "There had not been substantial compliance with the provisions of Article 13:54 concerning holding conventions." RUP Attorney Richard J. Clarkson had argued that the secretary of state had recognized the petitions as having fulfilled all election requirements and the Texas attorney general had concurred. Furthermore, Clarkson pointed out the apparently contradictory legal opinions and stressed that if ballot status was not granted, substantial numbers of Mexicanos would be disenfranchised and would have no voice in the November election.[70]

In its ruling the state Supreme Court denied RUP's petition for recognition in all three counties. RUP took the case to federal court, claiming its candidates' civil rights had been violated because county officials had placed stricter requirements on RUP than on the Democratic or Republican parties. But RUP's lawyers were unable to get the federal court to agree, and the party remained off the ballot.[71] (Years later RUP officials acknowledged that they had made a series of small technical errors that had in fact violated the state statute.)

Angry but not discouraged, RUP's tricounty leadership decided to use a write-in campaign for the November elections. Shockley describes the next-to-impossible hurdles RUP faced:

Owing to the nature of the procedures for write-in votes under Texas law, such a campaign had little chance of success. Stickers could not be used; names had to be written in. In a community where many of the Mexicanos were functional illiterates, getting them to write all their candidates' names correctly and in the proper place became an insuperable task. Although the courts did rule that election officials could help illiterates vote if they requested, the Anglo election officials refused to do so since they were not required to.[72]

RUP's monumental task was to educate Mexicanos on the intricacies of a write-in campaign. The party held rallies and town hall meetings and conducted classes to teach voters how to write in the names of RUP candidates. This was difficult because the median level of education for Mexicanos in Texas in 1960 was 2.3 years in Cristal and 1.3 in Cotulla and had not changed much ten years later. Men and women who had never before voted, some of whom were illiterate, practiced writing the names of RUP candidates. *La Verdad* carried many articles explaining the write-in procedures. Article after article focused on educating the Mexicano electorate on the specifics of the write-in campaign: "Study well the ballots that we illustrate in the newspaper so you can learn how the 'write-in' campaign is conducted. If all of us do our humble effort, we can create a triumph for the Raza Unida Party against those who seek to destroy it. We have a great opportunity to put an end to the political training that gringos here in Texas call democracy."[73]

Although they had managed to keep RUP candidates off the ballot, whites also launched a high-powered campaign. They were resolute in their efforts to stop RUP from expanding its community control movement to the county level. Some Mexicanos reported that certain people in county government had threatened to take citizens off the welfare rolls and surplus food lists if they voted for RUP candidates.[74]

La Verdad reported that the county head of the state welfare agency, Ben Ivey, accompanied by Bessie Taylor (Mrs. Irl Taylor), had visited welfare recipients and told them that voting for Judge Irl Taylor was a prerequisite for an increase in their welfare payments. This action sowed fear and confusion among Mexicano voters. Gringos also relied on what Shockley describes as "the Puppets"—people who were out in force, taking "unrequested absentee ballots to the sick and elderly [Mexicanos], getting them to sign their names, and then voting the ballots for them."[75]

An integral part of the strategy was to instill fear in the white voter. The Democrats of the tricounty area relied on TV ads, mailers, and paid newspaper advertisements. Their media blitz targeted the changes being made by RUP both in Cristal and Cotulla and depicted RUP as a radical party and a propagator of hate and separatism.[76] The Democrats' ads described RUP candidates as unqualified to serve and suggested they would harm the counties' economy and raise property taxes. In a specific effort to foster a high white voter turnout Judge Taylor mailed a "confidential" letter to all Anglo voters registered in Zavala County. The letter noted that only 1,450 of 3,996 registered voters in the county were Anglos. Judge Taylor argued that "every single one of these 1,450 should be a committee of one to be sure and vote." He continued:

Of these 2,546 registrants who bear a Spanish surname, I cannot believe that all of them are "Chicano." I proudly claim many Mexican-Americans as my friends. And I know many of those people do not go along with this "kill the gringo," "squash the gringo like a beetle" philosophy that is so freely preached by this small, militant group for their own glory and personal financial gain. I also know each of you have many friends among the same people. So why include them when we bad-mouth these people? It would be better and we would feel better, if we would think twice and refer only to the individual militants. We need these clear thinking progressive people in our communities and they need us. With them we can win in November. . . . The cold facts: we must have 600 Mexican-Americans added to the 1400 Anglos to win, and they live among us. Why not work with them and show them they are appreciated? After all they are responsible American citizens.[77]

Another mailer emphasized the accomplishments of the current county administration. Written in both English and Spanish, it mentioned the construction of the new courthouse and jail, the surplus commodities program, and road improvements and welfare services that county and state officials had brought to the area.

RUP immediately disputed these so-called accomplishments, asserting that the construction of the courthouse and jail could have been completed much sooner and for a lot less money had the county not pulled out of a joint venture with Cristal after Los Cinco won in 1963.

RUP officials noted that people preferred food stamps to the commodities program; the county's refusal to dispense food stamps became a RUP countercampaign issue.[78] Throughout the county campaigns RUP organizers emphasized the importance of winning control from whites, stressing that the changes made in Cristal had to be extended to the county level of government.

On election day RUP ran a vigorous grassroots get-out-the-vote drive in all three counties. Some Mexicanos walked precincts, while others worked tables set up by polling places to provide last-minute instructions or assistance to voters. Local election judges and police intimidated and harassed RUP precinct workers and poll watchers all day. For example, claiming that the poll watchers' credentials carried the wrong precinct number, a white election judge prohibited poll watchers from entering a polling place in one precinct in Cristal. The number of the precinct had been changed shortly before the election. When the poll watchers insisted, the sheriff threatened to arrest them.[79] Harassment by deputies was also commonplace.

In Cristal deputies stopped a truck with a sound system as it wound through the barrios exhorting Mexicanos to vote. The deputies claimed the broadcasts could be heard in the polling places. Texas Ranger patrol units pointedly cruised the barrios. Mexicanos who asked election judges questions about write-in procedures were treated with indifference. Some voters in Cristal arrived at the polls only to be told that they had already voted. Only if they insisted or argued were some allowed to vote.[80] Scores of similar incidents occurred throughout the Winter Garden Project area.

RUP's write-in campaign managed to elect only one of the party's sixteen candidates. Raul Rodríguez of La Salle County was elected to the court of commissioners from Precinct 3. In Zavala County Julian Salas received 925 votes to his opponent's 1,502; Carmen Flores received 811 votes to her opponent's 1,496; Isaac Juárez secured votes 776 to his opposition's 1,502; Ramón de la Fuente got 528, his opponent 774; Manuel Palacios garnered 524 to the opposition's 804; Esteban Nájera received 97 votes to his opponent's 234; and José Serna, who came closest to winning, got 288 votes while his opposition got 346.[81]

Illiteracy among Mexicanos of the area, coupled with the inherent difficulties of organizing a write-in campaign, doomed the effort from the start. Many votes were lost because names were misspelled. For instance, José Serna's name was spelled in various ways—José Serna, Joe Serna, José Cerna, and so forth. When the votes were counted, José Serna had won the most votes but lost the election because each different spelling of his name was tallied for a separate candidate. The election judges refused to recognize the variations of write-in names. An editorial in *La Verdad* noted that RUP's candidates had won the election but lost on technicalities, proving the party's political viability. With RUP officials educated about the fine points of Texas election law and how it could be used to thwart an upstart party, and with eighteen-year-olds to be permitted to vote in 1972, even in defeat the party had reason to be confident of its eventual success.[82]

Gutiérrez declared, "We proved our point. The party is something visible, meaningful, and attractive to the Chicano voter. We'll go state-wide in 1972. We start work in January 1971. The party has got no-where to go but up."[83]

3

The Emergence of RUP's Machine Politics (1971–1972)

After a year of RUP's struggling to consolidate its community control of Cristal's city council and school board and make major policy changes and implement various programs, Ciudadanos Unidos (CU) was evolving into a full-fledged political machine. José Angel Gutiérrez understood and applied Saul Alinsky's dictum that "the most powerful weapon in the arsenal of the poor and oppressed is organization." In doing so, he organized CU into a powerful family of community-based organizations that became the vanguard of the peaceful revolution and of RUP in the area. CU now was the most powerful organization in and around Zavala County. By late 1971 CU, with its big base of constituents and its ability to deliver the Mexicano vote, was evolving into a partisan political machine rather than a community organization. And at the top was Gutiérrez, who functioned increasingly as CU's political boss. For the next four years Boss Gutiérrez and the invincible CU controlled and directed local election after local election.

Political Machines: Instruments of Control

Machine politics began in the United States in the mid-1850s with the arrival of various ethnic groups in the growing urban areas of the nation. Many arrived in cities that were cauldrons of extreme poverty and alienation. Scholar Eugene Lewis writes about the horrid conditions that fostered the emergence of political machines.

Nineteenth century America was a horror for many of urban citizens. Slums in the large cities were worse than they are today. There was incredible overcrowding and disease; crime and poverty characterized every urban center. Starvation was frighteningly common. Millions . . . arrived in America poor, hungry, diseased, and completely unable to cope with life in the New World. . . . Social disintegration and alienation from public institutions were real problems for urban dwellers—both old and new.[1]

The strength of the political machine lay in the low-income ethnic communities adjacent to the commercial and industrial heart of the city. Political machines also emerged as a result of the social disintegration and alienation created by the horrors of the cities—immense poverty, overcrowding, epidemic disease, and crime. The machine was a reaction to the federal, state, and local governments' inability or lack of desire to rectify the many social and economic problems that immigrants faced.[2]

City machines are hierarchical private organizations grounded in political party organizations that rule cities by controlling nominations to council and executive offices, including that of mayor. They offer city council members benefits and special privileges in return for unified action. Bryan T. Downes describes a political machine as a "hierarchical party organization within the context of mass suffrage." Political scientists Harlan Hahn and Charles Levine define and differentiate between the two interrelated terms *machine politics* and *political machine.* Accordingly, to engage in machine politics is to manipulate certain incentives to partisan political participation: favoritism based on political criteria in personnel decisions, contracting, and administration of the laws. They define a political machine as an organization that practices machine politics—that attracts and directs its members primarily by means of incentives.[3]

Mexicanos in Texas were not unfamiliar with machine politics. Historian Rodolfo Acuña describes the pervasiveness of gringo-controlled political machines:

In South Texas, machine politics also became popular after the Civil War. It handed out patronage—for example, city jobs, contracts, franchises, and public utilities, and, for the poor Mexicanos, it meant a primitive form of welfare. The machine won elections by turning out the vote. In the border towns, the machine controlled the custom houses. The indiscriminate use of the Texas Rangers bolstered the machine's political hegemony.[4]

Political machines held sway in most cities in south Texas, including Brownsville, Laredo, San Antonio, and El Paso. Brownsville's, led first by boss Stephen Powers and then by his replacement, Jim Wells, was the most powerful. These machines were products of "controlled franchise," wherein Mexicanos voted according to the dictates of the local patron, or boss. Because these political machines delivered sizable blocs of votes in state and national elections, the Anglo patrones (among them Sam Rayburn and Lyndon Johnson in this century) acquired influence far beyond that of backwater county politicians.[5]

All these machines depended on inducements that were specific as well as material:

A specific (as opposed to general) inducement is one that can be offered to one person while being withheld from others. A *material* inducement is money or another physical "thing" to which value attaches. *Nonmaterial* inducements include especially the satisfactions of having power or prestige, doing good, the "fun of the game," the sense of enlarged participation in events and a pleasant environment. A machine, like any formal organization, offers a mixture of these various kinds of inducements in order to get people to do what it requires. But it is distinguished from other types of organization by the very heavy emphasis it places upon specific, material inducements and the consequent completeness and reliability of its control over behavior, which, of course, account for the name "machine."[6]

Robert Merton differentiates between "manifest" and "latent" functions of an activity. Manifest functions are those that are intended and recognized, whereas the latent functions are unintended and unrecognized despite the machine's involvement in "honest graft" (legal inducements).[7]

Furthermore, machines filled a real need: social welfare.

To the poor in the slums of cities, the machine provided needed services: It found jobs, or tided the family over during the periods of unemployment; it buried the dead; it cared for widows and orphans; it organized youth activities; it provided a multitude of neighborhood social functions; it contributed to the churches of the poor neighborhoods; it provided bail bonds and legal advice; it furnished assistance in finding housing and tried to help tenants talk their landlords out of rent increases. It provided literally hundreds of services, the need for which was not recognized by much of the middle class.[8]

The political machine was an instrument of employment and service in exchange for votes. It was led and controlled by a boss who was often the mayor, although sometimes the boss was a unelected leader who operated behind the scenes to control local government. Assisting the boss were ward leaders, precinct captains, and block leaders who presided over a disciplined party. Ward leaders were often city council members who were responsible for several precincts. Most precincts were by-products of a political party, usually the Democratic Party. Some were the epitome of centralization and discipline. Others were merely coalitions of divergent interests at the ward level. Sustaining the machine was more like running a family-owned business than a corporation. The vast array of party workers, favor seekers, and office seekers operated on an informal understanding. They were not bound by contract or collective agreements. No formal organizational chart delineated their relationships. Machine politicians cultivated personal bonds, social relationships, and, above all, "friendship." Thus political machines obtained their power and control of the spoils of office through the systematic use of patronage.

Political machines were not advocacy vehicles for social change. Political machines seldom, if ever, got directly involved in working-class union struggles or protest movements. They usually stood on the side of law and order and the status quo. By the midtwentieth century most political machines had disappeared from the nation's urban areas, casualties of changing political and economic conditions, especially the reform movement, which perceived the machine as a corrupt and immoral political force that needed to be eradicated. In the belief that machines were antithetical to urban governance, reformers successfully pushed such changes as the council-manager form of local government, nonpartisan at-large elections, recalls, initiatives, referendums, and the New Deal, all of which diminished the stature and power of political machines.

Ciudadanos Unidos: A Political Machine

The very nature of politics, as practiced in Cristal from 1970 to 1975, created conditions and circumstances conducive to the practice of machine politics. During these years Cristal was in a perpetual state of mobilization, focused on either impending elections or battling issues. Gutiérrez explained that "we found out quickly that once you won, the next day you have to start running for reelection. We were constantly on the campaign trail. . . . We had to overcome the poll-tax mind-set, even though it was no longer in effect. . . . We had to overcome the people's cynicism that we're going to fail. We had to show them that we could get the power, hold the power, make enough changes to overcome their cynicism."[9]

Gutiérrez realized that creating and maintaining a successful third party at the state or county level would not be enough to secure real political change. Maintaining community control requires organization and readiness. Gutiérrez recalled,

For the sake of our survival, we had to keep organizing more people. We had to make sure that the organizing process continued to refine itself in terms of how we recruited new members, how we trained our leaders, how we recruited candidates, how we perfected the political machine to enable us to win elections, how we raised the money, how to give the party line, and how to begin to develop a political information program so that everyone could understand what was happening, instead of being victimized by rumor, innuendo as had been the case with Cornejo.[10]

It was clear to Gutiérrez that to maintain control of Cristal's city, school, and county structures, the paramount concern had to be "getting votes and winning elections."

As Gutiérrez has acknowledged, by 1975 CU had evolved into a full-fledged political machine, and he was its boss. From CU's formation in late 1969 he had envisioned it as the community political organization. That year it was chartered in Zavala County as a political association. The early members elected officers and approved its by-laws. As Gutiérrez intended, CU became the organizational foundation of the Winter Garden Project, which included forming the Raza Unida Party. Gutiérrez chose not to seek nonprofit status for CU for two reasons. First, he wanted a full-fledged political entity at the community level that would not be vulnerable to attack because of its nonprofit status. Second, he sought to create a multifunctional political entity; its duties would include developing a grassroots membership; selecting and running candidates; conducting voter registration and get-out-the-vote drives; raising of money to finance campaigns; mobilizing the community for direct action on issues; and arbitrating political disputes.

CU was RUP's organizing arm. In some respects this system did not differ from that of the Democrats and Republicans. Both major parties have had a variety of independent political entities at the local level, such as Democratic and Republican clubs, as well as at state and national levels, that work to advance the interests of their particular party. But unlike the clubs of the major parties, which tend to draw a small membership from the middle class, RUP's political associations, which included CU in Cristal and Familias Unidas in Robstown (in Hidalgo County), among others, sought large memberships and recruited from among the poor, the working class, and the middle class. Moreover,

RUP's political associations had dual agendas—electoral politics and social change. They functioned as interest groups that dealt with public policy issues.

RUP's structure, like that of the Democratic and Republican Parties, was mandated by the Texas Election Code. The law required RUP to have a traditional structure of state and county entities. At the county level the party was led by an executive committee that was comprised of a county chairperson and precinct chairperson from each of Zavala County's seven precincts who were elected in the May primary. For the most part the executive committee was active only in partisan elections (county, state, and national elections—Cristal's city and school board elections were, officially anyway, nonpartisan). Candidates who sought to run on the RUP county ticket had to file with the executive committee—and receive the sanction of CU.

CU was formally led by its board of directors and three standing committees. In 1974 it came to have an informal body, which I call the "directorate," that included representatives of four sectors: elected officials; school and county administrators; community organizations such as the Mexican Chamber of Commerce, IMAGE, and the Barrio Club; and community leaders. Each sector was important to RUP's peaceful revolution, and the influence of the constituents of each sector depended on the positions they held or their reputations. The directorate met en masse once a week to discuss pertinent administrative and community matters and to make recommendations to CU (see Chapter 5).[11] But the leadership of RUP and CU leadership came primarily from the poor and working classes. Important to Gutiérrez's early success was this cadre of loyal party officials who resorted to the use of material and psychological incentives for maintaining community control. Although some held office—including Gutiérrez, who served on the school board in 1970 and became county judge in 1974—the holding of public office was not the primary source of RUP's strength.

The foundation of CU's (and RUP's) political power was its massive membership, which by early 1975 included about five hundred families in Cristal. This was especially true for the "nonpartisan" city council and school board elections. Nonpartisan elections became partisan. All candidates for city council and school board openly and deliberately declared themselves as RUP adherents and ran on a RUP slate. In election years CU meetings were more like miniconventions. Any candidate wishing to run for local office under the aegis of RUP had to go before CU during its biweekly Sunday meetings to solicit the membership's support. Candidates who failed to win CU's endorsement could not run as RUP candidates. For those candidates that CU endorsed, it would take over the organizing, fund-raising, and other aspects of the campaign.[12]

During the first five years a few RUP members tried to win office without CU backing and were soundly defeated. When it came to tackling various issues, RUP's leadership relied on CU to apply pressure, usually by mobilizing members for a protest. In some ways CU functioned as RUP's rapid deployment force—it was always ready and prepared to send its legions of supporters to protest or support issues and causes throughout south Texas. No other political association organized by RUP supporters equaled CU's organizational and mobilizing capacity.

Thus with its well-organized membership CU was the political machine that propelled and sustained RUP's peaceful revolution in Cristal. Like other political machines, CU relied on material inducements—patronage in the form of jobs, contracts, appointments, and grants. Job opportunities, especially, went to those who were loyal to and supportive of RUP. From 1970 to 1975 the city, school, and county structures were purged of most anti-RUP personnel and replaced with RUP supporters. Consequently, by 1975 few of RUP's adversaries remained employed by these governmental structures.[13] Another material incentive was the services and programs offered by schools and the city and county governments. Theoretically, of course, most residents of Cristal benefited from public services, but in practice neighborhoods that were loyal to RUP got priority. In addition, CU's Committee on Social Action provided assistance to members through the organization's volunteer-run day-care center, credit union, and various self-help programs.[14]

Like traditional machines, CU also relied on nonmaterial or psychological incentives. Beginning with the Winter Garden Project in 1969, Gutiérrez gradually but systematically began developing a community mind-set, or psyche, for change and for building RUP. The success of the school boycott and especially the second revolt began to dispel the widespread cynicism, distrust, and lassitude that had characterized the years that followed the first revolt of 1963.

The years up to early 1975 were typified by an esprit de corps and a sense of community unprecedented not only in Cristal but perhaps throughout Aztlán. Political apathy gave way to a fervor for participatory democracy and political discourse. Cristal was the most politically alive community in Aztlán. CU's large membership became active on school board and city council committees and commissions. Members attended rallies, marches, demonstrations, fund-raisers, city council and school board meetings, and turned out to vote on election day. The greatest psychological reward for Mexicanos was that they were no longer afraid of gringos. RUP's peaceful revolution fostered a sense of courage, pride, and belief that Mexicanos were in control of their own destiny.

All this was masterminded and led by Gutiérrez, the boss of the political machine, a role he actively embraced:

I was the person the people came to [to] solve problems, to mediate disputes, allocate patronage . . . give advice and counsel. I was the only [one] ever elected over and over again as its *consejero legal* [legal counsel]. All the officers changed, yet I was always in the same position. I was the one who was well known because of the media. I was the one who did most of the traveling. I was very much the only individual who could ultimately veto things that were popularly decided by Ciudadanos Unidos.[15]

Gutiérrez was an eclectic activist, but he was also, at times, a pragmatist. His ideology was a hybrid of capitalism, cultural nationalism (Chicanismo), and socialism. Take, for example, the language he used in many of his speeches. He usually larded them generously with an extreme criticism of capitalism for its exploitative nature. He often alluded to the need to create a more equitable distribution of wealth and power. Yet he espoused and used the capitalist system's federal and state funding to finance the programs and projects of RUP's peaceful revolution. In addition, he and a few other RUP leaders became involved in profit-making ventures.

Gutiérrez's use of CU and its directorate is an example of his willingness to allow others to participate in what political scientist David Easton called "the authoritative allocation of resources."[16] However, the bottom line was that during the period of 1970 to early 1975, Gutiérrez was the boss, the person with the power, the purveyor of patronage, and the person piloting and navigating RUP's peaceful revolution. The legitimacy of Gutiérrez's role as boss was predicated on his ability to deliver change that benefited the overwhelming majority of the Mexicanos in Cristal.

While Gutiérrez did at times act like a traditional boss, he had a unique style of bossism, such as his idea of power sharing. With few exceptions he never vetoed any decision made by CU: "I never did it because I knew that would be a very big mistake. So I always managed to avoid . . . having to make a decision contrary to what was already done." Gutiérrez said there were times when he voiced opposition to CU decisions. For example, in 1970 he supported the women when they sought full membership in the theretofore all-male CU. And during the school walkouts he prevailed on the demands made of the school board, despite opposition from some CU members.[17]

RUP's decision-making process was pyramidal. Gutiérrez solicited ideas from a few trusted confidantes, such as Viviana Santiago, Luz Gutiérrez, and Nano Serna, but he made the critical decisions on general policy issues. However, all decisions were open to scrutiny and discussion at CU's Sunday meetings. This provided a certain amount of power sharing and checks and balances. Richard A. Schaffer, reporting for the *Wall Street Journal*, describes how CU's membership participated in policy formulation and debate:

[CU] meets every other Sunday in the high-school cafeteria. At the meetings, every elected official and the heads of each governmental agency must give an accounting of what he has done since the last meeting and must outline his plans. All major policies are decided by a vote of the committee in sessions that often last four and five hours. In addition, the committee has the authority to recommend the hiring and firing of any governmental employee, and its recommendations are usually followed. After the reports, the meeting is thrown open to whatever the citizens wish to discuss.[18]

He concluded that "if Ciudadanos Unidos resembles a political machine, it's because it is, and many observers fault La Raza for their reliance on it." Gutiérrez acknowledged that CU sometimes had to arbitrarily exercise its power: "Sometimes we have had to force things on people because they didn't know what was good for them. Pestering people at all hours, forcing the literature on them, making sure that they voted. It shouldn't [be], but it is necessary at this time."[19]

In election years CU became what Gutiérrez described as a political party apparatus. For five years (1970–1975) CU was politically invincible, defeating its opponents through the power of organization. CU's political mobilization committee was responsible for recruiting candidates, registering voters, and getting out the vote. Gutiérrez or his designee usually coordinated the committee's get-out-the-vote mobilization. Every precinct had its captain, every captain had block leaders, and every block leader had an abundance of volunteers. Every polling place had poll watchers, and amplified vehicles would travel through designated precincts urging people to vote, while local radio stations carried scores of spots exhorting people to go to the polls.[20]

To finance all this activity Gutiérrez instituted a CU income tax that was based on the ability to pay and funneled to the organization through payroll deductions from the paychecks of all members—particularly from those who benefited from the patronage jobs doled out by Gutiérrez and CU. Gutiérrez contributed 10 percent of his salary to CU after the organization instituted his income tax plan in 1975.[21] CU also relied on dances, dinners, fiestas, and the like to raise money.

Whites' Reaction to RUP's Machine Politics

In 1973 I interviewed a dozen white residents of Cristal whom RUP members and other whites identified as leaders or "power holders" in the city. They generally perceived CU as a political machine and RUP as a "communist revolutionary movement." Most described CU as a political machine that used patronage to buy political support on behalf of RUP. "I don't think it will catch on as a movement," said Dale Barker, editor of the *Zavala County Sentinel*. "It does not have much of an appeal because of its racially separatist orientation. It will function more as a political machine and be limited essentially to Crystal City."[22]

Ronald Smith, one of two doctors in Cristal, described several problems he had with Gutiérrez. He objected to Gutiérrez's "ruling a small town like this Crystal City with an iron-clad political machine entirely based on patronage where the first criterion for a job is political affiliation."[23]

Some saw RUP as a communist organization bent on fomenting a revolution in south Texas. They used such words as *dictator, despot,* and *radical communist* to describe Gutiérrez. Some likened RUP to the Communist Party. Barker described RUP both as a political machine and as revolutionary movement that sought to foster major change in the political and economic establishment of Texas. He said that RUP's effective involvement of many people in the making of decisions and its grassroots orientation were indicative of its revolutionary posture.[24]

Gloria Bookout, a businesswoman, said, "Anglos have objected to the Marxist and Trotsky political doctrine of the Raza Unida plus the hatred promoted for political purposes." Guin Carey, a schoolteacher, depicted RUP as a leftist radical movement, entirely foreign to the true democratic sense of the United States. He added, "I have no doubt that there are others above him [Gutiérrez] somewhere controlling him." Businessman Jack Kingsberry not only agreed with Carey but added that he had heard that Gutiérrez and some RUP leaders had been trained in Cuba by Fidel Castro and his cadres.[25]

All the whites I interviewed were hypercritical of Gutiérrez. They saw him as a power-hungry and opportunistic radical dictator with ulterior motives who used people for his own ends. They resented the fact that Mexicanos now controlled the politics of the community. All showed signs of anger, if not outrage. This was evident in their tone of voice, facial expressions, and hand gestures. Clearly, after generations of being in control they were not willing to accept their political powerlessness. Although they were still economically omnipotent, economic squeeze-plays no longer worked against the "maverick Mexicanos." All acknowledged that defeating RUP was going to be a slow and difficult task.[26]

The 1971 Local Election and Issues

In 1971 and for much of the four years that followed, Gutiérrez kept RUP members in a state of constant readiness, following Alinsky's strategy of polarization and a multi-issue approach to maintain the ferment of activism.[27] The political struggles and the county elections of 1970 had further educated, organized, and strengthened CU's grassroots base. By the 1971 local elections CU had about two hundred families enrolled as members and was fast becoming an invincible, well-organized, and well-lubricated political machine. This was complemented by its success in working with other community organizations, such as the Mexican Chamber of Commerce. At least symbolically, RUP's agenda of economic empowerment required that it include an organization that was business oriented. The chamber was perfect because by 1971 it had become nothing more than a social club. Anyone could join, so RUP supporters became members and ousted the existing middle-class, moderate leadership that sought coalitions with whites.[28]

In 1971 Cristal's three other city council seats, including that of Mayor Francisco (Frank) Benavides, were up for election. Also facing reelection were the two CASAA holdovers, former mayor Paulino Mata and his friend, schoolteacher Santos Nieto. In the school board election Eddie Treviño, the holdover who had crossed over to RUP, and Malcolm (Buddy) Maedgen, a wealthy rancher, were up for reelection.

In preparation for the upcoming elections CU announced at its weekly Sunday meetings that it would be seeking candidates. Because the city council and school board elections were nonpartisan, RUP had to leave the responsibility for organizing local elections to CU. As we have seen, CU's candidate selection process combined participatory democracy and machine politics.

For the school board CU endorsed Treviño and Rodolfo (Rudy) Palomo, who had just been appointed to the city's Urban Renewal Commission. CU also reaffirmed its support for Benavides and endorsed José Talamantez and Roberto Gámez for city council. All the RUP candidates were local products who had been graduated from Crystal

City High School, and some had college degrees. Three were teachers in the school district.[29]

Partly because of RUP's success in consolidating its power, whites were in political disarray. They resorted to the politics of subterfuge. According to Shockley,

> The older Anglo leadership seemed to withdraw in pain, disgust, and impotence. Some of the new leadership, many who were new to the area, were willing to admit confidentially that many Anglos in Crystal City were racists and that these people were the worst enemies of moderate Anglos. . . . Because of their political moderation, they decided not to run any Anglos for either the city council or the school board. This was illustrated by Buddy Maedgen's decision not to run for re-election.[30]

Instead, the whites encouraged the "old guard"—conservative Mexicanos—to run candidates under the banner of Better Government (BG), which was nothing more than the old CASAA coalition. However, BG was not a formal organization, as CASAA had been. It was essentially an ad hoc group of Mexicanos and whites who were zealous anti-Gutierristas. BG recognized that it did not have the votes to beat CU and that it therefore would be a mistake to run white candidates under BG.

Thus BG fielded Teodoro Muñoz and Alfredo Ramon for the school board. The two men happened to be related: Muñoz was Ramon's stepfather.[31] Both were ardent adversaries of Gutiérrez and RUP. They had openly opposed the school walkout. When RUP targeted Muñoz's grocery store for an economic boycott, gringos came to his rescue by patronizing the store. For the city council the BG backed incumbents Mata and Nieto along with Gilberto Salazar, the owner of a bakery located in the same building as Muñoz's grocery store.[32] Throughout the campaign CU and RUP supporters disparagingly categorized BG's candidates as *vendidos* (sellouts) and *cocos*, or coconuts (white inside and brown outside).

Three other Mexicanos decided to run for the city council seats as independents. They were former city councilman Roberto Cornejo (brother of Juan Cornejo), Ralph García, and his mother, Mariana García. Some CU members claimed that Cornejo and the Garcías were receiving gringo support because the gringos saw the trio as a way to split the RUP vote.[33] But if BG had little organization, the independents had none.

The elections were important to all three forces because control of both the city council and school board were on the line. Winning the three city council seats, for example, would give the BG a 3–2 majority.

If BG won the two school board seats, it would have a 4–3 edge over RUP. CU was determined to not only maintain control but to solidify its hold by controlling all five seats on the city council and six of seven seats on the school board. With the stakes so high, both the city and school board campaigns were hard fought.

The BG election strategy was to try to discredit RUP's management of the schools and the city. BG's central theme throughout the campaign was that both RUP-dominated administrations were permeated with mismanagement, incompetence, and corruption. The incidents cited by BG included the school district's firing or retirement of twenty-three white teachers in early March, and the high school's temporary loss of accreditation by the Southern Association of Schools and Colleges (see Chapter 8 for extensive discussion of these developments). Although no one was ever charged or found responsible, BG alleged that RUP school personnel had run a cafeteria deficit of about $15,000 and that a $1,200 shortage existed in the city's petty cash fund. Implicit in BG's allegations of corruption was that some RUP supporters were stealing money. A letter to the editor focusing on the alleged corruption, written by Ann Ladner, a teacher who had just been fired by the RUP-controlled school district, and published in the *Sentinel*, stated: "It would appear that the only ones receiving any benefits from the Gutierrez administration in the school and city are the political stooges and whoever got the money from the cafeteria fund. . . . Some of the hardcore Gutierrez supporters have no viable means of support."[34]

BG also attacked the involvement of thirty high school students in an antiwar protest. On February 27 the high school's MAYO chapter went to Houston to attend an antiwar rally organized by the Texas Peace Action Coalition. CU, which owned a bus, provided the transportation; high school coach Ramiro Jaime drove. Supporting the local MAYO chapter on its stance against the Vietnam War was an important statement by CU and RUP that was anathema to most of BG's conservative supporters—who viewed such protests as radical and un-American.

Still, Gutiérrez became the main target of BG's attacks, denounced as a ruthless power-hungry dictator who used patronage to sustain his following. Schools superintendent Angel Noe González also came under attack for the high school's temporary loss of accreditation, pulled after the district failed to submit a required annual report with information about such areas as curriculum and qualifications of professional staff. Barker accused González of "muddying up the water over the school's loss of accreditation."[35] To no one's surprise the *Senti-*

nel endorsed the five BG candidates, concluding, "These candidates merit your support and vote."[36]

CU's overall strategy was predicated on two tactics: stressing the accomplishments of its one year in office and creating a massive voter turnout. CU sought to counteract BG's negative campaign by emphasizing the many achievements and reforms of RUP's first year of control and stressing that these were merely the beginning: bilingual-bicultural education; free breakfast and lunch programs; hiring of Mexicano school administrators, teachers, staff; dramatic changes in curriculum; construction of low-income housing; paving of streets; better delivery of city services; and the control and political participation of Mexicanos. RUP candidates constantly reminded Mexicano voters that the BG coalition was but a front for gringos whose agenda was to regain control by using their puppets, or cocos, to govern. CU relied heavily on this use of polarization politics, emphasizing that there was no room in Cristal for neutrality against RUP's adversaries.

Throughout the campaign CU exercised its barrio precinct mechanisms. Every targeted precinct had a group responsible for conducting door-to-door canvassing, distributing literature, and getting out the vote on election day. It held numerous organizational meetings and social functions such as picnics, receptions, dances, and huge political rallies. These events were used to demonstrate the organization's political power to reinforce a sense of community power, pride, and RUP's invincibility. The rallies were ways to instill confidence, a sense of security, and feelings of self-worth and empowerment in RUP's supporters.[37]

On February 6 César Chávez, president of the United Farm Workers (UFW), came to Cristal to participate in a number of festivities, including a rally held at City Park and attended by hundreds of RUP supporters. Chávez lauded Cristal's rich political history, referring to the first revolt by Los Cinco in 1963: "It was here in '63 where a political explosion occurred that brought about many changes. Today, you continue giving all of us an example that we can follow. We can do something for ourselves, by ourselves, when we are disposed and determined to do so."[38]

Chávez also alluded to the importance of family unity and a redefinition of machismo and spoke of the UFW's lettuce boycott. Gutiérrez also spoke and praised Chávez's commitment to change and nonviolence. After the rally CU held a reception for Chávez at which he reminded the crowd that it was important for Mexicanos to join other groups and work toward collective change.[39]

At another RUP rally on April 2, hundreds came out to support RUP's local candidates. Speaking at the rally were Bexar County commissioner Albert L. Peña, state senator Joe Bernal, and other officials from outside Cristal. Their participation reflected MAYO's tactic of bringing in prominent forces or individuals to legitimize the issues or projects at hand. Gutiérrez addressed the rally and reminded the people of what Cristal meant to Mexicanos across Aztlán: "Cristal is a symbol. It is a symbol of the Chicano Movement. . . . Chicanos throughout the nation know well we will not give up. . . . The communities have heard about the victory we are going to realize here in Cristal as Chicanos."[40]

The school board elections were held on Saturday, April 3. A record number of voters turned out. The *Sentinel* described the turnout as the result of the most spirited political campaign in the city's history. As during the second revolt, RUP's get-out-the-vote political machinery was in high gear. Scores of RUP volunteers worked the precincts and served as poll watchers. The results were impressive. RUP school board candidates Palomo and Treviño won decisively—Palomo with 1,657 votes and Treviño with 1,688; BG candidates Muñoz and Ramon received 1,236 and 1,218, respectively. Palomo and Treviño had received 58 percent of the vote. The victory gave RUP a 5–2 majority on the school board.[41]

Victorious, CU redirected its resources and energies at the Tuesday, April 6, city council elections. On election night hundreds of RUP supporters gathered downtown to await the results. When the final count was announced, RUP had another victory on its score card. The party's candidates had won by an impressive 2–1 margin. The crowds celebrated noisily with music, honking horns, and yells of "Viva La Raza!" Benavides got the most votes, 1,649. Gámez and Talamantez followed with 1,626 and 1,622 votes, respectively. Of the BG candidates, Mata did best, garnering 911 votes. Nieto and Salazar received 891 and 890, respectively. The independent candidates did poorly. Cornejo got only 40 votes and Ralph García and his mother each received a mere 4.

The election results proved that Gutiérrez and CU had solidified RUP's power base. The RUP victories sent a powerful message: Mexicanos were zealously and widely supportive of its peaceful revolution. The high turnout of Mexicano voters was a sign of La Raza's political and organizational prowess, sophistication, and power. The local white community responded with disgust and apprehension. BG asked District Court Judge Ross E. Doughty to impound all ballots and records from both the school board and city council elections, but the recount did not alter the results.[42] Some gringos repeated the charges that RUP was communistic, radical, and racist. Yet for Mexicanos throughout Aztlán, Cristal continued to be the matrix and catalyst of the Chicano Movement's struggle for empowerment and change.

Salient Issues of 1971

RUP took on a variety of issues during the remainder of 1971. City Manager Bill Richey resigned to go to Harvard Law School, and Francisco Rodríguez was hired as his replacement. Rodríguez, a former resident of Cristal, had returned to the city after college and served as an assistant to Richey for a few months before being appointed to the top job. Confident in its capacity to exercise power, the RUP-controlled city council accelerated its efforts to solidify both its control and power base. In doing so several issues arose that further exacerbated the city's political polarization.[43]

In April 1971 the city council sought control of the segregated Crystal City Country Club. Built just before World War II, the country club property had housed a Japanese internment camp. After the war whites used city money to buy one building from the federal government and convert it into a clubhouse for the exclusive use of whites. Although the city owned the property, in 1956 it gave the whites a thirty-year lease, and they operated it as a private venture, which meant that the facilities, including the swimming pool, were off-limits to the city's Mexicanos. In 1971 it remained one of the few bastions of white omnipotence and racial exclusivity. Now the city refused to recognize the lease and demanded $14,400 in back rents.[44] Gutiérrez saw the racial exclusivity of the club as a symbol of the "racial dictatorship" that had governed Cristal before RUP's takeover.

The issue became more conflict ridden when vandals broke into the country club facilities and committed hundreds of dollars in damages to the cabana area surrounding the pool. The *Sentinel* reported that they painted obscenities, and slogans such as "Chicano power" and "Viva La Raza," on the walkways and walls.[45] The city barricaded the clubhouse, locked the swimming pool gate, and removed the water meter. The city placed a sign on the barricade that read: "Notice— Closed by order of the City Manager . . . discrimination in the use of services and facilities on this airport property is prohibited by Title VI of the Civil Rights Act of 1964." City officials contended that the facilities belonged to the city and to the public at large, regardless of their race, creed, or national origin. They emphasized that the property did not belong merely to the fifty members of the Crystal City Country Club Cooperative.

The country club members secured a restraining order from 38th District Court enjoining the city from preventing access to the country club and sued the city for $350,000. The city retaliated by seeking a judgment against the Crystal City Country Club Corporation for $544,500 (including $500,000 in punitive damages). The city argued first that the lease was invalid. Its second position was that the lease was void because the membership discriminated by denying the use of the facility to all residents of Cristal.[46] The case continued in the courts for several years (see Chapter 4). Gutiérrez later said, "They won the suit, but in the end we won through the city's use of eminent domain." Years later the city gained control of the property and built schools, housing, and city maintenance facilities on the land.[47]

Although the country club was among the most volatile issues of the year, other matters kept RUP's city council busy. In June the city responded to a tax strike by some of the major white landowners. The tax strike affected municipal revenues, hindering the city's ability to proceed with planned improvements. City Manager Rodriguez told the Sentinel what he thought was behind the tax strike: "This large increase in delinquent taxes is due to the irresponsible attitude of those residents of Crystal City who have decided to boycott the payment of their taxes simply because their political beliefs are not necessarily those of the officials who have been elected to public office."[48]

Nonetheless, the city went ahead with the improvements. In August the city announced it would spend $700,000 for plans for a variety of new projects, including a legal services center, a communitywide health insurance plan that would provide maternity and death benefits, a career program in health that would provide jobs for both underemployed and unemployed residents, and a jobs training program. A few weeks later the city announced the availability of emergency ambulance service. In September the city sponsored a three-month citywide clean-up during which residents would remove trash, weeds, and discarded items from their yards.

The city also moved to further professionalize the all-Mexicano Cristal police department with a new training program and to integrate Cristal's all-white fire department. Through the summer months the city continued its control and consolidation efforts. The Urban Renewal Agency, for example, continued to be purged of non-RUP supporters. The agency's new executive director, Juan Cotera, hired Mexicanos to replace eleven whites who had resigned in protest of RUP policies.[49]

In November a Cristal delegation went to Washington, D.C., to participate in the National Coalition of Spanish-Speaking Conference. The delegation included José Angel and Luz Gutiérrez, Ninfa Lozano, and Angel Noe González, the schools superintendent. Conference participants praised Cristal as a symbol of "Chicano Liberation." Resolutions praised and supported RUP's efforts in Cristal to promote self-determination and rejected the racial and political harassment efforts by state and federal agencies, media, and politicians.[50]

The 1972 Local Elections and Issues

Cristal's 1972 local elections became an exercise in continuing the controlled politics of the RUP machine. Only two seats on the school board and two on the city council were in contention in 1972, which did not threaten RUP's majorities. In February CU held its special meeting to nominate candidates, and incumbents Buenaventura González and Pablo Puente were selected without challenge. But minor friction developed within CU's membership over the school board candidates. The conflict was a result of CU's procrastination in choosing candidates. Luz Gutiérrez said that CU's delay was attributable to a lack of candidates.[51] Because of a school district policy barring the candidacy of anyone who had relatives who had been employed by the school district for less than two years, few CU members who were interested in running were eligible. City council candidates were not hampered by such restrictions, so candidates were plentiful.

The first major schism in the CU membership surfaced in February 1972. At a CU meeting José Mata declared his candidacy for the school board and filed soon after that. A few days later, without consulting the CU membership, Ester Ynosencio and Police Chief Alberto Sánchez also filed. Consequently, by March CU had three members running for the two seats. A political tug-of-war broke out. Initially, Sánchez sided with Ynosencio because he believed that she had been treated unfairly by CU. However, other CU members sought to persuade Ynosencio to withdraw from the race. When she refused, CU endorsed Sánchez and Mata and initiated its ostracism procedure for dealing with maverick candidates. Then fourteen disgruntled CU members who became known as *Los Catorce* resigned in protest. (Gutiérrez was not in Cristal when this occurred. He was living part-time in Austin where he was working on his doctorate at the University of Texas. Periodically, he returned to Cristal to attend school board meetings, troubleshoot problems affecting the peaceful revolution, and ensure that a generally approved course of action was being followed.)[52] Although very much in a position of control, CU in 1972 had not yet evolved into a full-fledged political machine because of Gutiérrez's absence. While he was away,

Gutiérrez relied on CU's internal leadership to guide the peaceful revolution.

Believing that the disagreements within CU would work to their advantage, the white community ran candidates whom CU denigrated as puppets. The white community's nominees for the school board were businessmen Julian Saldívar, owner of the J&J Shoe Store, and Emmett Sevilla, manager of White's Auto Store. Opposing RUP's city council candidates were Hector Ramon and Eusevio Salinas. Unlike the 1971 local elections, in which RUP's opposition ran under the aegis of BG, in this election they ran as independents. The voters of Cristal also had to decide on a $2.8 million bond issue for the construction of a new high school, which became a central issue in the school board campaign. Because the approval of the bond meant an increase in school district taxes, the independent candidates were adamantly against it. Conversely, because the RUP-backed school administration had proposed the bond, RUP's candidates were in favor of it. Barker, backed the independents and his editorial page told readers: "Although the school district's building program has not kept pace with current needs, the plans outlined in the proposed bond issue are much too ambitious, and the Sentinel does not support it. . . . A bond issue calling for the paying of nearly three million in principal, and interest, will put a burden on tax payers in the district."[53] Explaining the rationale for the *Sentinel's* endorsement of all four independents, Barker wrote of Sevilla and Saldívar, "These two businessmen will provide strong leadership and merit your support."

The central theme of the independent school board candidates was "Patriotism is a virtue." In a political advertisement in the *Sentinel* they declared that "a vote for us is a vote for freedom to express your own beliefs regardless of race, creed, or nationality." A common allegation was that many of the new teachers were radical, possessed loose morals, and represented a negative influence on the children. The political advertisement in the *Sentinel,* printed in both English and Spanish, went on to claim that "the present administration has chosen to overlook or ignore drug abuse and unscrupulous teachers, whose morals are not in the best interest of the students . . . dismissed qualified teachers, therefore depraving the students."[54] Indeed, there was more to these allegations than RUP cared to acknowledge (see Chapter 8).

The independent candidates were asserting that the school district had hired many unqualified teachers and that the schools were discriminating against whites and those Mexicano students who were not supporters of RUP's agenda for educational change. Not unexpectedly, Gutiérrez also became a central issue in the campaign. Again, he was depicted as a *cacique* [boss]. A paid advertisement in the *Sentinel* declared, "We are not seeking honor or glory but we firmly believe that you should be informed of people who are only interested in their own gain." The ad went on to declare, "Enough of oppressive bosses, men who are greedy and cruel who only care about their own self-interests."[55]

The campaign for the city council was equally contentious. However, although the two independent candidates directed a barrage of accusations against the RUP candidates, their polemics were less virulent than those of their school board colleagues. The independent council candidates stressed promises that RUP had made in 1970 and had not kept. The independents also were critical of what they referred to as RUP's "unrepresentativeness." They declared that they would represent the "total community" and attacked RUP for being dictatorial and for representing only its supporters. The independents relied on newspaper advertisements, a few meetings, and fund-raisers to reach voters. Unlike RUP and CU, the independents were unable to mount a comprehensive voter mobilization and had no organizational capability.[56]

CU, on the other hand, was well prepared. With its vast network of families it made sure that every precinct was set up with captains, block leaders, and volunteers. On Saturday, April 1, CU scored one of its most impressive political victories. RUP school board candidates José Mata and Alberto Sánchez won impressively, with 1,707 and 1,727 votes, respectively. Independent candidate Sevilla received only 840 and Saldívar 845 votes. Ester Ynosencio, former member of CU, polled an embarrassing 67 votes. CU's position also prevailed on the bond issue, which voters approved 1,737 to 867.

The city council election results were no different. CU again produced a massive turnout on April 4, and RUP incumbents Buenaventura González and Puente prevailed over independent challengers Hector Ramon and Eusevio Salinas. González led the balloting with 1,745 votes, followed by Puente with 1,741. Salinas received 522 votes, whereas Ramon got 517.[57] RUP candidates had a 3–1 margin of victory. The reelection of González and Puente reaffirmed RUP's control of the city council's five seats.

The elections were important to RUP because the votes were an opportunity for people to express their support for the myriad political, social, economic, and educational changes that had been implemented—and they did so ardently. The election results legitimized RUP's peaceful revolution. The defeated independents reacted by alleging fraud, claiming that some people who had voted for RUP candidates were not actual community residents or were ineligible to vote. The ballots and all other election records were impounded, but the results did not change.[58]

Salient Issues of 1972

RUP remained busy on other fronts in 1972. In January Reverend Sherrill Smith, a long-time social justice advocate who had just been assigned to Cristal's Catholic parish, and four others were arrested after picketing the Warren Wagner Farms. The dispute arose when spinach workers were paid $1.30 per hour instead of the $1.60 they had been promised (see Chapter 10).

The official charge was blocking a public road. Zavala County Sheriff C. L. Sweeten ordered the picketers to return to Cristal. The crowd, which had grown from thirty initially to about eighty, refused to board the bus provided and instead marched to town. Upon their arrival more than four hundred people joined the protesters. Most of them were high school students who had joined the march as it circled the courthouse square. Smith and his colleagues peacefully resisted their arrest. At the end of the march the five arrestees reported to county authorities while a crowd of about 350 waited outside. Justice of the Peace Frank Moreno Sr. charged the five with blocking a public road and released them after attorneys Jesse Gamez of San Antonio and Ray Perez of Eagle Pass, representing the Mexican-American Legal Defense and Education Fund (MALDEF), posted their bonds.[59]

While neither CU nor Gutiérrez had officially sponsored the picketing, the actions clearly had their support. The two indicators of this were the high school students' involvement and the appearance of the MALDEF attorneys. Amancio Cantu, assistant superintendent of the Cristal schools, told a San Antonio reporter that the students were allowed to leave their classes "because they (students) said they were going whether we let them or not." Students played a significant political role during the five years of RUP's community control of Cristal—they were a rapidly deployable force of activists for RUP, always ready to respond to the call for mobilization. Smith became a member of CU and a strong supporter of RUP's peaceful revolution.[60]

Shortly after the election the city council adopted a budget of $625,510.79 for the upcoming fiscal year. The new budget was $4,000 less than the city's budget in 1971. Cristal's new city manager, Francisco Rodriguez, submitted various recommendations that the council approved: an increase in the tax rate; a 5.5 percent pay increase for city workers; additional staff training; and extending health insurance coverage to the mayor and city council members (city employees already were covered). Rodriguez reported to the council that the future of Cristal had never looked brighter.

For the rest of 1972 the council continued to focus on urban renewal, housing, the Del Monte annexation, and the expansion of social services, among other issues. In particular, the efforts to seek federal funding for a health center became an issue during the presidential election campaign. Democratic candidate George McGovern charged that RUP had sold out to the Republicans in exchange for federal funding for the clinic (see Chapter 10).[61]

In the summer of 1972 Mexico's president, Luis Echeverría Alvarez, met with Gutiérrez and a delegation of RUP leaders in San Antonio. As a gesture of goodwill Echeverría Alvarez delivered to the city of Cristal a bust of Benito Juárez, the nineteenth-century Mexican statesman. The Mexican president also ordered several visits by Mexican government officials, including the Eagle Pass consul; consul general of San Antonio; Maria de la Paz Beceril, a member of the Mexican congress; academician Jorge Bustamante; and José Juan de Olloqui, Mexico's ambassador to the United States.[62] The visits were part of Gutiérrez's efforts to secure support and assistance for RUP from the Mexican government and catapult the Chicano Movement into foreign affairs.

By 1972 Cristal had a growing national reputation as a dynamic rural community undergoing massive change. The Nixon administration sent representatives to Cristal to investigate the problems of Mexicanos in rural Texas. Mexicano scholars such as Rudy Acuña, Ralph Guzman, José Angel Cardenas, Simon Gonzales, Blandina Cardenas, Juan Aragon, Salmon Flores, Gloria Zamora, José Gonzales, and Nick Vaca visited Cristal to learn about RUP's peaceful revolution as well as to offer their assistance.[63] Politicians like New Mexico's lieutenant governor, Roberto Mondragon, along with scores of activists from throughout Aztlán and the midwest, made political pilgrimages to Cristal. With the county, state, and national elections that November the RUP movement reached its apogee.

The 1972 County, State, and National Elections

Cristal's second revolt and RUP's peaceful revolution spurred RUP's growth as a state party and as a movement throughout Aztlán. By 1971 RUP had scores of organizing committees throughout Texas, although most were in south Texas. In October RUP held its first statewide convention in preparation for getting RUP on the 1972 ballot. The issue of going statewide nearly split the RUP movement. Gutiérrez, who represented primarily the rural perspective, wanted RUP to develop on a county-by-county basis, whereas Mario Compean, who held a more urban point of view, believed RUP was ready to go statewide.[64] Compean prevailed, and the party moved quickly to nominate candidates for county, state, and federal offices.

In Cristal CU had begun preparing in January for the county elections in November. RUP held its county convention in May and began a petition drive to get the party placed on the ballot statewide in November. The convention's agenda focused on the election of permanent county and precinct chairpersons and the nomination of county candidates. RUP nominated the following for county offices: Rey Pérez for county attorney; José Serna for sheriff; Armando G. Barmea for tax assessor–collector; and candidates for a number of lesser offices.[65]

To ensure that RUP would be on the statewide ballot in November, CU worked hard to get signatures from the scores of migrants who left Cristal in early summer.[66] On another front, four RUP members filed suit in U.S. District Court, claiming that the election code discriminated against minority parties by not providing for their members to cast absentee ballots, whereas it was easy for members of the major parties to do so. At the same time RUP and CU stressed to their constituents the importance of not voting in the Democratic and Republican Party primaries on May 6: anyone who voted in these primaries would be ineligible to register as a RUP member. Under the Texas Electoral Code, RUP had only from May 8 to June 30 to obtain the twenty-two thousand notarized signatures required to get on the ballot for the November elections. RUP secured about thirteen hundred signatures in Zavala County alone during the month of May.[67]

While RUP prepared for the upcoming county elections, so did its opposition. In April RUP's Zavala County adversaries began their own preelection organizing. They held a meeting to create a countywide political organization that would oppose RUP. Approximately one hundred people from throughout the county attended and established Amistad ('friendship' in Spanish). The *Sentinel* explained the purpose of Amistad: "The organization is for keeping more than one political entity available in Zavala County to insure that all people have a true opportunity to express themselves through elective representatives." Amistad was nothing more than the old RUP adversaries of CASAA of 1970, BG of 1971, and independents of early 1972 with a new label. According to Dale Barker, Amistad was similar to CASAA in orientation, but its membership was much younger.[68]

By May Amistad was well on its way to becoming a functional political organization. Elected to its board of directors were Essal Johnson, Emma Servia, Julián Rodriguez, Jack Kingsberry, Yolanda López,

Wayne Hamilton, Bernard Brown, and David Dalerod. Membership in Amistad was open to both Mexicanos and whites of the county. To become a member a voter had to be anti-RUP and had to follow Amistad's better government credo.[69]

For all intents and purposes Amistad became synonymous with Zavala County's Democratic Party. In June the Democrats held their primary and nominated R. A. Taylor for county attorney, C. L. Sweeten for sheriff, Martha Cruz for tax assessor–collector, Felipe Torres for commissioner from Precinct 1, Santos Nieto for commissioner from Precinct 3, and a host of others for lesser offices.[70] After the June primary Amistad endorsed and openly supported the Democratic Party's candidates. Because Texas at that time was essentially a one-party state, the Democratic candidates in Zavala County had no Republican opposition. Their main opposition came from RUP.

After weeks of arduous work on the petition drive, in August RUP organizers succeeded in garnering sufficient signatures to place RUP on the ballot. They did it by relying on the newly created state structure and on the quota system devised by Gutiérrez. With more than twenty county RUP entities organized and a quota assigned to each, by the end of the petition drive RUP had 22,365 acceptable signatures, thus guaranteeing it a place on the statewide ballot.[71] MAYO leaders such as Mario Compean, Alberto Luera, and others had headed the petition drive. By 1972 MAYO's absorption by RUP was almost complete, and MAYO leaders were the driving force behind RUP's organizing throughout Texas.[72]

Even though RUP had succeeded in getting on the ballot statewide, the petition drive had its problems—workers, money, and getting the petitions notarized were chief among them. RUP county committees participated in the drive, but not all were effective. According to Luera, some counties only got fifteen signatures, whereas others, such as San Antonio, secured thousands. Second, because so little money was available, RUP's staff, headed by Luera, was small. In fact, volunteers were the backbone of the petition drive. Getting the signatures notarized was a serious problem. The few full-time staff members and volunteers had to scrutinize every petition for errors and for authenticity of signatures before the petitions could be submitted.[73] Some RUP supporters were convinced that the petition drive would fail. According to RUP's gubernatorial candidate, Ramsey Muñiz, "Before August, people really didn't know what was going to happen. We didn't know if we were going to be on the ballot or not. People had already given up and they were saying we are not going to make it. There were rumors [of] *que si y que no* [of yes and no]."[74]

During August RUP's political campaigns throughout Texas gradually began to pick up momentum. In three months, lacking money and sufficient staff, among other things, RUP sought to become the balance of power in Texas electoral politics. The objectives of the campaign were several: to run Ramsey Muñiz for governor; to elect RUP candidates; to make sure that RUP received enough votes to secure a place on the ballot for the 1974 elections; and to expand RUP's power base to the other counties with large Mexicano populations throughout Texas. From August to November RUP's state and county candidates were busy spreading the word that RUP was now on the ballot and that it was an official party.[75]

By 1972 RUP as a third-party movement had spread to several states within Aztlán and the midwest as well. Wherever there were significant pockets of Mexicanos, RUP organizing committees were formed. Some functioned more like pressure groups contending with community issues, whereas others worked exclusively to get RUP on the ballot as an official political party. In an effort to formulate a national strategy Gutiérrez called and organized a national convention in September in El Paso. It drew about three thousand Mexicanos and other Latinos from throughout the nation. Eighteen states sent delegations: Arizona, California, Colorado, Illinois, Indiana, Kansas, Maryland, Michigan, Nebraska, New Mexico, Texas, Washington, Wisconsin, Wyoming, Utah, Washington, D.C., Missouri, and Oregon. There were 268 delegates, and they cast 441 delegate votes.

Joining Gutiérrez at the national RUP convention were several national, state, and local activist leaders. Among the national CM leaders who attended were Rodolfo "Corky" Gonzales, who headed RUP in Colorado as well as the Crusade for Justice, which espoused formation of a Chicano nation, and Reies López Tijerina, leader of the land grant movement (which sought the return to its original Mexicano owners of lands taken by the federal government) under the aegis of New Mexico's Alianza Federal de Mercedes.[76] Also in attendance were Muñiz, the Texas gubernatorial candidate; Mario Compean, RUP's Texas state chairperson; Salomon Baldenegro of Arizona; and Juan José Peña of New Mexico. These national and state RUP leaders were joined by numerous other local and regional leaders, especially the Californians—Raul Ruiz, Herman Baca, and me. The convention proved to be RUP's high point on the national political stage. From this point on Gutiérrez and Gonzales became involved in internecine power struggles that became a major factor in the party's rapid decline and ultimate end as a regional or national third party.

The convention had all the trappings of a traditional major party convention. In jockeying for delegates both Gutiérrez and Gonzales relied on a combination of tactics to win RUP's national leadership— from parliamentary maneuvering to one-to-one or group persuasion, and sometimes even arm twisting, friendly persuasion, and physical intimidation. Both Gutiérrez and Gonzales used the power of oratorical persuasion from the podium.

Gonzales gave the keynote address at the convention, emphasizing the importance of building RUP into a national party. He described the Democratic and Republican parties as a two-headed monster feeding from the same trough. Gonzales berated Mexicanos who remained Democrats and Republicans. He accused them of being stooges, *vendidos*, *Tio Tacos*, and *malinches* (all three terms are pejoratives generally meaning sellouts). His message to them was "you're not free because you're licking the white man's boots."[77]

Gutiérrez's address stressed the importance of building unity within RUP. He emphasized the need to avoid internecine politics:

We must resolve our own problems with this political party.... Some say it is impossible.... Ask these same people if they saw fighting at the gringo conventions and they'll say, "Oh, that was discussion, argument." In that case, he doesn't know Mexicans. We're not fighting. *Nos estamos poniendo de acuerdo* [We are reaching a consensus]. We will leave here a united party.... I hope, to fight for one another.... We should stop concerning ourselves with Chicano power ... and build power for Chicanos here today.[78]

López Tijerina's role at the convention was one of neutrality. He also worked to be a unifier, staying clear of endorsing any proposal relating to the power struggle between Gutiérrez and Gonzales. In his address he spoke of unity before ideals, organization, and leaders. He cautioned the delegates not to get into a fight over political purity.[79] In addition, Tijerina stressed the need for what he called "brotherhood of awareness," warning delegates to avoid hatred in their search for cultural identification.[80]

After a heated debate and acrimonious attacks the convention held its election for the national leadership of RUP. Gutiérrez won by a vote of 256⅙ votes to Gonzales's 170⅚. The convention delegates also approved the establishment of the Congreso de Aztlán. During the convention RUP's national platform was drawn up and approved. The *El Paso Herald* summarized the platform:

The adopted national platform called for bi-lingual and bi-cultural education, wage and employment parity, a fight against drugs in Chicano communities, the appointment of Chicanos as judges, the providing of free legal aid for Chicanos, the redistribution of the nation's wealth, a break-up of monopolies, the honoring of original Mexican and Spanish land grants in the southwestern United States, an end to real estate taxes, complete Chicano self-determination, an endorsement of Ramsey Muniz for Governor of Texas, and no-endorsement of a presidential candidate.[81]

Refusing to endorse Nixon or McGovern for president, the RUP delegates opted for complete political independence for Mexicano voters.[82] This meant a symbolic boycott of the presidential election. The delegates decided to concentrate on local and state elections instead.

Throughout the convention Gutiérrez had relied on his cadre of MAYO leaders, the Texas RUP delegation, and leaders from CU, as well as his supporters in the other delegations, to muster the necessary delegate votes to confirm his leadership. He relied on Voluntarios de Aztlán and members of the Barrio Club for his personal security as well as for organizing the convention.[83]

Back in Zavala County RUP redirected its political energies toward the county elections. At the same time the Democratic Party, backed by Amistad, began preparing for the inevitable political showdown. The Democratic strategy was identical to that of the local RUP's gringo-versus-Mexicano position during the 1971 and 1972 local elections. Once again whites worked to discredit the accomplishments of RUP through allegations of *caciquismo* [bossism], corruption, reverse discrimination, high taxes, incompetence, control by outside opportunists, poor public service, and poor public schools.

Both Amistad and the Democratic candidates bought half-page ads in the *Sentinel* that contained all these allegations. The Democratic-Amistad program emphasized local people handling local community interests, local people employed in local jobs, community harmony, industrial progress, reasonable tax rates, and good schools.[84] Their strategies relied on the old gringo tactic of divide and conquer, this time by airing a radio spot recorded by Mike Pérez, the former RUP school board member and one of the fourteen CU members who dropped out of CU when it refused to endorse Ester Ynosencio for the school board in early 1972.

A common criticism of Pérez within CU was that he defected because he was envious of Gutiérrez.[85] A week before the election, Pérez, in a lengthy radio spot, denounced Gutiérrez as a ruthless dictator and alluded to the cruelty of the cacique, or political boss. For a week this spot, which was more of a commentary, was played several times daily by the local radio station:

Here we must remember the philosophy of the political boss that some must die so others can live . . . and today . . . he applies the same philosophy to his own people. . . . Who authorizes this individual to condemn a fellow human being, designating him of being culpable, sacrificing for the errors of others, and be so callous as to ask the community to not employ him because he was a bad Mexican? . . . This is what sustains and gives this political boss pleasure—by killing people economically, socially, and mentally.[86]

The radio spot made no mention of Democratic candidates or of Amistad. Apparently, the strategy was to confuse and divide the RUP electorate. Supposedly, Pérez was speaking for the fourteen people who still considered themselves RUP supporters. He concluded by declaring that "the intention of this program is to clarify our position within our Raza Unida Party."[87] Pérez was thus careful not to criticize RUP or CU but directed his remarks solely at their political boss.

Lacking CU's grassroots machinery, the Democratic Party candidates relied heavily on both the radio and paid advertisements to organize their county campaign. By October Amistad had come out with a newsletter entitled *El Camino Recto* [The Right Road] as a counterpoint to RUP's *La Verdad*. Amistad explained the title as meaning "the right road . . . the road of the truth and ideals that merits your attention and support." Distributed every two weeks, it summarized Amistad's activities and focused on various campaign issues. Reacting to a study conducted by the University of Texas that concluded that only 6 percent of La Raza identified themselves as Chicanos, *El Camino Recto* stated: "It could mean the majority of Americans of Mexican descent are fed up and sick of the separatism and racism practiced by the people pushing the use of the word Chicano."[88]

The Democratic Party candidates were backed by the *Sentinel*. In an editorial against RUP, *Sentinel* editor Barker wrote:

If our government is to continue to be stable and to serve all of the citizens, it is of utmost importance that these capable Democrats be elected. . . . La Raza Unida has brought nothing but hate, distrust, turmoil and complete financial irresponsibility to our community. The only way to stop this disruptive force that is attempting to gain complete control over people's lives is to refuse to vote for candidates supported by La Raza Unida.[89]

RUP's strategy was predicated on maintaining a positive and aggressive posture in regard to its accomplishments. Since the second revolt in 1970, CU had relied on its emphasis on community control and participatory democracy to thwart a return of political apathy or complacency. RUP's overall strategy had been to socialize Mexicanos into changing their apolitical and fatalistic attitudes. RUP commonly stressed attitudes of pride, self-worth, and antigringoism.

Integral to RUP's offensive posture was its tactic of not retaliating when the opposition made charges. However, when Pérez came out with his long anti-Gutiérrez commentary, RUP was caught by surprise.[90] *La Verdad* retaliated by mounting a political attack against Pérez, Amistad, and *El Camino Recto.*

On election day both political camps mobilized to get out the vote. As was customary, RUP had its people running tables at every polling place. Amistad also had its table. RUP sound trucks canvassed the Zavala County communities of Cristal, Batesville, and La Prayor. Precinct workers went door to door. Election day was marked by a number of incidents. Early in the morning Sheriff Sweeten attempted to prevent RUP's candidates from placing poll watchers at every polling place. He also arrested Gutiérrez and Eliseo Solis and charged them with disturbing the peace.[91] According to the Texas Election Code, RUP was entitled to seven poll watchers; Sheriff Sweeten would allow only one. Before the incident was over, deputy sheriffs and Texas Rangers were involved in verbal skirmishes with more than sixty Mexicanos, who were supported by Cristal's local police force. In an article entitled, "Election Night in Crystal City" for a national church publication, John Fry describes the scene: "There was a lot of pushing, lots of threats, lots of cussing in the best bilingual tradition of South Texas . . . the issue to be decided along the strict machismo lines of 'who's got the most balls?' The sheriff's lethal presence had been apparently neutralized by the sub-lethal means of an Election Code, standing behind . . . the guns of the municipal police."[92]

Before the second revolt it was the common practice of gringo power holders to allow its opposition only one or no poll watcher at all. This was one method they used to maintained their power. They would threaten and harass the Mexicano majority. If that was insufficient, gringos would steal Mexicano votes after they had been cast. But the sheriff's efforts to intimidate the RUP poll watchers failed because of the explicitness of the Texas Election Code on the issue. In most precincts the RUP poll watchers won their points.

On the evening of election day, while people waited for the results, the sheriff tried to intimidate a RUP absentee ballot watcher. Another fracas resulted. Fry describes it: "Sweeten tried to arrest José Serna! Serna tried to arrest Sweeten! 'A citizen's arrest,' he said, not without a touch of macabre humor, since Serna was an optimist and was superbly confident he had already won. That's where I heard, 'get a rope.'"[93]

There were many other incidents before and during election day. Amistad rented a helicopter that had a public address system and blitzed Cristal with a five-minute extract from Pérez's radio infomercial, berating Gutiérrez as a dictator and a bandit. RUP countered by alleging that local gringo employers were coercing Mexicanos into not voting for RUP candidates. According to Fry, they came right out and threatened, "'You vote for Raza Unida and you ain't got a job anymore.'"[94] For these reasons this election proved to be the most heated and hotly contested. Amistad was determined to keep RUP from expanding beyond Cristal and especially from winning control of Zavala County's court of commissioners.

RUP won five of the nine contested offices. County Attorney R. A. Taylor lost to Rey Pérez by 37 votes (1,949 votes for Pérez to 1,912 votes for Taylor). In the sheriff's race Serna won with 2,005 votes to Sweeten's 1,883. RUP candidate Elena Díaz won the commissioner's post for Precinct 3 with 403 votes to Democrat Santos Nieto's 303. Rodolfo (Rudy) Espinosa Jr. won the constable post for Precinct 2 by 9 votes—557 to his opponent's 548. Moses García, RUP candidate for constable of Precinct 3, ran unopposed and received 487 votes. The Democrats won four offices: for county assessor Martha Cruz got 2,026 votes to A. G. Barmea's 1,871; for commissioner for Precinct 1, Felipe Torres, received 466 votes to Juan Guzmán's 338 votes; for constable for Precinct 1, M. L. Blackman garnered 404 votes to Héctor Mata's 351; and for constable of Precinct 4, Lonzo Bostic received 628 votes to Antonio Ríos's 593.[95]

Although the RUP did not win all nine county offices, it gained a strong foothold in county government. The Zavala County elections were a power struggle over who was going to control and govern. A precinct-by-precinct analysis of the county returns showed that only a handful of Anglos could have voted for the RUP candidates. Many Mexicanos voted for the Democratic candidates.[96] Some RUP supporters felt that in other circumstances RUP would have won all nine seats. The following factors hurt the RUP's county efforts: Mike Pérez's speech confused many RUP supporters; RUP failed to generate sufficient interest in the campaigns outside Cristal—in, for example, Batesville and La Prayor; a strained workforce—some of RUP's workers were dispatched to assist the state effort in San Antonio; and Gutiérrez, the campaign strategist, was out of the area managing Ramsey Muñiz's campaign for governor.

At the state level RUP's political scorecard was not one marked by victories. RUP's efforts proved to be more symbolic than real. Muñiz, hoping to deny victory to Democrat Dolph Briscoe, was able to secure only 219,127 votes, or 6.43 percent of the vote. Briscoe, however, won by beating his Republican opponent, Henry Graves, 1,632,287 to 1,532,075. Of the 254 counties in Texas, Briscoe carried 223, whereas Graves won 23 and Muñiz 3. Muñiz won Zavala, Brooks, and Jim Hogg counties against Briscoe but lost the other twelve predominantly Mexicano counties in south Texas.[97] The other RUP state candidates also went down to defeat, receiving no more than 10 percent of the vote, even in counties where Mexicanos were a majority.

However, RUP scored a symbolic victory: Muñiz got enough votes to give RUP official party status for the 1974 state elections. RUP was now required by law to hold a party primary, with the state picking up most of the tab. The election also gave credence to the belief of Gutiérrez and others that RUP had the potential to become a power broker in Texas state politics.[98]

After the November county elections RUP found itself harassed by grand jury indictments and suits. In December a RUP candidate for constable and seven others were indicted by the Zavala County grand jury on charges of illegal voting in the November 7 general elections.[99] That same month a suit was filed by four defeated Democratic candidates against RUP candidates. The suit alleged that 1,800 votes had been cast illegally. It stated that the votes came from people who were convicted felons, who lived outside the county, and noncitizens. The plaintiffs also asked that the election boxes be reopened and the votes recounted. They further sought to have all illegal ballots subtracted from the total votes cast for each candidate to establishing which candidates won the election.[100]

The RUP candidates categorically denied these charges. RUP attorneys Paul Rich, who worked for the Crystal City Legal Aid Society, and Jesse Gamez of MALDEF and San Antonio, filed the first response. This was followed by a brief filed by attorney Ray Perez from Eagle Pass. Both briefs claimed that there was no legal procedure for learning which voters, if any, had voted for RUP candidates.[101] RUP's four county elected officials were sworn in in January 1973 but were required to post bonds because of the ongoing suit. The suit was not litigated until 1974; the outcome favored RUP—only the office of constable went to the Democrats.

4

The Calm Before the
Political Storm (1973–1975)

The years between 1973 and early 1975 were the apogee of RUP's community control in Cristal. During these years Ciudadanos Unidos (CU) developed into a full-fledged political machine. After three years of community control RUP succeeded in effecting many changes that improved Mexicanos' quality of life. Politically, it defeated all challenges to RUP's control of the city council and school board, and in 1974 it captured control of the Zavala County Court of Commissioners. These were also the years of RUP's continued expansion as a statewide party. But it was during these two years that RUP's peaceful revolution began to experience internal schisms, nascent power struggles, and conflicts. By 1975 these difficulties had led to its political rupture and eventually its demise.

Cristal's 1973 Local Elections: An Observer's Perspective

RUP kicked off 1973 with confidence. Already assured of its control of Cristal's city council and school board, the party had won a seat on Zavala County's Court of Commissioners, and its members had taken three other county elective offices in the November 1992 elections. In early January 1973, despite the lawsuit initiated by the defeated Democratic candidates, the four RUP victors were sworn in. But before the

117

swearing-in ceremony they were required to post bonds in connection with the lawsuit, as stipulated by the Texas Election Code. The bond amounts set by the district clerk of the 38th District Court ranged from $28,000 for Sheriff José Serna to $4 for Constable Rodolfo (Rudy) Espinosa Jr.[1]

Although January was politically uneventful, Dale Barker, in his *Sentinel* column, The Barker, reminded readers of the upcoming April elections:

> With only a brief rest from the November election, the political machines are being oiled up for the city council and school trustees elections in April. Candidates are currently being selected in hush-hush meetings for another all out confrontation at the polls between Amistad and La Raza Unida. And this spring's political bout will bring to light some new and, perhaps, surprising alliances as the maneuvering for control of the city and school continues.[2]

The city council elections were crucial to both sides, because control of the city council was on the line. Three of the five council seats were in contention. On the school board three of seven seats were open. The terms of José Angel Gutiérrez, Arturo Gonzales, and RUP defector Mike Pérez were expiring.

In February a long-simmering controversy surrounding the school district's bilingual education policy started to boil (see Chapter 8). It led to the first serious internal schism to plague RUP's peaceful revolution. The district had established a bilingual education program in 1970, and some Mexicanos were openly opposed to it. The district's policy was to develop a bilingual-bicultural program that was different from the program developed under federal guidelines, which was to use a child's native language in instruction only until the child gained proficiency in English. Instead, the Cristal district would develop a program that called for each student to become proficient in both Spanish and English before being graduated from high school.[3] This was a pet project of José Angel Gutiérrez, who was president of the school board. Now the district was making twenty-two recommendations for improving the program.[4] On January 22 about six hundred people from the community met with the school board to discuss the list. Some parents felt that their children were not learning English well enough. Some felt so strongly that the bilingual policy was to blame for their child's lack of progress in English that they walked out in protest when the board refused to take a vote to reject its bilingual policy. Ponciano Hernández, an anti-Gutierrista and outspoken member of the community, explained the reaction of some parents: "That night I got home and I must have received over thirty calls. . . . They would ask, if they are not going to listen to us, then what are we going to do about it?"[5]

On February 1, the board held a third community forum on its proposed bilingual policy. School trustee Mike Pérez, who had split with RUP in 1972 over CU's candidate-endorsing policy and joined the breakaway *Los Catorce* in Amistad, sided with the angry parents. Despite the parental opposition, the school board the next day adopted the recommendations for improving its bilingual education policy. Pérez, Hernández, and others who opposed Gutiérrez seized the opportunity and continued to hammer away at the problems with bilingual instruction. They immediately circulated a petition criticizing the school board's actions and held several strategy-planning meetings. At one meeting someone proposed a school boycott such as the one held in 1969. This idea was rejected because of the likelihood it would fail or backfire.[6]

At a community meeting held on February 25 about one hundred disgruntled Mexicanos met to discuss political alternatives, including the viability of creating another political party to counter RUP. They decided that it was not a realistic option because it would require too much money, workers, and time. Instead, the group decided to run candidates for both the school board and city council as independents and chose Mike Pérez, José R. Mata, and Elfego Martínez. For the city council the group nominated Eliseo Sanchez, former Cristal police chief; Roberto Cornejo, a former city council member; and Manuel Garza. Those in attendance also signed a petition rejecting the district's bilingual education policy and decided to circulate it. By the end of the month they had collected about one thousand signatures, which they sent to the Texas Education Agency as well as to several state representatives and senators.[7]

Meanwhile, CU began preparing for the most serious challenge to its power since RUP members won control of the school board in 1970. The bilingual policy had cost CU some supporters. Nevertheless, CU was confident that it could beat the electoral challenge. The three RUP incumbents for the city council, José Talamantez, Roberto Gámez, and Francisco Benavides, decided not to seek reelection because CU had promulgated a "desire to break the traditions that the gringos had established in Texas of staying in public office for 10, 20 and 40 years."[8]

Thus CU endorsed Ramón "Monche" Mata, José D. Cuevas, and Richard Díaz to RUP as candidates for city council. Two RUP school

board incumbents, Gutiérrez and Arturo Gonzales, also chose to follow
CU's no-reelection policy, and Ernesto Olguín, Viviana Santiago, and
Ramón Garza became RUP's candidates for the school board.[9]

One of CU's strategies for mobilizing voters was to continue to stress
the plethora of changes brought about by RUP since the second revolt.
From February through April 1973 CU's literature and principal newspaper, *La Verdad*, maintained a steady flow of information about
the educational and municipal achievements under RUP leadership.
Moreover, CU's propaganda was calculated to isolate gringos and independents and polarize the community by depicting them as the enemies of RUP's peaceful revolution. It described the former gringo
power holders as standing in the background, manipulating discon-
tented Mexicanos in order to thwart RUP's peaceful revolution. CU
caricatured the independent candidates in *La Verdad* as puppets of the
gringos. Of all the independents, Mike Pérez was the special target of
CU's relentless onslaughts. In *una carta abiertä* [an open letter] to Mike
Pérez, a *La Verdad* reader wrote (as translated):

> This letter is directed to all the comrades, friends . . . of my pal Mike Perez
> and his skirted dogs, to tell them that they are a bunch of traitors who want
> to win control of the power so that they can turn it over to the gringo. . . . Did
> you know that backing the independent candidates, is the most racist gringo,
> Jack Ware and other gringos? They are the ones giving money to the indepen-
> dents for their propaganda. . . . That is why I am alerting all parents to not
> vote for them because we will be betraying our own children. . . . May God
> help us in this struggle against these traitors from our own people.[10]

Complementing CU's character assassination tactics was a concerted effort to neutralize the controversial issue of the bilingual education policy in the schools. After adopting the twenty-two recommendations that made Spanish the main language of instruction, school
officials held several more community meetings in February and
March to explain that bilingual education was beneficial and to stifle
the independents' efforts to use the bilingual policy as a campaign
issue.[11] *La Verdad* carried several articles that bitterly attacked the independents while justifying the district's bilingual policy. In addition, the
superintendent of schools wrote to parents to explain the board's rationale for approving the bilingual policy. CU initiated a radio campaign
that alluded to the success of the bilingual-bicultural program and
stressed the many accomplishments of RUP's peaceful revolution.

RUP's campaign strategy relied on special events to solidify the party's support. Rallies were particularly successful. They resembled those
held in Mexico by the Partido Revolucionario Instituciónal (PRI). The

party provided free food, drink, entertainment, and plenty of Tex-Mex music for hundreds of people. More than a thousand people attended another rally at a local park on the Sunday before the elections. The air was one of jubilation and excitement, which was intensified by the speeches of various RUP candidates and dignitaries. At the rally Ramsey Muñiz, RUP's 1972 candidate for governor, gave an impassioned speech on the importance of RUP's struggle in Cristal. Gutiérrez also spoke, and he denigrated the independent candidates as cocos. People shouted, "Viva La Raza Unida!" throughout the rally. RUP banners, Mexicano flags, placards, people wearing buttons, and cars with bumper stickers were everywhere. The community reacted with pride and purpose, confident in its power and in its ability to defeat the opposition.

Propaganda and symbols were basic to RUP's mobilization strategy. This was evident at another rally at the Luna theater just before the election. It too drew about one thousand supporters. As usual, there were speeches, banners, flags, and placards. Adding to the spirited ambiance was the award-winning Cristal City High School marching band. Its musical program included "Jalisco," "Guadalajara," "La Negra," and "La Marcha Zacatecas," just like a campaign rally in Mexico.

In an attempt to neutralize the controversy over bilingual education RUP had a six-year-old girl deliver an eloquent, inspiring oration in both English and Spanish. This was followed by several school officials who expounded on the progress made since RUP's takeover. Gutiérrez spoke against the gringos he claimed were propping up the independents.[12]

Throughout the campaign RUP relied on spots on the local station, KBEN. The spots, one a day, began airing on March 16. By election day, April 3, the party was running forty spots a day. One spot, directed by Monche Mata, a RUP candidate for city council, said in part,

In the city of Cristal our party has started projects and programs to develop our capacity to provide our people with medical assistance. The Winter Garden Research project is in the process of developing health programs for our community and for the nine Winter Garden counties. . . . Zavala County Health is in the process of developing a health clinic for our people and for our brothers of neighboring communities. This is nothing more than a few of the projects we have seen started for our people by the Raza Unida Party.[13]

In another spot RUP council candidate Richard Díaz addressed the benefits of the district's bilingual policy: "The bilingual program is excellent and is highly respected by federal government officials." Viviana Santiago also participated, stressing the high number of Mexicanos who were being graduated from high school and were attending universities and colleges through the nation. The spot ended with her vitriolic attack on the independents as propagators of lies and for misleading the electorate. The spots reminded listeners not only of RUP's successes but of its future projects, such as the construction of a new high school and a health clinic that would provide medical care for the area's poor. Other spots addressed RUP's accomplishments in housing, mental health services, and civic participation.[14]

But, as always, the backbone of CU's mobilization strategy was its grassroots political machinery. Its political action committee emphasized that every CU family and individual member was expected to vote and participate in the get-out-the-vote drive. Even before election day, RUP's headquarters in Cristal was coordinating the voter registration drives, door-to-door canvassing, and all other aspects of the campaigns, including organizing rallies. As an activist organizer, I had orchestrated and organized a similar takeover of a school district in Cucamonga, California, in 1969, but I had never witnessed such a sophisticated exercise of organizational power as I did in Cristal. Placards, house signs, and bumper stickers were everywhere in all the barrios. CU instructed people to call their immediate and extended family members as well as friends to remind them to vote. CU was truly a political machine, capable of delivering the vote.[15]

The independents' strategy was similar if not identical to that used by RUP's adversaries in earlier elections. The independents attacked RUP's leadership and candidates and tried to discredit its reforms, particularly the school district's bilingual-bicultural program. In a one hourlong radio spot Mike Pérez attacked the bilingual policy as regressive, not progressive. He characterized Gutiérrez as a power-hungry dictator who was using the Mexicano community for his personal aggrandizement. He expressly stated that the independents did not oppose RUP but Gutiérrez. The following is representative of the Pérez's acrid attacks on Gutiérrez: "Unfortunately we have fallen in the hands of a true caudillo [chieftain or boss] who is without justice and morality. For this reason we are no longer a few who are against Gutiérrismo or who are not from the Raza Unida. These are two things as distinct as day and night."[16] Pérez asserted that Mexicanos should not be puppets manipulated by a ruthless dictator. Acting as the point person for the independents, Pérez included other RUP leaders in his character assassinations in the radio diatribe. He described Viviana Santiago as a single woman of loose morals. He caricatured Richard Díaz as a loser who came to Cristal out of desperation. He depicted RUP school and city officials as selfish money-hungry outsiders who were reaping the benefits of Mexicanos' long struggle. But more than anyone, schools superintendent Angel Noe González was the target of the independents' attacks. In addition to accusing him of opportunism, they questioned his commitment and his credibility.

Asked in an interview about Pérez's charges, Santiago said, "Pérez and other independents made incredibly hateful and scurrilous allegations against my character and that of other Raza Unida leaders that were totally untrue. Since I was a single, they spread malicious rumors that I was having affairs with men and in essence a loose woman. They were so desperate that they resorted to blatant lies."[17]

The other independents held community meetings, small rallies, passed out literature, and ran radio spots, focusing their attacks with sixteen criticisms:

- lack of discipline in the schools
- application of political pressure to all teachers
- dissension within the school district's administration
- bad conduct by some teachers
- adoption by the school board of the twenty-two recommendations for bilingual education
- raising wages for the district's high-ranking education professionals while providing no increases for support staff
- lack of improvement in the cafeteria's food services
- showing favoritism to professionals from outside the school district
- selection of local public officials without consideration of their qualifications or lack thereof
- lack of communication between parents and teachers, a result of the district's inattention
- threatening faculty and students who do not agree with the administration
- lack of representation of diverse opinions on the school board, whose members' only concern is advancing their political interests
- lack of certified teachers
- teachers who teach subjects outside their professional expertise
- political problems suffered by teachers who do not agree with the administration
- teaching Spanish slang[18]

The independents also alleged that RUP was trying to intimidate Mexicanos who were neutral or who were aligned with the independents. The barrage of accusations also hit hard at the city's loss of about twenty white-owned businesses. The businesses had closed since RUP's political takeover in April 1970 (for more detail see Chapter 9 on the economics of RUP's peaceful revolution). The independents blamed RUP for creating an unstable political situation that made Cristal a haven for radicals. From the independents' perspective this negative image was having a disastrous effect on Cristal's economic development. Throughout the campaign they accused RUP of corruption, dictatorial practices, extortion, intimidation, and patronage. The independents also claimed that "outsiders" were in control of the administration of the school district. Although the independents' strategy clearly was to discredit RUP's leadership, they were careful not to attack some of the peaceful revolution's changes and reforms, such as homes under construction, street paving, and new school construction.

The independent platform offered few, if any, alternatives. Except for the new bilingual education policy, Mike Pérez supported many of RUP's educational changes and programs. He directed his most severe criticism at Gutiérrez and RUP administrators. Ponciano Hernández generally concurred with the changes on RUP's agenda for peaceful revolution, again except for the bilingual policy. His other main criticism was directed at Gutiérrez's antigringo biases. José Mata also expressed concern over what he perceived as RUP's extreme posture of cultural nationalism. In interviews for this book none presented real alternatives. They stressed improving existing RUP-initiated programs, such as the hiring of better-qualified teachers. Hernández remarked that all programs would have to continue unchanged, except for the new bilingual program. He was especially critical of the RUP leadership's use of patronage and claimed the party also used intimidation to maintain its political control.[19]

Amistad was supporting the independent candidates covertly. According to Jack Kingsberry, Amistad members decided after the November elections that standing back and letting the independents lead would be the most advantageous strategy. Most whites perceived the independents as the lesser of two evils. The whites generally saw the independents as fair and kind-hearted people who had the best interests of the total community in mind. Yet gringos believed that RUP and Gutiérrez were part of a national subversive leftist organization.[20]

The independents' campaign headquarters was a building owned by Jack Ware, a major economic force in Cristal, a situation that gave credence to RUP's allegations that the independents were in thrall to the white community. Hernández, Pérez, and Mata denied receiving any financial assistance from gringos.[21] However, throughout the campaign gringos were spotted doing campaign work from the building and displaying the independents' bumper stickers on their vehicles.

The *Sentinel*, predicting doomsday, endorsed the independents:

Voters will make an important decision. . . . They will decide whether or not the future of Crystal City will remain in the hands of La Raza Unida Party and its philosophy, or turn away from the path that has stopped progress in what was once a growing community. Voters have it in their power to stop the deterioration of the city that is leading to its eventual destruction by voting for the . . . independent candidates.[22]

The independents spent hundreds of dollars on newspaper ads, buying full pages in the *Sentinel*. Their central theme was "your vote is needed to return sound, honest, and responsible administration to our city and school."[23] They also took out several full-page ads in *El Diario*, a newspaper from Piedras Negras, Coahuila, Mexico. The ads contained excerpts from Pérez's hourlong radio talk. One ad was entitled, "Independent Candidates Guarantee Prosperity and Huge Guarantees for All the Citizens of Crystal City, Texas." The text continued, "In the communities, and in the cities we have children, elderly, women we should help without distinction to classes. We love prosperity. We love our community. We respect our authorities and we struggle for a general collective betterment."[24]

Although they were too young to vote, some high school students who supported the independents published a newsletter, *La Mera Verdad* [The Real Truth], an underground newspaper that was hypercritical of RUP school administrators and district policies. One article redefined the word *vendido* and said it described certain RUP school administrators:

The word "vendido" or "coco" means a person who is a sell out, but specifically, what is a vendido? He may be defined as someone who goes out and yells, "Viva La Raza" all day long and at the end of the day drives home in his new Cadillac, which he was able to buy from his tremendous salary while the rest of the community is barely surviving. A vendido is a person who is more concerned about his job and his social status than he is about the people of La Raza.

The newsletter accused RUP administrators of brainwashing students and of using Mafia tactics against RUP dissidents. In an obvious jab at Superintendent González, another article admonished, "Think for yourself this time and 'vote.' Remember, Chicano Power doesn't mean Gonzalez power."[25] The newsletter urged those seniors who had turned eighteen to register and vote.

Like RUP's, the independents' attacks relied on propaganda, primarily newspaper ads, radio spots, and pamphlets. They were not, however, as successful as they would have liked. Whereas CU could effectively mobilize hundreds of people for rallies, the independents drew only a few to theirs.

Three days before the April 3 city council elections, a school assembly was disrupted by shouting and fistfights between pro-RUP students and students who sympathized with the independents. The assembly was a question-and-answer session for the candidates. Most students there were ardent supporters of RUP. Tempers flared when Mike Pérez lost his temper and insulted the students. Amid the shouting and fighting, several students who favored the independent candidates were beaten up.[26] The local police were called in to restore order. Later that week the independents summoned Texas Rangers from Uvalde to investigate the imbroglio. Texas Ranger Joaquin Jackson reported that three male students and one high school teacher had been assaulted. His investigation revealed that a group of only ten or fifteen boys had been involved in the scuffle. Although no one was arrested or charged, the incident heightened political tensions in the community.

On election day more than three hundred people worked on the get-out-the-vote drive. Their enthusiasm was impressive. Every designated precinct had people walking the neighborhood. Others staffed tables at every polling place. Several trucks with sound systems patrolled neighborhoods throughout the day to remind residents to vote. The local radio station, KBEN, continuously broadcast RUP radio spots exhorting RUP supporters to vote. Scores of students volunteered for a variety of campaign tasks after school. Teachers and school and city administrators participated, and even some Anglo teachers worked for RUP candidates.

Gutiérrez's get-out-the-vote drive was like a well-coordinated military operation. Before the election CU's political action committees identified RUP voters and sympathizers. They computerized the pertinent voter data and organized it according to precinct. This enabled the precinct captains and block leaders to identify and focus on RUP voters. Poll watchers carefully monitored who had voted and who had not. Free food and drinks were provided for the workers as well as RUP voters.

Conversely, the independents' get-out-the-vote drive was hampered by a lack of workers, organization, and general know-how. Unable to muster a sufficient number of Mexicano volunteers, they resorted to using white residents, especially at campaign headquarters. Their get-out-the-vote drive was essentially dependent on radio spots on KBEN. Their use of this medium far exceeded that of the CU.

On election night CU held a large rally while the votes were counted. Hundreds of jubilant and confident people listened to speeches and Tex-Mex music. They were not disappointed with the results of the city council races. RUP's José Cuevas was the top vote getter with 1,543 votes. Ramón Mata followed with 1,542 votes and Richard Díaz with 1,526. RUP's city council candidates won approximately 60 percent of the vote. The independents' top vote getter was Eliseo Sanchez with 1,024 votes, followed by Manuel Garza with 991, and Roberto Cornejo with 990.[27] At the RUP rally that night people were overcome with excitement. Young and old shouted, "Viva La Raza Unida!" and honked horns all night long.

Four days later, on April 7, CU's candidates were once again triumphant, this time in the school board elections. However, the April 7 victory over the independents was narrower than in earlier school board elections. In fact, the margin was smaller than it had been in the 1971 and 1972 elections. The vote spread was only 400 instead of the 555 votes of the 1972 election. The top RUP vote getter was Ramón Garza with 1,661 votes. Ernesto Olguín followed with 1,657 votes, and Viviana Santiago received 1,642. The top independent vote getter was Mike Pérez with 1,223 votes, followed by José Mata with 1,205 and Elfego Martínez with 1,201 votes.[28]

Voter turnout was the highest in the history of Cristal. RUP held a victory celebration on election night at the Oasis Drive-in that was attended by five hundred people and followed by a dance held at the Campestre Ballroom.

About a week after the election there was an incident involving witchcraft. Three influential members of RUP received small boxes, each containing a dead bat covered with long strands of hair covered by a waxy substance. A cross of gold ribbon was pinned to the bat's body. Two boxes also contained curses, which predicted marital problems for one recipient and family problems for another. The third box went to Virginia Musquiz, a principal leader of the party in Zavala County, with a note that read, "To Musquiz speaking for the Raza Unida. The wrong that has been done will fall on you little by little, you dog."[29] Although the curses failed to instill fear or apprehension among RUP members, they did suggest the desperation of RUP's adversaries. After the school board meeting that night, two bats were burned in a bonfire attended by scores of RUP supporters. The third bat was put on public display by Musquiz at RUP headquarters.

Throughout the April elections poor Mexicanos had enthusiastically supported CU. It was apparent that the power of RUP in Cristal was predicated on its accomplishments and the capacity of CU to mobilize supporters, most of whom were poor. Conversely, the independents' power base lay in the small Mexicano middle class and whites of the area.

Most of the independent Mexicanos I interviewed were unequivocally opposed to Gutiérrez and RUP's political agenda. Few identified with the word *Chicano* or with the Chicano Movement. They were very conservative and dependent economically on the area's white elite. The whites of Cristal had become powerless politically, but they remained powerful economically and pragmatically sought to use the disenchanted Mexicanos in their efforts to wrest community control from RUP. This electoral strategy was almost identical to the one used to defeat PASSO in 1965.

Defeated electorally, the independents resorted to litigation to try to overturn the city council and school board election results. In early May the independent candidates for the school board and city council sued in 38th District Court to contest the results of both elections. The *Sentinel* reported, "The wording of the two suits is almost identical, with the contestants alleging that illegal voting took place in both elections and contending that if all votes illegally cast should be subtracted from the total vote received by each contestant and by each contestee the total vote received by each contestant would exceed the total vote received by each contestee."[30] Specifically, the suits, which ultimately were unsuccessful, alleged that noncitizens, felons, and nonresidents of the county or precinct had voted.

Meanwhile, with community control of the city council and school board assured for another two years, RUP continued to solidify its power base in Cristal. Although the margin of victory was smaller in the school board election than it had been in the past, RUP boasted of its success and omnipotence in an editorial in *La Verdad:*

Like everyone can see, the Raza Unida Party is stronger than ever and will continue to progress. Be certain that in next year's coming elections, the Raza Unida will have a voter turnout of 60 percent so that it will be a complete defeat for the Gringo party. Why? Because the Chicano people of this community know because of our political unity we have begun to resolve our immense problems that have been placed before us. We will overcome.[31]

Salient City Issues of 1973

In 1973 the political issues that faced Cristal's city government were the Del Monte annexation suit, begun in 1970, urban renewal efforts to build additional housing, providing health care and building a clinic for low-income residents, funding of mental health care and other services, reassessing real estate, and economic development projects (for details see chapters 9 and 10).

One issue that carried over from the preceding year was the country club controversy. In February the Texas Supreme Court ruled that the city of Cristal could not break its lease of city land to the country club. It ruled that the city council, then controlled by whites, had acted legally when it leased the land in 1956. As reported in the *Sentinel*, the court, without writing an opinion of its own, upheld the decision of the 38th District trial court and the U.S. Ninth Circuit Court of Civil Appeals. The court's validation of the lease of the land on which the country club and swimming pool were located ran until 1986. But the setback was only temporary. Using its power of eminent domain, the city gradually regained control of the property.[32]

In June 1973 City Manager Francisco Rodriguez resigned, and the council unanimously accepted his decision. Rodriguez was replaced by Ezequiel Guzmán. The change in city managers had little effect on policy because both Rodriguez and Guzmán were strong RUP supporters and had the backing of the city council, Gutiérrez, and CU.

The 1974 Local Elections

During 1974 CU continued to flex its organizational muscles. Since 1971 Gutiérrez and the CU leadership had worked to consolidate and expand CU's membership base. By the April 1974 city council and school board elections in Cristal CU's membership had grown to approximately four hundred families.[33]

Gutiérrez also continued to promote the Voluntarios de Aztlán. College students from various parts of the country continued to help in RUP's peaceful revolution. Some universities, such as California State University at Northridge, had agreed that students could receive academic credit for their time in Cristal.[34] The media still periodically reported on RUP's reforms. But because CU had been successful in defeating every electoral challenge, the national media no longer gave RUP, Gutiérrez, and Cristal much coverage. By 1974 the novelty of beating a heretofore unbeatable machine apparently had lost some of its media appeal.

The consolidation of CU's community control of local politics was evident in appointments by the school board and city council of CU members as key officials responsible for overseeing various aspects of the elections.[35] So few seats on the council and school board were to be contested in 1974 that RUP's control was not at stake. On the school board the terms of Eddie Treviño and Rodolfo (Rudy) Palomo were expiring, as were those of Pablo Puente and Ventura Gonzalez on the city council. But neither CU and RUP nor their adversaries took the elections lightly. For example, Barker wrote an editorial about the declared candidates, gleefully reporting, "Ya basta [That is enough] is emerging again, but this time it is within the ranks of the Raza Unida itself. Apparently some of the early followers have become disenchanted with the way things have been run by the party leadership and are in the process of breaking away from the party."[36]

By February RUP's opponents were no longer calling themselves the independents. They had reorganized under the aegis of La Raza Libre [The Free People]. On February 24 they held their first rally at Ranchito Avila, a ranch just outside Cristal. The purpose of the rally was to announce formation of the organization and introduce members of its executive board and its candidates for the upcoming city, school, and county elections. Sitting on its executive board were Juan Dominguez, chair; Cesario Duran, president; Carmen Hinojasa, vice president; Maria Moreno, secretary; Ray Alvarado, treasurer; Richard Avila, sergeant-at-arms; and Henry Flores, adviser.

La Raza Libre backed Pedro Contreras and Marina Balboa Avila for city council and Dora Palomo Garza and Roberto Hernandez for school board. Like some members of La Raza Libre's executive board, Contreras and Avila were employed by the school district's Career Opportunities Program (COP; see Chapter 8 for additional information about the program). The various speakers who addressed the few hundred participants at the rally explained that La Raza Libre's membership included laborers, school faculty, young people, and veterans. One unidentified speaker said, "La Raza Libre, as its name implies, welcomes all persons who seriously wish to be free free from oppression, free from domineering forces, free to be themselves."[37]

The *San Antonio Express* described La Raza Libre as a new party, although it was not. The paper reported that some of La Raza Libre's leaders and supporters were former RUP members. It went on to say that La Raza Libre was the first major indicator of dissension within RUP's ranks in Cristal. But according to Rudy Espinosa, president of CU, La Raza Libre was not an offshoot of RUP, and some of its leaders had never been members of CU. Another RUP spokesperson remarked, "We're not worried. They don't have much going for them." La Raza Libre's Gregg Barrios, maintained, "We are getting strong. We will win."[38]

One aspect of La Raza Libre that made it different from earlier groups formed to oppose RUP was that a good portion of its leadership was employed by the RUP-controlled school district. In addition to the two city council candidates, three of the seven members of La

Raza Libre's executive board were employees of COP. The board's chair, Gregg Barrios, was a high school teacher in the district.[39]

Dora Garza, one of the school board candidates, alleged that Gutiérrez, former president of the school board, had placed people loyal to him in high-paying positions. She attacked the inferiority of the school system, blaming Gutiérrez and schools superintendent Angel Noe González. She also claimed that she had once supported RUP, adding, "If it had not been for us, Gutiérrez and González would not be here."[40]

La Raza Libre did not embrace, at least openly, any accommodation with the gringos or Anglos. La Raza Libre was simply gunning for Gutiérrez. Dora Garza told the *San Antonio Express,* "We were better off when the gringos were in power." Cesario Duran, president of La Raza Libre, said he had once been a strong supporter of RUP and charged Gutiérrez with "totalitarianism."[41]

In an effort to broaden its base of support beyond Cristal, La Raza Libre sided with Gutiérrez's arch rival, Rodolfo "Corky" Gonzales, the RUP leader from Colorado who had challenged Gutiérrez for RUP's national chair. In fact, on March 17 a La Raza Libre delegation traveled to Denver, where it participated in a national march organized by Gonzales's Crusade for Justice. The delegation included Duran, Roberto Hernandez, Juan Mendoza, Roy Lopez, and Lorenzo Ortiz. A press release from La Raza Libre announced, "These people will represent Crystal City as freedom, peace, and justice delegates." Other Chicano Movement leaders who attended the national march were Mario Cantu of San Antonio and Bert Corona of Los Angeles. La Raza Libre's participation was an obvious political slap at Gutiérrez and RUP in Texas.

By March La Raza Libre appeared to be gaining organizational strength and showed signs it would be a more formidable adversary than RUP had faced in the past. La Raza Libre's campaign headquarters were open to the public day and night. When there was no electricity at night, the group resorted to kerosene lamps. La Raza Libre accused RUP city officials in charge of the utility department of turning off the electricity at its headquarters (the accusation was accurate). "This is just another move against this local organization," a La Raza Libre spokesman told the *Sentinel.* "However, these moves were expected and have no effect in diminishing the strong determination of the organization to fight on."[42] In March La Raza Libre held fundraisers, meetings, and a rally at which Cantu was the keynote speaker.

In the closing days of the April election campaign La Raza Libre made it clear that it sought the support of "all" voters. In an expensive half-page ad in the *Sentinel*, La Raza Libre expounded on its campaign objectives:

1. An education that will prepare our youth and this to consist not only of a sincerely dedicated and well-qualified faculty but with a just yet firm discipline.
2. Prevention of any increase in taxes in the city as well as the school district.
3. A police department which we can expect to protect us all equally without favorites over any person or groups.
4. An environment free from political pressure so that our city and schools will discontinue being the subject of political jokes throughout Texas.[43]

Although Barker tried to depict RUP as in dire political straits, the opposite was true. CU was confident in its ability to mobilize Mexicano voters. Running on the RUP platform for the vacant city council seats were Lupe Cortinas, a former city tax assessor–collector, and Arturo Gonzales, a former school board member. For the school board CU endorsed Raul T. Flores and Mercedes "Chachi" Casarez.

Between February and the election in April CU gradually mobilized the Mexicano community, using its usual rallies, town hall meetings, radio spots, fund-raisers, precinct canvassing, vehicles with sound systems, and its massive family network of volunteers. On election day both CU and La Raza Libre launched energetic get-out-the-vote drives. Barker, who sometimes doubled as a reporter, wrote, "Voting went at a steady pace Saturday, with the two opposing factions setting up their tables and umbrellas early near the polls. Cars with signs backing the candidates were busy bringing voters to the polls; and both were busy with telephone committees in an effort to get the vote out."[44]

CU had its grassroots political machinery of precinct and block organizations humming as usual. Although La Raza Libre had a headquarters, a telephone committee, and some volunteers, it was no match for CU. Although the *Sentinel*'s coverage was such that La Raza Libre candidates appeared to be mounting a serious electoral challenge, the opposite was true, and they lost resoundingly.

RUP's two city council candidates won impressively. Arturo Gonzales was the top vote getter with 1,442 votes. His running mate, Lupe Cortinas, received 1,440 votes. La Raza Libre candidates Pedro A. Contreras and Marina Balboa Avila received 789 and 779 votes, respectively. RUP candidates had a more than comfortable edge of 653 votes, a 2–1 margin.

RUP's school board candidates also won handily but not with the same spread as in the city council election. Raul T. Flores received the highest number of votes, 1,478, followed by Mercedes "Chachi" Casarez with 1,471 votes. The margin of victory was 539, smaller than it had been in the city council elections. In 1973 RUP had won by about 400 votes, half its margin in the 1972 election. One reason for the smaller margin in the school board race was that the area covered by the school district was larger than that of the city, so it included more white voters. Before both the city council and school board elections, the Raza Libre candidates asked 38th District Court Judge Ross E. Doughty to impound the absentee ballots, which he did. Although the papers ordering the impoundment were delivered to election officials, his order was not carried out. He issued another order before the school board election, impounding the absentee ballots on the ground of suspected fraud. This time the request was filed by two RUP officials, Amancio Cantu, presiding judge of absentee balloting for the school board election, and Angel Noe González, superintendent of Cristal's school district. When the absentee ballots were counted, they favored RUP's candidates by a 4–1 margin.

Although whites maintained a low profile through both the city and school board elections, on election day they came out in large numbers to support La Raza Libre candidates. Barker, always hypercritical of RUP, acknowledged the white participation: "Although Anglo participation was apparently lacking in this year's campaign, they turned out in large numbers Saturday. Most had their vote challenged, with the challengers contending that they were not residents of the school district. . . . Some Anglos were required to sign affidavits attesting to their residency. The challenges were apparently harassing tactics being used by election personnel."[45] Except for the county clerk, all election officials were RUP supporters.

The election results were something of a vindication for RUP because they showed that its community control agenda was still popular. As during the second revolt RUP supporters paraded on election night through the city's streets, sounding their car horns and shouting slogans. They were particularly conspicuous in the neighborhoods where La Raza Libre leaders lived. To Gutiérrez and the CU leadership the 1974 election results meant that the capability and sophistication of CU's political machinery was undiminished.

City Issues of 1974

During 1974 the city's agenda continued to revolve around the Housing Authority, urban renewal, and other projects involved in securing federal funding. However, perhaps the most significant action in 1974 was the annexation of the Del Monte plant. After legal battles and protracted negotiations the city and Del Monte finally reached an agreement. It called for Del Monte to pay $8,000 a year in back taxes for the years 1970 to 1974 and $17,000 a year until 1981.[46] In return, the city agreed not to annex the plant until 1981. The city and Del Monte concluded this pact as the CU-organized labor union, Obreros Unidos Independientes (OUI), won a three-year agreement with Del Monte (see Chapter 10).[47]

During the elections RUP lashed out against its opponents by threatening to sue the electric and telephone companies for furnishing power and service to La Raza Libre's headquarters. The city claimed its Urban Renewal Agency owned the building. The building had been owned by Mariana M. Garcia but was taken over by the city and condemned by the agency. But after RUP's victories in the elections, it dropped the threat to sue.

That summer the city council enacted four bills related to the sale of alcoholic beverages, including providing longer hours during which sales would be permitted. In June the city announced receipt of a federal grant for $49,824 under the Library Services and Construction Act to create resource centers. Established in various barrios, these functioned as tutorial centers, emphasizing reading, library use, storytelling, and the like.[48]

In December Cortinas, the newly elected council member, was charged with resisting arrest after he became involved in a scuffle with police at a lounge in Cristal. This followed a fight with a former city council candidate. Cortinas was jailed and released within a few hours.[49]

The 1974 Zavala County Elections

By January CU had announced its candidates for the May 4 primary. Running on the RUP platform were Gutiérrez for county judge; Virginia Musquiz for county clerk; Carmen Flores, county treasurer; Rosa Mata, district clerk; Hortencia Treviño, commissioner from Precinct 2; Benito Perez, justice of the peace for Precinct 2; Esteban Nájera, commissioner from Precinct 4; Rosa Quijano, justice of the peace for Precinct 4; and Irene Morales, justice of the peace for Precinct 1. Candidates for RUP precinct chairs included José Luis Balderas, Precinct 3; Rudy Espinosa, Precinct 5; Elipidio Lizcano, Precinct 6; and Eliseo Solis, Precinct 7.

As usual, the real contest for power and control was not between Democrats and Republicans but Democrats and RUP. Historically, the Democratic Party had controlled Zavala County and state politics.

Since the Civil War Texas had been essentially a one-party state. For many years the Republican Party had not fielded candidates at the county level. Barker described the situation: "Before the emergence of the Raza Unida Party, which gained recognition and was placed on the ballot in 1972, local races were usually decided at the Democratic primary with the Democratic nominees running without opposition at the general election."[50] This 1974 primary in Zavala County was unprecedented—the Democrats had such serious opposition that control of the county was at stake.

Two years earlier the four defeated Democratic candidates had contested the election, claiming that noncitizens and felons had voted. After nearly six months of intermittent hearings that became entangled in legal procedures and challenges, Judge Ernest Belcher of the 38th District Court moved the trial to Uvalde, citing the possibility of violence in the courtroom if the case continued in Zavala County. At the crux of the suit were 65 votes.[51] The trial began May 14, and CU packed the courtroom with its supporters. They cheered and jeered so much that the judge recessed the trial early that afternoon. Barker, who reported on the trial, wrote:

The courtroom was packed, including the standees in the aisles and along the wall, with crowd overflowing out onto the courthouse lawn. The judge noted that the spectators on [at] least two occasions demonstrated in favor of the contestees and their counsel by loud laughter, cheering, and clapping of hands. Judge Belcher also noted that his action in recessing the trial . . . was greeted with laughter and jeers, adding that the evident tension might have led to longer and louder demonstrations and physical violence if the trial had continued [in Cristal].[52]

Outside, demonstrators gathered and threw a picket line around the courthouse. RUP protesters bore placards reading, "Justice Is Overruled in Cristal," "Brown Will Be Beautiful in the Courthouse," and "Ballots Are Bull . . ." Someone raised the RUP banner on one of the flagpoles.[53] The trial, covered by print and electronic media, received national publicity.

For reasons that are unclear RUP's attorneys, Pat Malone and Jesse Gamez, removed themselves from the case and were replaced by Zavala County Attorney Ray Perez as lead attorney (he was also a party to the suit), and Paul Rich of La Oficina de la Gente [Office of the People], the legal aid office in Cristal, as co-counsel. After a series legal skirmishes the Democrats agreed to drop their suit against County Commissioner Elena Díaz because not enough votes were at stake in her race to change the outcome.

Judge Belcher found that although some illegal ballots had indeed been counted, the only result that would change was in the race for constable of Precinct 2. The court determined that Democrat Cecil Holt was the winner over RUP's Rudy Espinosa. In correcting the vote Holt lost 10 votes and Espinosa lost 27, so Holt ended up with 538 votes to Espinosa's 530.[54] RUP's adversaries consistently used litigation to test the validity of RUP's triumphs at the polls. This posed a major problem for Gutiérrez and CU. They were compelled to respond legally, which was expensive and time consuming.

Meanwhile, Gutiérrez was facing political opposition from within RUP's ranks for the upcoming May 4 RUP primary from Manuel Espinosa Jr. for county judge. Hortencia Treviño and José Talamantez also squared off, challenging each other for the RUP nomination for county commissioner from Precinct 2. This was the first time since RUP's formation in 1970 that candidates not endorsed by CU broke ranks and ran for office. Their candidacy represented a minor schism in the party (see Chapter 5 for more detail).

In February the RUP County Executive Committee refused to accept the applications of Espinosa and Talamantez, citing typographical errors. They promptly sought a writ of mandamus in 38th District Court to get their names placed on RUP's primary election ballot. Both candidates alleged that Manuel Cortinas Jr., RUP's county chair, had wrongfully refused to accept their applications on the ground that the applications did not comply with the requirements of the Texas Election Code concerning the loyalty affidavit.

In early March District Judge Ross E. Doughty ordered Cortinas to place Espinosa and Talamantez on the RUP May primary ballot.[55] The problem was that both Espinosa and Talamantez had found a way around CU's candidate selection process. Additionally irritating to CU were public statements from Talamantez and Espinosa regarding their candidacy. Before the May primary Talamantez, a teacher, granted an interview to the *Sentinel*. The article, written by Barker, was complimentary, which was uncommon for any candidate associated with RUP. In an obvious attempt to separate himself from Gutiérrez and the CU machinery Talamantez declared, "I will serve all the people of the community and county, as I have done in the past, and will make my own decisions for the benefit of all." Espinosa also talked to the *Sentinel* and revealed that the real reason he was running was to open the door to all Mexicanos who wanted to run for public office instead of leaving it to CU to decide who would be a candidate. Espinosa explained, "We have opened that door, and that has never been done before. The people now have a choice instead of being told who they are to support."[56] His candidacy was perceived as a direct challenge to Gutiérrez and to CU.

But the perception was wrong. Gutiérrez won by a landslide, receiving 1,764 primary votes to Espinosa's 213. In the race for commissioner Treviño pulled 427 votes, whereas Talamantez received 139. The other RUP candidates running for state and county party officers were unchallenged. This meant that Ramsey Muñiz was once again RUP's candidate for governor. Now Gutiérrez and CU had to prepare not only for the upcoming county elections in November but had to broaden their efforts to include RUP's statewide campaigns.

According to Mario Compean, state RUP chair, a major goal of RUP's 1974 campaign was to challenge Mexican-American Democrats. Two months later Muñiz officially entered the race for governor, paying his $1,000 filing fee in one dollar bills, a symbolic representation of individual contributions. "When we say we are going to run a people's campaign, we mean just that," he explained. However, unlike in 1972, RUP was running candidates in only ten counties in 1974.[57]

Muñiz tirelessly traveled the state. On September 21 and 22 RUP held its statewide convention in Houston. The contest for state chair was heated. Compean withdrew from the race in favor of Guadalupe Youngblood of Robstown, who easily defeated his opponents. This was perceived as a major victory for Muñiz, who had joined forces with Compean against Gutiérrez two years earlier over the strategy for developing RUP. At the convention Muñiz adopted a populist theme, reminding delegates that RUP's main objective was to improve the quality of life for Mexicanos in Texas.[58] Gutiérrez addressed various themes:

In electoral politics, we must remain an independent party beholden only to our goals. . . . We should not look to Wall Street or Washington for our destiny, our destiny is to the south with people like us. . . . We must pledge ourselves not to be misled or confused by all who would like to see us fail. . . . We must address ourselves to building our own Chicano nation. . . . We've got to begin building our bases and capturing control in those areas where our majority is inevitable.[59]

As the November county and state elections approached, Gutiérrez and CU focused on the Zavala County contest. Gutiérrez had managed Muñiz's campaign in 1972, but this time Gutiérrez himself was on the ballot, for county judge. CU's machinery was in full battle dress by early fall, conducting a voter registration drive and working the absentee ballot campaign. CU also was pressuring La Raza Libre with tactics that resulted in the resignation of its president, Cesario Duran, in October. He said he was resigning because of untrue allegations that he had stated that La Raza Libre was backing RUP in the November elections. A week later the *Sentinel* quoted a La Raza Libre spokesperson as saying that the organization was not committed to any candidate or party and charging that RUP was lying about receiving an endorsement from La Raza Libre.[60] CU had managed to put La Raza Libre on the defensive and to depict the organization as weak.

The Democrats unleashed a barrage of newspaper ads, radio spots, and literature attacking RUP's leadership and Gutiérrez personally. In a letter published in the *Sentinel* on October 31 incumbent county judge Irl Taylor fiercely attacked RUP's leadership, describing them as "money hungry people" who wanted to control the county. He exhorted the voters to stop RUP from expanding its power base to the county. He added, "The stopping of these leeches will stop many things—intimidations, harassments, discriminations, boycotts, hate, fighting among ourselves, name calling, division of people, exorbitant taxation and the exorbitant unnecessary spending of money, along with other things."[61]

The *Sentinel* endorsed the Democratic slate. In a blistering editorial Barker depicted RUP as a purveyor of hate:

If our government is to continue to be stable and to serve all of the citizens, it is of utmost importance that these capable Democrats be elected to the offices for which they are candidates. This is especially true of the county offices. The Raza Unida Party has brought nothing but hate, distrust, turmoil, and financial irresponsibility to our county. The only way to stop this distrust and destructive force in its attempt to continue complete control over people's lives and livelihoods is to refuse to vote for the Raza Unida candidates.[62]

RUP responded by emphasizing its accomplishments during its nearly four years of community control of the city council and school board. On election day CU, using RUP's county structure, responded with great efficiency, delivering the vote in the county and statewide elections.

The effort paid off. In Zavala County RUP candidates won most of the more important races. Gutiérrez defeated incumbent Taylor 1,968 to 1,702. Virginia Musquiz beat Democrat Georgia L. Price for county clerk 1,950 to 1,742. Carmen Flores polled 1,977 votes to Pernla Dennis's 1,714 for county treasurer. In the race for commissioner from Precinct 4, incumbent E. A. Easter lost to RUP's Esteban Nájera by 2 votes. The final count was 590 for Nájera to Easter's 588. And RUP's Irene Cuellar received 370 votes to defeat Bert Banter in his reelection bid for justice of the peace from Precinct 1. The RUP victory left Democrats with one member of the court of commissioners, the tax assessor–collector, and three justices of the peace. The victory gave RUP a 3–2 majority on Zavala County's court of commissioners for the first time.

In the statewide races Muñiz carried Zavala County with 2,034 votes to Democratic governor Ralph Briscoe's 1,613. Republican candidate Jim Cranberry polled only 114 votes. But Muñiz fell below the vote totals he had received in 1972, garnering 24,000 fewer votes, although the percentage of the total vote was the same, 6 percent.[63]

Adding to the excitement of election day were the actions of the Texas Rangers. District Judge Doughty ordered them to impound all the ballot boxes, which were placed in the Zavala County Bank for recount. The three Democratic candidates alleged that unqualified persons had voted. But the recount produced no changes in the results of the general election. Each of the three Democrats received only one additional vote.[64]

Cristal's 1975 Local Election: A Pyrrhic Victory

RUP had accomplished what no other Mexicano group in the country had—that is, it had won control of the school board, city council, and county court of commissioners. Now the county judge, Gutiérrez continued to function as the boss of the county RUP and CU's political machine. By 1975 CU's membership had increased to nearly five hundred families, the highest ever.[65] The 1974 county elections represented for Gutiérrez and CU the apogee of their mobilization efforts and power.

Gutiérrez may have been kingpin of Zavala County in 1975, and he was still RUP's national chair, yet he had not managed to consolidate his power on the national level. RUP was riddled with tension from the internal power struggles between Gutiérrez and Rodolfo "Corky" Gonzales; dissension over ideology, strategy, and structure; and an increasingly conservative political climate. At the state level, although Muñiz again had secured 6 percent of the vote, RUP was under attack from gringo and anti-RUP Mexicano politicians, specifically Governor Dolph Briscoe. Moreover, by 1975 the number of counties in which RUP had organizing efforts had declined.[66]

Nationally, Gutiérrez was faced with the rapid decline of RUP and the Chicano Movement. Yet, as the 1975 city and school elections approached in Cristal, its local power base appeared to be impregnable. The 1975 city and school elections would, however, be the last local election before a disastrous rupture occurred. The 1975 Cristal elections produced few controversies or serious challenges to Gutiérrez's and CU's political machinery, although control of the city council was at stake. The opposition again organized under the umbrella of La Raza Libre, electing as president Roberto Cornejo, a brother of Juan Cornejo, who had led the first revolt. Alberto Sánchez was elected vice president; Beatrice Espinoṣa, secretary; Javier Ramon, treasurer; and Richard Avila, sergeant-at-arms.

The terms of the three RUP council members—Mayor Ramón "Monche" Mata, José D. Cuevas, and Richard Díaz—were expiring. Political control of the school board was not in jeopardy because only two seats were in contention—that of Alberto Sánchez, who had defected to La Raza Libre, and RUP's José O. Mata.

In March both political organizations announced their candidates for the city council and school board. La Raza Libre supported Juan Cornejo, Beatrice Espinosa, and Henry Flores for city council. Cornejo had served as mayor of Cristal from 1963 to 1965. Beatrice Espinosa was married to Manuel Espinosa, who had made an unsuccessful run against Gutiérrez in 1974 for the RUP nomination for county judge. Flores was a prelaw student at the University of Texas at Austin.

RUP's city council candidates included José D. Cuevas, business manager of the school district, who filed for reelection. This was unprecedented for CU because of its no-reelection policy. The other two RUP city council candidates were Eugenio "Gene" Ruiz and Ambrosio Melendrez, both employed by the school district. Filing for the two school board seats on the La Raza Libre slate were former RUP supporters Alberto Sánchez and Javier Ramon. Sánchez, who had been elected to the school board in 1972, broke with the pack and decided to run for reelection with the support of La Raza Libre. Although the reasons for Sánchez's change in political affiliation are unclear, one can deduce that he objected to CU's policy of barring its members from seeking reelection. CU fielded Abelardo Marquez and José Luis Balderas.

Both camps duplicated their 1974 campaigns. La Raza Libre had yet to develop the sophisticated political machinery possessed by CU and continued to rely on disgruntled Mexicanos and the covert backing of whites. The issues and themes of its campaign strategy were unchanged. La Raza Libre still emphasized ads in the *Sentinel*, a phone bank, and a weak get-out-the-vote effort. If anything, its 1975 campaign was more disorganized than its campaign of the previous year. CU, meanwhile, took nothing for granted and continued to rely on its massive grassroots mobilization.

RUP's candidates won decisively. Ambrosio Melendrez was the highest vote getter with 1,541 votes. José D. Cuevas and Eugenio

"Gene" Ruiz won with 1,522 and 1,519 votes, respectively. La Raza Libre's Juan Cornejo, beaten 3–1, got 560 votes, followed by Beatrice Espinosa with 554 votes and Henry Flores with 550.

CU had once again devastated its opposition. On the down side the election produced the lowest voter turnout since the second revolt in 1970. Only 2,100 people voted, 140 fewer than in 1974. In contrast, Cristal residents had cast more than 2,500 votes in 1973, 2,250 in 1972, 2,500 in 1971, and 2,161 in 1970.

RUP also triumphed in the April 5 school board election. RUP's José Luis Balderas won with 1,565 votes, and Abelardo Marquez followed with 1,563. La Raza Libre's Alberto Sánchez received only 431 votes and Javier Ramon 430. (Interestingly, Sánchez, first elected on the RUP ticket in 1972, had received 1,727 votes that year.)

Again, fewer voters went to the polls. This election drew only 2,000 voters, whereas in 1974 about 2,400 ballots were cast, and in 1973 the total was 2,880.[67] Both RUP and CU were increasingly plagued by internal schisms.

5

Schisms Emerge in Cristal's
Power Structure (1972–1974)

During the first two years of the politics of community control José Angel Gutiérrez relied on the organizational power of his emerging political machine, CU, to build RUP locally and to develop the peaceful revolution's many changes and programs. However, as he consolidated his power, CU became part of RUP's local community power structure. By 1974 this centralization of power was causing internal schisms that were weakening CU. The schisms reflected a simmering discontent that emerged between 1972 and 1975 among CU's contentious power elites.

RUP's Elitist Power Structure

Who governs in the United States has been the basis of an often emotional and controversial debate among social scientists. Political scientists, especially, have been caught up in the controversy for years, attempting to answer several pertinent questions: Who makes the important political policy decisions? How widely is political power shared? What influence do economic and other elites have on government policies? How accountable are these elites to the public?[1] The question of power distribution has been vigorously addressed by those who advocate pluralist theory. Pluralists assert that power is widely dispersed among the various competing power groups, all held in check by the public and by each other. Conversely, ruling elite theorists contend that power is concentrated in the hands of a small group, subject to little or no control by the rest of society.[2]

During its first three years the peaceful revolution produced a quasi-monolithic community power structure headed by what can be described as a "demosocratic elite." The phrase, which refers to a combination of various aspects of pluralist and elitist theories with a slant toward pluralism, was coined by Harold Lasswell and Abraham Kaplan in their work, *Power and Society*. They explain that a demosocratic elite is

a form of rule in which the base value of the predominant form of power is affection. Since this must be widely dispersed to serve as a basis of power, demosocracy is rule by the popular, the favorites of the people. Rule is always by an elite; but the principle of elite recruitment and the relations between elite and mass differ considerably from one form to another. A demosocracy is constituted as such, not by its having no elite, but by the fact that the elite owes its position to popular affection.[3]

Thomas Dye defines *elites* as those few that have power in society as opposed to the masses that do not. His definition buttresses the work of prominent elite theorists such as Vilfredo Pareto, Gaetano Mosca, Robert Lynd, and Harold Lasswell and Daniel Lerner, who concluded that every society is governed by an elite. However, Robert Michels's Iron Law of Oligarchy best describes RUP's power structure:"He who says organization says oligarchy." According to Michels, the Iron Law of Oligarchy governs any social system.[4]

Elite theory posits that elitism is endemic to all societies. Cristal's power structure was no exception. By 1974 Cristal's power structure was demosocratic in theory, but in practice it had evolved into a much more hierarchical and oligarchical power elite. In orchestrating the second revolt and RUP's peaceful revolution Gutiérrez deliberately developed CU as an elite political machine comprised of the most supportive and influential families and the leaders of the community.[5] In theory, public policy was a function of the elected officials, but in practice power emanated from Gutiérrez. Gutiérrez was the elite of elites. No one else within CU's multilayered elite infrastructure exercised the influence and authority that he wielded.

Throughout the golden years of the peaceful revolution (1970–1975) Gutiérrez relied on a form of democratic centralism in the decision-making process. This meant that within CU's various tiers of power, debate and discussion of issues or criticism of individuals were tolerated until a decision was reached. However, once the decision was made by Gutiérrez, the board, and especially the membership, the decision was binding. Attempts by recalcitrant members to buck a decision were condemned as "fractionalism" and subjected to some form of censure by CU. This process of decision making was in part what Gutiérrez's adversaries used to describe RUP's peaceful revolution as "communistic and a dictatorship."

As the political boss Gutiérrez exercised power in a way that made it appear that CU was pluralistic in its decision-making process. But there was never really any question about who actually influenced or determined the direction of RUP's peaceful revolution. Gutiérrez was the ultimate source of authority for RUP's local, national, and, to some degree, state agenda. His authority was derived from his intellect, articulateness, assertive personality, and ability to create tangible change. Although he was not an attorney, he served as CU's legal counsel for five consecutive years.[6] His national prominence as a major leader of the Chicano Movement contributed significantly to the perception of his power.

During the five years of community control he used his positions as legal counsel, school board president, national RUP chairperson, and county judge to influence CU's direction, issues, and policies. His tenure as CU's legal counsel was a flagrant violation of CU's no-reelection policy. According to Gutiérrez, the rationale for making an exception for him lay in the nature of the position. CU members felt few had the capacity to fill such a position. Another member of the elite, Virginia Musquiz, RUP county chairperson, acknowledged the importance of Gutiérrez's leadership in a 1973 interview: "We have tried to help him, morally and physically, in the struggle to help the Mexican people. We know the worth of his leadership. Without him to guide the party [RUP], I don't know how much we would have accomplished. He has shown his talent and intelligence by helping his community."[7]

The second tier of power within CU was its board of directors. Gutiérrez exercised his influence in the selection of CU's eleven board members. At first, Gutiérrez groomed and nurtured the board's leadership. Later, the board established a nominating committee. Its function was to present a slate to the general membership, which elected board members from that slate. Loyalty to Gutiérrez and RUP was a prerequisite for holding office in CU. Most board members were middle class. They were either businesspeople such as José Serna (1969–1971) or administrators or politicians like Ambrosio Melendrez (1975). (Yet Gutiérrez described most board members as "working class.") Their occupations limited their power because they had little time to attend meetings during the workday. Gutiérrez explained that the board was a "balancing mechanism": "We made sure that all the power centers and sectors of the community were represented on the board. It was a form of ticket balancing."[8]

The board's role within CU represented a division of labor, and board members' power depended on their position in the community. According to the articles of incorporation and CU's by-laws, the board was its governing body, yet in reality it served as a governing mechanism for Gutiérrez. With few exceptions, the board never opposed Gutiérrez's decisions or recommendations. This did not mean that he ruled by decree. On some occasions CU members challenged him successfully. But the board used Article 3, section 4, to dilute those challenges. Under this provision a project or position presented by the board to the membership was practically guaranteed passage. The membership could overturn or reject a board proposal only by a two-thirds vote.[9] CU's membership had other opportunities to participate in decisions, but once a decision was made, it was final.

Although the board set the agenda for the membership, once an issue was brought to the floor, "they [board members] had no role—it was whatever the membership decided on," Gutiérrez said, understating the importance of the two-thirds vote required to change a board decision. Also, under Article 6 the board could by majority vote oust a general member for misconduct and then present its decision to CU members for approval at a regular Sunday meeting.[10] Thus the board was the second most influential level of power in CU.

The third tier was what I call CU's directorate. The idea for it arose soon after the political takeover, but it was not formed until 1973. The directorate consisted of CU members who were key city, school, or county administrators and elected officials; organizational representatives; and RUP's county party officials. They were key policy makers in their respective fields. Gutiérrez met with the directorate almost every Wednesday.

In his study of Atlanta Floyd Hunter concluded that power there was held by a small upper class of "economic dominants." He categorized office holders and influential people from the private sector mainly as second-level leaders whose major responsibility was execution of decisions made by the economic dominants.[11] In Cristal the economic dominants were no longer in control of the power structure. The directorate was the closest thing to an economic dominant by virtue of its members' well-paying jobs, created as a result of the peaceful revolution. Nor did the directorate fit the profile described by Robert Dahl in *Who Governs?*—his study of New Haven, Connecticut, found that the dominant power holders there were the city's elected officials. Gutiérrez designed the directorate as a "supercentral committee" without absolute power. Members had to meet at least one of the following criteria: election to office, administration of an agency, or recognition as a community leader.[12]

For those who measured up, entry into the directorate still was contingent on approval of its sitting members. They were fairly strict in demanding that an aspirant have some degree of popular support, recognized expertise, or demonstrated leadership ability. Even aspirants championed by Gutiérrez were ultimately voted up or down by a majority of those present at the Wednesday meetings, so Gutiérrez allowed a semblance of power sharing. Within CU the directorate wielded considerable influence over policy. At first members would bring issues to the attention of the directorate for discussion and direction. That didn't last long. Increasingly, by 1975 the directorate was making decisions at the Wednesday meetings rather than at the CU general meetings on Sunday.

Some members of the directorate held several positions. One was concurrently a school board member, director of a city agency, member of the city's Industrial Commission, secretary of CU, member of the G. I. Forum, and a member of the Barrio Club (the latter was a non-profit organization set up in 1971 to provide security at RUP events). He was not an exception. Others held several positions simultaneously. Arthur Vidich and Joseph Bensman encountered a similar situation in their study of Springdale, New York: "Interlocking, duplication, and overlapping of leadership roles tend to channel community policy into relatively a few hands. This results in a wide range of community activities being coordinated simply because a small number of individuals are engaged in a wide range of leadership positions." In an interview Gutiérrez acknowledged this interlocking form of decision making in setting the direction and priorities of the peaceful revolution.[13]

The directorate had thirty to forty members at any given time.[14] Interviews with its members revealed the following breakdown:

Elected officials: Five school board members, one city council member, the mayor, one county commissioner, and the county sheriff
Administrators: Superintendent of schools, assistant superintendent of schools, director of urban renewal, director of the housing authority, director of mental health, director of the health clinic, and the city manager
Political operators: RUP national chairperson, RUP county chairperson, and CU chairperson
Community leaders: Former mayor and former school board members

Information gleaned from biographical questionnaires the directorate members filled out for me in 1973 provided the following profile:

their median age was thirty-five; they were essentially low-income and middle class; most had annual incomes between $7,000 and $9,000, although some made considerably more; they were mostly male, married, renting, and had worked as migrant workers at some point in their lives; and all had been Democrats before they registered as RUP members.[15]

On Wednesday mornings they would assemble to discuss and troubleshoot general policies and problems and to set a general direction for their respective spheres of power and influence. The sessions dealt with general strategy concerns and were used for simply exchanging information. As head of the directorate Gutiérrez coordinated and chaired the meetings. He would call upon each member to report on the problems, progress, and priorities of her or his particular area of endeavor.

After one member gave a report, other members would ask questions or make suggestions. If an individual reported a problem, the group would attempt to resolve it. Most meetings had no formal agenda, and the members generally dispensed with parliamentary procedures. Gutiérrez made decisions and asked for consensus. If the members disagreed, they discussed the topic until they reached a decision collectively. Decisions were final and binding. The members would then follow the decisions in carrying out their professional programs or services (Texas had no open meetings law that would have opened this decision-making process to public scrutiny).

When matters under discussion were considered controversial or required the opinion and consensus of CU's membership, the directorate would present a report and make recommendations at CU's Sunday membership meetings. The membership would discuss the situation and vote on a decision. But within a year of the directorate's formation its members had become highly selective in what went to CU's general membership for approval. Gutiérrez explained the rationale for the change:

The Wednesday meetings started when we first took control of the schools and the city. We found ourselves besieged with problems that people normally would not understand nor care to understand, such as bonds, taxes, and fire rates and insurance rates. Matters that the community simply leaves to administrators. It's grown into such [a] large body that the supercentral committee of the area and the decisions are made a month in advance.[16]

Peter Bachrach and Morton S. Baratz's theory of "nondecisions" is a good way to describe CU's power structure. To these political scientists power has two faces. One manifests itself in the outcome of the overt decision-making process. The other is apparent in the capacity of individuals and groups to prevent issues or contests from entering into the policy debate. In their book, *Power and Poverty*, Bachrach and Baratz explain their concept of nondecision making: "Nondecision making is a means by which demands for change in the existing allocation of benefits and privileges in the community can be suffocated before they are even voiced; or kept covert; or killed before they gain access to the relevant decision-making arena; or failing all these things, maimed or destroyed in the decision-implementing stage of the policy process."[17]

That was how the CU board and membership, and especially the directorate, made all decisions. All three levels of CU's power structure at one time or another practiced nondecision making—some matters never made it to the appropriate level or entity for policy consideration or approbation. Nondecision making was also Gutiérrez's practice. If Gutiérrez, the CU board, or the directorate determined that general discussion of certain policies, issues, or projects might lead in a direction that the three levels of power disapproved of, those items never surfaced at CU's general meetings or the school board, city council, or county commissioner meetings.

The directorate's control over routine administrative decisions was ironclad. Asked whether the directorate was comparable to a power elite as described by C. Wright Mills, Gutiérrez replied, "Yes, definitely, somebody has to make decisions." He explained that collective community decision making is utopian and idealistic.

Directorate members were required to function as a disciplined collective body that adhered to democratic principles. To maintain their power position they had to work as a team, advancing RUP's peaceful revolution. Gutiérrez stressed that individualism was tolerated only to the extent that it did not interfere with the directorate and CU's other levels of power. If a member failed to comply with the policies and decisions of the directorate or if the member lost favor with the community, that individual was subject to disciplinary action. Offending members would receive a warning and, if they continued in their maverick ways, they would be dropped from the directorate and CU. Then they were subject to job loss and social ostracism.

Within the directorate was what political scientist Gaetano Mosca calls the "circulation of elites." Once a directorate member ceased to hold a position of influence, she or he was replaced by whoever had assumed that position of leadership. This was particularly true of elected officials and administrators. The few exceptions ultimately were decided by Gutiérrez. A few people were allowed to continue as part of the directorate because they were community leaders despite their "emeritus" position and because they were perceived as vital to the progress of the peaceful revolution.[18]

The fourth tier in the RUP's power structure was CU's membership. Theoretically, this was the primary level of power. It held CU's other three levels accountable. This was CU's base of authority and legitimacy. CU's membership of nearly five hundred families by 1975 was the foundation upon which RUP's peaceful revolution was built and developed. Initially, neither Gutiérrez, the CU board of directors, nor the directorate could expect to make decisions without the approval of the full membership. They voted on key decisions and selection of candidates for the various school, city, and county races. This was especially true during the first three years of CU's community control, the period of CU's demosocratic governance.

During much of 1970 and into 1974 CU's family membership was active in all aspects of the peaceful revolution. Its dynamic participation was evident in RUP's high voter turnouts, on the numerous city commissions and school committees, and when CU mobilized to protest or support an issue. In essence, CU's mass membership was the heart that pumped the blood to its powerful body.

Although the membership remained the most influential tier within CU, by 1974 its power had been eroded by the ubiquitous influence of Gutiérrez as the political boss. Gutiérrez's power grew with his election in 1974 to county judge. That position made him boss of a countywide political machine. The directorate's loss of influence became more evident in 1975 with the emergence of the directorate's "secretariat," which was comprised of even fewer members of RUP's elite (see Chapter 6 for more information about the secretariat).

In 1975, with the peaceful revolution increasingly under internal and external attack and facing growing bureaucratic problems, Gutiérrez tried to strengthen the decision-making power of the directorate by streamlining it. And as the members gained experience in leadership and management, and consolidated their power and influence, they sought additional power. By 1975 Gutiérrez was allowing the directorate to share more of his power by emphasizing collective decision making. That decision that later proved detrimental to Gutiérrez.

Thus in 1974–1975 a power structure parallel to that of CU began to emerge. An elite developed within the power elite. Fewer and fewer people held more and more power. Whereas Gutiérrez relied on the influence and support of CU's membership and board, the directorate became increasingly self-reliant—not surprising, given the resources the members controlled, the people they directed, and the authority of the positions they held. Cristal's elite within an elite affirmed Harold Lasswell and Daniel Lerner's dictum: "Government is always government by the few, whether in the name of the few, the one, or the many."[19] And this elitist power structure became increasingly vulnerable to internal schisms and dissension. The members of the elite were redefining the pursuit of community control and empowerment as the pursuit of individual control and power over the allocation of patronage and material inducements.

Early Schisms in RUP

According to V. O. Key, politics involves mutual relations of control between leaders and followers of superordination and subordination, dominance and submission, and governors and governed. Cristal was no exception. Between the second revolt of 1970 and the political rupture in 1975 schisms developed among RUP supporters, CU's membership, and its power structure. Gutiérrez responded to a comparison of Key's thesis and Cristal's realpolitik by saying, "It was and continues to be natural that in politics people are not always going to agree. We were not exempt from this." Lupe Cortinas, the main leader of the Barrio Club who by late 1975 would become Gutiérrez's nemesis, supported that appraisal. In a 1975 interview he said, "There has always been conflict. It was not ever brought out into the open. There was always the ability to work out differences among ourselves. We were going along in that manner up until a year ago" (1974).[20]

The peaceful revolution was never free of schisms. The roots of discontent were evident in the 1970 protest by women, who had been excluded from CU membership. Supported by Gutiérrez, the women pressured the men into granting them full-fledged membership in CU. Although this particular incident produced no lasting political divisions, it shows that CU's members had serious differences from the beginning.

Politically significant schisms did not begin to surface until 1972. Several developed as preconditions, or endogenous antagonisms, between 1972 and 1974 that precipitated the final split in RUP.[21] The first major public split occurred during the 1972 local elections in Cristal when CU's membership split over the endorsement of candidates for RUP's school board slate. In February CU's nominating committee recommended Alberto Sánchez and Ester Ynosencio for approval by the membership. A procedural dispute developed over the late submission of José Mata's name. The committee decided that Mata was a much stronger candidate than Ynosencio and replaced her with Mata.[22] Ynosencio refused to accept the decision. Supported by Sánchez, she took the position that the committee's action violated CU's candidate endorsement procedures. The dispute escalated at the Sunday meeting of CU at which the general membership voted to endorse Mata and

Sánchez. As a result, Ynosencio and thirteen other CU members resigned; they became known as Los Catorce [The Fourteen]. Despite
efforts by the membership to persuade her to drop out of the race,
Ynosencio ran on her own, receiving a mere 67 votes.[23]

The dispute over Ynosencio precipitated the defection of Mike
Pérez, a RUP school board member and part of Los Catorce, to CU's
adversaries. Pérez had played an important leadership role in the second revolt, which made his defection from CU in 1972 especially significant. Some RUP adherents saw Pérez's departure as stemming from
leadership differences with Gutiérrez, not the Ynosencio candidacy.
For the next two years Pérez was Gutiérrez's nemesis.

After he left CU Pérez and the rest of Los Catorce became supporters of Amistad. Pérez again became a leader, this time within Amistad,
which was comprised of gringos, Anglos, and the old guard Mexicano
elite that opposed RUP. He used the organization as a platform to
make vitriolic attacks against Gutiérrez in particular and CU in general. On the school board he opposed RUP's educational changes. In
1973 he ran for reelection as an independent. Although he failed in his
bid for reelection, he remained a critic and ardent foe of Gutiérrez.[24]

The next schism, of which Pérez's defection was a part, was the
RUP-controlled school board's adoption of the twenty-two bilingual
education recommendations in 1973. Many parents were concerned
that their children were not getting enough instruction in English. To
address their concerns the school board held several community meetings that were attended by as many as six hundred very upset and
concerned parents. Most parents were RUP supporters, but some were
allied with Amistad, including Mike Pérez.

For the first time hundreds of parents were mobilized against one
of RUP's educational programs. Although RUP continued to direct
community control of the schools, discontent clearly was beginning
to develop within its grassroots supporters. CU managed to diffuse
the potentially explosive situation by mounting a massive well-
coordinated community outreach effort. Although CU prevailed on
the changes to the bilingual education program, it cost the organization some community support.

In 1974 the former RUP supporters who had backed the slate of
independents in the school board and city council races in 1973 and
other anti-Gutierristas formed La Raza Libre. Some, especially the
press, interpreted the formation of La Raza Libre as reflecting a major
fracture with the ranks of RUP. According to Rodolfo (Rudy) Palomo,
the various factions that were anti-RUP simply came together and
formed La Raza Libre, which was made up of "mainly disgruntled

people who didn't like José Angel."²⁵ The split attracted media coverage from near and far and included stories in the *Arkansas Gazette* and
San Antonio Express, as well as the *Sentinel*. The *Express* reported, "The
new party [La Raza Libre] may become strong because there is much
dissatisfaction with Gutierrez."²⁶

La Raza Libre fielded candidates in both the 1974 and 1975 local
elections against CU. Although its candidates lost, the emergence of
La Raza Libre contributed to the development of a much more volatile
political climate in Zavala County.

Manuel Espinosa, a RUP member, decided to challenge Gutiérrez
for the party's nomination in 1974 for county judge of Zavala County,
a move that reflected yet another fracture within RUP. Joining Espinosa
was maverick José Talamantez, a candidate for county commissioner
from Precinct 2. Both refused to accept the decision of the CU nominating committee and membership to back Gutiérrez, and Hortencia
Treviño for county commissioner from Precinct 2. Espinosa and Talamantez decided to run in the RUP primary.²⁷ This issue was finally
resolved in court; the brouhaha was significant because it made public
the strength of the disenchantment within CU.

On the night of the April 1974 school board elections an incident
occurred that exemplified the growing rift between Gutiérrez and
Manuel Espinosa, the RUP member who was challenging him for the
party's nomination for county judge of Zavala County. According to
Espinosa, he was hosting a small gathering at his home when drivers
passing his house started honking their horns and yelling obscenities
at him. He also said that rocks were thrown and two shots were fired at
his house. Some rocks were thrown by passengers in a yellow Pontiac
Firebird, Espinosa said. He further claimed that among the passengers
was José Angel Gutiérrez.

Espinosa told the *Sentinel* that a deputy sheriff had followed and
stopped the yellow car. The paper quoted Espinosa as saying that he
saw Gutiérrez and the officer exchange a few words and that the officer
subsequently turned off his headlights and let the car go. Gutiérrez
categorically denied any involvement, saying he had spent the evening
at the Cross Y Restaurant, then at the No Esta Aqui Lounge, and later
at the home of high school coach Frito Salinas where Gutiérrez had
remained until 4 A.M.²⁸

Although the media gave heavy coverage to the Espinosa incident
and his challenge to Gutiérrez, Espinosa gained little politically. Lacking the support of CU, both Espinosa and Talamantez lost badly.

Then there was the issue of Jesse Gamez's legal fees, which precipitated a rift between Gamez and Gutiérrez. In 1972 the RUP-controlled

school board had retained Gamez and his law partner, Pat Malone, to represent the district in litigation involving the passage of the $3 million high school construction bond. The bond was being challenged by irate white farmers. After spending a considerable amount of time in litigation, Gamez and Malone billed the board $68,000 for their work, which the board considered exorbitant. Viviana Santiago, a school board member at the time, recalled, "I was amazed. I called the Texas Bar Association and explained the matter. I told them there was no written contract and that [Gamez and Malone] were charging the district an unreasonable amount. They [the bar association] agreed with me."[29]

The school board met in executive session to resolve the issue. Superintendent Angel Noe González and Santiago argued against payment in full. Santiago argued that paying the bill would require the district to cut back on a school building program funded by the 1972 bond issue that the lawyers had been hired to defend. She believed that $10,000 would be fair payment for the limited legal services Gamez and Malone had rendered.

On a 7–0 vote the board agreed to pay Gamez and Malone $15,000. Gutiérrez explained that events moved so swiftly that CU never had a chance to resolve the problem quietly. While in court on the bond litigation, Gutiérrez had spoken to Malone about the bill and they argued. According to Gutiérrez, "I fired them on the spot, and Malone told me that they quit." Gamez had been a good friend and political ally of Gutiérrez's since the second revolt; now there was a rift between them.[30]

The precarious relationship between Gutiérrez and Gamez further disintegrated in late 1974 in a struggle over who controlled Zavala County's beer market. This issue created a fissure within CU. Some CU members took sides. Gutiérrez, Gamez, school superintendent Angel Noe González, and others had gone in together on a number of business ventures since 1973. Luz Gutiérrez explained that every week the group would get together to discuss ways of promoting economic empowerment. From that informal process came Gamez's decision to buy a Budweiser beer distributorship. Gutiérrez subsequently decided to become part owner of a Falstaff distributorship.[31]

As a result, an intense economic war ensued between the two men. Initially, both Gutiérrez and Gamez felt that there was more than enough business to sustain the two distributorships. This was true until "sales of Budweiser took off and Falstaff didn't," Arturo Gonzales recalled. Gamez's distributorship was more successful than Gutiérrez's because, Gonzales said, "Budweiser [was] doing national advertising and Falstaff was doing none."[32] However, the *Corpus Christi Caller* reported in June 1975 that Gutiérrez's distributorship was making a profit.

The economic power struggle escalated to the point that it was brought up before CU. Gutiérrez lobbied for support and got it. "Angel [Gutiérrez] took it before Ciudadanos Unidos and a boycott against Budweiser was started," Arturo Gonzales explained. Arturo Gonzales's father worked for Gamez at the time; although the senior Gonzales was making good money, he quit his job when CU decided to boycott the product Gamez was distributing. In September 1975 the *Wall Street Journal* reported, "Whatever the case, there's no question, the town is split. Where you eat, where you buy groceries, even the beer you drink is a political decision. According to party regulars, for example, Lone Star is gringo beer; true believers drink Falstaff. (It's only coincidental, they say, that the county judge has the local Falstaff franchise.)" Within a year of the boycott both franchises went under. According to Arturo Gonzales, "The boycott cut down on Budweiser sales, and Falstaff sales never really took off. Both lost."[33]

But of all the many schisms forming within CU, one of the most serious was the "outsider issue." The transfer of control and power from whites to Mexicanos in 1970 created a dilemma for Gutiérrez. Cristal needed capable, qualified, and experienced administrators and technicians. But few Mexicanos in Cristal possessed such qualifications. Thus Gutiérrez was compelled to recruit from out of the area. Outsiders' filling of the well-paying jobs became an explosive issue and serious point of contention among long-time RUP members who wanted a bigger slice of the economic pie.[34]

RUP's peaceful revolution produced many relatively high-paying jobs. Most whites were replaced with Mexicanos who were loyal to RUP. In the four years between 1971 and 1975 the peaceful revolution changed the staffing of the county's largest employer, the public schools, from 34 percent Mexicano to 90 percent Mexicano. The city and county government workforces underwent similar transformations. Community control translated to control of jobs. "We turned things upside down in favor of Mexicanos," Gutiérrez said.[35]

"We were making a transition from laborers, migrantes [migrant workers], onion clippers, cafeteria workers, bus drivers to teachers, principals, and CEOs," Rodolfo (Rudy) Espinosa Jr. recalled. Consequently, the peaceful revolution created an insatiable demand and competition for jobs.[36] No matter how many programs Gutiérrez, Viviana Santiago, Luz Gutiérrez, and others brought into Cristal, there were never enough jobs to accommodate all the seasonal migrant workers, who comprised 40 percent or more of the Mexicano population of Zavala County.

As early as 1972 some RUP supporters were complaining that most administrative and principals' positions in the school district were being filled by outsiders and not Cristaleños.[37] The outsiders were for the most part from well-educated middle-class families and spoke more English than Spanish. By contrast, the Cristaleños were primarily sons and daughters of migrant farmworkers and had only recently received a college education and achieved middle-class status.[38] Consequently, their résumés were not as impressive.

The outsider issue was also a manifestation of the parochialism of many RUP adherents. Carlos Reyes, a Gutierrista at the time, described the outsider issue as a major contributor to the growing factionalism within RUP: "If you're not from there, if you were not born and raised there, you're considered an outsider, regardless. In Cristal outsiders were called *cucarachas* [cockroaches]."[39]

By 1975 a growing perception among anti-Gutierristas and even some RUP supporters was that only a handful of RUP members, and especially outsiders, had profited from the five years of community control. This perception in itself helped induce distrust, jealousy, and greed among the members of CU's directorate and general membership. Although many RUP supporters passionately touted the socioeconomic progress made by the peaceful revolution, RUP's adversaries had an antithetical view, especially with regard to Gutiérrez himself. Roberto Cornejo, the Raza Libre leader, told a Corpus Christi paper that Gutiérrez's success had spoiled him: "This atmosphere he is living gives him comfort, money, and prestige, and it has gone to his head. He has forgotten the true value of human status, which is to help those who need help, asking nothing in return—especially loyalty."[40]

On September 5, 1975, the *Wall Street Journal* ran a major exposé of RUP's peaceful revolution in Cristal. One section of the article was devoted to a look at Gutiérrez's finances:

Only a few years ago he was a struggling graduate student. Today he is doing well. His gross family income last year was about $47,000, or more than 11 times the $3,984 median level of Mexican-American families in Zavala County. He received about $11,000 as director of a Carnegie Foundation program for training Chicano school administrators. He grossed about $15,000 from a Falstaff beer distributorship and earned about $5,000 from lecture fees and from teaching political science in South Texas junior colleges. (Mr. Gutiérrez holds a master's degree in political science and is working on his doctorate.) His wife, Luz, was paid $16,000 as acting director of the county health clinic. This year Mr. Gutiérrez became county judge on Jan. 1 ($11,500 a year). He no longer holds the $11,000 Carnegie post, but his wife's salary has risen $2,000, to $18,000 a year. He estimates this year's gross family income at $45,000 to $46,000.[41]

Gutiérrez's response was not at all apologetic: "Sure . . . my income is right up there with the gringos', but it comes from sources they can't touch. If it didn't, how long do you think I'd be able to go on with my (political) work? I think I can articulate very well the frustrations and the aspirations of our Chicano community, and as long as I can do that, it doesn't make any difference whether I'm a millionaire or making a dollar a year."[42]

Individuals such as Angel Noe González and Amancio Cantu, who were outsiders, and Jesse Gamez, an insider, also attracted criticism. González was targeted for his supposedly lavish lifestyle. In 1974 González was paid $29,000 a year as the school district's superintendent. His wife, employed by the school district as director of the Right to Read Program—a federally funded program for pupils in grades four through eight—received $13,000 per year. The *Texas Observer* reported that "the Gonzalez's are not the only husband-wife team around Cristal these days." This statement implied that other RUP couples, such as the Gutiérrezes, were also benefiting economically. During González's three-year stay in Cristal, the *Texas Observer* reported, he bought three new Cadillacs with his own money. He justified the purchases by saying he was constantly on the road to San Antonio and Austin on school business. Gamez defended González on the ground that he was effective in bringing in federal grants.[43]

Gutiérrez's adversaries had been claiming since before 1974 that the wealth of the peaceful revolution was concentrated in the hands of a few RUP members. They voiced these complaints in the press, thereby providing a constant source of ammunition to Gutiérrez's external as well as internal enemies. Gutiérrez unequivocally rebuked his adversaries for alleging that transactions by RUP's leadership bordered on the illegal. He further said that such innuendos were predicated on pure petty jealousy. This impression among anti-Gutierristas and some RUP leaders, that RUP's leadership was getting rich, created an insatiable hunger for control and power among them. Some RUP leaders wanted what Gutiérrez appeared to have: power and wealth, and they were determined to topple him from power.[44]

These were the most salient schisms. It is important to note, however, that the leaders of the Barrio Club, who became the power between late 1975 and 1977, mention other issues they believe contributed to the rupture. Arturo Gonzales referred to a conflict with Luz Gutiérrez over his inability to obtain a major staff position with El Centro de Salud [The Health Center]. Another was the expulsion of Eliseo Solis from CU: "He was kicked out of town because Ciudadanos Unidos accused him of spying at its meetings," Lupe Cortinas said. Barrio Club members also cited the expulsion of Marcos Esequiel and his wife from CU because they enrolled their children in the local private school controlled by whites.[45] From 1970 to 1975, although RUP's Mexicano opponents never posed a serious challenge to Gutiérrez's power or CU's control, they were successful in fostering an anti-Gutierrista mind-set. RUP's critics constantly depicted Gutiérrez as a ruthless and selfish dictator who only cared about himself.

Throughout the first five years of community control Gutiérrez's adversaries vehemently criticized the authoritarianism of CU, which they perceived as a *dictadura* [dictatorship] and political machine. The Mexicano critics did not use the terms *boss* or *machine politics* in describing or referring to Gutiérrez. Instead, they referred to him in the context of Mexican politics. To some, RUP was the equivalent of Mexico's governing party, the PRI (El Partido Revolucionario Institución al) and Gutiérrez was its caudillo [chief]. from 1970 to 1975 the critics changed their banner but not their opposition to RUP's peaceful revolution and its main architect, Gutiérrez. In 1970 they were the Citizens Association Serving All Americans (CASAA). In 1971 they became the Better Government association. For the local elections in 1972 and 1973 they called themselves independents. For the county elections in 1972 they opted for Amistad. And in 1974 and 1975 they became La Raza Libre. No matter what they called themselves, they zealously opposed Gutiérrez and RUP. Thus by 1975 the political climate was such that CU's power structure was showing visible breaks.

6

The Political Rupture (1975)

By 1975 the peaceful revolution's schisms had become major fissures. The discipline, organization, and unity of action that had characterized RUP's politics of community control since 1970 came to an abrupt end. Instead, competing bellicose factions resorted to the politics of self-destruction. Their differences became so irreconcilable that they became precipitants, ushering in the calamitous political rupture—a series of events so devastating that RUP broke apart and ended its peaceful revolution. As a result, the peaceful revolution's politics of community control was replaced by the politics of self-destruction.

Theoretical Aspects of the Political Rupture

The political rupture did not occur spontaneously or in a vacuum. It was a product of antagonisms that by 1975 had created a volatile political climate. This change in Cristal was induced by endogenous schisms and exogenous antagonisms.[1] Exogenously, at the national level the epoch of protest (1956–1974) was essentially over. The massive demonstrations, marches, sit-ins, and picket lines had diminished considerably. Mexicanos had adopted a much more conservative mind-set that rebuked militancy and protest and embraced a politics of accommodation in its approach and thinking.[2]

This dramatic change in the nation's politics was precipitated by the demise or decline of the protest movements—the civil rights, New

Left, antiwar, Black Power, and Chicano movements. Contributing to their decline were the end of the Vietnam War; the neutralizing of activist leaders and organizations through their infiltration, destabilization, and, in some cases, incarceration or physical elimination by law enforcement agencies; the co-opting of activists into federal and privately funded programs; the prevalence of fractionalization and power struggles among the activist groups and leaders of these movements; and the alienating political effects of Watergate. These and other factors contributed to the development of apathy, complacency, and a growing alienation felt throughout the nation.[3]

The Chicano Movement, a product of exogenous and endogenous antagonisms, was moribund by 1975. Texas historian David Montejano writes, "By 1975 the [Chicano Movement] in Texas and the Southwest had largely been exhausted. Many of its aims had become institutionalized and its more dramatic elements accommodated. Exhaustion, however, came from internal friction about leadership and tactics and from external pressure applied by state authorities." Its protest generation had been replaced with the "Viva Yo," or the Me Generation.[4] This meant that the notion of community, so wholeheartedly embraced by the Chicano Movement, had been replaced by individualism.

Although some vestiges of protest remained after 1975, they were hardly radical or militant. With the exception of César Chávez and the United Farm Workers, the three most prominent leaders of Chicano Movement organizations had lost their power.[5] Reies López Tijerina, released from a federal penitentiary in 1971 after serving a two-year term for destroying federal property in a national park in New Mexico, was no longer the head of the Alianza Federal de Mercedes. The Alianza and Tijerina had spearheaded the land grant movement, which had sought the return to its original Mexicano owners of lands taken by the federal government. After his release from prison he had lost much of his militance and now preached "brotherhood and love." According to historian Juan Gomez-Quinonez, "Tijerina was no longer willing to organize in vehement protest of the system's practice." Rodolfo "Corky" Gonzales, leader of the Crusade for Justice and the Raza Unida Party in Colorado, was barely holding on to his operation in Denver. After a disastrous electoral showing in 1970 and 1974, RUP in Colorado was essentially defunct by 1976.[6]

The Brown Berets, a separate paramilitary organization that promoted the establishment of a Chicano nation (Aztlán), were disbanded in 1972 by their leader, Prime Minister David Sanchez, after a series of power struggles. In frustration, Sanchez explained, "Words were no longer a mediator, fighting in the organization was sometimes gang-like."[7] Increasing factionalism, infighting, and apathy also plagued the Chicano student organizations. Those who had been in the avant-garde of the Chicano Movement either faded away, like the Mexican American Youth Organization (MAYO) in Texas, or became much less active, like the Movimiento Estudiantil Chicano de Aztlán (MECHA) based in California. In many of these student organizations the splits occurred between cultural nationalists who still espoused Chicanismo and Marxists.[8] Students began shifting from activism to mainstream activities and career building. They began forming organizations oriented to enhancing their personal careers and focused on law, engineering, business, medicine, and other fields. These groups by and large were antithetical to the Chicano Movement's activist politics. Chicano fraternities became popular.

RUP was also in decline. At the national level RUP was split into the Gutierristas (those loyal to José Angel Gutiérrez) and the Corkyites (those loyal to Rodolfo "Corky" Gonzales).[9] As in the past the struggle was over who would be *el líder máximo* [ultimate leader] of RUP nationally and over differences in RUP's orientation, ideology, and strategy.[10] According to historian Ignacio Garcia, "The years 1975 through 1977 were disastrous for La Raza Unida Party. Not withstanding the pledges of commitment to the rural strategy and to the development of ideology, the party failed to make any significant advances in political victories or in new conversions. The party began to decline rapidly after 1975."[11] RUP's national politics of self-destruction would also consume RUP in Cristal.

The decline of RUP both nationally and in Texas weakened Gutiérrez's leadership in Cristal.[12] Not even his energy and adroit leadership could stop RUP's decline. Besides, he was overwhelmed and overextended—embroiled in power struggles at the national level, plagued by organizing problems within Texas, and confronted by schisms in Cristal, even as he served as RUP's national chairperson, county judge (a full-time position), and county political boss. As RUP national chairperson, he traveled extensively to give speeches and attend meetings and conferences. He also had several meetings with Mexico's president, Luis Echeverría Alvarez, and government officials.

This situation forced Gutiérrez to delegate some of his leadership responsibilities to people he believed were his trusted lieutenants or leaders within CU.[13] Many were members of the directorate. Several belonged to the Barrio Club or were part of the technocracy emerging within the school district and city government.[14] A few perceived themselves as equal to Gutiérrez. For example, his nemesis, Lupe Cortinas, said the Barrio Club members (hereafter referred to as the *Bar-*

rioistas) wanted it "all."[15] They wanted to take control of politics in Cristal. Although CU leaders like Cortinas continued to articulate the line of the Chicano Movement, they did not practice it with the same zeal.

The Rupture: A Product of Relative Deprivation

RUP's fatal rupture was a product of "relative deprivation." Scholars such as Alexis de Tocqueville, James Davis, and Ted Gurr counter Marx's misery theory of revolution—which holds that worsening social conditions, especially the standard of living, are the decisive cause of revolution—with the so-called prosperity theory.[16] In advancing this theory Tocqueville writes, "It is not always in going from bad to worse that one falls into revolution. It happens most often that a people, which had supported the most crushing laws without complaint as if it did not sense them, rejects them violently when their burden is lightened. The regime that a revolution destroys is always better than the one that immediately preceded it."[17]

Complementing Tocqueville's analysis is James Davis's J-curve hypothesis. According to this theory, "Revolutions are most likely to occur when a prolonged period of rising expectations and rising gratifications is followed by a short period of sharp reversal."[18] Davis believes that a revolutionary situation exists when a gap between expectations and reality, produced by a cyclical downturn that weakens confidence in the existing regime, generates frustration, which then creates the climate for revolution.[19]

The theories of both Tocqueville and Davis depend on the notion of relative deprivation. Gurr explains that the term *relative deprivation* refers to the gap between what people get and what they think they should get. Specifically, it is, "a perceived discrepancy between men's value expectations and their value capabilities. Value expectations are the goods and conditions of life to which people believe they are highly entitled. Value capabilities are the goods and conditions that they think they are capable of attaining or maintaining."[20] Social discontent is a function of the scope and intensity of relative deprivation among various strata and groups of the population.[21] When the frustration between what people want and what they get becomes intolerable, a situation ripe for revolution exists. This was the case in Cristal.

Although the theory of relative deprivation has several shortcomings, it is useful for analyzing the etiology of RUP's political rupture. Politically, each endogenous schism and exogenous antagonism stimulated among some RUP leaders rising expectations that could not be satisfied. A gap developed between the leaders' value capabilities and their value expectations. As a result, irreconcilable differences developed between Gutiérrez and his followers on the one hand, and leaders such as Lupe Cortinas, Rodolfo (Rudy) Palomo, Arturo Gonzales, and Rodolfo (Rudy) Espinosa Jr., among others, from both the Barrio Club and the local technocracy, on the other. By late summer 1975 these two factions had coalesced into what I describe as the "new guard" that led the overthrow of Gutiérrez as boss of the peaceful revolution.[22]

The overthrow of Gutiérrez unleashed an unprecedented wave of conflict and political unrest that ruptured the peaceful revolution politically. I use the word *rupture* because it connotes a sense of coming apart or, in the case of Cristal, an overt and uncontrollable bursting of rising expectations among the new guard that resulted in the emergence of a self-destructive mode of politics. In addition, the power struggle between the new guard and Gutierristas became so severe that the rupture became synonymous with an all-out internal political war. As a result, the peaceful revolution became so disrupted that a power realignment occurred, with the new guard winning control of both the schools and city while the Gutierristas retained a tenuous hold on county government. The Gutierristas became casualties of what political scientist Chalmers Johnson describes as power deflation and a loss of authority.[23]

Theoretically, the political rupture that dismembered RUP and its peaceful revolution was a form of what Harry Eckstein has called "internal war."[24] The term refers to the use of violence to create change in government policies, leaders, and organization. Although the transfer of power to the new guard was relatively nonviolent because it occurred through an electoral coup, it nevertheless entailed a change in the policies, leaders, and organization of Cristal's politics. At the same time the rupture brought an end to the golden years of peaceful revolution. In fact, the political conflict became so intense that some violence did ensue that involved the leadership and supporters of both of RUP's contentious power blocs.

What happened in 1975 that led to political rupture? Essentially, the rupture was a product of concurrent exogenous and endogenous antagonisms. Exogenously, the nation was becoming more conservative politically. Endogenously, the prevalence of schisms within CU by 1974 had fostered a form of relative deprivation among a part of CU's intelligentsia; this proved to be self-destructive. In 1975 the schisms became more acute, creating conflict, unrest, and divisions to varying degrees. Those that emerged during the first six months or so were preconditions, whereas those that surfaced in July and August became precipitants of the rupture.

Preconditions to the Rupture

The RUP Delegation's Trip to Cuba

Among the major preconditions that exacerbated an already bad situation was Gutiérrez's efforts to organize a RUP delegation to visit Cuba in 1975. That January 1975 Gutiérrez accepted an invitation from the Cuban ambassador in Mexico to lead a RUP delegation to Cuba. Following the usual procedure, Gutiérrez brought the invitation to CU's membership for approval and got a strong endorsement. It became a problem only as people began to discuss who was going to be part of the delegation.[25] Seeking to give it a national focus, Gutiérrez invited RUP leaders from California, Arizona, Wisconsin, Illinois, Indiana, Michigan, and New Mexico. Because he was embroiled in a power struggle with Rodolfo "Corky" Gonzales, Gutiérrez invited no one from Colorado.

In explaining the purpose of the delegation's trip to Cuba, Gutiérrez told the press that it would gather valuable information in Cuba that would be helpful as RUP developed programs in education, housing, health care, and farming.[26] He was especially eager to learn more about Cuba's collective farming, because a cooperative farm was being proposed for Zavala County.

Gutiérrez delayed the trip, which had been scheduled for late January or early February, at the request of the Cuban government. In January some of RUP's adversaries told reporters that Zavala County was going to pay for the trip to Cuba. Viviana Santiago, a confidant of Gutiérrez's, unequivocally denied the allegation on his behalf, telling reporters, "Obviously no county money is being used because these aren't county officials. It's Raza Unida money. Actually, each one who is going is bearing the burden of travel expenses." But that wasn't true—Fidel Castro's government was going to foot the bill for the RUP delegation from Mexico City to Havana and back. Travel expenses from their homes to Mexico City and back were the responsibility of each delegate. The delegation would leave from Mexico City to circumvent the U.S. economic embargo of Cuba that banned air travel to Cuba from the United States.[27]

Winter became spring, and Gutiérrez still had not named the members of the delegation. He wanted people who could represent Zavala County. Supported by CU, he selected his wife, Luz; Ezequiel Guz-

mán, Cristal's city manager; Amancio Cantu, who had become superintendent of schools in 1974; and Elpidio Lizcano, director of one of
the school district's bilingual programs.

Not everyone in CU was happy with those choices. Some members
began to question Gutiérrez's decision and became upset that they
were excluded. Others objected to the number of bureaucrats. Carlos
Reyes, a Gutierrista, said, "Gutiérrez took bureaucrats like Lizcano
who were not committed to making changes."[28] Thus the selection of
the Cristal delegates fostered discontent among some members of the
new guard.

The delegation that left for Cuba in late April also included RUP
representatives from various parts of Texas, the Southwest, and the
Midwest: Abel Cavada and Roberto Maggioni from Texas; Daniel Zapata, Sharon D'Aiello, John Ramirez, and Marisal Cordoy from California; Manuel Sepulveda from Michigan; Ernest Chacon of Wisconsin;
Angel Moreno of Illinois; and Lupe De Leon of Indiana. Raul Ruiz of
California joined the delegation just a few days before its departure.

A master of manipulating the media, Gutiérrez also invited a few
reporters on the trip. This maneuver was calculated to ensure that he
and the delegation got a lot of ink, which would give him a boost on
the national and international political stages. The media contingent
included Ed Rable of CBS News and his two-member crew and Guile
Gonzales of the *Corpus Christi Caller-Times*.[29] Ever the glib radical, Gutiérrez spoke at length about what he expected to learn from the trip:
"In seeing the Cuban model, we will see how we can apply the improvements they have made, despite the differences that exist between
communism and capitalism. . . . It has been noted that Cuba has made
great strides in wiping out illiteracy, poor housing, discrimination and
other problem areas that South Texas Chicanos also face."

Asked about the State Department's restrictions on travel to Cuba,
he responded sarcastically: "We have not prejudged how U.S. authorities may react to our visit upon our return. We do not presume we
need State Department clearance, okay or blessing to visit Cuba . . .
since no national policy reflects our view." He also juxtaposed the Cuban Revolution and RUP's peaceful revolution in Cristal: "Despite our
differences there is a certain similarity between their revolution and
our rise to power in South Texas. Although their's was a bloody revolution and ours was not, we do have several things in common, like agricultural production."[30]

The delegation arrived in Cuba on April 21. During the ten-day stay
the RUP delegation met with various high-ranking Cuban government
officials and were able to discuss various aspects of the Cuban Revolu-

tion. Specifically, the delegation toured a farm cooperative, school, hospital, university, and Radio Venceremos, and attended Cuba's May Day parade in Havana and a reception at which Fidel Castro was present.[31]

Upon the delegation's return Gutiérrez held a press conference in San Antonio. Newspapers across the country reported his remarks and observations. He invited criticism from whites and some Mexicanos, especially his adversaries, and got it.

Gutiérrez's comments proved incendiary. He alluded to how Cuba in some areas was more advanced than the United States: "There's no crime, no illiteracy and few health problems." At another press conference a few days later he stated that he was not a communist but that he would like to use some of Cuba's socialist ideas in Zavala County and within RUP "as soon as I can convince them they are good ideas." One reporter asked, if he liked Cuba so much, why didn't he and other Mexicanos live there? "Because we have to make a Cuba here," Gutiérrez responded.[32] In another statement he defended his desire to bring socialism to south Texas: "The specific applicability (of socialism) to South Texas or any place would depend first of all on local initiative—the people wanting to change their own situation by whatever means necessary, ballots or bullets or whatever. . . . I really don't think there's going to be a revolution anytime soon in the United States. So, leaving that out, it reduces the options one has to ballots or peaceful change."[33]

Not surprisingly, the newspapers' headlines reflected his remarks: "Raza Chief Would Try Socialism in Zavala" (*San Antonio Express*); "Socialism a Better Way of Life Than Capitalism" (*Corpus Christi Caller*); "Raza Unida Wants to Create Little Cuba in South Texas" (*Alice Echo News*).[34]

Ventura Gonzalez, a former Gutierrista mayor, complained years later that reporters and others who had used the issue of Cuba to attack the peaceful revolution were misinformed: "They might have misunderstood what José Angel meant was the purpose of the trip to Cuba. It was only to see how it was over there and to take the good and not the bad and use it here."[35]

The controversy played right into the hands of whites in Zavala County. Jack Kingsberry, a businessman, attacked Gutiérrez for using the fruits of capitalism—federal funds—to perpetuate his power and control. "We didn't think he [Gutiérrez] was going to continue leading if he were going to try to make another Cuba here in Zavala County," Kingsberry said. In an editorial in June Dale Barker quoted Dr. Carlos D. Carbonell, who was born in Cuba and who remarked that life in Cuba was not as pleasant as the RUP delegation reported.[36]

According to both Gutierristas and the new guard, the Cuba trip added to the growing discord within CU. According to Reverend Sherrill Smith, the long-time civil rights activist, Gutiérrez's "trip to Cuba made a lot of people nervous." Moses Peña reported that during the Cuba trip a rumor circulated that Gutiérrez would use his connections with the Cuban government to fill his pockets. Even José Mata, one of Gutiérrez's trusted allies, acknowledged the negative effect that the Cuba trip had on Cristal: "Yes, it affected us because of the negative national publicity. Even the president of the United States spoke on national TV against Cristal. . . . Governor [Dolph] Briscoe [of Texas] labeled us as a little Cuba. It affected us badly even though we were a movement and free to exercise our rights. But because we were Chicanos and were a new movement that was growing rapidly, well, the government didn't like it."[37]

In fact, there was dissension within CU's ranks even before the delegation left in late April. Abel Cavada, a delegate, said the problems had "nothing to do with the Cuba trip," but the trip was a "convenient excuse for them" (the Barrio Club) to raise complaints.[38]

Barrio Club member Arturo Gonzales said that the Texas Rangers showed him a video of the Cuba trip and then interrogated him. The rangers claimed they were investigating allegations that the delegation had given school property, a video camera, to the Cuban government. Gonzales told the *Corpus Christi Caller* that Gutiérrez "brought back some stupid ideas from Cuba."[39] Another Barrio Club member, Rudy Palomo, recalled that some CU members researched the trip to Cuba and concluded that it was illegal. In addition, he said that the trip served to foment infighting among RUP's ranks. José Luis Balderas, a technocrat, concurred that the Cuba trip contributed to the breakup of RUP: "[It] started when he went to Cuba and came back with some communistic ideas that could have worked but not in context of how we were doing it. We wanted a system that was dictated by the community and not by one individual."[40]

Juan Cornejo said, "The trip to Cuba didn't hurt everyone, just Angel." Reverend Smith explained that the new guard used the Cuba trip effectively against Gutiérrez: "They [the new guard] were totally *Mexican*. They were also citizens of Texas and the United States. I don't think ideologically they identified with Cuba, Nicaragua, or even Mexico."[41]

CU's Income Tax

Yet another precondition to the rupture was CU's 1975 imposition of a progressive income tax, which exacerbated the already growing tensions and divisions. Gutiérrez sought to enrich CU's political war chest by taxing its membership. Although members agreed that the tax was necessary, they disagreed about how to implement it. In theory each family was to be taxed 10 percent of its earnings. However, in practice the amount was really based on ability to pay, especially for the hundreds of low-income families. Within three months the tax brought in $18,000 to $25,000, which the treasurer deposited in CU's account. All the money was used to sustain Gutiérrez's and CU's political activities. Some RUP leaders and the emerging new guard believed the income tax was inequitable and part of Gutiérrez's patronage system. They believed that he was using the money to support his national RUP organizing activities and that little of the money would be spent in Cristal.[42] Years later Gutiérrez addressed the negative reaction by explaining, "Some who resisted were teachers who had been promoted to program directors and staff and others who had benefited from the RUP. . . . They had no problem with giving to the church voluntarily, but they didn't want to be obligated to paying into the CU."[43]

The income tax controversy weakened Gutiérrez's hold on CU. Most of the new guard opposed the 10 percent tax, their resistance partly motivated by a change in their political ethos. The *we* of group solidarity of RUP's peaceful revolution was being replaced by the *I* of individual acquisition of capital. Moreover, the new guard did not want to do anything that might strengthen Gutiérrez's control of CU.[44] Even after CU split in two, the Gutierrista CU continued to impose its income tax. At a CU meeting on October 12, for example, forty-four members contributed $194, or approximately $4.30 per family.[45]

The Committee of Nine—The Secretariat

Upon his return from Cuba Gutiérrez also moved to establish the *Comite de Nueve* [Committee of Nine], which became another precondition of the rupture. According to Ignacio Garcia, the paramount function of the Committee of Nine (which I call the "secretariat") was to "make decisions on hiring and firings in the city and schools and . . . be the top policy maker in the party."[46] Gutiérrez said the secretariat was set up to expedite streamlining of the public policy process. Using CU, especially the directorate, as the public policy clearinghouse had become too cumbersome. Gutiérrez explained, "What was happening with Ciudadanos Unidos was that it was getting too large. The reports were getting too long because we were adding more programs and people. The meetings were getting to be unproductive . . . people were getting tired of listening to all the reports. It was getting more and more overwhelming." He added that directorate was not up to the job: "It was difficult to get all these agency, political public offices, heads

together, there were just too many of them. Those Wednesday meetings
... were attended by all bosses because there were no supervisors
over us."[47]

He explained that directorate members usually took fifteen minutes
each to make their reports, which would be followed by discussion.
With seventeen to twenty people present, the morning meetings held
in the school district conference room went well into the afternoon.

As an alternative Gutiérrez established the secretariat, or what he
called the supercentral committee, to downsize the peaceful revolution's overall bureaucracy and improve its capacity to make public policy. Furthermore, the formation of the secretariat meant that RUP's
power structure had become increasingly oligarchical and elitist. Each
of the following policy-making entities had one representative on the
secretariat: city council, school board, county, urban renewal, Housing
Authority, Centro de Salud (the health clinic), Ciudadanos Unidos, the
county RUP, and Renteros Unidos (Renters United, a tenants' union).[48]
But some CU members thought that Gutiérrez had devised the secretariat as an attempt to further consolidate his power in response to
growing internal dissatisfaction and opposition.

As he tried to get the secretariat going, Gutiérrez encountered opposition, cynicism, and distrust, especially from the new guard's Barrioista faction. The summer was a period of internal infighting among
CU's Gutierristas and the increasingly hostile Barrioistas. Because the
secretariat, at least in theory, was to have the same, if not more, power
over public policy than the directorate, people scrambled for control,
which heightened the conflict between Gutierristas and Barrioistas.
The Barrioistas were certain that the creation of the secretariat
was illegal.[49] They also were concerned with the scope of its power—
Gutiérrez had even endowed it with the power to mediate political
disputes.[50]

By July the differences between the factions were becoming clearly
defined. Schools superintendent Amancio Cantu acknowledged the
presence of three clashing factions within RUP. He explained, "Within
Ciudadanos Unidos there were three groups that emerged: the Gutierristas, the people who followed José Angel, who still believed that he
was on the right track because of the many things that he had done for
Mexicanos in Cristal and the nation. Then there were the 'Barrioistas,'
who totaled to twenty-five members. The 'Oportunistas' [opportunists]
were a small group of fifteen to twenty people."[51]

Cantu explained that the alliance between the Barrio Club and what
he labeled the *Oportunistas,* or, as I call them, the technocrats, was precarious at best. He said he called the technocrats Oportunistas because

they were the middle- to upper middle-class individuals who perceived themselves as sophisticated because they were administrators or technicians. As Cantu saw it, these people had done absolutely nothing to bring about RUP's peaceful revolution—they were the beneficiaries.[52] The new guard was really an unholy alliance of the anti-Gutierrista factions that had essentially one thing in common—both wanted Gutiérrez's power and control of patronage.

By summer the conflict within CU over the secretariat had become intense. According to Barrio Club member Arturo Gonzales, Gutiérrez initially was a formal part of the secretariat because he was its organizer. "He represented the county. But he gave up the position to one of his friends, so he could get appointed by Renteros Unidos."[53] But Gutiérrez failed to secure his appointment to Renteros Unidos, and he was left out of the secretariat.

As a result, Gutiérrez suffered his first major political defeat at the hands of the new guard. According to Rodolfo Palomo, the new guard, of which he was a member, had the controlling 7–2 majority and voted to disband the secretariat. "Gutiérrez got excluded from the committee. . . . The first action item that we had as a committee was to disband it. He [Gutiérrez] didn't like that, and that is when the fights started." Gutiérrez's adversaries claimed the secretariat was illegal. They felt it took power away from the city council, school board, and commissions. José Luis Balderas, another member of the new guard, elaborated: "I went all out against him [Gutiérrez]. I didn't want Cristal to become communist. We wanted to be known for our political contributions."[54] City Manager Guzmán echoed Balderas and added that some RUP leaders in Cristal had compared Gutiérrez to Fidel Castro.[55] By July the political schisms were severe enough to precipitate the political rupture.

The Chief Garza Controversy

All these events helped induce a volatile political climate. The resignation of Cristal's chief of police, Antonio Yanas, was an important endogenous antagonism that precipitated the rupture. Yanas resigned in July in protest of Guzmán's suspension of two city patrol officers. Yanas said Guzmán was usurping the chief's powers.[56] Guzmán had suspended the two officers, Ruben Gonzalez and José Luis Jimenez, for two weeks for failing to respond to a break-in. Yanas told reporters that rather "than allow that violation, I prefer to resign." Guzmán responded by appointing Tony Jimenez, the assistant city manager, as acting chief of police. Guzmán also accepted the resignation of Officer Jimenez and appointed a temporary officer in his place.[57]

The police chief's resignation created a window of opportunity for the anti-Gutierrista new guard. But it was the Barrioistas who led the power struggle that followed. By late July Cristal's political climate had become extremely precarious. Gutiérrez and CU were caught in a power deflation spiral, losing authority and power over the city and school decision-making structures and processes.[58]

The Barrioistas in particular were no longer willing to play second fiddle to Gutiérrez and his supporters. In August the divisions became public. Confident that they had the votes on the city council, the Barrioistas maneuvered to appoint Ramón Garza, who had been with the county sheriff's department, as the city's new police chief. As before, the appointment of a city official was first discussed and decided within CU. CU backed Victor Castillo, a deputy sheriff, for police chief.

Although CU's endorsement went to Castillo, the new guard refused to honor the decision, and the city council on a 3–2 vote gave the job to Garza. The three new guard council members—Arturo Gonzales, Lupe Cortinas, and Eugenio Ruiz—voted for Garza. Voting against him were Gutierrista council members Ambrosio Melendrez and José Cuevas.

Before the city council vote, someone informed Dale Barker of the *Zavala County Sentinel* of the impending split. Barker wrote in an editorial:

You can just say that the natives are restless, an anonymous caller who said he was a Raza Unida member told us Wednesday afternoon. Our caller said he was talking about a split in the local Raza Unida Party, and that we would be hearing more and more about it during the next few days. The informant went on to say that local party supporters are objecting to new faces being brought in here to work for "la causa."[59]

Barker's editorial was in part predicated on the "outsider issue." From the beginning of RUP's peaceful revolution, the issue of outsiders taking jobs in Cristal was a major preoccupation and concern to some of its supporters.[60] The Barrioistas, all natives of Cristal, used the issue effectively against Gutiérrez. The level of conflict within CU was so great that there was no longer room for compromise.

The Barrioistas were no longer willing to be mere recipients of patronage. They wanted to control and dispense it. After months of internal posturing over the myriad schisms and preconditions, by late summer 1975 they moved methodically to topple Gutiérrez. Their intent was to become Cristal's new power structure.[61] During the turbulent days before the rupture the new guard attacked Gutiérrez on the issue of patronage. Gutiérrez rationalized that the Barrioistas were upset because outsiders had gotten the highest-paying jobs and because the Barrioistas believed that Gutiérrez was introducing communist ideas.[62]

The Ruiz and Casarez Defections

The Ruiz and Casarez defections became a precipitant of the rupture. This issue had its roots in January 1975 when CU endorsed José Herrera, and not the Barrio Club's Isaac Juárez, for city council. According to Gutiérrez, the Barrio Club then alleged that Herrera was a fraud—that he had faked his school record and credentials. CU called an emergency meeting, and its members decided not to support Herrera.

Believing that they had scored a victory, Barrio Club members reintroduced their original candidate, Juárez. But Gutiérrez and the overwhelming majority said no and opted for Gene Ruiz, brother of the CU school board member Mercedes "Chachi" Casarez. Gutiérrez said that some people were concerned about having a brother and sister in office at the same time. But there was not enough time to redo the entire nomination process "so we went with it."[63] Ruiz won his race for city council.

For the time being, Gutiérrez had gotten his way. But by that summer both Casarez and Ruiz had defected to the new guard. Their defections meant that the new guard was in control of the city council. The shift in control was a result of a well-executed electoral coup. Gutiérrez explained how the new guard set the stage for its revolt against him: "Chachi and Ramón Garza were on the school board along with Raul Flores, who was the head of Ciudadanos Unidos. Felipe Flores was his brother and was running the CAP agency—these were all very key positions. The Barrio Club was able to convince the Ruizes by convincing them that they would get better jobs and more pay if they supported the Barrio Club."[64]

The Firing of Superintendent Cantu

With majorities on the city council and school board and confident of its new power, the new guard moved to oust the school district's Gutierrista superintendent, Amancio Cantu. This action was the final precipitant to the political rupture. At a special meeting on August 18 the school board voted 4–3 to fire Cantu, who had been superintendent since September 1, 1974. Voting for removal were board president Raul T. Flores and trustees Ramón Garza, Mercedes Casarez, and José Luis Balderas. Ignacio Mata, an administrator in the school district, was named acting superintendent on a 4–3 vote. He had come up through the technocracy. Balderas and CU's president, Raul Flores, were employees of the Urban Renewal Agency, which was directed by Barrio Club leader Rudy Palomo.[65]

The alliances that marked the votes on the police chief and school superintendent heralded the new world order in Cristal. What followed was an all-out internecine political revolt that may be better described as the politics of self-destruction. This new mode of politics put an end to RUP's politics of community control and its peaceful revolution.

The Political Rupture

The political rupture unleashed what I describe as the politics of self-destruction. What occurred was reminiscent of the first revolt (1963–1965). Both power blocs engaged in a relentless power struggle that at times became violent. Five years of community control and a plethora of changes hung in the balance. The animosities, differences, and frustration that had been growing among the new guard burst into an outright power confrontation and revolt against Gutiérrez. The political fracture split control of the schools and city and county governments: the new guard controlled the schools and city council, while the Gutierristas controlled the county. Their differences became so acute they wound up in court.

Numerous lawsuits were filed alleging everything from nepotism to libel and slander. As the polarization became more severe, so did the infighting. Cantu retaliated against the three new guard school board members responsible for his firing with a slew of unsuccessful suits. On August 20 he filed a complaint with Deputy Sheriff Victor Castillo against three of the four new guard board members, lodging against each two counts of nepotism (nepotism was against district policy). The three were Chief of Police Ramón Garza; Mercedes "Chachi" Casarez; and Raul Flores, president of the school board. Bond was set at $1,000 each for Casarez and Flores, and $200 for Garza.[66]

Cantu took his case to U.S. District Court, but Judge John H. Wood denied his request for a temporary restraining order and temporary injunction. A hearing was set for September 9 in the U.S. District Court in Del Rio on Cantu's suit for reinstatement as superintendent or payment for the remaining two years of his contract. He also sought $50,000 in actual damages and $50,000 in punitive damages.[67]

On September 2 Judge José Angel Gutiérrez of the Zavala County Court dismissed the nepotism charges against three of the four board members on the ground of defective complaints. San Antonio attorney Pete Torres, who represented the three, successfully argued that the dates of the alleged offenses were different than those on their complaints, which had been prepared by County Attorney Richard Arroyo. The three school board trustees were back in Zavala County Court on September 17. On the day that Gutiérrez had dismissed the defective complaints, Cantu had filed thirty-three separate new complaints against the trustees. These charges involved the hiring of school district personnel at board meetings in May, July, and August 1974 and during March, May, and July 1975. The new complaints referred to the same events as those detailed in the charges that had been dismissed. School board president Flores claimed that Cantu was motivated by vindictiveness because he was no longer superintendent. Flores pointed out that it was Viviana Santiago, a Gutierrista school board member, who had made the motion to hire Eugenio Ruiz at a meeting in May 1974.[68]

But once again the trial produced a legal and political victory for the new guard. On September 20 a six-member county court jury, with County Judge Gutiérrez presiding, found the three school trustees not guilty of the charges of nepotism. During the trial Cantu asserted that he had been fired because he had suggested that school board members were guilty of nepotism. He also brought the matter to the attention of the Texas Education Agency. According to Gutiérrez, the jury heard tapes of board meetings during which Chachi Casarez acknowledged that she had voted for other board members' relatives in exchange for their votes for her brother. However, the jury refused to take her statements into account. Although it was a setback for him, Gutiérrez recalled, "I said, 'That's it, we're not going to do this again,' so they were exonerated." Like the dismissal, the verdict drew cheers from supporters of the three trustees.[69]

During the court proceedings a frustrated Gutiérrez had sent a letter to County District Clerk Rosa Mata, an anti-Gutierrista, demanding her resignation. In the letter dated September 3 and printed verbatim the next day Gutiérrez accused Mata of bringing embarrassment to the county court. The day before the trustees' trial he had accused her of negligence because a new jury list had not been prepared, among various other complaints. Mata told the Sentinel, "He's blaming me for his inefficiencies and the inefficiencies of the County Clerk and her deputies. I don't take his orders. He's not my boss and I have no intention of resigning my office. I was elected by the people."[70] Interviewed twenty years later, Gutiérrez said, "It's not true. That's ridiculous. If I were going to retaliate in any way it would be with an employee I could fire and hire. . . . I don't know who wrote the story, but that's just crazy."[71]

On September 9 U.S. District Judge Wood ruled that his court would not hear the suit for damages until Cantu had exhausted all administrative remedies. "I don't want to referee a squabble in this party (La Raza Unida)," Wood explained. He asked for progress reports and assured Cantu's attorney, Frank Herrera Jr., that Cantu could always come back to court if he could gain no satisfaction through administrative proceedings. The school board set a community hearing on the matter for September, then rescheduled it for late October.[72]

Not to be deterred, Cantu on October 26 again filed charges of nepotism against the new guard's four school board members who had fired him. Six white jurors were impaneled and found the trustees not guilty on November 26. Gutiérrez said that he did not think any Zavala County jury would find the defendants guilty of charges of nepotism. Gutiérrez ordered the other charges of nepotism against the trustees dismissed.[73]

From late August to late October the *Sentinel* carried vivid accounts of the political machinations. In one editorial in early September Barker wrote, "Local political observers say that the split in the Raza Unida's united front is the deepest since its organization. And it's not likely to heal over as quickly and as smoothly as some of the leaders claim." He proved to be correct. Gutiérrez was quoted as pessimistically saying that RUP could lose some of its clout in Zavala County because of the split, but he added, "What the hell, we'll start all over again."[74]

The conflict continued to escalate in the courts. On September 17 the Barrio Club filed a $3 million slander suit against Gutiérrez. The suit was filed in the 38th District Court by his one-time friend and RUP local legal counsel, Jesse Gamez. The Barrioistas claimed that at a meeting held at Miguel Hidalgo Hall on August 23 Gutiérrez had claimed that the "schools were infested with drugs, that the Barrio Club sold them to the students." Furthermore, the suit claimed that the statement was made before one hundred people with the intent of injuring the plaintiffs and depriving them of their good name, thus causing them malicious harm. They claimed that they were held up to public contempt and ridicule by their neighbors, business acquaintances, and other citizens and had suffered business losses and endured great humiliation, shame, embarrassment, and mental pain and anguish, which should be compensated with a damages award of $3 million.[75] The suit apparently was nothing more than a political ploy: the Barrio Club never filed the usual motions, and the court dismissed the action.

On September 21 the rupture intensified, with CU formally splitting in two at the weekly Sunday meeting. Both factions were present and they went toe to toe. The verbal exchanges were heated and tempers flared. In a reference to the Barrioistas, the *Sentinel* editorialized that "at the crux of the contention was the expulsion of five members of the organization—Lupe Cortinas, Arturo Gonzales, Eugenio Ruiz, Ezequiel Guzman and Ramon Garza." The editorial further stated that the purge was "a little party discipline against the five" for going against CU's decision not to back Ramón Garza for chief of police.[76]

José Luis Balderas, a participant of the new guard, said that the meeting became utterly polarized after Gutiérrez said, "We are going to do what I say or I am going to take care of all of you." Balderas explained that the situation deteriorated to the point that Gutiérrez led a walkout of his supporters.[77] The result was the existence of two CUs, each with its own leadership, membership, and newspaper called *La Verdad*. The walkout by the Gutierristas so polarized the membership that reconciliation was impossible.

The Gutierristas quickly met and regrouped. They elected new temporary officers and board members. On September 28 they met again and elected the following permanent officers: Ambrosio Melendrez, president and treasurer; José Mata, vice president; Tita Marquez, secretary; Pablo Puente and Cornelio Flores, parliamentarians; David Mendoza, legal counsel. For the first time in five years Gutiérrez was not elected legal counsel.

They recruited many people to serve on the three major standing committees: politics, chaired by José Mata; fund-raising, chaired by Olivia Serna; and research, chaired by Viviana Santiago. They decided to continue the controversial income tax and collected a total of $194 from forty-four members. They approved a motion to publicize that they were the original and legitimate CU. As was customary, each elected official and administrative leader reported on the status of his or her respective sector or entity.[78]

In the weeks that followed, the Gutierrista CU initiated a major membership drive that expanded its membership base. This was important because the split had cost it members. Among the new members recruited were several high school students who belonged to MAYO. The Gutierrista CU continued the old rule that new members had to be sponsored for membership.[79] The existence of two CUs meant the end of the once monolithic political machine with its grassroots base of nearly five hundred families. Both organizations were considerably smaller and, more important, less effective.

Meanwhile, the political battle continued at other venues. The salient issues of 1975 became those ignited by the rupture. One fight was

over control of the city's urban renewal board. This battle was important to both power blocs because the winner would control substantial
resources, including the awarding of contracts and jobs. According to
Rudy Palomo, the trouble escalated when Gutiérrez, in his position as
urban renewal commissioner, tried to suspend Palomo from his job as
executive director of the Urban Renewal Agency on charges of favoritism in the issuance of urban renewal grants for new homes.[80] At a
morning meeting on September 22 Gutiérrez, Zavala County Sheriff
José Serna—who chaired the commission—and Tito Salinas voted to
suspend Palomo, who was also a key leader of the Barrio Club. Julia
Palacios De la Cruz, a secretary for the agency, was named acting director. Rudy Espinosa, a technocrat and the commission's vice chairman,
voted against the suspension; Reyes G. Cook abstained.

Although Gutiérrez won the vote on the Urban Renewal Commission, the new guard city council met that evening and reversed the
action. The council voted 3–1 to expand the size of the commission
from five to nine members. Cortinas, the leader of the Barrioistas and
a city council member, questioned Gutiérrez's appointment to the commission. He said Gutiérrez did not live within the city limits and therefore should not have voted. The new guard council voted on a motion
to remove Gutiérrez and then replaced him with Marcos Esequiel.[81]

The city council then moved expeditiously to make new appointments, naming four new urban renewal commissioners: Victor Lopez
and Juanita Santos for one-year terms and Marcela Cavazos and Manuel Costina Jr. for two-year terms. Cortinas also called, without success, for the resignation of Melendrez from the city council. The next
day, September 23, the council held a special meeting and removed
Gutierrista José D. Cuevas as mayor, replacing him with Arturo Gonzales. The vote was 3–0 because neither Melendrez nor Cuevas was present. Indicative of the new guard's confidence and power were Cortinas's comments regarding Cuevas's ouster: "The mayor we have does
not want to work with the majority of the council. In effect, we do not
have a mayor because a mayor without four votes is no good, he will
never get anything done."[82]

That evening the terms of the members of the city's Housing Commission became an issue. As with the Urban Renewal Commission, the
new guard city council, motivated by retribution, moved swiftly to
purge the Housing Commission of Gutierrista commissioners and replaced them with political allies. The dislodged commissioners, Ventura Gonzalez, Juan E. Hernandez, José Mata, and Leticia Torres, retaliated by suing the city council. The suit, which did not succeed, alleged

that their removal was illegal because the Housing Commission had no vacancies.[83]

By early October the conflicts were so intense that the technocrats, who had sided with and supported the Barrio Club, began disassociating themselves by stating publicly that they were not members of the Barrio Club. In the *Sentinel* Barker clarified their position—that opposition to Gutiérrez was broader than just the Barrio Club.[84]

Then, on October 8, came the "snake attack" on Gutiérrez. Sometime earlier the Barrio Club's *La Verdad* had published a cartoon that carried the implied threat that a snake was going to get Gutiérrez. The drawing was of a man with a snake entwined around his head. The caption read, "The End." By the time the cartoon appeared, Gutiérrez had received several threats on his life. The snake attack involved three people in a car who were circling the courthouse. They were spotted by police officers. One man, who was carrying a burlap bag, got out of the vehicle and was intercepted by an officer. In the bag the officer found a "very agitated" five-foot, seven-inch diamondback rattlesnake with its rattler cut off. Two of the three men, Santos Puente and Gilberto Gonzales, were subsequently identified and charged in county court with perpetrating a "terroristic threat." Puente was also charged with aggravated assault on a peace officer. Whether the snake was alive, dead, or just sleeping then became a matter of debate. At a CU meeting on October 12 one of the arresting officers reported that the snake was very much alive. As a result of the incident, Gutiérrez secured a gun permit and publicly stated that the next person who threatened him was "going to get killed."[85]

On same day that the officers intercepted the snake in the bag, Gutiérrez filed charges against twenty-five members of the Barrio Club. He claimed that the members had good reason to believe that an aggravated assault was about to be committed against Gutiérrez and his family. Among those arrested were Mayor Arturo Gonzales; Councilman Lupe Cortinas; schools superintendent Ignacio Mata; Rudy Palomo, former director of urban renewal; and former mayor Ramon R. "Monche" Mata. All posted the $1,000 bond set by Justice of the Peace Frank Moreno Sr. On October 17 Moreno held a hearing and dismissed the charges. Gutiérrez said he told the court that there were actually three snakes; years later he explained why he lost the case: "You know why I lost? The judge ruled it was not a loaded gun [that he had no proof]. So I lost the case."[86]

The snake incident was a perfect example of the deterioration, polarization, and the conflict that characterized the rupture. Cristal's politics had devolved into warring factions impelled not by ideology or a moral high principle but by greed, self-aggrandizement, unbridled ambition, and rising expectations. Reverend Smith's words in describing the rupture were appropriate: "Down here there are no shades of tan; everything is brown or white. Everything is terribly polarized." To him the rupture was simply "a question of who's going to call the shots."[87] The polarization and conflict between the warring CU factions escalated to the point that Gutiérrez in retaliation called for a school walkout to protest the new guard's control of the schools.

As Gutiérrez and the Barrioistas squared off in court over the snake incident, about two hundred students walked out of class on October 17. The protesting students, wearing t-shirts that bore the word *Gutierrista* and a clenched fist encircled with an ammunition belt, set up a picket line around the high school campus. They demanded the resignation of trustees Raul T. Flores, Mercedes "Chachi" Casarez, and Ramón Garza, and the firing of Superintendent Ignacio Mata. They also demanded that former superintendent Amancio Cantu be reinstated. From the school the students marched to the justice court where the hearing involving Gutiérrez and the Barrio Club was underway. Gutiérrez addressed the students and gave his support to their boycott of classes.[88]

Ten school staff members, among them Gutierristas Ambrosio Melendrez, Juan Salinas, and José D. Cuevas, echoed the students' demand for resignations of the three Barrioista trustees in a letter dated October 9. They accused three trustees of jeopardizing the district's accreditation: "We feel that your actions while serving on the school board of trustees have seriously impaired the education of the students enrolled in the Crystal City Public Schools. We have decided that unless the three of you resign from the Board of Trustees of the CCISD, very little can be done to regain the credibility of the administration, teachers, students and the community."[89]

In late October the Texas Education Agency said it had determined that sixteen teachers had improper credentials. On November 6 Texas Education Commissioner M. L. Brockette placed the Cristal schools on probation, basing his decision on an April audit by the Texas Education Agency.[90]

On October 28 the school board held a public hearing on the Cantu firing. It was chaired by new guard leader Lupe Cortinas, who was a member of the city council, a law student, and arch foe of Gutiérrez. Appearing for Cantu was attorney Frank Herrera; Jesse Gamez represented the district. The hearing required several sessions and focused on twenty-two charges leveled against Cantu. The board dropped ten of the allegations in its last session on November 12. But a week later the school board, meeting on November 19, upheld Cantu's firing on a 4–3 vote.[91]

The new guard trustees in early November retaliated for Cantu's incessant litigation by asking the Texas Rangers and FBI to investigate the possibility that Gutierrista school officials had misappropriated school district funds. More than three hundred students and three hundred parents signed a petition, drafted and circulated by students, in support of the new guard. The demands included the resignation of trustees Viviana Santiago, Abelardo Marquez, and Ernesto Olguín, allegedly because they had been absent from board meetings, had incited students to boycott classes, and might have engaged in improper activities as board members. The board voted 4–0 to seek their resignations.[92]

The remaining weeks of 1975 saw no let-up in hostilities. On November 18 council member Cortinas was stabbed twice in the back while at a bar in one of Cristal's barrios. Cortinas was treated for the wounds at the hospital and released. But no charges were filed because he refused to name his assailant. Nonetheless, Cortinas was named in an aggravated assault complaint filed in the Justice of the Peace Court on November 17 in connection with the beating of Roberto Díaz. The complaint was also filed against Juan Flores Jr. and Ezequiel de la Fuente, all members of the Barrio Club. Díaz alleged that he had been struck in the head with a tire iron, causing a deep cut that required stitches.[93]

Both factions made charges and countercharges regarding the use of violence. Barrioista Arturo Gonzales, for example, claimed in an interview with a *Sentinel* reporter that Gutiérrez had ordered some former convicts to beat up on Barrio Club members. Although the allegation was never corroborated, it was a good example of how the politics of self-destruction had deteriorated into violence. By late 1975 the political conflict had become such that knifings and fistfights between the power blocs were not uncommon.[94]

After more than four months of internecine conflict, in December the power blocs began preparing for the upcoming 1976 city and school board elections. Gutiérrez, growing pessimistic, responded to a query about the possibility of losing the local elections by saying, "Whoever wins or whoever loses is not going to change materially what we have accomplished. Chicanos are in control. I know that whoever wins it is not going back to the conditions that existed prior to 1970." Asked the same question, his nemesis, Lupe Cortinas, said, "I think that if he risks putting up a candidate against us, he's going to risk losing whatever semblance of leadership he might still hold. We have nothing to lose, not a damn thing to lose."[95] The *San Antonio Express* reported in October: "The split in the Raza Unida Party has reached the breaking point with both sides wooing outsiders to regain power." It went on to say that both sides were negotiating an alliance with the Raza Libre Party.[96]

Media Reaction to RUP's Political Rupture

The Texas media covered the political rupture avidly. They seemed to savor the fact that RUP was disintegrating. According to historian Ignacio Garcia, the coverage "thinly veil[ed] a condescending and stereotypical view that insinuated that 'envidia' [envy or jealousy] was the motivating factor behind the dispute." Garcia cites as an example a *Texas Monthly* piece by Tom Curtis that began by retelling Gutiérrez's version of the "crab syndrome": "An anglo fisherman on a coastal jetty has caught a bunch of crabs and has put them in a shallow bucket near him. When he turns his back on the bucket to return to crabbing, the people next to him cry that the catch will escape. It's okay, he reassures them. They are Mexican crabs–they'll pull each other back down." RUP, Curtis concluded, had become a "testimony to the enduring power of . . . ambition, vanity, greed and envy."[97]

The *Alice-Echo News* ran an in-depth story on the troubles in December headlined "Fight to Death Power Struggle Invades La Raza." Asked about the coverage the fireworks were attracting, Gutiérrez told the *News*, "This happens every year, no big deal. This is our sixth opponent . . . called the Barrio Club." Speaking of the upcoming local elections in April, he said, "I'm confident that the community residents are going to be able to analyze this situation correctly and recognize that these people are wrong and proceed to vote them out of office in April." He acknowledged, however, that the new guard had much more political clout than any previous opponent.[98]

The *News* story also quoted several new guard leaders. Lupe Cortinas called Gutiérrez "crazy," adding, "I think he's paranoid. He's not very stable. He may even have an inferiority complex." Arturo Gonzales added: "His attitude is that if you're not for me, you're against me." City Manager Ezequiel Guzmán, a member of the new guard, referred to how some RUP leaders compared Gutiérrez to Fidel Castro after his return from Cuba. Guzmán then qualified his assessment by saying, "That's not fair to Castro. . . . Gutiérrez is acting more like Francisco Franco (the late dictator of Spain)." Gutiérrez was somewhat facile when the reporters asked him to respond to the new guard's comments: "I don't have any army; I don't have any police; I don't have anybody in brown shirts going around beating people. . . . We expect everyone's support. If you don't support it, you're expelled. . . . That's how you keep a strong, disciplined, militant organization together and I make no apologies for that whatsoever."

Even the parishioners of the local Catholic church were not immune to the conflict. Reverend Smith told the paper how the rupture had affected his congregation: "I had people who came to Mass every Sunday: good, solid parish family people. . . . They're not coming anymore because I supported the four [new guard members on the school board] in their efforts . . . so I've taken a side."

Cristal resembled a nation torn apart by civil war or revolution. Even the local bars became segregated according to faction. One reporter interviewed a gas station attendant who complained, "Hell, I don't even know where to go to get a drink."[99] Gutiérrez's boss rule and his political machine were not the only casualties of the rupture. The biggest casualty of all was RUP's peaceful revolution.

7

The Political Decline of the
Peaceful Revolution (1976–1978)

The political rupture replaced RUP's politics of community control with a new mode of politics—the politics of self-destruction. After five years of centralized community control guided by CU's political machinery, the second phase of the Cristal experiment succumbed to internal antagonisms. For the next two years Cristal's politics was characterized by divisiveness, confrontation, and conflict. Factionalism, crass self-interest, and power struggles among the shifting and competing factions dominated Cristal's local politics. It was like a replay of the first revolt of 1963–1965. From 1976 to 1978 CU, the once invincible and omnipotent political machine, was fractionalized and transformed into two smaller competing political organizations or "mini-machines." Politically, what followed was the decline of RUP's peaceful revolution.

Cristal's Hostile Political Environment

As 1976 began, Cristal was an extremely polarized community. The two warring CUs prepared for the next major clash, the school board and city elections. The modus operandi for conducting politics in Cristal was a continuation of the politics of self-destruction, characterized by what many describe as *maldad*, greed, and blatant individual power acquisition. The pursuit of power by both factions was relentless. Community control no longer connoted participation by citizens. Increasingly, it meant control by competing elites. Consequently, citizens' political participation declined as the competing elites from both power blocs struggled for power and control. The cultural nationalism that had impelled RUP's peaceful revolution was essentially replaced with politics of the *I* and the personification of unbridled greed. This new mind-set had a deleterious effect on the capacity of both power blocs to mobilize. Neither CU commanded the hundreds of families that made up its grassroots infrastructure from 1970 to 1975. Both paid a price for their internecine political warfare—both entered a state of decline.

From its genesis in 1975 to late 1977, the politics of self-destruction produced so much hostility that some nuclear and extended families became divided.[1] The divisions were reminiscent of civil war. As a result, Gutiérrez's emphasis on the importance of family unity, which had characterized the first five years of community control, was virtually gone. Neither power bloc was open to mediation or compromise, and the conflict reached a level of physical confrontation. Political purges and back-stabbing politics became commonplace.[2] One Barrioista, Arturo Gonzales, said that between late 1975 and 1976 "it was a war, it was bad." José Mata, a Gutierrista, told of leaving a bar and encountering some Barrioistas. Without saying a word, "Bam, bam— we went at it." Both Gonzales and Rudy Palomo, also a Barrioista, alluded to several instances when people used fists instead of words as weapons for retaliation. Gutiérrez too was involved in situations that led to altercations with the Barrioistas.[3] The politics of self-destruction in Cristal increasingly resembled the personality-driven and macho politics of Mexico, where intimidation, violence, and death threats are commonplace.

The Battle of the Egos

Cristal was deeply divided. Leading the political wars were two assertive, relentless, and recalcitrant personalities, José Angel Gutiérrez and Lupe Cortinas. The press depicted Cristal's hostile political climate in quasi-military terms. Kathy Clasgow of the *Corpus Christi-Caller Times* identified the two prominent power blocs: "The Raza Unida Party in Crystal City split into two warring camps by 1975. Gutiérrez, the brilliant uncompromising ideologue, led one army. On the other side, that of equally brilliant Guadalupe Cortinas and a social organization called

El Barrio Club." The struggle between the two leaders was not so much one predicated on ideological or strategic differences. It was based, essentially, on clashing personalities and egos.[4]

The two acted as if they were two generals determined to strategically out-maneuver each other. Each controlled a different political territory or turf. As a consequence of the political rupture, Gutiérrez lost control of both the schools and the city government. His sphere of influence was reduced to the county, whereas Cortinas was successful in forging the new guard coalition that controlled Cristal's city council and school board. One paradoxical aspect of the conflict was that both power blocs claimed to be "the" RUP.[5]

My visit to Cristal in September 1975 and my follow-up research led me to conclude that beyond the previously discussed schisms and endogenous antagonisms, the power struggle between Gutiérrez and Cortinas was at the heart of the political rupture. In interviews the leadership of both power blocs made reference to the ongoing ego clashes of the Titans. This became more evident when I interviewed Gutiérrez and Cortinas. Neither had a kind word to say about the other. Cortinas, using plain language, made it clear that he did not like Gutiérrez. He perceived himself as Gutiérrez's equal in intellect and leadership capacity. Asked whether the differences between him and Gutiérrez were personal, Cortinas replied, "The personality conflict between us has always existed. It's hard to explain why we don't get along." Gutiérrez responded acrimoniously. He perceived Cortinas as arrogant, reckless, power hungry, and motivated by selfishness. Gutiérrez saw Cortinas as driven not by a commitment to help empower the people of Cristal but by a crass pursuit of the benefits, especially patronage, that control brought to him and his power base, the Barrio Club.[6]

When others from both political camps were asked what they thought was the basis of the conflict between the two, all acknowledged that the political rupture was partly the result of the intransigence of the two leaders. Palomo, a Barrioista, said, "Lupe just liked to aggravate the shit out of him." Palomo cited as an example Gutiérrez's election to county judge in 1974. One day Cortinas parked his 1954 Chevy in Gutiérrez's designated parking space. Cortinas reasoned that no county judge had an exclusive right to a parking space because it was city property.[7]

Moses Peña agreed that the differences were personal. He said Cortinas could not match Gutiérrez's charismatic personality and oratorical ability. Yet in some ways they were much alike. Peña described both as intelligent and competitive. He recalled that Cortinas once told him,

"Hey, man, nobody is better than I am." José Luis Balderas, an anti-Gutierrista, added, "José Angel and Lupe were always clashing. They had the same character—neither wanted to admit that they could be wrong."[8] Thus at the heart of the politics of self-destruction was the clash of two leaders who wanted to be Cristal's controlling boss.

The Barrio Club: Power Contender

From late 1975 to 1977 the Barrio Club was the dominant political force behind the new guard and within RUP. Formed in 1971, its initial purpose was to function as a RUP security force. Some members provided personal security for Gutiérrez. Organized as a nonprofit corporation, the Barrio Club was a by-product of RUP's peaceful revolution, reflecting RUP's emphasis on building multiple organizations that promoted "people participation." Gutiérrez noted that he was initially supportive of the Barrio Club. He and some of the Barrioista leadership, such as Rodolfo (Rudy) Palomo and Arturo Gonzales, had been friends since childhood. In fact, from April 1973 to April 1974 Palomo served as president of the school board, replacing Gutiérrez.[9] Palomo was a principal leader within CU.

Until 1974 Gutiérrez had no reason to suspect that the Barrio Club would become a Trojan horse. "I didn't see a problem with the Barrio Club organizing," Gutiérrez explained. "We had a lot of different groups, and this was just one of them. They were very defense oriented, pulling security at fund-raisers. . . . It was useful for us to have this type of group around. They saw themselves as our very own Brown Berets."[10] In fact, the Barrio Club had been a loyal supporter of RUP's peaceful revolution and had produced several major leaders.

Many people, including Barrioistas, agreed with Gutiérrez's appraisal of the Barrio Club. Yet some Barrioistas describe its general orientation as more toward self-help and community service. Arturo Gonzales explained that people in Cristal thought of the Barrio Club "in a hundred different ways." From his perspective the Barrio Club was a charitable, nonprofit organization comprised of CU members who sought to "help the needy" by raising money. Despite some attempts to project a different image, most agreed that it was essentially a tightly organized security group. Some were hypercritical of the Barrio Club's activities. Severita Lara, leader of the student walkout, said, "They were a group of men that just got together to party and drink and became political. I don't remember them doing anything good." Moses Peña described them as a "bunch of tough guys" who pushed their weight around.[11]

Regardless of how it was perceived, the Barrio Club had become increasingly political by 1975. The year before, both Cortinas and Gonzales were elected to the city council. Impelled by their rising expectations and growing appetites for power, they were instrumental in fostering some of the schisms and precipitants that led to the rupture. The club had a core of twenty-five members whose power rested on their ability to control the key political and administrative positions within the city and schools. Lacking the organized grassroots power base of the original CU, the Barrioista CU relied on bringing other disgruntled Gutierristas, such as the technocrats, into the fold. Together they forged what I described in Chapter 6 as the new guard.

Of the two wings of the new guard, the Barrio Club was the better organized and led. Barrio Club members were more knowledgeable, experienced, and better trained in the art of politics. After all, for nearly five years they had been students of the master organizer, José Angel Gutiérrez. In other words, Gutiérrez, who was perceived by some as being Machiavellian, was outfoxed by some of his pupils. The technocrats were also students of Gutiérrez. José Luis Balderas elucidated: "When José Angel said he was going to beat the hell out of us, all of us . . . and that he was going to show us . . . I was the one that said, 'Listen, José, you showed us, and you trained us too, and the one that is going to lose is you.' And he did."[12]

The technocrats were products and beneficiaries of programs that Gutiérrez designed and arranged the funding for: the Teachers Corps, the Carnegie Foundation's School Administrators Internship Program, and the Career Opportunities Program (COP). The staffs of these programs formed a powerful clique of administrators, teachers, and technicians and became an influential elite within CU. Because they lacked some of the practical political experience of the Barrioistas, they took on a supportive role, backing the Barrioistas until 1977. Thus in both cases the pupils came back to haunt their teacher. They seized power through a well-orchestrated coup d'état, displaying their political prowess. In the April 1976 local elections in Cristal they once again displayed their political acumen.

The 1976 Local Elections: The New Guard Wins

In January both RUP factions began to map out their campaigns and select their candidates. RUP's Zavala County Executive Committee was made up of both Gutierristas and new guard. Despite the bitter infighting, both claimed RUP as their political affiliation. Moreover, hard feelings did not prevent them from meeting. On January 14 the executive committee met to discuss the upcoming RUP convention in May and the strategy to be adopted by RUP's state executive committee for the Democratic primary, also scheduled for May. The race for sheriff of Zavala County drew the most attention as well as most candidates—four Mexicanos and one Anglo. With Sheriff José Serna, a member of RUP, not running for reelection, the Gutierristas made it known that they were supporting Deputy Sheriff Crispin Treviño as his replacement. The new guard countered with Ramón Garza, Cristal's chief of police.[13]

Both CUs met in convention to select their candidates. Whereas the new guard did not contest every seat open at the county level, the Gutierristas ran a candidate for every office. The new guard focused on those races that fell within the political boundaries of Cristal. Beyond the sheriff's race, the most coveted seat was that of county commissioner for Precinct 3. The Gutierristas nominated incumbent Elena Díaz. In a strategic maneuver the new guard nominated Rodolfo (Rudy) Espinosa Jr., the school district's COP director and RUP chairperson Zavala County's fifth precinct.[14]

Running unopposed were Gutierrista candidates for county attorney (Paul Avila, director of the Oficina de la Gente, the legal aid office) and school board (Richard Díaz, former tax assessor–collector). But the two factions went nose to nose for some lesser offices, such as constables and justices of the peace. The Gutierristas had more candidates running than did the new guard. Balderas explained why the new guard placed more emphasis on the city and school elections: "We didn't want to touch him [Gutiérrez] at the county level. The reason was that we as a community needed to keep control of it."[15] Balderas seemed to suggest that the new guard's power and base of support was limited to Cristal.

Control of the city council and school board was a different matter. Running on the new guard's slate for city council were Victor Lopez, deputy superintendent of the Cristal school district, and Francisco Benavides, former Gutierrista mayor and businessman. Gutiérrez attributed Benavides's defection to the new guard to anger at not being designated RUP's point man for dealings with the Mexican government. Between 1972 and 1976 Gutiérrez had sought to develop a collaborative political, economic, cultural, and educational relationship between RUP and the Mexican government. RUP's leaders and Mexican presidents Luis Echeverría Alvarez and José Lopez Pórtillo and other officials met several times. According to Gutiérrez,

Benavides got pissed off because he was not getting the limelight in our relations with Mexico. In his mind, he thought he had started all the relationship with Mexico because he had gone to Piedras Negras and talked to the local mayor there . . . supposedly who talked to the governor, who was going to talk to the president. When we went to President Echeverría in San Antonio, Benavides thought he had made it all possible. When we started going to Mexico, he never went so he got [angry]. He thought he should be going and leading the delegations. He also had some crazy ideas of how to make money in terms of economic development.[16]

The new guard, especially the Barrioistas, had learned well how to manipulate the community's anger, frustration, and restiveness. They also were effective in nurturing some of the anti-Gutierrista sentiment.

For the school board the new guard fielded José Luis Galvan, an employee of the Housing Authority; Henry Rivera, an automotive body repairman; and Palomo, executive director of the Urban Renewal Agency. All the new guard candidates worked for either the city or the schools. In an editorial in the *Sentinel* Dale Barker sarcastically described the Gutierrista candidates as "Los Angelitos" [the little angels]. The Gutierrista city council candidates were Olivia Serna, wife of outgoing county sheriff Serna, and Pablo Puente, a former city councilman. For the school board the Gutierristas ran incumbent Ernesto Olguín, former school trustee José O. Mata, and Jesús Salas.[17] Olguín was running for reelection, whereas Mata and Salas were seeking to fill the expiring terms of Ramón G. Garza and Viviana Santiago.

The city council race also drew two independent candidates: Juan Cornejo, the leader of the first revolt and a former mayor, and Roberto Díaz, a former police chief. Barker all but set up a popcorn concession, writing, "It will be interesting to see how many votes the two 'independents' will siphon off from the two factions." The candidacies of Cornejo and Díaz were significant. They represented the traditional Mexicano old guard, which was anti-Gutierrista but not supportive of the new guard. Instead, they stood in opposition to the two CU factions. But then the independent slate became a slate of one, Cornejo. In March Díaz formally withdrew from the city council race because of personal and health reasons. He said that he was not pressured to withdraw from the race.[18] Because of the lateness of his withdrawal, his name remained on the ballots, which had already been printed.

As both RUP factions organized for the April local elections, they also prepared for the RUP primary on May 1. At stake was control of RUP's county apparatus. Running for the chair of RUP in Zavala County were Benito Perez Jr. and José A. Frito Salinas. Juan Garza ran unopposed for chair of RUP's Precinct 1 in Batesville. But RUP had six other precinct chairs and all were contested: Irene Juarez and Enriqueta Palacios for Precinct 3; Alejandro Perez and Mario Barmea for Precinct 4; Isabel Valdez and Griselda Flores for Precinct 5; Ninfa Moncada and Hortencia Treviño for Precinct 6; and Pedro Contreras Jr. and Ignacio Hernandez for Precinct 7.[19]

Barker underlined the importance of the May 1 primary:

Who controls the local Raza Unida Party will be one of the big decisions facing the party's voters. . . . The Gutierrista faction has apparently lost its hold on the County Executive Committee and is running candidates in all the precincts except for No. 1. . . . Although Barrio Club members don't like for their club's name to be used as the faction which opposes the Gutiérrez group, it is the name most often used to point out the opposition. Probably because most of the anti-Gutierristas leadership comes from the ranks of the Barrio Club members.[20]

Organizing for the April 1976 local elections was relentless and confrontational. Both CUs were well versed and experienced in the art of organizing campaigns. Each sought to legitimize itself by casting aspersions on the other's candidates. In January several Barrioistas—Police Chief Ramón Garza, Chachi Casarez, and Raul T. Flores—asked Earle Caddel, the district attorney, to investigate whether the county had reimbursed Sheriff José Serna for meals never served at the county jail. It was Lupe Cortinas who publicly levied the charges against Serna, which went nowhere.[21] By February both power blocs claimed that they had the support of the majority of voters and stated publicly that they were going to be victorious. One Gutiérrez supporter claimed that the Gutierristas would sweep all the elections with at least 60 percent of the vote and predicted it would be easy.

During the rest of February and March both power blocs mounted a preelection grassroots mobilization in CU tradition. Both held rallies, town hall meetings, and fund-raisers, exercised their *La Verdad* newspapers, canvassed precincts, and distributed their campaign paraphernalia to their respective targeted voters.[22] The Gutierristas focused on the accomplishments of RUP's peaceful revolution, whereas the new guard hammered away at what its members perceived as Gutiérrez's dictatorial politics. Meanwhile, the *Sentinel* and other papers in south Texas continued to focus on the ongoing power struggle. All the activity stirred people's interest in politics, as evidenced by the absentee ballot drive. In 1976 525 voters returned absentee ballots in the school district, whereas in 1975 only 217 voters had done so.

On the Sunday before election day the two factions held competing social-political events. While the Gutierristas held a rally with free food and drinks at the county park, the new guard held a dedication ceremony for the new high school.[23]

Election day saw Cristal in a state of full mobilization. Carlos Reyes said, "The politics were hot and heavy." Using the traditional CU get-out-the-vote drive strategy that involved scores of volunteers, both worked arduously to mobilize their respective constituencies. The final showdown, however, boiled down to who was the better organized. As Reyes explained, "Both sides were well organized . . . had computerized lists, [and] winning became a game of who got to the voters first and got them to the polls."[24]

During the day Mark White, the Texas secretary of state, flew into Cristal to visit the various polling places, election personnel, and party workers stationed outside the polls to determine whether there were any voting irregularities. Most election officers were loyal to the new guard. This was a tremendous advantage, especially in counting absentee ballots and determining who was eligible to vote. With the new guard in control, the election returns were posted at the Blanca Gamez Food Store; the Gutierristas gathered at the Oasis to learn the returns. Large numbers gathered at both sites. The *Sentinel* reported that bottles and rocks were thrown at the people attending the Gutiérrez gathering.[25]

The school board and city elections were disastrous for the Gutierristas. The *Sentinel's* headline read, "Voters Reject Gutierrista Slate." The new guard's José Luis Galvan, Henry Rivera, and Rudy Palomo swept the school board races. Galvan was the top vote getter with 1,450. Rivera polled 1,444 votes, and Palomo received 1,438. Gutierristas Ernesto Olguín garnered 1,149 votes, José O. Mata, 1,139, and Jesús Salas, 1,125. The new guard also prevailed in the city elections. With two seats up for grabs Francisco Benavides won with 1,271 votes, followed by Victor Lopez with 1,231. Gutierrista candidate Olivia Serna got 1,056 and Pablo Puente, 1,042. As for the independents, Juan Cornejo received 65 votes and Roberto Díaz got 18 votes.

The total number of votes was 2,581, more than the number cast in 1975 and 1974 (2,000 and 2,400, respectively). The returns showed that the new guard candidates received a higher percentage of votes within the school district than within Cristal. There was a 300-vote, or nearly 12 percent, spread between the slates of the two power blocs. This suggests that the new guard's school board candidates were successful in garnering white support because the school district included areas outside Cristal that had large white populations. The spread for the city council race was narrower, with approximately 200 votes separating new guard member Benavides from Gutierrista Serna. Statistically, the new guard candidates produced an impressive victory over the more experienced Gutierristas.

Reaction to the election varied. At the request of the Gutierristas, Judge George Thurmond of the 63d District Court ordered the school and city ballots impounded. Richard C. Arroyo, Zavala county attorney, asked the judge to impound the ballots on the ground that election fraud had been committed. But a reexamination of the ballots did not change the outcome. In fact, Gutiérrez subsequently commented that he did not expect any further challenge to the election results. Gutiérrez attributed the loss of both the school board and city council to whites who voted for the "Barrio bunch."[26]

To Gutiérrez and the Gutierrista CU the power behind the new guard was the Barrio Club. "The Barrio Club became the last group to make up enough of a critical mass with the support of the gringos to be able to defeat us," Gutiérrez said. He added that the so-called cocos, vendidos [sellouts], and La Raza Libre (the group of anti-Gutierristas that had broken away from RUP in 1974) all were factors in the loss.[27]

Overall, the 1976 school board and city council results strengthened the control of the new guard. In both elections the Gutierristas were dealt a disastrous political defeat. The election results further solidified the power shift that had resulted from the rupture. The Barrioista faction of the new guard controlled a majority on both the school board and city council. The Gutierristas had only a tenuous control of Zavala County. Gutiérrez said that after the firing of schools superintendent Amancio Cantu (see Chapter 6) and the 1976 elections "we never again had a city manager or school superintendent."[28]

For the new guard the swearing-in of the new city and school officials was a time to demonstrate the consolidation of their power. Francisco Benavides replaced Arturo Gonzales as mayor. The position of mayor pro tem went to Gene Ruiz. Gutierristas José D. Cuevas and Ambrosio Melendrez remained on the city council as the opposition. On the school board the new guard had total control; Raul T. Flores was reappointed as president of the board.[29]

Next came the county primaries. Both contentious RUP power blocs prepared for the showdown, again in a contest of organization and strategy. Both factions stressed absentee voting. By April 21 about six hundred RUP voters had cast absentee ballots. In contrast, only eleven Democrats had done so. On April 27 Judge Jack Woodley of the 38th District Court ordered the absentee ballots impounded and placed in the Zavala County Bank. He also ruled on a request from Rodolfo (Rudy) Espinosa Jr., the new guard candidate for county commissioner for Precinct 3, to impound the election ballots. Espinosa alleged a number of violations of the Texas Election Code: electioneering near polling places, people marking ballots for voters, candidates helping voters, and so on.[30]

Then the new guard candidate for the RUP nomination for county sheriff, Ramón Garza, filed suit in 38th District Court, challenging the eligibility of his opponent, Crispin Treviño. Garza petitioned for a temporary restraining order and a permanent injunction against Treviño and Manuel Cortinas Jr. as county chair of RUP. Garza claimed that Treviño's permanent residence was in Pearsall in Frio County and that he maintained a temporary residence in Batesville. Judge Woodley did not grant the restraining order but agreed to hear the case on May 7.[31]

The RUP primary held on May 1 produced surprising results. In a come-from-behind victory the Gutierristas defeated the confident new guard. Barker wrote, "The Gutierrista faction of the Raza Unida Party dominated their primary election in a show of strength that surprised many voters who had aligned with the anti-Gutierristas to win both the city council and school board races last month."[32]

Gutierrista Treviño won the nomination for sheriff, receiving 1,254 votes to 1,071 for new guard candidate Garza. But Treviño still had to prevail in the suit brought by Garza before Treviño could plan his fall campaign. Espinosa, of the new guard, lost by 9 votes to incumbent Gutierrista Elena Díaz for the RUP nomination for county commissioner of Precinct 3. Espinosa received 360 votes to Díaz's 369. Lupe Cortinas of the new guard, who was the absentee vote judge, reported that Espinosa got 128 votes to Díaz's 227 absentee votes, for a combined total of 356 votes.[33]

The reinvigorated Gutierristas in control of RUP's Zavala County structure held a countywide convention in Cristal on May 8. Sixty-five delegates attended. Gutiérrez was elected permanent convention chair and Carmen Flores permanent secretary. Delegates elected to represent Zavala County at the RUP state convention in September were Gutiérrez, José O. Mata, RUP County Chair Tito Salinas, Mario Bermes, Jesús Salas, and Francisco Prado.[34]

The Garza and Espinosa suits were not settled until June. On June 14 Judge Woodley ruled in favor of Crispin Treviño, declaring him a resident of Zavala County and entitled to be on the November ballot.[35] The Gutierristas also prevailed in the suit brought by Espinosa.

The defeat of the new guard in court served to further the politics of self-destruction. In September Raul T. Flores, the new guard school board president and president of the anti-Gutierrista CU, announced a write-in campaign for county commissioner of Precinct 3 by attorney Jesse Gamez, who was now a municipal judge. Their rationale for staging the write-in campaign was utter rejection of what they saw as Gutiérrez's dictatorship. "The reason we are going to launch a write-in campaign is because the people need an alternative to one-man rule," Flores said.

The new guard tried to use the indictment of former RUP gubernatorial candidate Ramsey Muñiz on drug charges to discredit the Gutierristas. Muñiz was indicted in September by a federal grand jury in Nueces County on charges of conspiring to smuggle and distribute six thousand pounds of marijuana. Muñiz was a good friend and supporter of Gutiérrez's, and the new guard had a field day. Flores pointed out that Muñiz had paid a campaign visit to Cristal in support of Elena Díaz.[36] The irony was that in 1972 and 1974, when Muñiz ran for governor, Flores and other new guard members were ardent supporters of his.

On election day Jesse Gamez, the new guard candidate for commissioner, purchased a quarter-page ad in the *Sentinel*. It showed a sample ballot and exhorted voters to write in his name. The Barrioistas also made a strong get-out-the-vote effort. The Gutierristas likewise mobilized their supporters throughout the county. They continued to rely on the family networks, emphasizing the targeting of voters, canvassing, and poll watching, to get out the vote.

The Democrats dominated the November general elections. Zavala County Democrats came out in record numbers to sweep all four races in which they had candidates running against both RUPs. Democrat Elfego Martínez took the race for sheriff by a vote of 2,079 to Crispin Treviño's 1,425. For the position of tax assessor–collector Democrat Martha Cruz beat RUP's Richard Díaz by a vote of 2,172 to 1,313. Incumbent Democrat Felipe Torres won reelection as commissioner of Precinct 1 by a vote of 406 to 328 for RUP's Francisco Prado Jr. Incumbent Democrat Cecil Holt, constable for Precinct 2, won reelection by a vote of 503 to 375 for RUP's Ventura Gonzalez.

RUP victories were few. In a hotly contested race involving both power blocs (the Democrats did not field a candidate) the results were close. Gutierrista Elena Díaz, challenged by the Gamez write-in campaign, won by a mere 19 votes. Díaz received 376 votes to Gamez's 357. RUP's candidate for county attorney, Pablo Avila, ran unopposed, as did RUP candidates Gregoria Delgado, for justice of the peace, Precinct 1, and Guadalupe C. Mata, for constable, Precinct 1. Although the Democrats made significant inroads, Gutiérrez's RUP continued to maintain control of the Zavala County Court of Commissioners by a tenuous 3–2 margin. The Gutierristas' three votes consisted of Gutiérrez, Díaz, and Esteban Nájera. Gutierrista reaction to the election was subdued but came to life after hearing "a rousing pep talk" from Gutiérrez, where the main point was «*adelante con la Raza Unida*» [forward with RUP]. The new guard reacted by demanding a recount.

Although the results of the November elections were not devastating for either power bloc, the race foretold RUP's diminishing power base in a presidential election year. With a total of 3,600 ballots cast, the turnout was much lower than for the 1972 presidential election, which had marked the high—4,000 votes. Moreover, the margin of victory for Democrats over RUP was much wider than that secured by RUP against the Democrats during the last county election, in 1974. The impact of the election results was essentially none. However, the infighting and polarization of the two RUP power blocs continued unabated, with Gamez contesting Díaz's victory.[37]

The Gutierrista-controlled county board voted 3–2 on October 26 to present a bond issue to voters on November 20. The $500,000 bond was for the construction of a county park. In addition, it would authorize the county to levy, assess, and collect an annual property tax surcharge while the bonds were outstanding. The tax was sufficient to pay the interest on the bonds and to provide a sinking fund to redeem the bonds at maturity. The proposed park consisted of an earthen dam with a channelization system to create a fifteen-hundred-acre lake in the Bayouque area of the county. Democratic commissioner Frank Guerrero Jr. opposed the bond on the ground that financing it would require a 29 percent increase in property assessments over the three-year period.[38]

Both the Raza Unida Party and the Democratic Party mobilized their forces for the bond referendum. The Democrats used ads in the *Sentinel* and campaign literature to argue that the county would not be able to handle its finances or operate within its budget, yet it still wanted to saddle taxpayers with an additional million-dollar debt. Before the referendum District Court Judge Woodley signed an order impounding the bond ballots. Badly divided, RUP lost the referendum. Of the 2,266 votes cast, 1,484 were against it and 782 for it. The *Sentinel*'s publisher wrote: "The vote against the bonds was another defeat for the Gutierrista bloc which rallies around County Judge José Angel Gutiérrez. Candidates backed by the group have been defeated by the opposition's candidates at all elections held this year."[39]

Barker was incorrect. The Gutierristas had just won some county seats in the November elections that gave them continued control of the county board. This was typical of the *Sentinel*'s biased and anti-Gutierrista editorial slant.

Salient City-County Issues of 1976

While the elections dominated Zavala County and Cristal's politics, some city and countywide issues surfaced in 1976. One was a libel suit filed at the 38th District Court on March 1 by Lupe Cortinas, then a member of the Cristal city council and the Barrioista leader. The defendants included José Angel Gutiérrez, Luz Gutiérrez, Virginia Musquiz, and Leticia Torres. Cortinas alleged that Gutiérrez was the owner of the RUP newspaper *La Verdad* and that the other three defendants were its editors. In his petition Cortinas stated that on or about February 7 *La Verdad* carried an article accusing him of misappropriation of public funds and of making illegal bank loans. Cortinas further alleged that the defendants, after publishing the statements, republished and repeated them when talking to individuals. Cortinas asked for a judgment of $750,000.[40] The suit, which Cortinas did not pursue, was one of many to come against Gutiérrez. The suits were politically motivated and designed to irritate and pressure Gutiérrez while keeping him on the defensive. Most were dismissed or languished for lack of follow-through by the plaintiffs.

Meanwhile, Ramsey Muñiz's indictment on drug charges continued to affect the Gutierristas in Cristal and RUP statewide. The new guard continued to try to use the Muñiz indictment against Gutiérrez locally. But statewide the impact was devastating. Alberto Luera, former state president of the Mexican American Youth Organization (MAYO) and RUP's state secretary, said, "When they busted Ramsey and put him in jail, the party was done in."[41] Muñiz and his brother Roberto, who was also arrested, had pleaded not guilty; both were released on a $75,000 bond. In November Ramsey Muñiz failed to show up for a docket call in U.S. District Court in Corpus Christi. Consequently, on Christmas Day Muñiz was rearrested by Mexican authorities in the border town of Reynosa and subsequently extradited to Corpus Christi.[42]

Neither the power struggle with the Barrioistas nor Muñiz's arrest deterred Gutiérrez from his dealings with Mexico. That September he headed a delegation of Mexicanos and met with Mexico's president, Luis Echeverría Alvarez.[43] From 1972 through 1978 Gutiérrez, under the guise of RUP, met several times with Mexico's presidents Echeverría Alvarez and Lopez Pórtillo and other government officials. His visits, particularly during the years of the politics of self-destruction (1976–1977), were significant because he and RUP were in political decline. A key reason for Gutiérrez's success had been the assistance and support he received from Mexican sociologist Jorge Bustamante, who was well connected with Mexico's PRI, the ruling party.

Then, in September, Texas governor Dolph Briscoe, while attending a state Democratic Party convention in Fort Worth, blasted the Gutier-rista-controlled Zavala County Economic Development Corporation (ZCEDC). ZCEDC focused on developing agricultural ventures; improving residents' technical and vocational skills; providing access to capital and technical assistance; and creating a viable, self-sufficient community development corporation that would benefit the people it served (see Chapter 9 for further details). Briscoe blasted the Ford administration for giving ZCEDC $1.5 million to establish a farm cooperative in Zavala County; according to Briscoe, the funding meant the establishment of a little Cuba in south Texas. A few days later Texas's attorney general, John Hill, sought a temporary injunction against a federal agency, the Community Services Administration (CSA), to stop the $1.5 million grant to ZCEDC to develop a farm cooperative.[44]

However, in an ironic turnaround the new guard–controlled city council sided with the Gutierristas against Briscoe's vicious attacks on ZCEDC. In a gesture of symbolic solidarity the city council passed a resolution calling upon Briscoe to apologize for the "little Cuba" remarks. Although the fighting between the two factions continued, both recognized the importance of securing ZCEDC's funding. By December Briscoe had managed to turn the issue into a personal political crusade by demanding that the Ford administration cut the grant.[45]

While Gutiérrez was under attack by Briscoe, the new guard–controlled city council dealt with several important local issues in 1976. That year the city's battles with Lo Vaca, the local natural gas supplier, became more acute. While the issue was in litigation, the city remained adamant in its refusal to make payment to Lo Vaca at what city officials considered usurious rates for natural gas (see Chapter 9). Furthermore, as in previous years, the council was preoccupied with issues that related to the budget, urban renewal, housing authority, new city council appointments, and utilities. In May the council rejected the proposed budget after inaccuracies in the general fund salary schedule came to light. The budget was not approved until June, when the council also delayed a pay raise for administrative employees that was scheduled for September and approved the monthly bills and monthly tax report. At the July council meeting Rudy Palomo, the urban renewal director, reported the construction of ten homes in the barrios of Mexico Chico and Mexico Grande. Reynaldo Mendoza, director of the Housing Authority, reported that there were rumors that some people living in the Housing Authority units had homes of their own. In September the council named Blanca Gamez to serve out the city council term of Gene Ruiz, who resigned because he was moving out of Cristal. She became the first woman to serve on the city council and was appointed mayor pro tem. That same month the council rejected a proposed rate increase by Central Power & Light Co.[46]

County government faced several important issues in 1976. The Gutierrista-controlled county board approved a 10 percent wage increase for county employees at its January 12 meeting. This was the second pay raise, as the board had increased salaries by 20 percent in January 1975. The board also approved the purchase of a fire truck for the Zavala County Volunteer Fire Department. In July the board pushed for a $900,000 county budget for fiscal year 1976–1977, the highest in county history, with an increase of $361,099 over the 1974–1975 figure of $496,234. The budget was finally approved at $672,090. By October, however, the board found itself in a financial crisis because the county did not have enough money to meet its payroll, even though it had borrowed $275,000 from the Zavala County Bank in September. The financial crisis was partially resolved when the county managed to meet payroll, but doing so forced the county to overdraw its general account by $5,000 to $6,000.[47]

The 1977 Cristal Local Elections

The 1977 school board and city council elections promised to once again be struggles for control. The new guard, still led by the Barrioistas, continued to control both the city council and school board, while the Gutierristas maintained a tenuous control of the county commissioners' court. As election activity got underway in January, the first to file were the new guard's candidates for city council, Ramon "Monche" Mata, Blanca Gamez, and Rudy Espinosa Mata had served as council member (1973–1974) and mayor from 1974 to 1975, when his term expired. Gamez, appointed to the council in 1976, sought her first elected term. Espinosa, a school administrator, had been an unsuccessful primary candidate for county commissioner in 1976. The new guard's two candidates for school board were Ramón Garza, Cristal's chief of police, and Jesse Gamez, municipal judge of Cristal and the unsuccessful write-in candidate for county commissioner in 1976. The new guard continued RUP's practice of recycling candidates who already held elective office or who had once done so. Consequently, it was drawing from a small elite pool. Both new guard slates had the support of the new guard CU headed by José Luis Balderas.[48]

Somewhat unusual was that the Gutierristas did not form their slates until February 22. Until then, the only Gutierrista candidate to file for any race was José D. Cuevas, who filed for reelection to the city council. However, by the early March deadline Hilario B. Lozano and Olivia Serna had joined Cuevas as part of the Gutierrista city council slate. The Gutierrista school board slate included Victor Castillo and Juan Guzmán. All five had the backing of the Gutierrista CU headed by José O. Mata.[49]

The election did not galvanize the same level of interest or participation as had the 1976 election. Both fragmented political machines sought to mobilize their forces. The intensity of the power struggle remained but not the community's political involvement or voting participation. Thus the politics of self-destruction appeared to have led to the cancerous growth of political alienation. For the first time the Gutierristas purchased a quarter-page ad in the *Sentinel*, an unusual move because the *Sentinel* had been Gutiérrez's media nemesis. The ad included sample ballots with Xs marking the Gutierrista candidates for the school board and city council. The message for the city council race was traditional: "Vote Saturday, April 2, for the City Council Candidates who are for progress, economic development, cleaner streets and parks, ambulance service, business expansion and the overall well being of our community." It reminded voters that the Gutierrista-directed peaceful revolution had brought many progressive changes to the community. The ad for the school board race stressed that a vote for Victor Castillo and Juan Guzmán was a vote for progress, better schools, better transportation, and a progressive curriculum.[50]

What once was an assertive, very Mexicano, nationalist message to Mexicano voters had mellowed and become more accommodating in tone. The change accommodated changing circumstances not only in Cristal but within the remnants of the moribund Chicano Movement. The new guard too had bought ad space in the *Sentinel*, showing sample ballots and urging voters to select the new guard slate but with no other message.[51]

Although the election was really a contest for control between the Gutierristas and new guard, a third faction, La Raza Libre, briefly re-emerged during this election. In "An Open Letter to Voters from Organizacion Raza Libre," written in English and Spanish and published in the *Sentinel*, Roberto Cornejo, president of the group, explained why it did not field candidates: "Ciudadanos Unidos, under the chairmanship of José Luis Balderas and other persons, had promised us a coalition for the coming elections on April 2, but at the last minute left us out of such slate. All this was due to the simple fact that they never had the intentions of complying on anything that we had agreed upon."[52]

Apparently, the new guard's leadership had learned well its lessons on the use of Machiavellian politics. Although the new guard gave La

Raza Libre the impression that its candidates would be part of the new guard slate, the new guard never had any intention of including them. This allowed the new guard to keep La Raza Libre members off the ballot, leaving it or any other faction few options but to support the new guard ticket. Both CUs held preelection rallies, canvassed house to house, and designated poll watchers, but neither possessed a strong grassroots capability comparable to that of the once unified CU.

The election produced no power realignment. The new guard kept control of both the city council and school board. The *Sentinel* headline trumpeted "Anti-Gutierristas Keep Control." Blanca Gamez was the top vote getter for the city council with 1,206, followed by Rodolfo Espinosa Jr. with 1,198, and Ramon "Monche" Mata with 1,140. Gutierrista Olivia Serna received 1,124 votes. José D. Cuevas, who lost his bid for reelection, got 1,121, and Hilario B. Lozano garnered 1,102 votes. The school board race was similarly close. New guard candidates Jesse Gamez and Ramón Garza won, with 1,238 and 1,126 votes, respectively. Gutierristas Victor Castillo and Juan Guzmán received 1,107 votes and 1,089, respectively. In what was becoming a postelection tradition, visiting district court judge Jim Weatherby ordered that the ballots for both elections be impounded.

The margins of victory were smaller than in 1976. Only about 130 votes separated the two slates for the school board. The city council race was even tighter. Top vote getter Blanca Gamez received 1,206 votes to Olivia Serna's 1,124, a margin of only 82 votes.[53] Although the school district continued to have more registered voters than Cristal, the turnout for the school board election was only 29 votes higher than for the city council races. The usual difference was 200 to 300 voters. A voter who had been a Gutierrista explained that citizens were tuning out Cristal's feuding politics.[54]

1977 Salient City-County Issues

While the politics of self-destruction remained the dominant focus in 1977, several other important issues emerged at the city and county levels that further fractionalized the power blocs, especially within the new guard coalition. The Cristal city council was preoccupied with the Lo Vaca natural gas supply, which led to a major energy crisis for the people of Cristal. In addition, the city early in the year focused on improving its infrastructure and securing additional funding. In January the city council received a federal grant for $764,359 from the Economic Development Administration of the U.S. Department of Commerce for the improvement of Cristal's sewer system. During February a rumor circulated that Gutiérrez was contemplating a run for Congress on the RUP ticket in 1978. Gutiérrez later denied the rumor and said that several people had approached him about running. In March RUP announced it was preparing to file a lawsuit against Governor Dolph Briscoe, Attorney General John Hill, and several state and federal agencies (the FBI and CIA). Gutiérrez explained that the suit would be based on a "compilation of incidents"—from Briscoe's sabotage of the $1.5 million federal grant for the farm cooperative to surveillance of RUP by the FBI and CIA. That month RUP leader Ramsey Muñiz was found guilty on one count of marijuana smuggling and of violating his bond provision. He was sentenced to a five-year prison term.[55]

The unholy alliance of the new guard began to unravel with the city's loss of a major federal grant. The technocrats began separating themselves from the Barrioista-led new guard and began to emerge as the more powerful faction. Differences began to develop over policy issues and administrative performance. In April the city submitted a proposal to the U.S. Department of Housing and Urban Development for its third year of funding for $674,000 to build new sewer, water, and gas lines and pave and curb some streets. It was rejected because the city's proposal was not submitted on time. Council member Rudy Espinosa, part of the new guard, strongly criticized the city's loss of funding. At a city council meeting in early May he once again went on record to publicly express his disgust over the loss. He asserted that it would not happen again and asked City Manager Ezequiel Guzmán whether he was going to resign. Guzmán told Espinosa that if he did resign, he would give fifteen days' advance notice.[56]

The loss of the grant continued to fester well into May. Mayor Francisco Benavides, Urban Renewal Director Rudy Palomo, and Housing Authority Director José Luis Balderas went to Washington, D.C., where they met with Rep. Abraham Kazen Jr. (D-Texas) and HUD officials. At a public hearing sponsored by the city council on May 20, Benavides reported that Cristal would receive only $174,000 for 1977 and would have to reapply for $500,000 in 1978. The council decided to use the $174,000 to complete the sewer project.[57] Although the city had managed to secure partial refunding, the issue became an antagonism that fostered a realignment within the governing and controlling new guard coalition.

Indicative of the emerging realignment in Cristal's local politics was the resignation of City Manager Guzmán. He resigned in June, effective July 1, and the council accepted his resignation. Guzmán had survived for almost four years as city manager. The fractionalization of the new guard became even more apparent when the Urban Renewal

Commission fired Palomo, the agency's executive director. Palomo was fired on a 6–1 vote, and the board cited a variety of administrative problems, including "causing irreparable damage to the Urban Renewal Agency and the community by losing federal funding and the failure to take necessary measures to prevent further loss of monies."

Palomo's firing also stemmed from alleged negligence to show in an audit report approximately $100,000 in expenditures not authorized by the city council. Balderas, a technocrat who had been part of the new guard as chair of the Urban Renewal Commission, presided over Barrioista Palomo's dismissal and the unanimous vote to appoint Francisco J. Martinez as acting director. Then, at a July 7 city council meeting, the Barrioista-led council voted 3–2 to appoint Palomo to the Urban Renewal Commission to replace a commissioner who had resigned.

The fissure within the new guard was also evident when Victor Lopez and Rudy Espinosa, both in the technocrat wing of the new guard, squared off at city council meetings against the Barrioistas over the appointment of Palomo to the Urban Renewal Commission. That same month Raul T. Flores, who had served for six years as assistant fiscal director of the Urban Renewal Agency, was named city manager. Flores also had served a three-year term as a school board member, including two years as its president.[58]

Although the Lo Vaca issue overshadowed almost all other city business, two new issues surfaced during the summer. The first was the city's agreement to receive $1,000 per month from the county to operate an ambulance service in the community. The second was the city council's decision at a special meeting to rescind Palomo's appointment to the Urban Renewal Commission. The council also voted to transfer administration of the community development grant from the Urban Renewal Agency to the city. This action reflected the growing schism within the ranks of the new guard and the ascendance of the technocrats over the Barrioistas.

While the power shifts were sorting themselves out, all of RUP's factions had to deal the problem of Lo Vaca, which had become a crisis of unprecedented proportions by September. After months of litigation and unsuccessful negotiations between city and Lo Vaca officials, Lo Vaca made good on its threat to shut off the gas supply to the city. The new guard put up little resistance or protest. The city council blamed Democrats for playing politics and being vindictive by making Cristal an example (they believed Briscoe and other Democrats were encouraging Lo Vaca's stance in order to sabotage the peaceful revolution). Gutiérrez was hypercritical of Lo Vaca and alleged that the company was racially motivated. In October Mayor Benavides went to Washington, D.C., at the invitation of Senator Edward Kennedy (D-Mass.) to testify before the Senate Committee on Anti-Trust Monopoly.[59] His testimony dealt with Lo Vaca.

In late October the Ku Klux Klan threatened to patrol the two-thousand-mile border from California to Texas to stop the influx of undocumented workers from Mexico. The Barrioistas, apparently not completely preoccupied with the Lo Vaca crisis and undeterred by their power deflation, took on the Klan. Mexicanos in California, led by Herman Baca from National City, pulled numerous groups together to protest the Klan's threat. In Texas the Barrio Club, led by Arturo Gonzales, set up a counterpatrol along U.S. Highway 83 and on a farm road near the Rio Grande River, using several cars and pickup trucks. The Klan never showed up, but the threat gave the Barrio Club a temporary fix of media coverage. The issue generated rhetoric and headlines for both sides. One San Antonio newspaper's headlines read "Crystal Army Can't Find KKK."[60]

In November the energy problem deteriorated to the point that, instead of natural gas, people were using expensive propane, wood stoves, and electric stoves for cooking and heating. During Thanksgiving the Gutierrista-controlled CU provided assistance to Cristal's elderly and poor. Under the leadership of José O. Mata, CU distributed electric blankets, hot plates, electric skillets, blankets, shoes, clothing, and some financial assistance.

During December the city council continued to focus its attention on the Lo Vaca crisis as the situation for the poor of Cristal worsened. Many were forced to prepare their meals outside on wood fires or propane stoves. The city council approved a resolution ordering Lo Vaca to turn the gas back on. The city also announced the expenditure of a $269,000 to pave streets in Cristal's Mexico Chico barrio. The contract went to George Ozuna and Associates of San Antonio, and work was to begin in January 1978.[61]

Zavala County also had its share of salient issues. Gutiérrez's control of t`e county board came into question with the firing of Gutierrista José O. Mata, the county road supervisor. In January the two Democratic commissioners and RUP commissioner Esteban Nájera voted to fire Mata and four other employees of the road department to save money. Opposing them were RUP commissioner Elena Díaz and Gutiérrez, the county judge. On this issue Nájera had crossed over to the Democrats, giving them a new majority, a development that was devastating for Gutiérrez. He had lost control of the county board, yet another blow to his influence and power. Worse, Nájera continued to vote generally with the Democrats. Nájera had maneuvered himself into being the swing vote on policy issues. The control of policy matters rested on the ability to negotiate with Nájera. Usually, the Democrats prevailed.

The shift became apparent during the Southwest Texas Junior College battle with the county over a tax collection dispute. The 38th District Court ordered county officials to pay disputed tax funds to the junior college. The suit stemmed from a move by the county to raise the charge to the college for collecting property taxes and delinquent taxes in the county and to drastically reduce the college tax levied in Zavala County—from 20 cents per $100 of assessed valuation to 5 cents. A second issue was the county board's unanimous vote the year before to increase the 1 percent charge to the junior college district to 45 percent for assessing and collecting the college's taxes, and to raise the charge for collecting delinquent taxes to 55 percent instead of 1 percent. The college sought to mediate the matter but failed. Under tremendous pressure the county commissioners agreed in August that the county would, under protest, collect the taxes for Zavala County's share of taxes for the junior college district. The vote was 3–2, with Gutiérrez and Díaz on the losing end.[62]

Another 1977 controversy that demonstrated the loss of control and power by the Gutierristas involved the use of a road and parcel of land next to the Nueces River. The county filed suit against Gerald Mann, an area property owner who had placed a fence and gate across the road. The county sought a temporary restraining order to prevent Mann from closing the road, an injunction ordering him to remove the fence and gate, and $50,000 in damages as well as legal fees and title to the road and the land.

In great part the flap stemmed from a dispute between Mann and RUP county officials over the ownership of the property. Mann claimed that he was the owner of the road and adjacent land. The county had long used the land as a public park and had used the road to haul gravel from the riverbed.[63] The suit, pushed by Gutiérrez, soon was the reason for a major political confrontation on the county board, with RUP commissioners squaring off against the Democratic commissioners.

Gutiérrez perceived Mann's action as a personal attack on him, RUP, and Mexicanos in general. According to Luz Gutiérrez, José Angel saw Mann's fencing of the road as an affront because the main users of the park were Mexicanos. In addition to pushing the county to file suit, Gutiérrez exercised his powers as county judge to deputize citizens and use them and county sheriff's deputies to break the lock on the gate and keep the road open. It was yet another power play, this time over who controlled access to the road and park.[64]

Ultimately, the Democratic commissioners prevailed. With Nájera's support they commanded enough votes to get the suit dropped in late June. Then they signed a five-year lease with Mann for $10 a year, subject to renewal every five years. The Democrats felt that their actions were justified because the county had been taxing the property all along, which seemed to acknowledge that the property belonged to Mann. Commissioner Guerrero could not resist a final jab at Gutiérrez, saying the county was dropping the suit because "to continue to waste taxpayers money because of selfish, capricious, egocentric attitudes is to deprive the public of many much-needed services."[65]

The decision to sign the lease was just one sign of the shift in power from RUP to the Democrats. RUP's power deflation at the county level became more apparent in the discussion of revenue sharing. The Democratic-controlled board of commissioners rejected most of Gutiérrez's funding proposals, such as the $25,000 earmarked for the Gutierrista CU for a butane gas business to provide Cristal's fuel needs and $10,000 for general support of the Zavala County Economic Development Corporation.[66]

In November Gutiérrez announced that he would seek reelection to county judge. Despite his serious political problems at home, he helped organize a national Chicano/Latino conference on immigration. Held October 28 to 30 in San Antonio, it was attended by hundreds of activists from throughout the nation. Gutiérrez and a host of other leaders called for action against President Jimmy Carter's immigration policies.[67]

1978 Local and State Elections: Year of a Temporary Détente

As the 1978 local elections approached, the various power factions began to maneuver. The politics of self-destruction continued. The difference was that instead of having two contentious power factions, Gutierristas and new guard, there were more. By 1978 the new guard, made up of the Barrio Club and the technocrats, had split, and the technocracy became the more powerful faction. The political relationship between the two was predicated on expediency and short-term returns. Going into 1975, the Barrio Club with its hard-core cadre of about twenty-five members, was better organized than the frustrated technocrats. However, with the formation of the two CUs, by 1978 the technocrats controlled the new guard CU. Moreover, the emergence of the technocrats as the more powerful faction was in part the result of the power deflation suffered by the Barrio Club in 1977. With the Barrio Club's main leader, Lupe Cortinas, away at law school, coupled with its "thug image," the technocrats in 1978 had consolidated and began to flex their political muscle. As the 1978 local elections approached, the technocrats became the main opposition to the Gutierristas.

The 1978 local elections, however, witnessed a new political power realignment that resulted in the formation of a new alliance. The tripartite coalition had no formal name (hereafter it is called the *alliance* or *CU alliance* for purposes of analysis). It opposed the Barrioistas and was comprised of the Gutierrista CU headed by Ezequiel de la Fuente; the technocratic CU led by Rudy Espinosa; and La Raza Libre, led by José Talamantez. However, the alliance did not surface publicly until late February. Before its formation, with the filing deadline just a few days away, no candidates from the various factions had filed.[68] Barker wrote of the uniqueness of the new coalition: "The alliance of the two Ciudadanos Unidos groups and the Raza Libre Organization to support a slate of candidates in the coming city council and school trustee elections is certainly a switch in the local political scene. There have been so many factions, most all spin-offs from the solid front of the early 70s, it was hard to keep up with all of them."[69]

With the emergence of the new CU alliance tensions and conflicts eased into a spirit of détente. The alliance did not mean the reinvigoration of RUP's peaceful revolution. By now the lofty idealism that had impelled the five golden years of community control had essentially been replaced by a mode of politics that stressed individual self-interest much more than community or collective self-interest. It was similar to the transitional politics of the years 1965 to 1969. Control of the spoils system per se became what Machiavelli described as the end and not the means to the pursuit of power.[70] It was not the empowerment of the people or community control that energized Cristal's politics. Despite the détente within the ranks of RUP, by 1978 the peaceful revolution in Cristal was largely history and had been replaced by a return to a more accommodationist and status quo–oriented mode of politics.

As the CU alliance sought to consolidate itself in February, it formed its slates of candidates for school board and city council. The slate for the city council consisted of Victor Lopez and Luis R. Avila. Lopez was the school district's superintendent, and Avila was a liaison officer for the school district. The school board candidates were Esmeralda R. Torres, employed by the city as an executive secretary, and José D. Cuevas, who served as acting director for the Centro de Salud, a public health clinic. Again, the candidates selected were part of the musical chair game, wherein key employees or elected officials from the city ran for the school board and vice versa. While formally introducing its candidates to the community, the CU alliance explained its reasons for forming this new coalition: "We have been made aware of the substantial hardships which our community has undergone in all efforts, due to lack of unity. . . . This year's natural gas crisis has indicated to all of us that we must unite, move ahead and implement economic strategies for our community."[71]

Opposing the CU alliance were Barrio Club–backed slates for both the school board and city council. For the school board the Barrio Club slate included Ramón Martinez and Jesús Menchaca. Incumbent mayor Francisco Benavides and Eliseo Sanchez, former chief of police, were the Barrio Club slate for city council.[72] But the Barrioistas were no match for the RUP alliance organizationally.

The three-faction CU alliance projected the semblance of a consolidated political machine. The difference was that it was a "trifurcated" machine without an omnipotent political boss in control. While Gutiérrez was still by far the most influential leader within the reinvigorated CU alliance, he shared power with others, especially Rudy Espinosa. In fact, because Gutiérrez was in and out of Cristal, it was Espinosa who provided the leadership in running both the school and city council campaigns.

Barrioista Rudy Palomo alleged that the primary reason that Espinosa broke with the Barrioistas and reconnected with Gutiérrez and the new alliance was that he wanted to be in a position to control the allocation of jobs.[73] Espinosa's campaign strategy rekindled RUP's grassroots mobilization, including several rallies, door-to-door canvassing, fund-raisers, radio spots, and the like. The Barrioistas could not match the alliance's organizational apparatus and ability to mobilize the electorate. If nothing else, the CU alliance's campaign succeeded in bringing about a transitory renaissance of political participation of RUP supporters in election activities.

The effects of the renaissance became apparent on election day. The CU alliance trumped the Barrio Club in both the city council and school board elections. The alliance put on an impressive get-out-the-drive that produced a lopsided victory. The results were so devastating for the Barrio Club that it was dead as a political force. The alliance's city council candidates won with nearly a 2–1 margin. In the city council races Victor Lopez secured 1,129 votes and Luis R. Avila 1,197, whereas Barrioista candidate Francisco Benavides received a mere 698 votes, and his running mate, Eliseo C. Sanchez Jr., got 665 votes. The results for the school board were nearly the same. Alliance candidates

José D. Cuevas and Esmeralda R. Torres won with 1,241 and 1,223 votes, respectively. Barrio Club candidates Ramón "Shaky" Martinez and Jesús Menchaca received 730 votes and 719, respectively.[74]

Separating the two slates was a 500-vote spread. The number of votes cast was smaller than in previous years. Only 1,927 people voted in the city council elections. The results for the school board election were no better, with only 1,971 votes cast. The results suggested growing voter alienation. Gutierrista José Mata explained that one reason for the dramatic decline was the community's alienation, brought about by the years of infighting and power struggles. This explanation was echoed by Barrioistas Gonzales and Palomo. The *Sentinel* reported that although voting was steady at the polling places, the lines of voters were short, and the heavy election day campaigning that had marked previous elections was missing. Barker concluded, "It was one of the quietest election days within recent years."[75]

1978 School Bond Issue Election

The next local electoral activity was a bond issue in October. The bond was for remodeling the old high school building and landscaping it. The proposed budget of $700,000 was to provide twenty-eight additional classrooms to alleviate overcrowding and provide air conditioning, new electrical systems, new plumbing, and auditorium remodeling. The alliance supported the bond. A committee for the bond referendum was formed, with Julian Moncada Jr. as its chair. The opposition to the bond consisted of whites and some old guard Mexicanos. Both sides ran aggressive campaigns, the alliance a more traditional CU grassroots campaign and the opposition one that concentrated on scare ads in the *Sentinel*. It predicted that if the bond issue passed, taxes would increase. On October 7 the voters of the school district approved the bond issue, 827–483.[76] For the CU alliance approval of the bond issue was an important victory because it showed that the coalition had popular support.

1978 Zavala County Elections

The culmination of the 1978 political year was the Zavala County and state elections. In January both the Gutierrista-controlled RUP and the Democrats began preparing for their primaries in May. The Gutierrista CU and Democratic Party Executive Committees each selected their respective slates of candidates. Ezequiel de la Fuente filed for RUP's county chair as part of a slate for the seven precinct chairs that had no opposition. The CU alliance followed past practice of vetting all nomination seekers before they filed as RUP candidates. In this case incumbent county commissioner Esteban Nájera, who filed for reelection to a second term under the aegis of RUP, did not secure the endorsement of CU and became the only candidate not sanctioned by CU. CU endorsed Alejandro Perez, a teacher in the Cristal school district. Nájera was denied the endorsement because Gutiérrez and others in CU believed he had defected to the Democrats, voting with them consistently in 1977. Withholding the CU endorsement gave Gutiérrez and CU a powerful sense of retribution for what they saw as Nájera's betrayal.[77]

The slates also reflected a realignment of loyalties among some candidates. A surprising maneuver by the Barrio Club was its decision to challenge Gutiérrez for county judge by running Arturo Gonzales as a Democrat. The Barrioistas were on their own because by late 1977 the new guard had fragmented. With few political allies left within RUP's ranks, the Barrio Club's challenge to Gutiérrez was predicated on winning new political allies. Gutiérrez was not surprised by this turn of events because, he said, the Barrioistas had been working quietly with some gringos and Mexicanos who were Democrats.[78] Gonzales's candidacy, however, was short-lived. Before the May primary he pulled out of the race. Speculation was that the Barrioistas had officially left RUP and had become Democrats. The significance of the political maneuver was that the Barrioistas' defection to the Democratic Party was no longer a rumor spread by Gutierristas.

Then RUP suffered two other major defections: Paul Avila, the county attorney, and Rosa Mata, district clerk, both filed for reelection, this time as Democrats. The May primary was uneventful. Alejandro Perez won the primary, soundly defeating Nájera's reelection bid with a vote of 401 to 191.[79] Perez now would face Democrat Matthew McHazlett in the fall.

The November elections, however, were intense. Espinosa, who had headed the CU alliance, continued to exert a dominant leadership role locally: "The way I ran the campaign was reminding them, 'Let's learn from the past, let's put things behind us, and let go and perform like we used to and win.'"[80] With the control of county government on the line, Espinosa and the alliance mounted a grassroots voter mobilization campaign. The electoral battle between the two partisan armies was reminiscent of the 1974 election, when RUP's CU machinery was intact.

On election day the alliance displayed its organizational might and efficiency by mounting an impressive grassroots get-out-the-vote campaign. Scores of volunteers canvassed the streets, ensuring that RUP voters cast their ballots. The Democrats mounted a weak voter mobilization, relying more on ads in the *Sentinel,* radio spots, and campaign literature that vehemently attacked Gutiérrez. To the Democrats the CU alliance was still an instrument controlled by Gutiérrez. Impelled by a reinvigoration of commitment to retaining control of the county, the alliance produced an impressive electoral victory. In his reelection bid Gutiérrez took 2,218 votes for county judge to Democrat Carlos Avila's 1,425. Other RUP victors included Margarita Gonzalez, district clerk; Diana Palacios Garcia, county clerk; Carmen Flores, county treasurer; and José L. Talamantez, commissioner of Precinct 2. RUP candidate Alejandro Perez edged McHazlett by one vote to become for commissioner of Precinct 4.[81]

The CU alliance secured additional victories for lesser county offices. This alliance's control proved transitory. The November election did not put an end to the political battle between the two partisan forces. Instead, it escalated. The Democrats filed requests for a recount for the two commission seats, the district clerkship, and justice of the peace for precinct 1. Meanwhile, RUP's victorious candidates sought and won a temporary restraining order from Judge Woodley to stop a recount. On November 28 Woodley dissolved the temporary restraining order, saying the court did not have the authority to maintain it.[82]

By now Lupe Cortinas, nemesis of Gutiérrez, had completed law school and had recently returned to Cristal to practice law. He represented the Democrats, who were defendants in the suit brought by the alliance. Then the county board, still controlled by Democrats, voted 3–2 to seek a recount, naming Barrio Club leader Arturo Gonzales to chair the Recount Committee.[83] The recount produced mixed results for RUP. McHazlett was declared the winner with 635 votes to Perez's 628, but that was the only race in which the outcome changed. The battle for control of the Zavala County Court of Commissioners continued relentlessly into 1979.

At the state level the Democrats soundly defeated RUP. Plagued by lack of resources, organization, infighting, and an increasingly conservative political climate, RUP gubernatorial candidate Mario Compean was defeated by Republican William Clements. Historian Ignacio Garcia writes of the devastating results: "By not receiving at least 2 percent of the vote, the party lost its ballot status and the state funds for its primary. More important, the dismal showing eliminated the party as an alternative to the Republicans and Democrats."[84] This spelled the end to the RUP third-party movement in Texas and beyond.

Other Political Issues of 1978

Although electoral politics seemed to dominate 1978, many issues were directly or indirectly tied to the elections. The Lo Vaca gas crisis continued in January to be a major concern of the city and county governments. Both governments were helping to provide residents of the county with propane and wood stoves. In the middle of that, the city council voted 3–2 to fire city manager Raul T. Flores. The vote reflected the disintegration of the new guard coalition and signaled that, at least for the time being, the Barrioistas were in control of Cristal's city politics. The motion to fire Flores was made by Ramon "Monche" Mata, a Barrioista, and seconded by Mayor Pro Tem Blanca Gamez, on the ground that Flores had played politics in dealing with the Lo Vaca issue. Council member Rudy Espinosa, part of the CU alliance, voted against the motion. Victor Lopez was not present. Flores supporters held a protest rally, and Flores responded by filing suing for reinstatement in 38th District Court. At the next city council meeting the Barrioista majority reiterated its decision to fire Flores.

Flores was not the only casualty of the disintegration of the new guard. Barrio Club leader Rudy Palomo was named city manager to replace Flores, and he fired the police chief, Ramón Garza. Palomo alleged that Garza had been fired because the city could not secure insurance for its police cars as long as Garza served as chief. The April 6 *Sentinel*, which reported on these events, did not elaborate.[85]

What followed was the end of the Barrio Club's brief control of the council. Espinosa, Lopez, and Blanca Gamez, who initially had supported the Barrioistas in the firing of City Manager Flores, called a special council session. With Gamez now siding with Espinosa and Lopez, the vote was 3–2 to override Palomo's decision to fire Garza.[86] The two no votes came from Garza's two former allies, Mayor Benavides and council member Ramón "Monche" Mata.

The election produced yet another realignment in Cristal's politics. With the CU alliance in control of both the school board and city council, it initiated a purge of Barrio Club members and sympathizers. Right after the elections in April the school board voted not to renew the contract of former superintendent Ignacio Mata, who headed one of the schools' federal programs. Moreover, the city council fired Palomo, who had been acting city manager.

By the end of April the council had rehired Flores as city manager. Once rehired, Flores promptly fired three city employees—assistant city manager Tony Jimenez; city building inspector Salvador Muñoz; and the director of the Mental Health Outreach Program, Juan Flores.

The purge continued into May with the replacement of five members of the Planning and Zoning Commission. That same month Luz Gutié- rrez, wife of José Angel Gutiérrez, got into a fistfight with Margaret Magucha Decker in the parking lot of a local supermarket; they filed assault charges against each other.[87]

The political conflict intensified at the county level too. With the November election for county and state offices taking center stage, RUP and the Democrats went at it. The differences between Gutiérrez and County Attorney Paul Avila had become personal. In February 1978 Avila had sued Gutiérrez, claiming that the county judge had "intentionally and knowingly threatened him [Avila] with imminent bodily injury." Municipal Judge Jesse Gamez (the Barrioista who once was Gutiérrez's friend) found Gutiérrez guilty and fined him $100. In April Gutiérrez appealed the ruling to the Zavala County Court. Be- cause neither he nor Avila could participate in the hearing, a special judge and prosecutor were appointed. The case was dismissed. Gutiér- rez then filed a suit seeking compensatory and punitive damages from both Paul Avila and Jesse Gamez, claiming that he (Gutiérrez) had been falsely and illegally detained and arrested.[88]

Avila promptly filed another complaint of aggravated personal in- jury against Gutiérrez in Justice of the Peace Court No. 2. The feud between the two spilled over into an open disagreement at a commis- sion meeting called to discuss the handling of a contract. On May 11 Avila filed yet another complaint against Gutiérrez, this one alleging aggravated perjury. In June Gutiérrez confronted not only Avila but the Democratic majority on the commission after the board cut the county's Child Support Program from the budget. Gutiérrez charged, "It's just cheap politics." Gutiérrez verbally attacked Avila, who worked with the unit, for not doing an adequate job of collecting sup- port payments from delinquent parents. Avila responded by saying that Gutiérrez was lying and distorting the truth.[89] At about that same time Avila dropped his suit in Justice of the Peace Court.

Joining Avila in the attack against Gutiérrez were the majority of the Democratic-controlled county commission. Gutiérrez had charged that cutting the child support unit was only the first of many moves the board would make to cut important programs. Commissioner Frank Guerrero Jr. responded, saying, "This is the judge's way to put fear into the minds of the people of Zavala County, but nobody is buying that poppycock any more." He explained that the Child Support Program was being run by Gutiérrez without authorization of the commission and claimed that the county had no written contract with the Texas Department of Human Resources for operating the program. The remaining months of 1978 saw a continuance of the conflict between Gutiérrez and Díaz against Guerrero, Torres, and RUP defector Nájera.[90]

Despite his local problems, Gutiérrez found the time and energy to continue RUP's efforts of *acercamiento* [coming together] with Mexico. In January 1978 Gutiérrez and a delegation of Mexicano leaders met with Mexico's President José Lopez Pórtillo in Mexico City. In the delegation were Eduardo Morga, national president of the League of United Latin American Citizens (LULAC); Antonio Morales, national president of the G. I. Forum; Reies López Tijerina, former leader of the Alianza Federal de Mercedes; and four others. Gutiérrez focused on the need for the Mexican government to support and defend the rights of undocumented workers in the United States, among other issues. President Lopez Pórtillo assured the delegation that Mexico would not endorse a bracero program (Mexicans working in the United States under contract to a grower) without the delegates' active participation in the negotiations.[91] Gutiérrez also came away with fifty scholarships for Mexicano students in the United States to study in Mexico.

Later that year, right after the November state and county elections, Gutiérrez and other RUP leaders met in San Antonio with Carlos Olamendi, foreign secretary for Mexico's Partido Socialista de los Trabajadores (PST, the Socialist Workers Party). In a joint statement they denounced the Immigration and Naturalization Service's plans to build fences in Texas, Arizona, and California to keep out undocumented Mexican workers. The statement also vehemently denounced the Carter administration: "RUP and PST wish to express our opposition to the unfriendly, unilateral and extortionist policies of President Jimmy Carter as demonstrated by the so-called 'Tortilla Curtain,' but what we prefer to call the 'Karter, Kastillo Kurtain' (KKK)."[92]

Supposedly, the San Antonio meeting resulted in an alliance between RUP and PST. Gutiérrez agreed to head a delegation to Mexico later that month to participate in a series of activities commemorating Solidarity Week Between Mexicanos and Chicanos in Mexico City, culminating with a visit with President Lopez Pórtillo.[93]

As 1978 came to an end, the political instability that characterized much of the postrupture years (1975–1978) persisted. The formation of the CU alliance merely brought an interlude of peaceful coexistence. Embers of discontent were ready to ignite. For Gutiérrez the political situation worsened to the degree that he no longer exerted the power he once had during the heady years of RUP's peaceful revolution. While still the most influential RUP leader in Cristal, he now had to share power with the alliance. Moreover, his Democratic adversaries had him on the defensive. The Democratic majority on the county commission refused to accept the November county election results. By December the battle for control of the county once again moved from the political arena into the courts.

The community no longer saw an organized effort to politically empower people by giving them control of their local institutions of governance. Instead, factionalism predicated on the pursuit of self-interest, greed, and control of the spoils were the driving forces of Cristal's politics. The deterioration of the peaceful revolution's politics also caused irreparable damage to the struggle for educational change.

Part Three

The Peaceful Revolution's Agenda for Change (1970–1980)

8

Revolution Through Education

During the golden years, from 1970 to the period in 1975 before the political rupture, a plethora of political, economic, and social changes were enacted as a consequence of the peaceful revolution. However, it was in education that the peaceful revolution scored its greatest triumphs. The second revolt had succeeded in taking control of the Crystal City Independent School District (CCISD) away from the white minority and giving it to the Mexicano majority. In general terms community control of Cristal's schools translated to empowerment and participation of parents; having Mexicanos as school administrators and teachers of Mexicano children; development of a curriculum and programs geared toward producing college graduates; and development of a mind-set among parents, students, administrators, teachers, and other school personnel that was predicated on Chicanismo. The five years that followed the second revolt produced the greatest educational change in the history of the Chicano Movement (CM).

Education Before the Second Revolt

RUP's educational revolution was grounded in the Winter Garden Project's efforts to decolonize the Winter Garden area, south Texas, and ultimately Aztlán. Its plan of action was largely engineered and carried out by José Angel Gutiérrez. Its foremost organizational goals were to achieve major educational change through political action and community control; bring democracy to the powerless Mexicano majority

217

by empowering it; organize Mexicanos for their decolonization; and promote the economic empowerment of Mexicanos.[1]

As previous chapters have discussed, the education agenda of the Mexican American Youth Organization (MAYO), sponsor of the Winter Garden Project, was greatly influenced by history. In writing of the educational aspects of internal colonialism sociologist Edward Murguía provides an analysis that was applicable to Cristal: "The area conquered and colonized is often rural and underdeveloped; its peasant people have few technological skills. . . . [The colonized] are not encouraged to become skilled, literate and educated because their chief benefit to the colonizers is to remain an abundant source of inexpensive labor. If they were to become literate and educated, they would rebel."[2]

Under internal colonialism educational institutions are purveyors of the colonialists' ubiquitous ideology, which controls the mental means of production and socialization. These pedagogical processes are effective instruments for controlling the colonized. Robert Blauner alludes to the colonialists' efforts to destroy the indigenous culture of the colonized and examines the colonialists' adherence to racism grounded in ethnocentrism. Pedagogically, they use segregation and a racist curriculum that is designed to denigrate and supplant the colonized culture, language, and heritage. The result is a "subsistence education" that keeps the colonized in a state of subordination, dependence, and poverty. Murguía points out that Frantz Fanon and Albert Memmi probably did not know about the plight of Mexicanos in the United States, yet their analysis of Algeria has some application to the internal colonization of Mexicanos in Aztlán, especially as it applies to education.[3]

The pertinence of the internal colonial model is evident when examining Mexicanos' educational experience in Cristal as well as throughout south Texas. Historically, Mexicanos throughout south Texas were subjected to de jure segregation from 1907 (when the school district was formed) until the 1950s. The 1954 Supreme Court decision in *Brown v. Board of Education* formally ended de jure segregation, yet segregation persisted in south Texas until the late 1960s. Despite this oppressive climate, Mexicanos managed to make some educational progress. In 1951 only 9 percent of all who entered the first grade in the Cristal school district were graduated from high school. By 1958 that figure had increased to 18 percent.[4] John Shockley provides a synopsis of the Mexicanos' educational attainment before the second revolt:

A dropout rate of over eighty percent was by national standards phenomenal, and the median increase for the population over twenty-five was such that if conditions continued at the same rate of improvement, by the turn of the century most adult Mexicans still would not have graduated from the fifth grade. The figure was made all the more outrageous to Mexicans because of their 2.3

years median compared to the Anglo median of 11.2 years. Concerning faculty change, the gradual increase in Spanish-surnamed teachers still left the faculty enormously unreflective of the composition of the student body. By the fall of 1968 eighty-seven percent of the student body were Mexican Americans. And, even as the faculty changed, all the principals remained Anglo. Thus, although there had been changes in the schools, tremendous differences between the two racial groups remained in faculty and administrative positions, in dropout rates and in Anglo domination of school board policies. These statistics seemed to reveal that a powerful barrier still existed which Mexican Americans could not cross.[5]

Before the second revolt Mexicano students were products of an imbalanced educational process. Although they comprised nearly 90 percent of the student population, they were victims of discrimination. Mexicanos were usually relegated to the lower levels of instruction. Discrimination was also evident in the schools' use of preschool testing; lack of counseling for higher education; absence of courses reflective of the Mexicano experience; tracking of Mexicano students; and the presence of ethnocentric teachers, administrators, curriculum, texts, and the like.[6]

The exclusion of Mexicano students was particularly apparent in the high school's extracurricular activities. White students dominated the football team, cheerleader squad, and band. For example, although white students were a minority, only one of the high school's four cheerleaders was Mexicana. When José Angel Gutiérrez returned to Cristal in 1969, the dialectical stage was set for the Cristal school walkout.

The First Year of RUP's Education Revolution

RUP's revolution in education did not begin with the second revolt. It began when Gutiérrez helped organize the Cristal school walkout of 1969. Gutiérrez understood that the community needed a crisis or issue if Mexicanos were to mobilize to take control of the schools. Gutiérrez used the cheerleader issue to initiate the mobilization (see Chapter 2). Student leader Severita Lara commented that some Mexicano students started questioning the education system. They asked: "'Why does it have to be that way? It shouldn't be that way.' So we started circulating a petition saying that we wanted the cheerleaders to be elected by the students. . . . They wouldn't hear of it, and that's when we started getting together."[7]

With Gutiérrez working behind the scenes, on December 9, 1969, the students unleashed Cristal's massive school walkout after months of meticulous planning, preparation, and organization. The mobilization involved hundreds of students and parents. In January 1970 they were victorious. As Herbert Hirsch and Armando Gutiérrez explain, "The victory, however, did not mean the death of the movement. . . . It had just started. José Angel Gutiérrez knew that the base to build a movement dedicated to the liberation of the Chicano people with the ultimate goal of a united movement to determine their own destiny and control their own institutions had been laid."[8]

By January the school walkout had produced a political climate that allowed Gutiérrez to take the next step—community control of the school board and city council. Control and redirection became the cardinal goals. Gutiérrez headed a slate running for the three positions on the seven-member board that fell vacant in 1970. During the campaign he did whatever he could to exacerbate the community's discontent, pointing out that the school administrators and school board were not carrying out the terms of the school walkout settlement and that they were giving in to pressures from the white community.[9] The walkout victory, coupled with the resignation of Cristal's superintendent, John Billings, did not sit well with much of the white community. Billings's resignation was effective June 30 when his contract expired.

The success of the second revolt created havoc among the white power holders, particularly as it affected the governance and control of the schools. The results of the school board election gave RUP supporters three votes, which meant that the gringos could still maintain control with the four incumbents. The critical swing vote was Eddie Treviño, who had been appointed three years earlier. He had gradually evolved into a quiet one-man opposition. In the beginning the whites perceived him as politically innocuous. Initially, Treviño thought that they were interested in helping him and the Mexicano community, but gradually he realized that they were not.[10] This became evident during the student walkout when Treviño was the only board member who voted against rejecting the students' demands. Shockley describes the political dilemma that the whites faced:

The Anglos . . . were desperately searching for a miracle, and were willing to do almost anything to keep Gutiérrez from becoming president of the school board. The board presidency was obviously the position that Gutiérrez wanted and expected, having masterminded the school strike and the spring campaign. Hoping to split the Mexican membership on the board in any way possible to prevent Gutiérrez from assuming leadership, the Anglos employed their incoming school superintendent, John Briggs, to approach Trevino about making him, rather than Gutiérrez, President of the Board with the support of the Anglos. Trevino told Briggs, however, that he was not interested in being President of the Board, and he refused to go along with this Anglo strategy.[11]

The white community's desperation continued until the meeting to swear in the board. School board meetings were usually held at the district's office, but the swearing-in was moved to the high school cafeteria because so many people planned to attend.

About 150 people were in the audience when the whites tried once more to prevent Gutiérrez from being designated board president. Using a divide-and-conquer tactic, one white board member nominated RUP trustee Mike Pérez for the board presidency. Pérez declined the nomination, saying he was not qualified for the position. He turned around and nominated Gutiérrez. The nomination was seconded by newly elected RUP trustee Arturo Gonzales. But Gutiérrez's nomination was ruled out of order on the ground that a motion was already on the floor. The board then voted on the Pérez nomination, which failed by a 4–3 vote. Gonzales then reintroduced his original motion, seconded by Pérez. Gutiérrez won the board presidency on a 4–3 vote. In both cases Treviño became the fourth vote, giving RUP the majority. The whites' efforts to divide the Mexicano majority failed and instead served to further unify them.[12]

With Gutiérrez assuming the board's presidency RUP's educational transformation began. At the swearing-in Gutiérrez described some educational changes that the district planned to carry out: "The school district would build houses for school employees . . . rent would be based on a percentage of the individual's salary. . . . School buses had to patronize all gas stations [previously all business had gone to white-owned service stations]. Employment of school personnel . . . must reflect the composition of the community which was 85 percent Chicano."[13]

The RUP majority began a purge of the district's top white administrators. The school district's attorney, R. A. Taylor, was replaced by Jesse Gamez. In executive session the board decided not to renew the contracts of thirteen teachers, including two Mexicanos. The district hired two new Mexicano teachers, Ambrosio Melendrez and Elpidio Lizcano, who by 1972 became important leaders in RUP's peaceful revolution in education. [14]

In the weeks that followed, the split school board clashed frequently. According to school board trustee Arturo Gonzales, "Anglos were on one side . . . and Chicanos were on the other." He recalled that at times tempers grew so hot that the police had to be called in to provide security. Luz Gutiérrez, wife of José Angel, elaborated on the the discord: "The key issue was the school. Before there had been a lot of emphasis on the city council. But the power . . . was in the schools. Because there was where you employed everybody. This was where all the teaching was done. . . . So that's why the school was so important."[15]

Another aspect of the conflict stemmed from RUP's efforts to democratize the school board meetings. The RUP majority encouraged citizens to participate and speak out. At the April 27 board meeting Armando Treviño, a Mexicano student, alleged that the selection process for the National Honor Society was discriminatory. A white board member objected to the allegation, saying that such a discussion was not on the agenda. Gutiérrez responded: "If there is any problem that any one student or parent has, we will always incorporate it into the agenda." For the first time in the history of the district the Mexicano community was running the schools. Dale Barker, publisher of the *Sentinel*, referred in an editorial to the community's participation: "If interest in the school board and city council sessions continues, both groups will have to look for larger meeting places."[16]

RUP's democratization efforts were in concert with Paulo Freire's postulation that authentic education is not carried on by A for B or by A about B but by A with B. He called this process *co-intentional education*.[17] Through the community's active participation the RUP-controlled board put in motion a series of major educational changes that would transform the district of Cristal from being a purveyor of maintenance of internal colonialism to one that sought the liberation of oppressed Mexicanos.

This fervor to propagate RUP's peaceful revolution in education was manifested in the board's actions to accelerate the application of the student walkout settlement agreement. Concomitantly, in April the board expressed its support for the Uvalde school boycott. The issue was whether the CISD should accept Mexicano students from Uvalde who were boycotting the schools there. The Uvalde boycott began April 14 over the all-white school board's refusal to renew a Mexicano teacher's contract. Organized by MAYO and influenced by the successful Cristal school boycott, Mexicano students drafted fourteen demands, including bilingual-bicultural education, more Mexicano teachers, and the replacement of a school principal. Because of the boycott, about five hundred students missed classes and faced the threat of failing or not graduating. The Cristal board, in a statement of solidarity, voted 4–3 to accept any Uvalde high school senior who might not graduate because of participation in the strike.[18]

Throughout the the Uvalde boycott scores of students from Cristal displayed their solidarity by actively participating in the picket lines and other protest activities. This was the precedent for using students as a rapid deployment protest force. For the next five years students from Cristal participated in numerous protest activities called by RUP's leadership. RUP's *La Verdad* wrote, "The students of Cristal support Uvalde. The Chicanos will never be those who close their eyes because of fear of the gringo."[19] Meanwhile, white board members went to court to try to stop the district's acceptance of Uvalde students. Gamez, the district's newly appointed lawyer, won the case. Although only three protesting Uvalde students enrolled in Cristal's high school, Gutiérrez and the RUP members of the school board used the Uvalde boycott to remind the people of Cristal that RUP's struggle was bigger than their school district.

With summer approaching and students out of school, the Uvalde school boycott fizzled out. By May the protest marches were sporadic and smaller, and a number of Mexicano students had returned to class. The Uvalde boycott ended in near total defeat—the district flunked all several hundred students who had participated in the strike. But Mexicanos from other neighboring districts began to seek help from RUP. Parents from the Asherton School District asked that their children be allowed to attend school in Cristal. In August the RUP majority voted to enroll thirty-nine students from Asherton, provided they supplied a driver for the bus that had been donated to the Cristal district by students at Wesleyan University in Middletown, Connecticut. Cristal's Ciudadanos Unidos (CU) organized a sixty-mile march from Asherton to Uvalde to highlight what was happening.[20]

A chief priority of the RUP-controlled school board was the removal of the "old guard." The intent was to replace Anglo and conservative Mexicano teachers and administrators with progressive, mostly Mexicano, supporters of RUP's peaceful revolution in education. To do this the school board refused to renew the contracts of some elderly teachers. This was tantamount to a purge—almost half the district's teachers, mostly white, left.[21]

Concurrently, the RUP school board embarked on an extensive teacher recruitment drive that would continue for the next five years. The board relied on myriad contacts and networks in making the "call for teachers." The white school board members became irate because the district placed some ads in ultraleft-wing newspapers and with organizations that they perceived as being radical and militant, if not subversive. One such ad appeared in the Socialist Worker Party's newspaper, the *Militant*. It read: "Chicano teachers who are interested in working in the first Chicano controlled district in Aztlán should contact José Angel Gutiérrez."[22]

In June, after an arduous search, the school board approved the hiring of seven teachers, five of whom were Mexicano. The need to recruit developed into a problem that would burden the district for years to come. Mexicano teachers willing to relocate to Cristal were few. By July the board was forced to hire Anglo teachers. Although the Anglos were politically sympathetic to RUP's peaceful revolution, they were not Mexicano. Despite the recruitment difficulties, nearly 40 percent of the faculty was Mexicano by the fall of 1970. "Many of the new teachers, both Anglo and Mexican, were quite different from their predecessors in outlook," Shockley observes drily.[23]

The RUP school board next moved aggressively to replace the white administrators with Mexicanos. For Gutiérrez this action was crucial to solidifying RUP's power and community control. However, this was easier said than done. Days before the April 1970 school board election the old board gave all the white principals and administrators a two-year contract. In late February 1970 the old school board had moved to replace John Billings as superintendent. During the school boycott gringos had criticized Billings for capitulating to the students' demands, and the old board perceived Billings as being weak. So the board hired John Briggs as assistant superintendent. Board members believed that Briggs would be willing to work with them to ward off the threat of Gutiérrez's taking over the school board. The board also fired a white junior high principal, J. F. Harbin, a target of striking students, and the principal of the high school resigned in protest.[24]

In August Briggs too fell victim to RUP's purge. Gutiérrez and other RUP board members had waited patiently for the right circumstances to oust him. Firing him was a delicate matter because the white school board had given Briggs a three-year contract in anticipation of losing the April school board election. The white board believed that any RUP victory would be transitory, so members wanted someone committed to them on board to weather the political storm. From April to June 30, 1970, Briggs served as assistant superintendent and officially became superintendent on July 1.[25]

During Briggs's brief tenure as superintendent, he sought to bring about a better working relationship among the two polarized power groups so that the district could function smoothly and effectively. He moved immediately to bring into the district a number of federally funded programs. He urged his administrators and teachers to become more involved in the community.[26]

On August 6, however, the RUP majority on the school board voted to suspend Briggs, returning him to the classroom. The vote demonstrated Gutiérrez's unwillingness to allow the white minority board members to run the district through the superintendent.[27] The firing was also motivated by RUP's cultural nationalist thrust, which required replacing white administrators with Mexicanos. RUP members felt these actions were mandatory if they were to bring about real change in education. They believed strongly that if Cristal was to be decolonized, they had to purge it of whites.

Briggs's ouster became both a political and legal issue. Politically, for the RUP board it was a difficult decision to make. In just a few months Briggs had brought the financially destitute district more than $250,000 in federal programs, hired a majority of Mexicano teachers, set up the student walkout agreement, and worked to achieve harmony among the board members.[28] Despite the extreme poverty and availability of federal resources to deal with the educational problems, earlier administrations had chosen not to go after the funding. Whereas earlier administrations were conservative and racist, Briggs's pedagogical philosophy was liberal.

That summer Briggs found himself in a power struggle. Concerned about the degree of educational change, the white school board members sought to block the changes by pressuring Briggs. Meanwhile the RUP school board majority was pressing him to accelerate the pace. Worse, the RUP board members looked on Briggs with suspicion because he was working closely with the three white board members.[29] Gutiérrez charged that Briggs was not so liberal as he appeared—Gutiérrez heard that Briggs had been keeping secret files on the four Mexicano board members and that he was seeking support for the white board members from anti-RUP Mexicanos.

The RUP board members fired Briggs in August, lodging thirty-nine complaints against him. At the top of the list were failure to carry out directives to establish a bilingual program; failure to develop a Mexicano history and culture class at the high school; interference in the politics of the board by maneuvering to deny Gutiérrez the board chair; an allegation that Briggs had tinkered with the board's minutes; and his opposition to the board's decision to hire former politician and civil rights activist Erasmo Andrade as a project director.

In late August Briggs secured a temporary restraining order and temporary injunction keeping the school board from reassigning him. However, in early September the court ruled that Briggs had not exhausted all his administrative remedies. On September 9 the school board held a public hearing. Briggs, his attorneys, and about three hundred people attended the nearly six-hour session. Briggs rejected the charges as "completely groundless," claiming "they were political and racial." The board acted on the matter by reassigning Briggs to the classroom. Briggs refused to accept his reassignment on the ground that to do so risked the appearance that he agreed with the changes to his contract. Moreover, he alleged that the reassignment would irreparably damage his reputation as an administrator. On September 14 the RUP majority board voted to dismiss him, claiming Briggs had been negligent, incompetent, and insubordinate.[30]

Briggs immediately appealed the board's decision to the Texas commissioner of education, Dr. J. W. Edgar. In December Edgar heard the case and in February 1971 ruled against the board. He held that the board had no bonafide reason to dismiss Briggs, that his contract was valid, and that he could not be legitimately reassigned. This meant that the board either had to allow Briggs to serve as superintendent or buy out his contract. The final showdown came in May 1971. The State Board of Education endorsed Edgar's ruling. Moreover, it ruled that the Cristal board had to honor the monetary terms of Briggs's contract, nearly $60,000.[31]

In response, the school district sued Briggs for refusing to accept the reassignment. Briggs counterclaimed for his salary and other costs. Ultimately, the Texas Supreme Court upheld lower court rulings by refusing to hear the case. It found no reversible error in the decisions. This meant Briggs was entitled to a $20,000 payment, because he had not found other employment. Briggs remained in Cristal and was a constant reminder of RUP's power and control. Throughout the political and legal struggle Briggs was strongly supported by whites from both within and outside Cristal. One sign of this was his legal counsel, Emerson Banack Jr., of the prestigious law firm of Foster, Lewis, Langley, Gardner and Banack of San Antonio. This was the same firm that represented several of Zavala County's large landholders in their disputes with the school district.[32]

The Briggs issue became the litmus test of RUP's power over the educational revolution. It was not, however, the only personnel issue the district confronted during the period. Mozelle Willmon, a teacher whose contract had not been renewed by the district in 1970, filed a suit seeking $200,000 in damages. This case continued well into 1971. Her suit was dismissed when the court ruled that she had not exhausted her local remedies and hearings.[33] Despite the litigation, the RUP board continued throughout 1971 with its educational transformation, especially the efforts to make the administration, teaching, and staffing predominantly Mexicano.

During August 1970 the RUP board replaced Briggs with Angel Noe González, a former employee of the Texas Education Agency. On August 6 Gutiérrez personally offered him the job of superintendent in a telephone call; after a brief discussion González agreed and arrived in Cristal the next day from Austin. (He had recently turned down another job with the district but had indicated an interest in the superintendent's job if it came open.) In an interview three years later González explained that he had decided to take the superintendent's job because he wanted to help Gutiérrez make the needed educational changes. The lead story in the *San Antonio Express* was "New Man Steps into Cristal School Hot Seat," and it carried pictures of both González and Briggs. Reporter Joy Cook wrote, "He has no contract yet, no salary guaranteed, no house for his family and that's just the start of the towering mound of problems."[34]

Reaction to González's hiring fell along racial lines. Although a number of homes, vacated by white families who had moved out of Cristal, were available for rent, the Gonzálezes, who had three children, could find no one willing to rent to them. They were compelled to live in a one-bedroom motel room for two months. Finally, they rented a house—at twice the rate charged the previous tenant.[35]

Malcolm A. Maedgen, one of the three white board members, told the *Express*, "I'm sure we are going to be in a complete state of chaos come the opening day of school." Gutiérrez was optimistic, saying that there would be problems only if people dragged their heels against the changes being made. He added, "We are going to carry out the changes that the people who are in the majority in this town expressed in supporting the school boycott in December and our election in April."[36]

In September González moved to hire ten teachers to teach kindergarten through second grade. He also hired Mexicano administrators—assistant superintendents, principals, directors of programs, band teachers, and athletics directors. And he dramatically expanded the district's staff, hiring more teachers' aides, secretaries, cafeteria workers, and other staffers. As the "browning" of school employees progressed, the white presence diminished.[37]

Gutiérrez began to use patronage as protection against the gringos' economic intimidation. When Del Monte fired Ventura Gonzalez, a member of the city council, Gutiérrez immediately hired Gonzalez to work for the school district.[38] The increase in federal funding created more jobs, and thus the use of patronage became Gutiérrez's modus operandi.

After one year of RUP's community control the figures regarding personnel were impressive: forty-one of the sixty-eight new teachers and administrators hired during the 1970–1971 school year were Mexicano. The changes in personnel suggest the effectiveness of RUP's purge. Table 8.1 shows that from 1969 to 1970 the district had twenty-four teachers' aides, thirteen of whom were white and eleven of whom

Table 8.1. Breakdown of School District Personnel by Race and Ethnicity

Personnel Category	1969–1970	1970–1971
White administrators	11	4
Chicano administrators	0	9
White teachers	91	78
Chicano teachers	27	50
[African American] teachers	0	4
White teachers' aides	13	3
Chicano teachers' aides	11	64
White cafeteria workers	12	4
Chicano cafeteria workers	4	21

Source: Adapted from John Staples Shockley, *Chicano Revolt in a Texas Town* (Notre Dame, Ind.: University of Notre Dame Press, 1974), 162.

were Mexicano. The next school year the district had sixty-seven aides—sixty-four Mexicanos and three whites. This showed Gutiérrez's incredible economic leverage to dispense jobs to the party faithful. The school board buttressed these changes in August 1970 by approving a policy that required staff members to be bilingual and bicultural. If they were not, they had to demonstrate that they were making progress toward becoming bilingual.[39]

From April through July 1970 the RUP board approved policies that affected both the administration and the curricula of the schools. Moreover, these policies reflected the board's understanding of the primary role that schools play in the political socialization of children. It moved to provide a free breakfast and lunch program and to ban military recruiters from school property, although they had always made routine recruiting stops at the high school. The board also approved a resolution opposing the Vietnam War; declared that student records were strictly confidential; made September 16, Mexican Independence Day, a school holiday; banned intelligence and English proficiency tests; adopted textbooks that described the manifold contributions of Mexicanos to U.S. society, even though the books were not "state approved"; and forbade the serving of nonunion lettuce in the cafeteria to express support for Cesar Chávez's lettuce-pickers' strike. In September the RUP board applied for federal funding for a bilingual program. That year, using local district monies, the district began a bilingual program for the first and second grades.[40]

In October 1970 some residents of German extraction made demands on the district designed to embarrass RUP. Shockley explains, "For some Anglos there was comic relief in the organization of a German American Parents Association (GAPA), modeled to ridicule the Mexican American Parents Association which had been organized in Uvalde during their unsuccessful strike." GAPA's fifteen demands were essentially the same as those presented by the Mexicano students and adopted in January by the white school board. The only difference was that they had substituted *German* for *Mexicano*. Some of the more symbolic demands were that Gutiérrez apologize for his racist remarks and resign; that the U.S. flag be displayed in every classroom; that the Pledge of Allegiance be recited every morning in classrooms; and that teachers speak English whenever they weren't speaking German.[41]

The symbolic protest was led by Gordon Erkfitz of Uvalde, president of GAPA. At a school board meeting in October the Cristal school board rejected GAPA's demands on a 4–3 vote. This orchestration of protest, although symbolic in intent, was a manifestation of an escalating racial polarization that was evident in many incidents that occurred during the 1970–1971 school year. White high school students began to withdraw from extracurricular and school-sponsored activities.[42] They dropped out of band, baton twirling, yearbook staff, and the journalism class. Some transferred to neighboring school districts. Some wealthy ranchers and farmers initiated an economic revolt that entailed not paying their school and city taxes.

The boycott carried over to the district's activities. White school board trustees and 75 percent of the retiring white teachers refused to attend the district's Superintendent Awards Banquet for retiring teachers. The white trustees also refused to attend the junior high and high school graduations. Graduating gringo seniors, as well as junior high graduates, refused to shake hands with the Mexicano trustees as they received their diplomas. When a young gringa student could not evade a board member's handshake, she made a display of wiping her hand on her gown with utter disgust, to the cheers of gringo students and parents.[43]

Polarization of the schools was an intrinsic part of Gutiérrez's strategic organizing. Well versed in Alinsky's theories of community organizing, Gutiérrez used polarization and racial conflict as tools for advancing RUP's overall peaceful revolution. Shockley addresses this point:

La Raza Unida was not interested in bringing about "harmony" in the community: they were interested in acting upon ancient grievances and in letting the Anglos know that things would never be the same again. Flaunting power and watching the "gringos" squirm was an integral part of their strategy, for it served to unite the Chicano community, to help them overcome their feelings of inferiority, and also to radicalize Mexican Americans by "exposing" the tactics Anglos would use in reaction.[44]

For Gutiérrez, making gringos squirm was integral to his decolonization strategy of "recognizing the enemy in all their involvements of policies, roles, and power manipulations." Words such as *compromise, reconciliation,* and *integration* were not in his lexicon. To use those words would be to accept the intolerable realities of the gringo colonial structure of south Texas. In order to promote his anticolonial perspective he relied from time to time on other Chicano leaders such as Cesar Chávez, who was invited to Cristal as part of the effort to validate the changes being made in education. At a rally before hundreds of parents and students in February 1971, Chávez praised RUP's peaceful revolution.[45]

The previous fall Angel Noe González had gone to Washington, D.C., on several occasions to seek out additional federal funding sources. He explained that it was difficult to get funding because programs were usually funded in the spring and not during the fall.[46] His efforts paid off. In November the district submitted a preliminary proposal for a bilingual program under Title VII, a vital component of the federal bilingual legislation enacted in 1968. The funding did not come until the 1971–1972 school year when a formal proposal was submitted, a setback that did not deter González. Using its own limited funds, the district began a bilingual program in the first and second grades.

In November 1970 José A. Cardenas, superintendent of the San Antonio Edgewood School District, offered Cristal his assistance in developing a bilingual program. The Edgewood School District sought an additional grant for its bilingual program in order to help Cristal's. Supported by the Texas Education Agency, in March 1971 the Edgewood district received a $32,000 grant from the U.S. Office of Education of the Department of Health, Education, and Welfare to begin a "satellite component" as part of the Edgewood's bilingual program.[47]

In the spring of 1971 the Cristal district applied for and received a $162,000-a-year grant for a five-year bilingual program. The grant allowed for the establishment of a bilingual curriculum center and hiring two curriculum specialists, two secretaries, eight teachers' aides, and an evaluator. By the end of the first year the Cristal district had expanded its bilingual program to include a bicultural component. The bilingual-bicultural education supplanted the old colonialist mind-set that had made the schools proponents of the elite's status quo. The bilingual-bicultural education became a powerful force in impelling RUP's agenda for change in education.

The RUP board sought other changes in the district's curriculum. The changes involved two important aspects: the extensive use of Spanish, including the local dialect, as the language of instruction and interaction, and the revitalization of Mexicano culture through a curriculum that incorporated Chicano studies (courses in culture, history, literature, regional folklore, politics, art, and so on). These changes were designed to create a "cultural renaissance." RUP's peaceful revolution, through its new curriculum, classroom and community activities, cocurricular events, and a new philosophy of bilingual-bicultural education, wanted "to create a unique 'Chicano view' of the self and society."[48]

Shockley analyzes the curriculum changes that occurred:

The school administration encouraged teachers to use new methods and new materials to reach the Chicano children and to try to stem the enormous dropout rate. Especially in civics, history, Spanish, English and journalism courses, changes were being made. Some teachers of English began to use more contemporary materials, including Chicano poetry and literature which had been written in English. The underground presses were studied and used. In journalism, questions of news slants and biases in the press were studied and explored. Spanish classes began utilizing Chicano literature and current events. History courses began emphasizing aspects of history which bore on Mexican and Anglo settlement of the Southwest. In this they emphasized aspects which had earlier been neglected such as the terms of the Treaty of Guadalupe Hidalgo in 1848 and the ways it had subsequently been violated. The focus of the agricultural program was changed from an emphasis upon such problems as cattle raising, which was useful mainly for farmers and ranchers, to questions facing migrant workers. Such problems as labor contracts, unionization and mechanization were being read about and discussed.[49]

RUP's educational changes had a positive effect on the district's other services and programs. Before the second revolt the school library had little or no literature on Mexicanos in the United States. After the second revolt, high school English teachers used *El Espego*, an anthology of Chicano writings, in their classes. During the first year the district purchased a number of books dealing with the Chicano experience, such as Rodolfo Acuña's children's books. By 1973 books like Acuña's *Occupied America*, Stan Steiner's *La Raza*, and Paulo Freire's *Pedagogy of the Oppressed* were popular among students, teachers, and administrators alike.

During the first year of community control the district instituted several new educational programs. One was Youth Tutoring Youth (YTY), which paid thirty slow learners from upper grades to tutor slow learners from lower grades. During the regular school year they worked ten hours per week. During the summer they worked thirty hours a week. The emphasis was on providing a learning experience for both tutor and tutee.[50] The district also hired a new high school counselor to guide students' career opportunities.

One priority of the RUP board was to ensure that its high school

graduates secured a college education. After a visit by members of the
National Education Task Force for La Raza in 1970, headed by director
Simon Gonzalez, the district secured outside scholarships of $3,500
each for four years at California State University at Sacramento for
master's degrees in education.[51]

The vast majority of educational programs set up in the 1970–1971
school year were products of federal funding. In the spring of 1971 the
district applied to the U.S. Office of Education for a planning grant of
$25,000 to establish the Urban Rural Program (URP). The district used
the grant to further the educational opportunities of administrators,
teachers, and staff. It provided in-service training and the opportunity
to earn credits toward a graduate degree. Most of the money paid for
professional staff training. Another grant provided money to facilitate
the integration and increase sensitivity to the problems of Mexicano
children in the school system. Erasmo Andrade, a long-time activist
and politician, was hired as its director.[52]

From the onset of the peaceful revolution in education the Cristal
school district became increasingly dependent on federal funds for
carrying out its educational programs. During the 1970–1971 school
year the district's federal funding nearly doubled, from from $417,000
to $720,000. Shortly after he took office in April 1970, Gutiérrez found
out that the white school board had returned $20,000 in unused federal
funds. He was outraged and declared, "This is tantamount to a
crime."[53] As beneficial as the federal funding was for the district, it
would become subject to the strict regulation that comes with federal
funding.

RUP's resocialization efforts to instill pride in Mexicano students
became particularly evident in the district's music program. Elpidio
Lizcano, hired as the new band director, made dramatic changes. The
high school no longer relied on the standard John Philip Sousa
marches and adopted a new repertoire that included Mexicano
marches and corridos, such as "Jalisco" as the new fight song, and "La
Marcha Zacatecas" and "Guadalajara," among others.

The changes in the music program met with resistance and criticism
from within and outside Cristal. It especially infuriated the gringos,
who alleged that such changes were un-American and symptomatic of
the peaceful revolution's radical nature. The high school band's half-
time programs were cultural and political in content and therefore created controversy. One half-time formation involved the spelling of R-
A-Z-A on the football field. While in formation, band members raised
clenched fists as their salute. (The football team also adopted the
clenched fist salute, which players would use after a successful play,

especially a touchdown.) The Mexicanos were thrilled, but the whites were furious. The half-time shows also were bilingual, which often caused altercations between Mexicanos and gringos. The noted author Calvin Trillin visited Cristal and wrote, "Of all the changes made, nothing has angered the Anglos more than the new practice of the band director announcing half-time formations at the high school football games in Spanish as well as English." With the cheerleaders and band clearly dominated by Mexicanos, football games were no longer bastions of white control. The Cristal schools were abruptly and deliberately being transformed into agents of Chicanismo.[54]

The band's supposedly radical program became a major issue in October 1971. State senator Wayne Connally gave a speech in San Antonio in which he charged that the clenched fists exhibited by Cristal's students were a "universal symbol of communism." He was also critical of the federal funding coming into Cristal to finance and support what he described as teachings of "anti-Americanism." Schools superintendent González categorically rejected Connally's characterizations. He said that the clenched fist was not a communist symbol but a sign of victory, of success, used by some American athletes. On the issue of federal funds, González said: "Federal funds are available to anyone who will fight for them, and we are working 24 hours a day to get such funds so we can cut our high drop-out rate." He claimed that RUP's educational changes had been effective in lowering the dropout rate, from 90.9 percent in 1963 to about 80 percent in less than two years. Moreover, he stressed that the school district did teach patriotism in the schools. In fact, he claimed that Cristal students said the Pledge of Allegiance more frequently than students in any other district in the state—"and we do it in two languages."[55]

The new-found pride and purpose were reflected in the community's participation at school board meetings. The board moved its meetings from the district office to the high school auditorium so that hundreds could attend. By the end of the 1970–1971 school year the RUP board had reenrolled about two hundred students who had been so alienated that they had dropped out. In less than a year the district, once a symbol of white control, was Exhibit A in RUP's plans for the rest of south Texas.[56]

By March 1971 the district was under increasing scrutiny and attack. That month Cristal's high school temporarily lost its accreditation from the Southern Association of Schools and Colleges. The loss of accreditation was attributable to the failure of Cristal's school officials to finish the required annual evaluation report. The report covered such areas as curriculum and qualifications of professional staff. The loss of accreditation meant that Cristal's graduating seniors might have some difficulty in being admitted to a college or university or participating in some programs once admitted. In addition, recruiting teachers would be more difficult.[57]

In fact, as Angel Noe González pointed out in a 1997 interview, membership in the Southern Association was purely voluntary and the only agency that could actually pull a school's accreditation was the Texas Education Agency. González charged that the action taken by the Southern Association, coming as it did a month before the school board and city elections, was purely political and designed to scare people. Although the Southern Association's action was a problem, it did not deter superintendent González from continuing to push RUP's agenda for educational change. This was especially the case in regard to recruiting more Mexicano teachers and administrators. To do that he forced the retirement of some anti-Gutierrista teachers. Moreover, before issuing contracts for 1971–1972 the school board adopted a retirement policy that mandated retirement age as sixty, with annual extensions allowed only until the age sixty-five, providing a teacher had a physician's approval. This policy affected thirteen white teachers and administrators.[58]

The district also decided to issue various types of contracts. The type of contract depended on the status of the teacher's certification from the Texas Education Agency (TEA). Ten white teachers did not receive new contracts. The reasons given for their dismissal were failure to relate to students and a lack of student discipline in the classroom. But the board could do nothing about the contracts for white administrators, who had received two-year contracts from the white-controlled board before the second revolt.[59]

The white community's response to RUP's personnel purges was immediate and dramatic. Before any formal announcement by the district regarding the Southern Association's action and just before the school board elections, the forty-five-thousand-member Texas Classroom Teachers Association (TCTA), joined by the Texas State Teachers Association (TSTA), announced that they were going to conduct an investigation of the district's firings and forced retirements of twenty-three teachers. TCTA and TSTA investigators interviewed only the affected teachers. According to Angel Noe González, the investigation was racist and politically motivated. He was not officially notified of their visit. In March the TCTA investigators submitted a negative report to their board, which voted in May to impose sanctions. Two members of TEAM (Texas for Educational Advancement of Mexican Americans) were in Cristal during the investigation and told the *Senti-*

nel for an April 1 story that González was ignored because he was Mexicano.

For the next three months a firestorm of publicity and controversy crackled around the sanctions, with charges and countercharges. The TCTA accused the Cristal school board of racism and of tolerating deplorable teaching conditions. TCTA president Oather Raynes told the *San Antonio Express*, "The teaching conditions in the schools of Crystal City are so deplorable that it is impossible for the teachers to render effective professional service."[60] As a result of the sanctions, various teacher associations blackballed the Cristal school district. They encouraged teachers in Cristal to leave the district and discouraged others from coming into the district to teach. TCTA launched a well-orchestrated campaign to discredit the school district's leadership. Texas newspapers, as well as papers elsewhere, carried stories that prominently featured TCTA's position.

The school district's response to the TCTA sanctions was both political and legal. Politically, Gutiérrez described the sanctions as a "fraud." He zealously attacked the credibility of the TCTA report, describing it as "another malicious document trying to discredit the Mexican American control of the school district.... This report plainly shows that the TCTA is for the gringo and is anti-Mexicano." Gutiérrez acknowledged that what he considered to be TCTA's "smear campaign" was going to have a negative effect on the district's efforts to recruit teachers. The RUP board retaliated legally by suing TCTA for $350,000 in damages and won. However, the court ordered TCTA to pay only $500 in damages and the district's legal fees. But with victory came defeat. The sanctions and temporary loss of Southern Association accreditation made it more difficult for the district to recruit teachers and administrators and encouraged others to join in the attack on RUP's peaceful revolution in education. How long the loss of Southern Association accreditation lasted is impossible to determine. González, whose records from that period have been lost, recalled that it lasted only a few months and never affected seniors' eligibility for college.[61]

Throughout the year RUP's board implemented its comprehensive educational change agenda on a consistent 4–3 vote. Federal and state agencies, however, became involved in monitoring the district's innovative changes. At the request of local whites the TEA investigated and found some deficiencies in the district's migrant program. In particular, it criticized the absence of the teaching of patriotism in the schools. An anonymous group called the Crystal City Citizens Committee was formed to served as a watchdog. This group wrote numerous scurrilous and deprecating letters to the editor of the *Sentinel* that were aimed at Gutiérrez and RUP's peaceful revolution. For example, one letter dated July 15 said:

> Under the "inspired" leadership of Angel Gutierrez, the trustees elected by La Raza were puppets, jumping to the strings pulled by Gutierrez. The school system deteriorated to the lowest possible depths that can be imagined. Disrespect for the American flag . . . communist publications advocating armed revolution and the overthrow of our government . . . plus civil disobedience to the laws of the land, disrespect for parents and religion—these became the important lessons to be learned in the Crystal City schools.[62]

Thus throughout RUP's first year of control of the schools, letters from irate whites and media coverage portrayed RUP as deliberately polarizing the community, especially the schools. They expressed concerns over what they perceived to be an "excessive use of power" by RUP school personnel. During the fall of 1970 officials from the Texas Education Desegregation Technical Assistance Center (TEDTAC) arrived in Cristal with the primary task of fostering integration, cultural awareness, and bringing greater unity to the community. The mission failed. TEDTAC called RUP board members "militants" who did not have the best interests of the children in mind and said the board was using the students.[63]

The next few years of RUP's peaceful revolution in education were even more intense, polarized, and change oriented. The first year of community control of the schools created the template for the myriad educational changes that would follow.

The Second Year of RUP's Education Revolution

During the spring and summer of 1971 González labored to hire more Mexicano teachers and administrators. Most of the district's professional staff had resigned. Of the 140 professional staff members, only 36 administrators and teachers returned for the 1971–1972 school year. The personnel crisis was so great that the district was left with too few school principals. Most were white, although some were Mexicano, carryovers from the earlier administrations. Amancio Cantu, who became assistant superintendent and director of Opportunities for Youth in Education (OYE, a program to combat dropping out) that year, shed some light on exodus: "During the first year [1970–1971] most of the gringo teachers stayed with us because they were thinking about winning the election in April and regain[ing] control of the school board. When that didn't happen, there was a mass exodus of teachers."[64]

In July 1971 the district found itself confronting several problems at once while still trying to recruit teachers: the TCTA sanctions and temporary loss of Southern Association accreditation. At the end of summer the district had hired only half the teachers needed to fill the positions of those who had resigned. As it had done in the past, the district advertised nationally. As RUP officials mounted their recruitment drive, the white community countered with a well-orchestrated media blitz, alleging that RUP in Cristal was racist and even communist. One letter to the editor of the *San Antonio Express* was typical:

You choose to ignore the fact that the liberals placed in the classrooms by La Raza this year circulated Communist propaganda publications advocating armed revolt against the U.S., pornographic literature among the students, and preached racism, communism, and immorality from the classroom floors until students, parents and dedicated teachers alike refused to accept it further and left the schools. The fact that your young liberals could possibly more accurately be called "young communists" and that Crystal City is being turned into a school for revolutionaries, preparing the students for their place in an armed revolt as was done in Cuba, is a racist way of thinking against an "unstoppable change." We do not believe the spread of communism is unstoppable at this point![65]

Roberto Fernandez, assistant superintendent, recalled that because of the negative publicity "it was hard to get recruits, so we really couldn't be selective." The teachers hired were mostly young, inexperienced, and lacked teaching credentials. According to Cantu, many recruits were Anglo ultraliberal hippies. Although they gave the Mexicano students a lot of love, they taught them very little. Angel Noe González recalled that the young teachers tried to preach "Viva La Raza" yet did not do a good job with basic instruction. "Some . . . came with the idea that they were coming to liberate us. They didn't last," González said. "They finally realized that we had already been liberated, that we were on top. So we ran them off."[66]

At times the young Anglo recruits were condescending to administrators. According to Fernandez, "Many of them were liberal but not liberal enough to take orders from Chicanos." Many came to Cristal wanting to experiment with their own teaching methodologies. The ragged appearance of some, with their long hair and beards, created apprehension among RUP foes and adherents alike. Some recruits indulged in continuous "partying," and their use of drugs added to the problem. Whites made the recruits an issue during the 1972 school board election. Guin Casey recalled, "The teachers that have been here, many of them, are radicals—dirty, long-haired, semi-ragged, and filthy mouthed and more. . . . Some of the group that was teaching in the schools were vocal in teaching the overthrow of the government."

Throughout the school year the press carried articles that quoted disgruntled whites who alleged that Cristal had become a sanctuary for radicals and communists. Cantu explained, "Because the gringo dished out the propaganda that Crystal City was communistic, it hindered our progress in education."[67]

Cristal's radical image led some students, mostly whites, to leave the district. In June 1971 the district received 178 applications for transfer: 144 from whites and 34 from Mexicanos. RUP school officials opposed the transfer of students to nearby districts. Assistant Superintendent Cantu, in a letter to the *Sentinel*, alluded to how the transfer violated the new state desegregation law. By September the students had transferred to schools in Carrizo Springs, Batesville, La Pryor, and Uvalde. In justifying the students' departure, Wayne Hamilton, a ranch business manager, stated, "In a town like this you can take the city and you can take the county, but when the schools go to hell, that's chaos."[68]

Yet the district eked out a symbolic political victory in the student transfers. State education commissioner Edgar instructed the affected districts that such transfers violated a federal court order stemming from a school desegregation case. In theory the students' transfers were denied. In practice, however, the ruling did not curtail the growing white exodus from Cristal. Dale Barker of the *Sentinel* reported that ninety-eight families had moved out of Cristal. To comply with the commissioner's ruling, residents of the Cristal school district erected trailer camps within the boundaries of other school districts. Mothers and children lived in the trailer camps during the week, while the fathers remained in Cristal.[69]

White parents also established a private school in Cristal under the leadership of retired Cristal superintendent R. C. Tate. The Crystal Community School welcomed whites and Mexicanos who opposed RUP's change agenda. Tate explained, "The school was established for the purpose of reintroducing the type of education and curriculum that had existed in the past. The student came here because the parents wanted more English taught." Its student enrollment was small, with approximately one hundred students attending grades one through eight. About 65 percent were white and 35 percent Mexicano.[70]

The school facilities were provided by the First Methodist and First Baptist churches. School funding was dependent on donations and tuition. Monthly tuition was $38 per student. No family paid more than $96 per month, regardless of the number of children enrolled. Of the fifteen full-time and part-time teachers, fourteen were white, one was Mexicana. The full-time teachers were paid no more than $250 per month. Most teachers were either retired or had been fired from the public school district. Santos Nieto's comment to a Corpus Christi paper was typical of Mexicanos who enrolled their children in the white private school: "I didn't like the politics going into the school."[71] His comments were representative of the feelings of conservative and middle-class Mexicanos who had sided with whites from the beginning of the RUP takeover.

In late July 1971 the district held a hearing as well as a subsequent meeting to discuss the teachers who were not rehired for the 1971–1972 school year. At the same time Superintendent González announced the existence of twenty-eight vacancies: twenty bilingual teachers, three school nurses, one librarian, three home economics teachers, and one head coach. After a difficult time recruiting for the position of head football coach, in August the district hired Gilbert Walker, a former player for the Denver Broncos.[72]

On August 30 the schools opened with an enrollment of 1,170, ninety students fewer than previous school year. In September the board approved the district's budget of $2 million, which represented an increase of about $800,000 over the 1970–1971 budget. Throughout the high school football season the Javelin Band continued to win awards, now under the direction of Roberto Botello.

In November the board unsuccessfully demanded the resignations of two white school trustees, Ed Mayer and Wayne Hamilton, on the ground that their children attended school in Uvalde.[73] After a court-mandated hearing that month the board offered a new contract to fired teacher Mozelle Willmon, who had sued the district for $200,000 in 1970.

In early December 1971 RUP school officials proposed a $2.8 million school bond issue to build a new high school and elementary school. The referendum on the bond issue coincided with the 1972 school board election and was heavily pushed by RUP's political machinery. Voters approved the bond issue 1,737–867. That same month U.S. District Judge John H. Wood Jr. dismissed the Willmon suit against the district because the plaintiff's lawyers had allowed the suit to languish.[74]

In January 1972 the district instructed its lawyer, Jesse Gamez, to seek an injunction against school trustees Hamilton and Mayer. The district sued to vacate their seats on the ground that neither lived in Cristal. Meanwhile, the Crystal Community School had extended its instruction to the ninth grade, and it continued to pull students from the public schools. It reported a 20 percent increase in enrollment. In May Jack Ware, a wealthy Zavala County landowner, filed suit the 38th District Court to contest the results of the bond referendum. He charged that the bond gained approval because unqualified voters had cast ballots.[75]

Despite a multiplicity of problems during the 1971–1972 school year, the RUP board continued to expand existing programs and create new ones. The bilingual-bicultural program continued. A new federal program, Opportunities for Youth in Education (OYE), was funded $502,413 for two years. It was designed to help students from low-income families finish high school and go on to college. It allowed the district to make curriculum changes, hire an assistant superintendent, a curriculum writer, two counselors, five teachers, and provided fifty stipends of $2,400 each to help 149 students further their education.[76] The program reflected the district's commitment to lowering student dropout rates.

The district also secured federal funds to initiate a summer program for six hundred low-income and migrant children. The program was designed to instill positive attitudes toward education. The district also received a $60,000 grant from the Texas Education Agency for testing students and providing more individualized instruction and a grant of $4,500 from the same agency for an adult education program. Evening classes offered adults the opportunity to acquire their GED (high school equivalency diploma). Another federal grant paid for in-service training for teachers on various aspects of Mexicano culture and historical experience, funding the Teacher Corps program for $365,000. A combined effort of the district and Texas A&I University at Kingsville, it allowed forty-two graduate students to work toward a master's degree in bilingual education.[77]

The turbulent school year produced positive results. During 1971–1972 the number of Mexicano teachers and administrators increased dramatically—from 41 percent in 1971 to 61 percent in 1972. Of the twenty administrative positions in the district, only one was filled by a white. By the end of the school year all the teachers were Mexicano. By 1972, 80 percent of the Mexicano students who were graduated were enrolled in college and received some type of financial assistance. But recruiting teachers continued to be a problem. The district was still hiring young inexperienced individuals, some of whom had no background in education, and some of whom were hired to teach subject areas in which they had no training. More than 40 percent held emergency teacher permits. Pressed for time, the district did not conduct careful background checks and was unaware that some new hires had drug problems.[78]

The Third Year of RUP's Education Revolution

As the RUP school board prepared for the 1972–1973 school year, so did the Crystal Community School. In June it announced that it was extending instruction to the high school level. But the private school's student population was changing dramatically. Its Mexicano student population doubled, now accounting for 70 percent of the student body. Angel Noe González explained that the dramatic shift was the result of white students transferring to neighboring school districts. The white parents felt that the education provided at Crystal Community School was inferior.[79] The loss of students translated to a loss of revenue for the private school. In July school officials announced a drive to raise $100,000 for a high school building.

On August 28 the public schools reopened with a reported shortage of fifteen teachers, an improvement over the previous year's. A record high of 1,932 students were enrolled. In September RUP school officials dedicated a new cafeteria on the high school campus. The Javelin Band continued winning award after award. In November it received a superior rating at the regional University Interscholastic League competition at Hondo. RUP school officials used the many successes of the band to promote the new agenda for education. In December the district sponsored a program to commemorate the Cristal school boycott of 1969. The program included speeches by principal Joe Talamantes and Diane Serna, a student; skits by the high school's Teatro Estudiantil de Cristal; performances by the ballet folklorico Cuadro de Danza de Cristal; corridos [songs] by various singers; and a concert by the high school stage band.[80]

RUP school officials scored a legal victory in December 1972. The lower court had dismissed rancher Jack Ware's challenge of the referendum on the school construction bond. Ware appealed, and in December the appellate court upheld the original ruling. (Ware took his appeal to the Texas Supreme Court, which ultimately rejected it.) A month later Gutiérrez, acting as an individual and as president of the school board, sued Ware in the 38th District Court seeking $450,000 in damages. Claiming "interference with contractual rights," Gutiérrez alleged that Ware, who was an attorney, had boasted that he knew that as long as litigation was pending, the attorney general of Texas could not approve the bond issue. This suit died for lack of follow-through by Gutiérrez.[81]

RUP school officials met their first major internal challenge in January 1973. Scores of Mexicano parents questioned the district's policies on bilingual education. At this time bilingual education was limited to the district's first three grades. Parents were concerned that their children were not receiving enough instruction in English. The policy of the district had been to teach students in their primary language until they could successfully make the transition to English. The Mexicano parents' protest came as the school district was seeking ways to improve and expand the nascent bilingual-bicultural program.

After several months of researching many other bilingual-bicultural programs, Superintendent González had proposed twenty-two recommendations designed to strengthen the district's program. The intent was to produce the most comprehensive and best bilingual-bicultural program in Texas, if not the nation. To defuse the growing discontent school district officials organized several town hall meetings that drew as many as six hundred parents. School officials also used the meetings to introduce the district's twenty-two recommendations for revamping the program. On February 1, despite some dissension from parents, the school board approved the recommendations, which guided development of the bilingual-bicultural program beginning with the 1973–74 school year. In essence the policy stressed

- learning, regardless of language
- oral proficiency in Spanish and English in all grades and reading proficiency in children's dominant language first before introducing them to reading in a second language
- limiting testing for verbal skills to the child's dominant language
- developing instructional materials in all subjects in Spanish and English
- developing a positive identity, self-assurance, and confidence in every child
- accepting Spanish and English on an equal basis as official languages of the district[82]

The primary long-term goal of the bilingual-bicultural program was to help students succeed in school through the use of two languages, Spanish and English, in kindergarten through twelfth grade.[83] The board saw strengthening the district's bilingual-bicultural program as paramount in the commitment to decolonize Cristal's schools and imbue students and school personnel alike with a Chicanismo mind-set. After several weeks of consultation with the community the RUP-controlled school board approved the twenty-two controversial recommendations.

The controversy over bilingual education led to the first major fissure within RUP. Although they were not successful, RUP's white and conservative Mexicano opposition sought to use the issue for political gain. Cantu described what happened: "The gringo has not blasted us as much as our own have. I am talking about the middle-class Mexicano that have gone against us [on], for example, bilingual-bicultural education. Many of them act as tape recorders for the gringos. The gringo himself doesn't come out and holler or shout at us. But they get the Mexicanos vendidos [Mexican sellouts] to do the shouting for them." González explained that "passage of the twenty-two recommendations became very controversial since at the time there was a law in Texas that prohibited teaching in any other language other than English. The idea that for teaching purposes English and Spanish were equal upset some people. Some reacted by saying publicly that we were communist for doing this."[84]

RUP school officials were embroiled in other internal and external issues. In April 1973 the district sued J. Paul Little and other white landowners in 38th District Court, seeking to collect delinquent taxes amounting to $46,650.04. These were the landowners who had refused to pay their taxes in the wake of RUP's takeover. The polarization on this issue carried over into the schools to the point that fistfights and other forms of confrontation became prevalent among students. On April 5 an altercation at the high school between pro-RUP and anti-RUP students resulted in injuries to seven students and two teachers. Over the next few days several more altercations and beatings occurred. The conflict became so acute that state and federal law enforcement officials, including Texas Ranger Joaquin Jackson of Uvalde, initiated an investigation.[85]

The violence was a product of tensions that had been building among the students. The polarization politics of their parents had carried over into the schools, especially the high school. The anti-RUP students clandestinely produced *La Mera Verdad*, a take-off on RUP's main newspaper, *La Verdad*. They alleged that Superintendent González yelled "Viva la Raza" all day and then drove home in his Cadillac at night. Another target of *La Mera Verdad* was band director Botello, who they compared to Hitler because of the band's extreme Mexicano cultural posture.[86] The tensions reached such a perilous level that rumors flew that the conflict would lead to a riot. By the end of April the student imbroglio faded, and the anticipated riot never transpired, but the polarization continued.

Pro-RUP students were expected to show their support through their presence at RUP protest activities. Students were a vital part of the party's mobilization capability. However, this did not sit well with anti-RUP students, who often felt the pressure and torment of the pro-RUP students. In May RUP school officials, as well as busloads of parents and students from Cristal, joined thousands of others from throughout Texas in a protest march in Austin. The protest was in response to the 1973 Supreme Court decision in *San Antonio Independent School District v. Rodriguez* decision that dealt with the disparity of funding levels between rich and poor school districts. The suit established that "fiscal neutrality" was not a right under the U.S. Constitution, although it might be a right under a state constitution.[87]

Despite the political difficulties, the district built up existing programs and brought in new ones. The district's Right to Read program was expanded in January 1973 with the hiring of nine more teachers. That same month the Carnegie Foundation gave the schools a $495,000 grant to fund the Carnegie Administration Internship Program, a two-year program to train Mexicano school administrators. Gutiérrez saw this as another vehicle by which to train an "administrative school cadre" that could in turn export RUP's peaceful revolution to other communities throughout Texas. The program entailed sixty-two units of coursework, an internship in Cristal, and field experience. Upon completing all the requirements, the eighteen interns would be awarded master's degrees. By October the district had secured federal funding totaling $872,485, up nearly $200,000 from 1969–1970.[88]

The RUP-controlled CISD had weathered the political storm for a third year. In late May the high school graduated 119 students, 80 percent of whom were college bound. Of the fifty who participated in the OYE program, twenty-five received grants of $2,500 for their college education. The board, having sold the $2.8 million in bonds in May, gave approval to build the new schools and remodel existing ones. As part of the district's commitment to direct community participation, school officials established fifty-seven building committees to gather ideas.[89]

The Fourth and Fifth Years

For RUP the years between 1973 and 1975 were the least politically intense. With its consolidated power base and total control of the school board, RUP witnessed continued educational change with its peaceful revolution. RUP's white and Mexicano adversaries struggled unsuccessfully to recapture control of the school board. But they were no match for Gutiérrez and the CU political machine. RUP's adversaries continued to be hypercritical of RUP's agenda for educational change. Yet, while they focused on electoral politics, they did little to stop or thwart RUP's educational policies or programs. This created a quiet period in which the level of conflict and polarization lessened.

The district continued to make positive changes. During these two

years two new schools were constructed. In August 1973 school officials selected the site for the new high school. Construction began in
October 1974. However, it was not completed until the summer of
1976. In 1975 Cantu said that because of construction delays, "We lost
about 25 to 30 percent of our buying power and now we can't finish
our high school. It's costing us $1.8 million but we don't have but $1.5
million." The construction of the Benito Juárez Elementary School went
more smoothly. Construction began in 1974 and was completed in
1975. In 1973 the district raised its tax rate to pay for building expansion. The new tax rate was $2.15 per $100 of assessed valuation, an
increase of 65 cents over the 1972 rate. The budget for 1973–1974, $3.69
million, was said to be the highest in district history. It was to be
surpassed by the 1974–1975 budget of $3.9 million. The district was
still ever dependent on federal funding, to the tune of $768,241 in
1974–1975.[90]

In August 1974 Angel Noe González resigned as superintendent to
become branch chief of the Title VII Bilingual Education Office of the
U.S. Department of Health, Education, and Welfare (HEW). González
was succeeded by assistant superintendent Amancio Cantu. Ambrosio
Melendrez was appointed assistant superintendent.[91] González's decision to resign was perceived favorably by Gutiérrez and other RUP
officials because the district would then have one of its own in a major
federal administrative position. They felt this could simplify the securing of additional federal funding for the district's expanding bilingual-
bicultural program.

Although 1973–1975 were quiet years, there was another controversy involving the high school band. In late October 1973 the band
elicited strong criticism from whites while performing in Uvalde. The
band based its half-time performance on the Cristal school walkout.
The band's clenched fist salute and heavily Mexicano repertoire alienated whites who felt its performance was too political. Conservative
observers claimed that the band's use of the salute smacked of May
Day parades and totalitarianism. The *Sentinel* ran a story quoting
sportswriter Charley Robinson of the *Uvalde Leader News*, who wrote,
"It is really sad that a half-time performance by the Crystal City band
coated with heavy political overtones had to overshadow a fine performance by the fighting Javelins."[92] A similar charge had surfaced two
years earlier in Del Rio.

A citizens committee formed by the school board took a look at the
controversy. Voting 12–1—the nay came from Superintendent González—the committee approved rules designed to constrain the band's
performance during half-time shows.[93] Although the rules changed the

high school band's half-time show, they did not eliminate the clenched fist salute or Mexicano musical repertoire. The band continued to be one of the best in Texas, winning award after award.

Another issue that rocked the two years was a taxpayers' suit against the Crystal City Independent School District. In January 1975 Judge Ross Doughty of 38th District Court signed a temporary restraining order that prevented the district from trying to collect taxes or declare them delinquent based on the valuations and assessments made on the 1974 tax rolls. Specifically, the plaintiffs contended that the school board had approved an increase in the valuation of their properties without notifying them, although the district had held a hearing on July 10, 1974, at which the plaintiffs had protested such increases, and a compromise valuation had been reached in some cases. The issue was tantamount to a taxpayer revolt. After two hearings Doughty ruled in favor of the plaintiffs, finding that the district's increase in the valuation of the plaintiffs' properties for 1974 tax year was invalid.[94]

Although the decision caused some setbacks, it did not hamper RUP's cultural and educational programs. In fact, they were so successful that they received recognition from the Mexican government. As a result of talks between Gutiérrez and Mexico's president Luis Echeverría Alvarez, a cultural exchange program was held in Cristal on September 16, 1974. The program consisted of art, theater, and dance. Some of Mexico's finest artists and performers participated. Another event that helped students celebrate the importance of their history of educational struggle was the commemoration of the 1969 school walkout. On December 7, 1974, the district declared a holiday from classes between 10:45 A.M. and 2:30 P.M. so that students could attend a special assembly. Speakers at the event included Gutiérrez, former student leaders of the walkout, and 1972 RUP gubernatorial candidate Ramsey Muñiz.[95]

The RUP school board continued to develop educational programs. This required a relentless pursuit of funding, the mainstay of which continued to be the federal government. However, the federal support declined from $872,000 in 1973–1974 to $768,211 in 1974–1975.[96] The reduction in funding was in great part the result of the politics of RUP's peaceful revolution. Although the board funded no major new programs during the 1973–1975 school years, it strengthened and in some cases expanded programs created before 1973. In January 1975 the district received a $234,733 grant from the U.S. Office of Education to fund the bilingual program for the Cristal high school. This funding was significant because Cristal was the only district in Texas with a secondary bilingual-bicultural program.

The purpose of the program was to extend the many benefits of the elementary bilingual-multicultural program to the high school. The emphasis was to be placed on learning rather than language. Moreover, the intent was to have students become proficient in both English and Spanish. According to Superintendent Cantu, the district was committed "to a kind of total immersion philosophy of bilingual learning, rather than the 'transitional' approach designed to get the Spanish speaker into the English language as quickly as possible."[97] By 1975 the bilingual-bicultural program was in full swing, reflecting the spirit of RUP's peaceful revolution in education.

The district's other programs continued up to 1975. The Urban Rural Program announced during the summer of 1974 that it would offer all professional personnel the opportunity to obtain a master's degree. At about this same time the Career Opportunities Program (COP) graduated thirteen students from Texas A&M University at Laredo. These students received bachelors' degrees in elementary education and were certified to teach in Texas. By 1975 thirty-one people had completed the program, but it ended in 1976 when its funding was discontinued. The Carnegie Foundation's School Administrators Internship Program had recruited seventeen participants from throughout Texas. After a summer residency at California State University in San Diego, they served as interns in Cristal's schools. Intended primarily for staff development, the district's Urban Rural Program trained eighteen people in bilingual education. The district's Adult Education Program had five teachers who offered two-hour classes two evenings a week. Scores of adults obtained their GED.[98]

Another of RUP's successes was the free meals program. In Cristal in 1975 the average yearly income of a family was less than $2,000, so the program affected almost all the district's students. Superintendent Cantu estimated that 90 to 94 percent of all students received free lunches, more than four hundred participated in the breakfast program, and more than three hundred in the supper program.[99]

Perhaps one of the most significant accomplishments of RUP's educational changes was the dramatic decrease in the high school dropout rate. Joyce A. Langenegger, whose master's thesis focused on Cristal's schools, writes, "In 1974 there are tangible results of the [RUP] efforts. Student dropout rates have remained in the 30 to 35 percent range since the [RUP] takeover. Although its statistic is still high, it is approximately the same as the national dropout rate for Chicanos nationwide. Compared to the 1970 dropout statistic of 82.8 percent, the change is imposing.[100]

In 1975 schools superintendent Amancio Cantu reported to the press that RUP's various educational programs and changes had had a major effect on the number of students going on to college: "The number of graduates going to college has ranged as high as 82 percent in the past four years, while dropout rates—which were as high as 94 percent among Chicanos pre-1970—have been trimmed back sharply."[101]

But 1975 was the year that RUP's revolution in education reached its pinnacle. It too began to decline as a result of the political rupture.

The End of RUP's Agenda for Educational Change

For five years RUP's peaceful revolution brought community control of Cristal's schools to Mexicanos. It ushered in an impressive array of changes in policies and programs. Journalist Brooks Peterson of the *Corpus Christi Caller* recognized, although perhaps not intentionally, the accomplishments of RUP's education agenda: "If Crystal City is the showcase of La Raza Unida, the gaudiest ornament in that showcase is the city's school system, the one institution most profoundly altered by the new regime."[102] But because the education revolution was a product of RUP's community control experiment, it too succumbed to the political rupture in 1975.

For the next five years the school board became a pawn in the game of chess being played by the competing power factions. The overthrow of Gutiérrez and his political machine by the new guard in late August 1975 threw the school board's governance and administration into turmoil. For the next four months the quagmire of divisive and polarizing issues (see Chapter 7) inevitably affected the schools, with the firing of Superintendent Cantu; the charges of nepotism against three new guard school trustees; Cantu's suit for damages against the trustees; the pro-Gutiérrez walkout; and school staff resignations, among others. In the midst of the rupture the school district was thrown into a panic over another threatened loss of accreditation. The Texas Education Agency (TEA) charged the school district with being in violation of its principles and standards after failing to submit some requested reports. TEA notified the school district of the problem.

TEA held a hearing on the matter on October 22, and about three hundred Cristal residents attended. In early November TEA notified the school district that it would have probationary status until the agency conducted another evaluation. Cristal's school board appealed the TEA decision in a vote that reflected the polarization and fracture created by the political rupture. The new guard carried the vote 4–2, with one abstention, for the appeal.[103] However, by January 1976 the district had dealt with most of the violations, and the board decided not to appeal. With the district in compliance TEA lifted its probationary status. The new guard coalition governed and administered the district via alternating superintendents and administrators until 1977.

But in 1978 the reinvigorated RUP alliance overthrew the new guard. However, this reassertion of control over the school board did not translate to a revitalization of RUP's peaceful revolution in education for several reasons. The pervasiveness of the factionalism that characterized Cristal's overall politics continued to make control of the school district the most coveted prize. It was still the county's biggest provider of jobs and therefore of patronage. As the political winds shifted, they rearranged the administrative chairs, especially the superintendent's position, which weakened RUP's educational reforms because of the lack of leadership and administrative continuity. RUP's loss of official party status in 1978 also accelerated the end of its educational revolution. And the pervasiveness of the "Viva Yo Generation" mind-set that had replaced that of the Chicano Movement gave rise to a more moderate, even conservative, pedagogical approach. The motivation for change was no longer based on decolonization but on maintaining the status quo. By 1980 the district was embracing a more traditionalist pedagogical approach that was "more integrationist."[104] Educator Armando Trujillo explains how the breakdown of RUP changed the district's espousal of cultural nationalism:

With the disbanding of the RUP the cultural nationalist ideology and philosophy were considerably weakened, and correspondingly membership and unity continued to dwindle without an organized political party that could espouse a strong nationalist line focused on the needs of the Mexicano community. As a result, many former RUP members became incorporated into the Democratic Party or remained unaffiliated with a political party. With this structured change the philosophy of the local Chicano movement was modified and its course of action reorganized.[105]

What followed was the dismantling of many Gutierrista tenets of educational change. By the time Gutiérrez departed from Cristal in early 1981, the schools no longer stressed Chicanismo. One example was the band. Although it continued to win numerous awards and still played some Mexicano music, its repertoire reincorporated John Philip Sousa and did away with the clenched fist salute and its controversial half-time shows. Student and teacher activism all but disappeared. Chicano studies courses nearly vanished. The changes and energy of the peaceful revolution were replaced by a stultifying apathy and cynicism among Mexicanos.

By 1980 most of the district's innovative educational programs created by the Gutierrista boards and school administrations had not been refunded. Between 1973 and 1975 federal funding averaged $800,000 a year. In 1976 it dropped to $589,193, and by 1980 it was at a low of $77,027. Yet from 1976 to 1980 the district's overall budget increased from $3.8 million to $5.5 million, thanks to increased state funding. In 1977 the Cristal district received $1.7 million from the state; by 1980 Austin was sending $3.9 million to Cristal, a record high. But in 1980 the board allocated only a small percentage of the district's $5.5 million for programs. It spent $2.6 million for instructional purposes, just under $1 million for general administration, and $657,000 to acquire and build facilities. The increase in state funding during the late 1970s can be ascribed to the end of RUP's peaceful revolution in Cristal. After 1975 the schools were no long a bastion of Chicanismo or radical change. They returned to a traditional system.[106]

One of the few federally funded programs of the peaceful revolution that managed to survive the political rupture was the district's bilingual-bicultural program. However, from 1976 through 1979 it too was weakened and transformed. In 1978 the Texas State Board of Education refused to extend mandatory bilingual education through the fifth grade. It adopted a policy requiring bilingual teaching only through the third grade for those who needed it. Funding for grades four and five was left to the districts. The Cristal district determined that only twenty students needed such education. In October 1979 Cristal received a $390,000 grant from the U.S. Office of Education for kindergarten through grade eight to continue bilingual education. Trujillo concludes that by 1981 "the program was only operative at the junior high level where students were required to take two years of Spanish as part of their course work."[107]

One program that Gutiérrez developed after the political rupture was *Becas para Aztlán* [Scholarships for the Southwest]. In June 1978 he announced the availability of scholarships to study in Mexico that fall, under the auspices of the Committee for Rural Democracy, a private nonprofit corporation. Mexican president Luis Echeverría Alvarez had started the scholarship program in 1972. In 1978 President José Lopez Pórtillo provided 250 scholarships, worth $9.5 million for the next five years; the scholarships earmarked for Cristal provided full tuition, books, and a stipend for living expenses and were the result of Gutiérrez's overtures to the Mexican government. The program was designed to send Mexicano students to study in Mexico in such fields as medicine, social services, history, political science, and anthropology, with the understanding that they would return to their communities to work upon graduation.[108]

Although the peaceful revolution in education was all but history, in 1979 Gutiérrez organized a whole week of activities commemorating the tenth anniversary of the 1969 Cristal school walkout. With the collaboration and support of the district the events ran from December 2 to 8. With a $5,000 grant from the Texas Committee for Humanities the Walkout Committee organized events that included art and literature awards, a disco dance, student open forums, a car show, a theater presentation, and speakers.[109] The program reflected the change in mind-set. Even those who had been in the vanguard of the peaceful revolution had, by 1979, given way to the district's growing integrationist and traditionalist pedagogy.

Nonetheless, in ten years the district had gone through a complete "browning." By 1980 nearly all students, teachers, staff, and administrators were Mexicano, which created a paradox. Although the board was totally governed and administered by Mexicanos, the schools were subject to oversight by the state and federal government. Pedagogically and ideologically, the district had reverted to espousing the status quo, which in turn helped to perpetuate the area's internal colonialism.

9

Struggle for Economic Empowerment

The scope of RUP's peaceful revolution was broader than attaining community control of the local political institutions or creating educational change. Another major thrust was economic empowerment. From the outset in 1970 the leadership of the peaceful revolution aimed for nothing less than the economic decolonization of Mexicanos in south Texas. RUP leaders tried to realize economic justice and democracy through the eclectic approach of "cooperative capitalism." Unlike other change-oriented efforts within the Chicano Movement (CM), RUP's peaceful revolution in Cristal was a more "holistic" struggle. Still, the peaceful revolution suffered its greatest failure in the area of economic empowerment.

Cooperative Capitalism: The Extrication from Internal Colonialism

RUP's peaceful revolution sought to extricate impoverished Mexicanos of Cristal economically from their internal colonial status. Gutiérrez and MAYO used internal colonialism as a conceptual framework by which to understand why Mexicanos in south Texas were poor, subordinated, and powerless.[1] Although Mexicanos comprised almost 73 percent of the population of Zavala, Dimmit, and La Salle counties, they were virtually landless. For example, in Zavala County whites owned 99.7 percent of all land parcels—and ten individuals owned 46 percent of the land. This meant that Mexicanos owned only three-tenths of 1 percent of parcels larger than three hundred acres. The same was true in Dimmit County, where whites held 99.1 percent of the land and in La Salle, where they owned 99.5 percent.[2] So there was no question that all economic power was wielded by a few whites.

In 1968 in Cristal alone 359 families earned less than $1,000 per year and 764 families earned $1,000 to $2,990. The average size of the Mexicano family was 5.6 people. In 1970 in Zavala County 52.7 percent of the population lived at or below the poverty level; in Dimmit the figure was 62.2 percent and in La Salle, 65.2 percent. As a comparison, the median income for whites in Zavala County was $8,076, whereas it was $3,984 for Mexicanos.[3] In 1970 Cristal did have a small Mexicano middle class of merchants, teachers, and bureaucrats, but the overwhelming majority of Mexicanos were poor and still dependent on migrant work for their economic survival.

At the start of the peaceful revolution in 1970 Gutiérrez recognized that winning control of Cristal's city council and school board would be much easier than wresting economic power away from the powerful gringos. "On the economic model you will never rid yourself of the colonialist imposition until you remove the economic pillar," Gutiérrez said in 1973. "We are only scratching the surface. We are going to have to fight the oil corporations, other major corporations, and the landowners. Its going to be a vicious fight, and violence may erupt."[4]

The struggle for economic decolonization in Cristal was guided by the goal creating a transfer of wealth from the white minority to the Mexicano majority. Yet in 1970, upon taking control of Cristal's city council and school board, Gutiérrez and other leaders had not formulated a plan of action for realizing this objective. Thus they developed their economic empowerment agenda as they went along. But in a 1971 article for *La Raza* magazine Gutiérrez appears to suggest that he had some general economic development steps in mind: "Under this economic development program the first step would be to replace the existing white managerial functions with Chicanos. . . . The transfer of existing businesses from gringo hands would be the second. In the last step, La Raza would set upon the agri-business, the oil and gas industry and the modern day land and cattle barons."[5]

An interesting aspect of RUP's economic agenda was that it was ideologically capitalist. Asked in 1973 to define RUP's economic development strategy, Gutiérrez described a three-step process: consumer education; immediate transfer of wealth by controlling jobs and setting up Mexicano-owned businesses; and changing the fundamental makeup of the area's economic order. "This is what we are trying to do, to push out the local colonialists," he said.[6] His approach was, in essence, to replace "white capitalism" with a modified version of "brown capitalism." "If capitalism is here to stay," he writes, "we might as well make it county capitalism."[7]

Gutiérrez's brown capitalist approach was infused with cooperativism. This entailed creation of self-help projects that required sharing in the labor and the profits. RUP's cooperative capitalism was predicated on the principle that whoever works the land and businesses should own and control them. His idea was not limited to the collectivist approach but included an emphasis on individual economic development.

For all the allegations made by anti-Gutierristas that RUP in Cristal was radical, Marxist, or revolutionary, at no time did he promote any "ism" other than capitalism, although he made facile use of progressive rhetoric and ideas, such as self-determination and redistribution of wealth. RUP's economic program was reformist, seeking to give Mexicanos greater access to the economic system. The irony was that although RUP sought to implement an economic empowerment agenda that, theoretically, was cooperative, in practice it worked within the economic framework of the very system that had maintained internal colonialism in Cristal and throughout south Texas.

RUP's Economic Empowerment Struggle (1970–1975)

RUP's struggle for economic decolonization began with the formation of Ciudadanos Unidos (CU) in late 1969. When meeting with Mexicanos, especially businesspeople, about the need to organize politically, Gutiérrez appealed to their economic self-interest. He stressed the economic benefits they could realize, provided they achieved community control of the local government structures. He convinced them that economic empowerment had to begin by forming nonprofit and profit-oriented corporations. With the support and participation of a few businesspeople CU formed Industrias Mexicanas (IM), a nonprofit economic development corporation. CU was the political action arm of RUP in Cristal; IM was to be the arm of economic empowerment. Gutiérrez saw IM as a catalyst for entrepreneurial and economic activities that could be propagated throughout south Texas.[8]

Incorporation of IM took until early 1970 to complete. The paperwork, handled by CU's attorney, Jesse Gamez, named Gutiérrez, his wife, Luz, and Gamez as incorporators. Serving on the initial board of directors were the Gutiérrezes, Julian Salas, Ramon Lomas, and Pablo Puente. On March 1 IM received its tax-exempt status and stated its general purpose and objectives:

(1) [to] provide relief to the poor, distressed and underprivileged; (2) lessen neighborhood tensions, eliminate prejudices and discrimination, and combat community deterioration and juvenile delinquency; (3) instruct and train individuals on methods by which to improve and develop their capabilities; (4) instruct the public on subjects useful to both the individual and the overall Mexicano community; and (5) conduct research for the purpose of attracting development or retention of current industry or business for the targeted community or area.[9]

Twenty people pledged to buy investment subscriptions in IM at $150 each. IM used the seed money to begin forming small-scale business ventures.

Gutiérrez also began organizing a nonprofit economic development corporation called Constructora Aztlán (CA, Construction Company of the Southwest). CA was formed to specialize in the construction of homes. By December 1969 Gutiérrez had convinced Victoriano Serna, Mike Pérez, Victor Serna, and Reynaldo Ramirez, all members of CU, to be its incorporators. The articles of incorporation were signed January 15 and sent to the Texas secretary of state for certification; however, CA did not receive its charter until October 1972 because of difficulties among the participating subcontractors.[10]

CA's purpose was to build new homes and to rehabilitate dilapidated ones. According to Gutiérrez, "Our interest in forming Constructora Aztlán was to take the experience of various Mexicano subcontractors, pull them into a consortium so that they could take on major economic projects." Individually, they lacked sufficient investment capital, so they pooled their resources and expertise to give CA the capability to undertake major housing projects. The incorporation of IM and CA was a public signal that RUP's peaceful revolution had an economic dimension to it as well. The two entities had overlapping boards and a centralized staff and administration. IM was the progenitor for the formation of other economic development entities.[11]

In January 1970, while Gamez was completing the paperwork for IM and CA, RUP moved its agenda for economic empowerment ahead on two fronts: boycotts of targeted whites businesses, and start-up of Mexicano-owned businesses. Boycotting began in December 1969 with the Cristal school walkout. With the Mexicano community in a state of mass mobilization CU and student leaders recognized just how vulnerable the opposing white businesses were to economic sanctions via economic boycotts.[12] The boycott had two objectives: to demonstrate the community's consumer power and to pressure the white-controlled school board. Antonio Camejo explains how the boycotts came about: "The involvement of the Chicano community quickly went beyond the issue of the schools. Students who were fired from their jobs in local stores for participating in mass marches and rallies were quickly backed up by the entire community, which proceeded to boycott these stores."[13]

Even after the school board agreed to meet the students' demands in January, the economic boycott continued, supported by CU. The boycotts were directed against those members of the business community who had either failed to go along with or had spoken against the walkout in some way.[14] Boycott organizers stressed the need to do business exclusively with Mexicano business owners who had supported the school walkout. Boycott targets included Urbano Esquivel, the Mexicano school board member who opposed the student boycott, and a white businessman who tried to pressure the students by firing two of his student employees involved in the walkout.[15] Esquivel owned a dry-cleaning business. "For about a week," Camejo writes, "the community went to the gringo cleaners in town to make the point that they would not tolerate one Chicano exploiting another." In a 1973 interview Gutiérrez explained, "We are the consumers. We are the majority. We can stop anything, and we can make anything in south Texas, providing we stick together and begin using common sense."[16]

On Saturday, January 10, local police arrested four of the thirty Mexicano students who had been picketing Spear's Mini-Max Market and Esquivel's cleaning establishment: Severita Lara, Mario Treviño, Linda Lara, and Cleofas Tamez. They were charged with intimidating customers and creating a general disturbance. The four were turned over to the custody of their parents on a $1,000 recognizance bond. The incident provoked extensive media coverage. Nevertheless, the students continued to picket the two businesses for about a week. They carried signs that read, "No compren con Spears" [Don't buy at Spears], "Ya basta" [Enough is enough], and "Chicano Power." Their protest actions got the whites' attention. Barker of the *Sentinel* wrote, "The picketing is evidently a part of the MAYO strategy as reported in recent news stories to attempt to turn the economic, political and social system of South Texas over to Chicanos . . . all in the space of two years."[17]

Mexicanos' use of economic intimidation was unprecedented. They had sent a powerful message to the white and Mexicano businesspeople of Cristal who were not supportive of RUP's peaceful revolution. Gutiérrez stated, "The fact that several businesses were the objects of effective boycotts made the [white] community cool the rhetoric of racism and reflect a bit for fear that their businesses might be hit next."[18] Although the official boycott ended, the community continued its economic boycott of both businesses. Concurrently, CU through IM sought to replace the three boycotted businesses, Spear's Mini-Max Market, Winter Garden Cleaners, and the Lone Star beer franchise.

IM tried to buy the Mini-Max. Gamez negotiated the signing of a one-year lease at $200 per month. Initially, the IM board was reluctant to sign a one-year lease because members were concerned about the extent to which the summer exodus of migrant seasonal workers would hurt business. Nevertheless, by February the market was in IM's hands, renamed the Mini-Mart. The IM board invested $3,000 in the store and hired Ramón de la Fuente and his wife to run the store. As part of the agreement the de la Fuentes invested an additional $1,000. IM would take 49 percent of the profits, and the de la Fuentes would received 51 percent. *La Verdad* made a formal announcement of its opening: "This store is the first effort for the economic development of the Chicano of the area. . . . The owners of the business are Mr. Ramon de la Fuente and Industrias Mexicanas. . . . This business is the result of the boycott. . . . The company who owned the store Mini-Max, Sweeney & Co., gave the people a franchise as a result of the boycott."[19]

After several months of operation the market went out of business because it was making only a small profit and had difficulty keeping its shelves stocked. Its supplier was located in San Antonio, 125 miles from Cristal. Viviana Santiago, explained, "The people would come to the store, and food items were not there, so we had to shut the store down."[20]

In January IM also moved to establish a dry cleaners, as an alternative to Esquivel's, and a Lone Star beer franchise, which the directors figured was a natural because Mexicanos drank a lot of beer. Why not control a product that would give IM a profit? But neither venture got off the ground because the board could not find investment capital or experienced people to run the businesses. CU continued to boycott the existing Lone Star distributorship on the ground that the franchise owner was anti-Mexicano.[21]

To fortify IM's economic development efforts Gutiérrez assigned Viviana Santiago to write proposals. Gutiérrez had recruited her at a MAYO state conference in December as part of the Voluntarios de Aztlán. From 1970 to 1976 when she left for law school, she was Gutiérrez's main technician in the development of economic, educational, and social programs and projects. When she started helping Gutiérrez, she was totally inexperienced in the area of economic development. Her background was in teaching. In March 1970 CU sent her to Washington, D.C., for three months of training. According to Santiago, she realized upon her return to Cristal that she was the only person in town who had such training and there simply was not enough capital to initiate projects. She commented, "The idea was to go and learn the movidas [moves] in Washington, D.C., because that was one of the chief resource centers. So I would spend time dealing with top people like Senator [John] Tower—learning about the power structure, who were the decision makers, who were the people with resources. Going right to the head instead of dealing with all the lower bureaucracies."[22]

She wasted no time in applying for funding, especially federal funding. At this point RUP still had no formal plan for economic development. "We would be in a restaurant talking when José Angel would get an idea and write it down on a napkin," Santiago recalled. "Other times, with Bill Richey and his wife participating, we would stay up well into the morning hours. . . . After a lot of discussion and sometimes arguing, he [Gutiérrez] would say to us, 'We really need to pursue this idea.'"[23]

Then it was up to Santiago to do the research, explore funding sources, write a proposal, and ultimately lobby for the funding. Santiago also assisted Gutiérrez and other administrators in developing and implementing RUP's educational and social programs. This left Santiago overextended, but there was no one else. The dependence on Santiago was symptomatic of a larger ill that pervaded RUP's peaceful revolution—the scarcity of qualified and committed technicians.

In July 1970 Santiago secured a $5,000 grant from Church Women United. The church group had been looking for a woman who was working on economic development projects along the border area of Texas. The project was named the United States–Mexican Border Economic Development Project and focused on problems plaguing the border area. But RUP used the money to maintain its other organizing projects, such as La Verdad.[24] The project did little to bring economic development to the community.

For RUP 1970 was not a particularly good year for its economic agenda. Gutiérrez was preoccupied with the political and educational arenas. Although IM and CA were functional, they accomplished little that year. Still, new Mexicano businesses were starting to spring up, the result of the flight of white-owned businesses from Cristal. That May, with the city council and school board under community control, RUP purged white personnel and replaced them with Mexicanos. This action enlarged Cristal's emerging middle class.

The next four years of RUP's economic empowerment struggle were plagued by problems and controversy. Although Gutiérrez and CU had made a strong commitment to focus on economic development, this aspect never attained the level of success reached by the political and educational efforts. In 1971 IM tried to establish a pig cooperative and restructured its board, increasing its roster to nine: Julian Salas, David Mendoza, Jesús Menchaca, Pablo Puente, Ramón "Monche" Mata, Ernesto Martinez, Natividad Granados, Beatrice Mendoza Piotter, and Viviana Santiago.[25]

The pig-raising cooperative gave some life and legitimacy to the largely paper corporation. The objectives were to provide pork to supplement the diet of members of the cooperative and create income and capital for them. Santiago prepared and submitted a proposal for a $31,635 grant that was approved by the Educational Systems Corporation in Washington, D.C. The IM board appointed an advisory committee made up totally of migrant and seasonal farmworkers to administer the project.[26] The committee recruited about fifty low-income families for the project and leased thirty acres for five years from a member of CU. Five acres were set aside for planting various vegetables, and the cooperative bought fifty sows. Shortly thereafter IM hired a full-time manager to help the member families run the cooperative.

The pig cooperative became IM's most successful venture. By 1973 the fifty pigs had become more than two hundred, and the cooperative made a profit of about $6,000 by selling pigs. The members of the cooperative divided the profits and received half a pig every Christmas for their own consumption. Then IM expanded the cooperative by buying sixty-five goats. According to Ramón "Monche" Mata, IM believed the goats would be a lucrative investment because goat meat was commanding high prices.[27] The cooperative received national and international attention from reporters throughout the United States, Mexico, and Europe. IM continued to provide technical assistance to the pig and goat cooperative until the cooperative fell apart and was dismantled in 1974.

The principal reason that the pig cooperative eventually failed was lack of cooperation from its member families. Each family was required to put in a set number of hours per week, but they began sending others to do their work. When the cooperative ended, only two families were carrying the full workload. To avoid divisions and more hassles IMs board sold the pigs and goats. The profit from the sale was divided among the ten families that remained as members; each received $300.[28]

CA did not begin its efforts to construct homes until 1971 because of infighting among the various subcontractors. The death of Reynaldo Ramirez, one of the key board members, exacerbated the scarcity of business leadership. Consequently, final incorporation of CA was not completed until October 20, 1972. Another problem that inhibited its development was the scarcity of capital. CA figured it needed about $125,000 in seed money to build several houses at one time.[29]

Although it did not contract directly with CA, the city's Urban Renewal Agency hired its member subcontractors between 1971 and 1973. "Instead of Anglo contractors reaping the profits, Mexicanos made the money," Gutiérrez said.[30] They built housing badly needed by the city's poor—twenty-seven brick houses on paved streets with curbs, gutters, sidewalks, and other improvements.

Gutiérrez's economic development scheme sought to maximize the use of public funds to promote economic development. This was very much the case in 1973 when the Zavala County Health Association, the organization formed by the community to provide health services, awarded CA the $277,000 contract to build a health clinic, El Centro de Salud (see Chapter 10 for further detail). Viviana Santiago was in charge of securing the bonding for CA for the building of the clinic and provided some assistance, but she was much too overextended to provide full-time support.[31]

After one year on the job CA abandoned construction of the health clinic because of internal fiscal, legal, and bonding problems. In 1974 the Texas Employment Commission (TEC) filed a lien of $4,655.76 for back taxes owed the TEC Unemployment Compensation Fund. There was also a $14,267.93 lawsuit filed against CA for a delinquent loan. One supplier of materials, Perry Shankel Co. of San Antonio, sued CA to recoup $5,852.74, plus $2,000 in legal fees; another supplier, Alamo Lumber, was owed $7,337.55. And the secretary of state filed a lien of $138.86 for unpaid franchise taxes. By 1975 CA had lost its corporate charter. Gutiérrez explained, "We were successful in putting them [Mexicano contractors] together, but the problem was their lack of experience. They were the best builders, but you put them in a position of leadership and control and they couldn't do it."[32]

CA was not the only housing venture organized by Gutiérrez and Santiago. In 1972 they developed a self-help housing cooperative. The pilot project, involving about twenty families, was funded by the U.S. Department of Housing and Urban Development through the National Spanish-Speaking Housing Development Corporation. The project was designed to help renters and homeless families become homeowners, and five actually did. The families received low-interest loans from the Farmers Home Administration. The program stipulated that all members of the cooperative had to help in the actual construction of all the houses. Sometimes people would not cooperate. They would take off for jobs in the north, and bickering ensued. According to Santiago, they would say, "You didn't come and help me put up the dry-wall," and arguments would follow. This venture folded in 1973.[33]

A third unsuccessful cooperative effort was the credit union. Formed in 1971, its membership grew to about 250 members. The credit union was organized to provide loans to both CU members and the area's residents. The average loan was $150. It was successful in that at one time it had as much as $6,000 in its loan fund. However, by 1975 the credit union too folded, another victim of bad management. Individual members recouped 95 to 100 percent of their investments.[34] That year IM too became defunct.

Other economic development entities were formed between 1971 and 1975. In 1971 Gutiérrez, Gamez, and Angel Noe González (the schools superintendent) formed a for-profit corporation, Dinero, Inc. Santiago and two other RUP leaders were also involved in the endeavor. Its corporate seal was the dollar sign, its name meant 'money' in Spanish, and there was no question about its purpose: to make money. "The purpose was to help people get into business, to become self-sufficient, and less dependent economically on the Anglo," González said.[35] But it never really succeeded.

Dinero's major venture was the purchase of about thirty lots in Cristal. One property was called the White House, a large two-story house once owned by B. H. Holsomback, a former San Antonio mayor and the brains behind the last successful white political machine in Cristal. With delicious irony it became the physical heart of the peaceful revolution. Until 1975 it housed the headquarters of RUP in Texas, the Texas Migrant Council's Human Development Project, the Carnegie Foundation's School Administrators Internship Program, Voluntarios de Aztlán, the Committee for Rural Democracy, and *La Verdad*.[36] Dinero charged the organizations rent, somewhere between $100 and $200 a month.

Gamez said Dinero never made a profit from the White House. He explained that most of the organizations and projects that operated out of the White House drifted in and out without paying a cent. "We had high hopes for it, but it never really took off," González said. "I know that we didn't make any money off of it. I don't think that any of the original incorporators made any money." Even the thirty-lot venture became problematic because construction costs turned out to be greater than the incorporators had thought. Local laws required that builders install curbs and gutters and figure the cost of such improvements into the price of each house. Without the investment capital, Dinero, Inc., never broke ground and became defunct by 1975.[37]

Gamez kept title to some of the remaining properties. "It went out of business almost as soon it started," Angel Noe González said. "If it stayed incorporated, it didn't do what we had hoped it would do because we had no resources, number one. Secondly, we didn't have the person power with the expertise to get out there and move it. All of us were too busy."[38]

Another profit-making corporation formed and incorporated in 1971 was De Zavala Businessmen's Association, Inc. Incorporated by Gutiérrez, Angel Noe González, Amancio Cantu, Rodolfo Palomo, and Erasmo Andrade, its purpose was "to deal with all kinds of personal property . . . to purchase or acquire, hold, own, mortgage, sell, convey, exchange, option, subdivide, or dispose of real and personal property of every class and description and any interest therein." As a profit-making corporation it was authorized to issue an aggregate of one thousand shares at $10 a share. Santiago again was the key technician in its development, and some shares were issued. But González said, "It didn't get off the ground because we were just too busy defending ourselves from one attack after another. Another problem was that we just did not make it work."[39]

Later in 1971 a group of Mexicano businessmen from the Mexican Chamber of Commerce of Cristal approached IM with a plan to build a shopping center in Cristal. After some deliberation the IM board decided that a local development corporation needed to be formed to handle the shopping center plan. It was named the Winter Garden Development Corporation (WGDC), and its officers were Richard Ortiz, president; Henry Flores, vice president; Moses Peña, secretary; Ventura Gonzalez, treasurer; and Reynaldo Mendoza, sergeant of arms. It was organized and structured to participate in the Small Business Administration's 502 Industrial Program. Its priorities were to build a shopping complex designed to serve the Winter Garden Area; finance (through SBA's 502 program) the purchase of land and a building for a local pickle-processing plant; negotiate with a leatherworks industry that was considering relocation to the city; and form a local crafts corporation designed to bring together the resources and expertise of local contractors.[40]

IM and the WGDC formed a joint venture that called for IM to purchase convertible debentures, meaning unsecured bonds, whereas WGDC was responsible for putting up the front money—about 10 percent of the total project to leverage the necessary 90 percent needed to complete the loan. In 1972 the joint venture submitted several proposals for funding to both public and private sources. It struck out with the SBA, then approached the Presbyterian Economic Development

Corporation, only to be rejected again. The failure to secure funding for WGDC meant its demise.[41]

Complimenting the economic development efforts were the many individual business ventures undertaken by CU leaders during RUP's five-year peaceful revolution. In 1973 Angel Noe González undertook construction of the Cross Y restaurant and trailer park, also the site of one of the two motels in Cristal. In February 1974 González tried to land a Chevrolet franchise in the Cristal–Carrizo Springs area but failed to submit the paperwork on time. When González left Cristal in August 1974, he transferred operation of his three businesses to one of his principal business associates. About a year later he sold the property to Eddie Treviño, the former RUP school board member, for $53,000. González claimed that he made only $2,000 in profit on the sale.[42]

Gutiérrez and Gamez likewise became involved in individual business ventures. In 1973 both went into the beer distribution business. With encouragement from Angel Noe González and Gutiérrez, Gamez and his sister purchased a Budweiser beer distributing company that serviced the Cristal area. Soon Gutiérrez, believing there was enough business to sustain two beer distributorships, became part owner of a Falstaff beer distributing company. His entry into the beer market created competition that ultimately split the two friends. Gamez felt Gutiérrez had betrayed him. The split became so acute that Gutiérrez went before CU and secured support for a boycott against the Budweiser distributorship. Arturo Gonzales, at the time a friend of both, explained that Gutiérrez called for a boycott because Gamez was making money and Gutiérrez was not. This was not necessarily true. The *Wall Street Journal* in 1975 reported that Gutiérrez's gross income for 1974 from his Falstaff distributorship was $15,000. By 1976 neither Gamez nor Gutiérrez was in the beer distributorship business. Both were victims of their intransigent competitiveness. For Gutiérrez this was his only major business venture, but for Gamez beer was merely the beginning.[43]

González, Gamez, and Gutiérrez were not the only RUP leaders to undertake business ventures. The economic boycotts proved effective against a grocery store, beer distributorship, car dealership, and tire store, and in general created an economic climate that benefited Mexicano entrepreneurship. Richard A. Schaffer, staff reporter for the *Wall Street Journal*, wrote, "In the past four years, an estimated 25 businesses have closed, and perhaps as many as 500 families—Mexican American as well as Anglo—have left town."[44]

Mexicanos moved in. They moved into what used to be all-white neighborhoods. The large numbers of families that moved out of Cristal created an oversupply of homes that in turn caused their prices to drop. The *Arkansas Gazette* in 1974 reported, "In one neighborhood of $25,000 homes, there are 11 for sale. One $35,000 house was on the market four years before it sold. More and more Chicanos are moving into what used to be solid white neighborhoods." All of sudden, homes were available and affordable for some of the emerging middle-class Mexicanos. Gutiérrez told the *Gazette*, "We've learned not to buy when they're ready to sell. . . . We want to break the . . . (SOBs)."[45]

While some of Cristal's white businesses closed and others withered, numerous Mexicano-owned businesses sprang up during the five years of the peaceful revolution. By 1973 RUP supporters had started about fifteen new businesses. Most were in the service industry—cafes, bars, markets, restaurants, gas stations, and auto body and automotive repair garages. If nothing else, RUP's peaceful revolution created a semblance of an economic awakening. However, not all the businesses became viable. Two such examples were headed by a school district employee, Adán Cantú—the Crystal Ready Mix (a cement supply firm) and the Winter Garden Publishing House.[46]

Cantú (no relation to Amancio Cantu, the former schools superintendent) formed Crystal Ready Mix to provide the cement for the schools the district was building. He created the Winter Garden Publishing House to be a supplier to the school district, city, and county offices and to function as a publishing house. Both businesses got off the ground in 1975 but were out of business by 1977 for different reasons. Adán Cantú and Angel Noe González were indicted on theft charges in June 1976 by a heavily pro–new guard Zavala County grand jury. One of González's chief accusers was Ramón Garza, Cristal's police chief and school board member. The charge against González stemmed from the school district's paying Cantú his school district salary of $12,000 a year while González was superintendent. According to the indictment, Adán Cantú did little or no work for his salary, spending his time developing various business ventures. From June 1976 to March 1977 the Texas media treated this as a major issue. Rick Casey reported in the *Texas Observer*, "The Texas press hadn't helped his reputation any. When González was indicted, most of the state's daily newspapers decided the story was front-page fare and played it accordingly; television and radio news departments followed suit. As the case moved toward trial, there were frequent reports in print and on the air that cast a lengthening shadow over Gonzalez's character."[47]

González spent months doing research for his defense, and the trial was moved from Cristal to Brownsville. The trial's political overtones became apparent when prosecutors tried to move the trial to Uvalde, home of Governor Dolph Briscoe. The case was being prosecuted by the Texas attorney general's office. The attorney general, John Hill, subsequently sought to wrest the 1978 Democratic nomination for governor from Briscoe and apparently wanted the trial held in Briscoe's hometown to highlight Hill's contention that Briscoe should have been more critical of events in Cristal.[48] For his part, between the indictment and the trial Briscoe was crusading to get the Ford administration to yank funding for RUP's cooperative farm and attacking Gutiérrez for his "little Cuba" statements, a flap that continued into the Carter administration and is discussed later in this chapter.

In March 1977 González was acquitted of all charges; prosecutors never pursued the charges against Adán Cantú. Despite the avid coverage of González's indictment, his acquittal was a nonevent, according to Casey: "Of the major dailies that had put the indictment on page one, only the San Antonio Express gave the acquittal front-page coverage."[49] The political and legal pressure was so intense that Adán Cantú sold the equipment and went out of business. "It didn't," Gutiérrez commented, "go because of lack of capital." With Adán Cantú bailing out of both business ventures, Eugene Monroe, a teacher in the school district, picked up the publishing aspect and sought to keep it going. Gutiérrez's 1976 book, *A Gringo Manual on How to Handle Mexicans*, was published by the fledgling Winter Garden Publishing House.[50]

Gutiérrez had begun courting the Mexican government for support in 1972. He said he intended to forge a series of ventures with Mexico. On June 19, 1972, he and a delegation of RUP leaders, mostly from Cristal, met with Mexican president Luis Echeverría Alvarez in San Antonio, Texas. The delegation included Francisco Benavides, mayor of Cristal; Francisco Rodriguez, city manager of Cristal; Ramon "Monche" Mata, board member of IM from Cristal; Jesse Gamez, city attorney of Cristal; and Ramsey Muñiz, RUP gubernatorial candidate. After a thirty-five-minute meeting Echeverría Alvarez agreed to send Pedro De Koster, director of industry in Mexico, to Cristal to provide technical assistance in establishing industries. During the ceremony the RUP delegation presented Echeverría Alvarez with a painting by a Cristal artist of Mexicano revolutionary hero Emiliano Zapata. Echeverría Alvarez reciprocated by donating about two thousand volumes of historical biographies of Mexicano political and educational figures to Cristal's Memorial Library. Gutiérrez used the opportunity to discuss the activities and politics of RUP. According to Gutiérrez, Echeverría Alvarez commented, "Keep on winning."[51]

Two weeks later De Koster arrived in Cristal for a three-day visit. He met with RUP city officials and business leaders. The discussions focused on the establishment of various types of industries. One was the "twin plant idea," which meant the development of interrelated industries on both sides of the border. Mayor Benavides told reporters that other ideas that had been discussed were a packing plant for such products as pickles, chiles, and even tomatoes; production of prefabricated flooring and wall covering; and the fabrication of straw beach hats that could be made at home by women who could not leave their families. An agreement was reached between RUP city officials and De Koster for promoting Cristal's industrial development. RUP city officials did not invite the white-controlled Zavala County Industrial Commission to participate.[52]

Whites were skeptical of Echeverría Alvarez's meeting with RUP officials and of De Koster's visit to Cristal. Jack Kingsberry, the local businessman, was one of several who openly criticized the De Koster visit. He said, "Since industry has completely shunned Crystal City since La Raza took over, this is just a cover-up to try to get people to thinking that they're something for the city." Some whites reacted as if Mexico had violated the sovereignty of the United States by meddling in its internal political affairs. Jack Ware, an attorney, said De Koster's visit was "unheard of in diplomatic protocol." He said that he was not opposed to the idea of cooperating with Mexico on developing new industry in Cristal. He felt, however, that Mexico should not have gone through RUP but rather through such channels as the U.S. State Department or an agency such as the Texas Good Neighbor Commission. Ware was also the former president of the Crystal City Chamber of Commerce, which became inactive as a consequence of RUP's second revolt.[53]

Echeverría Alvarez's agreement with RUP was politically unprecedented. Never before had the Mexican government agreed to offer technical assistance to Mexicanos on the U.S. side of the border. Of particular symbolic significance was Echeverría Alvarez's selection of Gut.érrez over other leaders of the Chicano Movement. This recognition enhanced his stature within the movement and RUP's political stock, giving national and international attention to both the leader and the nascent Chicano political party. This was the beginning of Gutiérrez's efforts to inject the "brown power" agendas of RUP and the Chicano Movement in the international political arena. Moreover, in an adroit and calculated manner he used the Mexican connection to strengthen his bid for the national chair of RUP against his rival, Rodolfo "Corky" Gonzales. At the RUP convention held in September

1972 in El Paso, Texas, Gutiérrez's strategy paid off. After a contentious power struggle for the chair, he prevailed over Gonzales.[54] As a result, Gutiérrez for most of the 1970s was recognized as the leader of the Chicano Movement by the Mexican government.

The high regard of the Mexican government for Gutiérrez became evident in November 1972 with the goodwill visit to Cristal of José Juan de Olloqui, Mexico's ambassador to the United States. De Olloqui explained to *La Verdad* the nature of his visit to Cristal: "I wanted to come to observe the political, social and educational reforms that have been made in Cristal on behalf of the Chicano, in spite of the domination and discrimination of the gringo in this nation." Officially invited by Mayor Benavides, the ambassador was taken on a tour of the city and schools by RUP city and school officials. At a luncheon held at SBANEDA Steakhouse, where de Olloqui was the guest of honor, students sang several Mexican songs.[55]

Gutiérrez gained a lot of media hype, but Cristal gained little economically from the meetings with Mexican presidents Echeverría Alvarez and José Lopez Pórtillo.[56] Pronouncements of support were abundant, but capital and technical assistance never materialized. Mexico's contributions to Cristal were more in the area of education, such as the two thousand volumes donated to Cristal's library, and cultural symbolism, such as the bust of Benito Juárez donated to the city.

Efforts by both the city council and the schools to foster Mexicano economic empowerment created hundreds of jobs for RUP's loyal supporters, through both direct employment and the awarding of contracts for housing and school construction. These actions gave a boost to Cristal's emerging middle class. In 1972 the city did a feasibility study of economic development and formed an industrial commission. The study, conducted by Urban Research Group, Inc., concluded that Cristal could become more industrial by wooing "labor intensive type industry." The report also recommended formation of an industrial development foundation and construction of an industrial park.[57]

Lupe Cortinas headed the Industrial Commission, and Elida Garza, Eddie Treviño, Rudy Palomo, Ramon "Monche" Mata, and Martha Cotera sat on its board. Its primary mission was to attract industry to Cristal. In March 1973 the Central Power & Light Company, then seeking permission to raise its rates, gave the city a $10,000 grant to use to attract industry to Cristal. The Industrial Commission then spent much of its time looking for a site for the proposed industrial park. It also began to meet with its white counterpart at the county level—the Zavala County Industrial Foundation (ZCIF). In February 1973 several RUP city and school officials attended a one-day industrial planning seminar conducted by the Texas Industrial Commission. For whatever reason, the Industrial Commission never managed to bring new industry to Cristal.[58]

Despite the grants and federal funding that brought some new jobs, the overwhelming majority of Mexicanos in Cristal remained poor.[59] Roughly 50 percent of the people were still dependent on migrant work for their economic survival in 1973. Although their quality of life had improved somewhat, most Mexicanos were still living under the economic yoke of internal colonialism. When RUP city officials met with Mexico's De Koster in 1972, the average annual income was about $3,200. The *Wall Street Journal* reported in 1975 on the pervasiveness of poverty in Cristal:

Putting party regulars in government jobs hasn't brought full employment, though the county unemployment rate has dropped from 17% "before Raza" to 13.3% in April, a 21.8% improvement. By contrast, the unemployment rate in neighboring Dimmit County, which has a similar ethnic makeup, declined over the same period to 9.3% from 13.7%, a 32.1% improvement. And the number of persons on welfare in Zavala County has doubled since the Chicano takeover, compared with a 60% increase in Dimmit County, though this may reflect more liberal administration of Zavala's welfare program.[60]

RUP zealots and adversaries alike concur that the greatest failure of RUP's peaceful revolution by 1975 was its inability to promote economic development for the impoverished of Cristal. Gutiérrez conceded that RUP in Cristal "failed miserably in economic development," but he placed much of the blame on its adversaries: "Instead of helping us attract new industry, the bankers and Chamber of Commerce types keep telling everyone that this is a politically unstable community. Hell, how long do we have to be in power before they see that we're stable? It's these people who are stabbing the whole community in the back."[61]

RUP leaders Angel Noe González, Santiago, and Luz Gutiérrez, as well as a host of others, echoed Gutiérrez's remarks. But González specifically blamed the lack of money, lack of expertise regarding economic development, and the lack of full-time staff to work on the projects. Santiago, who wrote many of the proposals, agreed with González's analysis.[62]

The Decline of RUP's Economic Empowerment Struggle (1975–1980)

The political rupture and the internecine conflicts that characterized the years 1975–1980 put an end to whatever economic empowerment efforts RUP's peaceful revolution had created. Instead of operating from a collective mind-set of economic empowerment, Cristal's leaders operated from the mind-set of "Viva Yo." The new emphasis was economic self-interest. The conflict was not over ideology or philosophical principles but over who or what group was going to control the spigot of patronage.

Gutiérrez continued to try to promote economic development. His pursuit was hampered, however, by powerful external political forces that decided to put an end to RUP's peaceful revolution. Adding to his problems was the cut-off of the city's gas service, causing great problems for the people of Cristal. These difficulties made it virtually impossible to attract funding capital and new industry and businesses to the area. Although they were on the defensive, the Gutierristas promoted economic empowerment with the formation of a new cooperative.

The Zavala County Economic Development Corporation

After experimenting unsuccessfully for nearly five years with several entities oriented to economic development, Gutiérrez in 1975 formed another nonprofit corporation, the Zavala County Economic Development Corporation (ZCEDC). According to Santiago, of all the nonprofit corporations formed, "this was Angel's baby. He spent a lot of time building it."[63] ZCEDC was chartered as an economic development corporation in Texas on September 19, 1975. The incorporators were Gutiérrez, D. M. Mendoza, and J. A. Perez. Led by a fifteen-member board headed by Gutiérrez, its membership consisted of about two hundred families who elected the board, attended meetings, and paid dues of $10 a year.[64]

ZCEDC had a level of administration and planning that IM, CA, Dinero, and others could only dream of. Compared to these other ventures, ZCEDC's goals personified much more the cooperative economic empowerment and development approach needed to extricate Mexicanos from internal colonialism. As a community development corporation, ZCEDC's goals focused on developing agricultural ventures; improving people's technical and vocational skills; providing access to capital and technical assistance; developing activities related to housing and real estate; promoting a safer and healthier local environment; and creating a viable self-sufficient community development corporation that would benefit the people it served.[65]

ZCEDC's priority was to use existing resources to create immediate employment. It sought to dramatically decrease the number of Mexicanos from the area still dependent on the migrant stream and whites for their livelihood. This strategy took into consideration the area's two unique resources: fertile land and the people themselves. RUP's research found fertile brushland that could be cleared for agricultural use. Zavala County also was home to about five thousand migrant farmworkers. Because their work was seasonal, about 38 percent were unemployed when they were home, which meant there was a surplus of skilled labor that could be recruited to develop the land. During its brief three-year existence ZCEDC's top priority was the development of a community-owned farm or, as its adversaries described it, "a communal farm." In an annual report Gutiérrez, ZCEDC's chief architect and subsequent chair, explained the rationale that impelled it: "Our people today, in 1976, are as poor as they were in 1946. Our people must leave home yearly and trek north in search of work. Our young must work in the fields harvesting tomatoes, strawberries, beets, corn and cucumbers for America to eat. We must continue to work in the fields. We must continue to feed America. But, we must own the land and our labor. We must own and shape our own destiny."[66]

The community farm was initially funded under the aegis of the Zavala County Economic Development Project through the federal Community Economic Development Special Impact Program. The request for funding was submitted to the U.S. Community Services Administration (CSA) in July 1975 and won a preplanning grant of $49,000. Then Gutiérrez shot from the lip again. On August 14 the *San Antonio Express* reported that Gutiérrez and RUP were "interested in starting some form of collective farming in Zavala County." To start the farm, Gutiérrez told the paper, the Mexicano community would have to buy land, lease land, or raise taxes so high that property owners would find it advisable to relinquish some of their holdings. In a story about Cristal that ran on the front page of the *Wall Street Journal*, Gutiérrez described the proposed community farm as a "people's commune." Gutiérrez threatened to exercise eminent domain to acquire the land needed for the farm: "It would be a sort of people's commune. The county would lease the land, or buy it. And, if the ranchers wouldn't sell, the county would simply take it through eminent domain, just like it condemns right of way for a new bridge. We're going to put the means of production back into the hands of the people where it belongs."[67] The article appeared only months after Gutiérrez's infamous trip to Cuba and its ensuing firestorm.

Despite Gutiérrez's provocative statements, in November 1975 CSA approved a grant of $150,000 for ZCEDC's Zavala County Economic Development Project. The grant was earmarked for development of a program that would improve the demographic and economic base of the area. In mid-1976 ZCEDC sought and won a $1.5 million grant from CSA for a two-year period.[68] The foremost objective, as summarized in ZCEDC's 1977 annual report, was to create a farm that eventually would become self-sufficient.

For Gutiérrez the grant offered a tremendous opportunity to put into effect his progressive ideas for economic empowerment. The agricultural venture underwritten by CSA was called Del Norte, Inc. (DN), and its developmental strategy called for

acquisition of 1,090 acres of highly productive land to commercially grow fresh vegetable crops (namely, onions, cucumber, bell pepper, cabbage, stalked cucumber and corn for grain) and development of both hydrocooling and packing operations to enhance profit potential and maintain control of products to meet market specifications. DN's basic mission is to obtain a respectable position in the fresh vegetable industry by: (1) producing a high quality product, (2) obtaining a market share in Texas of 1.4% for onions, 7.8% per cucumber, 3.6% for bell pepper, and 1% for cabbage, and (3) responding quickly to changing market needs. DN's employment estimates include 86 full-time employees for farm work, and 4 permanent staff positions. Said 86 employees will receive total compensation of $336,050. With the money multiplier estimated at 3.5 for Zavala County, the payroll impact upon Crystal City and its immediate vicinity is approximated to be $1.28 million in new money created.[69]

Del Norte was designed to be ZCEDC's main vehicle for its import-export venture. Julian Salas explained that Del Norte, as anchor, would bring in money to invest in import-export ventures with Mexico.[70] In December 1975 a dummy corporation named Chica Mex was set up in Mexico. It was headed by Salas's brother, Manuel, and Gutiérrez was listed as a board member. Alejandro Niere was sent to Mexico as a paid consultant to try to set up the import-export aspects. He succeeded in arranging a meeting with then Mexican president José Lopez Pórtillo. The president's statement of support for ZCEDC was symbolic and nebulous. He committed his administration "to cooperate in the development of the pueblo Chicano in the U.S., moreover [sic] specifically the established ties with La Raza Unida, especially through the proven leadership of Chicanos in Crystal City."

In Cristal as part of the import-export venture ZCEDC established another nonprofit corporation, the Southwest Trade Association. Membership dues were set at $5,000 per participating entity. Jesús Salas (nephew of Julian and son of Manuel) was selected as chair. By October 1976 ZCEDC's affiliation with RUP was an issue. Louis Ramirez, associate director of CSA, informed Gutiérrez that "you are here-by instructed that ZCEDC must dissociate its activities from La Raza Unida."[71] Gutiérrez ignored the warning.

With the symbolic support of the Mexican government ZCEDC officials felt confident that their community farm venture was viable. After all, its main goal was to improve dramatically the economic status of the farmworker families. About 450 workers would be making at least $3.50 an hour, significantly higher than the area's prevailing rate of $2.50. The plan was to provide year-round employment to the designated families, freeing them from the dependence and poverty of migrant work. In October 1976 ZCEDC's executive director proposed a business package that included community farm sites. One site was located west of Cristal in the vicinity of Caymanche Lake, and the other was land once operated by the Texas Vegetable Union.[72]

RUP's adversaries were angry about ZCEDC's $1.5 million grant. Texas governor Dolph Briscoe, for example, initiated a campaign to derail ZCEDC's funding. On August 17, 1976, Briscoe sent a telegram to President Gerald Ford informing him that funding ZCEDC violated the spirit, purpose, and express objectives of Circular No. A-95 from the Office of Management and Budget (OMB) and the authorizing Intergovernmental Cooperation Act of 1968. The governor asked that the grant be frozen until Texas could exercise its right to review and comment. James T. Lynn, director of OMB, responded to Briscoe and informed him that the matter had been discussed with the appropriate officials at CSA. He acknowledged that "apparently, there was considerable confusion at CSA and among applicants about the way in which the review requirements were to be applied to the CSA Community Economic Development Program." On September 1 Briscoe sent another letter to Ford, reiterating his arguments that funding ZCEDC's community farm was in violation of federal law and regulations.[73]

When Ford did not agree, the governor took his anticommunity farm and anti-Gutiérrez crusades to the courts. On September 21, 1976, Texas attorney general Hill sought a temporary restraining order against CSA. This action followed controversial remarks made by Briscoe at the state Democratic convention. Briscoe claimed that as chair of ZCEDC, Gutiérrez would use the grant to "establish little Cubas" in Zavala County. Such entities as the Bexar County Farm Bureau took up the cry, emphasizing its opposition to the idea of communal farms because they are socialistic.[74] At the core of Briscoe's crusade against community farms were two arguments: the grant had been approved without state or local review, and the farm would promote socialism in Texas.

In September Gutiérrez and RUP countered Briscoe's attacks. At the RUP state convention on September 18 and 19, RUP delegates approved a resolution "publicly censoring and condemning Governor

Briscoe for insulting the Mexican American people of Texas by calling [them] un-Texans and un-Americans." The resolution pointed out in strong language that Briscoe was the largest landowner in southwest Texas and sole owner of all savings and loan associations in the area. The former was particularly important because Briscoe's landholdings were massive. He owned at least 330,000 acres of ranch land in Uvalde, Zavala, and other surrounding counties. In Zavala County alone he owned twenty-two thousand acres.[75]

Briscoe and other powerful white farm and ranch interests, such as affluent attorneys Hayden Head of Corpus Christi and B. K. Johnson, were concerned about the implications of having a "communal farm" in their backyard.[76] In a interview published in the *Militant* Gutiérrez expanded on this point:

Why do we want the farm? Our people have to work all over now. We want this farm so we won't have to go on a "summer vacation" picking cherries in Michigan or potatoes in Idaho, or corn for Jolly Green Giant. . . . We plan to start out with our farm paying $3.50 an hour. Now that's "subversive." It's subversive because if you've got one farm in the midst of all those others paying $2.50, who in the hell is going to work for the other guy? . . . People are going to have the right to decide for themselves what they should do with their money and their labor! . . . It's good old fashioned capitalism. Except this time it's going to be the have not's who get a chance at it.[77]

Briscoe's crusade was also impelled by ZCEDC's commitment to establish a savings and loan that would be owned by Mexicanos. Briscoe was the major stockholder in the largest financial institution of the area, First State Bank of Uvalde, and it was apparent that he did not want competition, especially from a savings and loan controlled by RUP entrepreneurs pushing for the economic empowerment of Mexicanos in south Texas. Lisa Spann, writing in the *Texas Observer,* stated that the governor had involved in the campaign economic and political heavyweights who parroted his line—a veritable "Who's Who" of south Texas. John Muir reported in the *Texas Observer* that "as the reigning rancher/banker in the area, Briscoe is naturally upset to discover a model of collective farming right under his nose."[78]

Briscoe's crusade gained momentum. In October U.S. District Judge Jack Roberts in Austin granted the state's request for a temporary restraining order to stop further distribution of federal funds to ZCEDC. In November the state was given sixty days to review the controversial grant. Gutiérrez immediately moved to appeal the ruling before the Fifth U.S. Circuit Court of Appeals. Later that month the appellate court upheld review of the grant. In December the advisory committee of the Middle Rio Grand Development Council (MRGDC), headed by Dr. Alfredo Gutiérrez, the mayor of Del Rio, held a hearing on the matter and voted to disapprove ZCEDC's application. ZCEDC quickly submitted an appeal to MRGDC, which was denied on a 17–8 vote with one abstention. The irony of the vote was that several people voting to deny the appeal were Mexicanos.

That month a congressional committee recommended cancellation of the nearly $1.5 million grant on the ground of financial mismanagement. Rep. Floyd Hicks (D-Wash.), chair of the House Manpower and Housing Subcommittee, chastised CSA for not supervising ZCEDC and was hypercritical of alleged mismanagement by ZCEDC involving overpayment of consultants and other matters. In a letter to CSA Hicks expressed concern regarding Gutiérrez's Cuba statements: "We also find Judge Gutiérrez travels to Cuba and his reported statement that he would like to convert Crystal City into a 'little Cuba' to be ill advised in the light of the purposes of the Community Development Corporations and his position therein." At the state level Secretary of State Mark White sent certification to Attorney General Hill requesting dissolution of ZCEDC's articles of incorporation. With a mandated a thirty-day waiting period Gutiérrez publicly condemned the action and promised to fight in the courts. Despite the forces now standing in line to criticize ZCEDC, the court injunction that had frozen the funds expired on December 28, and ZCEDC was back in business.[79]

Despite Briscoe's best efforts, ZCEDC received a check for $67,000 from CSA in February 1977. It was a symbolic defeat for the governor. David had briefly triumphed over Goliath. In explaining the victory Gutiérrez alluded to the significant support of the grassroots community (letters, calls, meetings, lobbying): "Rather than trying to pull strings in Washington—which we didn't have to begin with—we took the only viable alternative, the grass roots support. And it worked. It always does."[80] The $67,000 covered the project's operating expenses for December, January, and the first half of February. Briscoe only intensified his campaign. He launched a well-organized lobbying effort aimed at the newly installed Carter administration.

A major reason that ZCEDC was able to weather Briscoe's firestorm of pressure was that, until now, Republicans had controlled the White House. Democrats charged that Republican administrators favored giving federal grant money to Mexicanos in an effort to forge political links with them. Angel Noe González concurred in an interview nearly twenty years later. He explained that much of the federal funding that RUP brought into Cristal was the result of Republican support. He added, "Particularly in my case, when I wanted something funded, I went to Senator Tower's office. I didn't dare go to Henry B. Gonzalez or

Chic Kazen or Kika de la Garza's office [U.S. Representatives Abraham Kazen and Eligio de la Garza, both Texas Democrats]. They were very anti–Raza Unida, very anti what we were doing. It was like it was an embarrassment for them what we were doing."[81]

Aware of this, Briscoe campaigned heavily for Carter and kept conservative Texas Democrats within the Democratic fold, squeaking past the Republicans in the presidential election. Lisa Spann of the *Texas Observer* described how the change in administration had strengthened Briscoe's crusade against ZCEDC: "No sooner was Carter installed in the White House than Briscoe began pestering top presidential aides to prevent the release of the grant. Dolph even showed up in person to plead his case and also used his clout to line up congressional support for his crusade to save South Texas from the Raza Unida–tied co-op."[82]

During 1977 CSA became supermeticulous in scrutinizing the community farm proposal. As a result, three problems surfaced: the transfer of ownership of the cooperative from the board to the farmworker members, alleged inadequacies in ZCEDC's management, and failure of the cooperative plan to sufficiently promote the economic well-being of Mexicanos in Zavala County—that it would merely create "a new class of stoop laborers." Gutiérrez and other ZCEDC officials categorically refuted CSA's findings. Gutiérrez argued that the cooperative would pump thousands of dollars into the area's depressed economy. But in late September 1977 CSA suspended the $855,000 allocated as venture capital for the purchase of the land. The agency justified the decision on the ground that ZCEDC had failed to follow the agency's instructions and to meet CSA's conditions in setting up its program.[83] But to Gutiérrez and RUP the Carter administration had caved in to Briscoe's crusade.

The decision flew in the face of two letters from CSA administrators that included positive remarks about ZCEDC's management. While on a quarterly monitoring visit to Cristal in April 1977, Eduardo Gutiérrez, program analyst from the Office of Economic Development, concluded:

Overall I believe that ZCEDC has made some very significant strides as it relates to administrative systems. The accounting and administration procedures manual is adequate in establishing fiscal and administrative control. It will now be very important for ZCEDC to follow these procedures to the letter. If this is done it will be unlikely that ZCEDC will face the administrative problems that have been faced in the past.[84]

Then on September 29 Gerrald K. Mukai, CSA's associate director, recommended release of the funds. In a memorandum to the court Mukai wrote: "The grant applicant has submitted a valid project and reunites the solicited conditions that were contested. . . . The investment proposal, as presented, has credible management and administration."[85]

ZCEDC's response to Briscoe's crusade was political and legal. Politically, Gutiérrez publicly blasted both Briscoe and Kazen in October 1977. Gutiérrez accused Briscoe of wanting to be a dictator and Kazen of being a "do-nothing congressman." In November Jesús Salas, ZCEDC's executive director, reported to the board that when he was in Washington, CSA officials had told him that the community farm would not be funded because of political pressures. The minutes of a report to the ZCEDC board by board member José Mata shows what happened:

Mr. Mata related that Mr. Mukai had related to them that the problems were not programmatic but political . . . that was why the venture had not been approved. Mr. Mata related that Mr. Mukai mentioned, several times, that it would be to the benefit of the ZCEDC if Mr. José Angel Gutiérrez resigned from the ZCEDC Board. Mr. Mata related that the ZCEDC Board was not in agreement with Mr. Mukai. Mr. Mukai related to them that he was not being malicious but that upon Mr. José Angel Gutiérrez's resignation the political pressures on CSA would lessen towards the ZCEDC. That's the way Mr. Mukai saw it, the political fight was between Mr. José Angel Gutiérrez and the Governor of Texas and that while Mr. José Angel Gutiérrez continued in the ZCEDC Board the Governor would continue putting up as many barriers as possible for the ZCEDC.[86]

With the situation rapidly deteriorating Gutiérrez spoke to some board members about submitting his resignation as a way to save the funding. At a meeting in December the board voted unanimously that the membership "was not going to accept Mr. José Angel Gutiérrez's resignation." The board also approved going forward with litigation against CSA.[87]

In November ZCEDC sued CSA to force the agency to release the money. The suit alleged that the denial of the funds was a political payoff to Briscoe by the Carter administration. Filed in U.S. District Court in Washington, D.C., the suit called for the release of the remaining $990,000 from the CSA's nearly $1.5 million grant. ZCEDC earmarked about $855,000 as investment capital for the purchase and development of the one-thousand-acre cooperative farm.[88] Using the Freedom of Information Act, ZCEDC received copies of eighteen memorandums dealing with its grant proposal. For the next few months the issue remained entangled in the courts.

U.S. District Judge Gerhard Gesell was assigned the case and exhorted CSA to settle with ZCEDC to avoid a trial. CSA presented

ZCEDC with a compromise that made release of the grant contingent upon the ZCEDC board's removing itself from running the project. Essentially, CSA's compromise called for the workers to be in control of management policies. ZCEDC officials agreed with CSA's offer. However, when ZCEDC's attorneys went to Washington, D.C., to complete the pretrial settlement, CSA officials reneged, saying that both Attorney General Griffin Bell and President Carter had personally objected to the agreement's language.[89]

On April 17, 1978, Judge Gesell, in a hearing that lasted a mere forty-five minutes, upheld Carter's claim of executive privilege in refusing to release internal documents related to the decision. He ruled that there was no evidence of "any wrong doing" by the White House in connection with the grant. The hearing produced several pieces of information. One was that Briscoe had written to President Ford on December 20, 1976, saying that giving a grant to ZCEDC was "un-Texan and un-American." Also, Briscoe had met with Carter eight days after the inauguration, and Briscoe's lawyers and aides had sent Carter a flurry of memoranda concerning the governor's objections to the grant. Further, on September 14, 1977, Frank Moore, assistant to the president; Margaret McKenna, deputy counsel to the president; and Joséph Aragon, special assistant to the president on Mexican-American affairs, had met with Graciela Olivares, director of CSA, at the White House to discuss the grant. Shortly thereafter Olivares announced that the money would not be released. Briscoe declined reporters' requests for comment on his meetings with White House officials.[90]

ZCEDC attorney Noe Flores said there was no way to appeal the judge's order. Jesús Salas charged that Carter was acting like Nixon in hiding behind the protection of executive privilege. In June 1978 Gesell dismissed the ZCEDC suit that alleged that White House pressure had influenced CSA's refusal to fund ZCEDC. The judge said he found "absolutely no evidence" to prove claims that Carter administration officials influenced CSA's decision to deny funding of ZCEDC's cooperative farm project. Dissatisfied with Salas's performance in the attempt to salvage the grant, the ZCEDC board asked for his resignation. When he refused, he was fired. Two other employees, David Ojeda and Miguel Delgado, resigned. Salas was replaced by Roberto Garcia, who had been the corporation's comptroller. In September 1978 CSA directed ZCEDC to come up with a plan for disposing of all its assets.[91]

In November the *Dallas Morning News* ran a provocative story under the headline "CSA Still Funding Texas Flop." The story attacked ZCEDC and criticized CSA for sending it $14,000 a month (the funding apparently continued because some agency officials thought the cooperative was a good idea). According to reporter Howard Swindle, ZCEDC had received more than $500,000 in two years but had failed to carry out the program for which it was funded. Garcia, ZCEDC's acting executive director, responded: "It's hard to come up with good programs when you don't know if you're going to have funding." In early January 1979 CSA discontinued all funding of ZCEDC's programs.[92] ZCEDC was the last hope of realizing the peaceful revolution's goal for economic empowerment. This occurred as RUP itself was becoming moribund. The ZCEDC leadership, acting in the belief that the organization could still secure other federal funding, decided to change its name as well as its focus and activity.

ZCEDC reemerged as the Community Agency for Self-Help (CASH). Gutiérrez remained the chair and Garcia the executive director, but the staff was cut. Although it remained committed to promoting economic development, the organization's activity shifted to housing and employment training programs. In a 1979 report from the chair Gutiérrez displayed a sense of historical perspective: "During the formative years of our CDC [community development corporation], we learned a great deal from CSA officials, President Carter, and Governor Dolph Briscoe about political deals. We lost our agricultural venture. We lost our real estate venture. We lost all support for refunding our CDC and were dropped by CSA. Nevertheless, we still exist, under a new name, Community Agency for Self-Help."[93]

Nevertheless, the end of ZCEDC was the final blow to RUP's economic development effort. The powerful farming, ranching, and Democratic political forces—the Goliaths of Texas—had collaborated to whip RUP, the David of south Texas. Because RUP was dependent on federal funding, the change to a Democratic administration in Washington was disastrous for Gutiérrez and RUP overall. The Democrats were determined to put an end to the Cristal experiment. By this time, even with the name change to CASH, nothing really was left of the peaceful revolution to motivate an interest in continuing the struggle for economic empowerment.

The Lo Vaca Issue: Cristal Loses Its Gas

The Lo Vaca gas issue exemplifies the powerful exogenous colonial economic forces that thwarted RUP's peaceful economic revolution. Lo Vaca was a thorn from 1975 to 1979. The issue engendered a protracted political and legal conflict between Cristal city officials and Lo Vaca Gathering Co., the city's natural gas supplier. For four years the flap received national media attention because of the skyrocketing increases in natural gas rates.

The conflict erupted in early March 1975 when the city council voted to repeal an ordinance passed in February 1974 that accepted a rate increase from Lo Vaca. Instead, the council decided to pay Lo Vaca its old contract price of 36 cents per one thousand cubic feet of gas, as stipulated in the 1972 contract. The city council's action was based on residents' inability to pay Lo Vaca's exorbitant rates. RUP mayor Ramon "Monche" Mata explained the rationale: "Too many of our citizens are on fixed incomes and can hardly cover their utility bill and have nothing left to buy food and for other living expenses. Small businessmen are likewise affected in that they are in business to pay for utilities." City officials gave another reason for the high tab: the city's gas system was plagued with leaks. According to City Clerk Teresa Flores, about 50 percent of the gas metered into the city's antiquated lines simply disappeared through leaks; the city and Lo Vaca disagreed about who was responsible for fixing the leaks.[94]

On March 17 the city council held a hearing on the rate issue. In attendance were representatives from the Railroad Commission (the state agency that regulated utilities and set rates), Lo Vaca Gathering Co., state representative Susan G. McBee, and state senator John Traeger. Robert Wells, vice president of Coastal States Gas Corp. and owner of Lo Vaca, informed city officials he did not have the power to reduce the rates. "The Texas Railroad Commission under the law sets the rates. We don't understand how they (the city) could change it," he said. The hearing produced no results. A few days later Lo Vaca gave city officials an ultimatum—pay the bill or the contract with the city would expire in thirty days. In April Lo Vaca filed a suit in Travis County District Court, asking for an order requiring the city to pay $1.35 per thousand cubic feet of gas metered into the city's distribution system. Again the company threatened to cut off the gas. In June the suit was moved to the 38th District Court in Zavala County. The city's debt by this time was $125,113. In August Lo Vaca filed a motion for a summary judgment, asking District Court Judge Ross E. Doughty to order the city to pay the fuel adjustment charges.[95]

A declaratory judgment by the 38th District Court in favor of the company allowed it to stop natural gas services to the city. Lo Vaca issued another ultimatum to the city for payment. In a letter Lo Vaca president and chief executive officer William E. Greehey informed the mayor that "if Crystal City does not make payment for past due amounts and agree to pay the interim rate for all future supplies, Lo Vaca will have no alternative but to terminate service. Should you decide not to meet the terms of the recent Court Order, service will be terminated November 7."[96]

The new guard coalition that controlled the city council was in the midst of the destructive turmoil of the political rupture and remained unyielding throughout 1975 on the gas issue. Mayor Arturo Gonzales felt the rates were unjust and pointed out that "they are threatening us now just before the winter season. . . . In the eyes of the law we could be wrong. But we are not going to pay." At town hall meetings in October the city took the issue to residents and asked them if they were willing to have their gas turned off. Council member Lupe Cortinas said, "I am willing to let them shut off my gas. This may be known as the town without gas." Despite the split within CU, people agreed that Cristal should fight Lo Vaca. On October 29 Mayor Gonzales announced that he was going to ask that Cristal be declared a disaster area if its natural gas supply was cut off. He stated, "I plan to write to President Ford, Governor Briscoe, the American Red Cross, and such organizations as the G. I. Forum for help in the event that the gas is shut off."[97]

In November 1975 the city responded to the 38th District Court ruling and Lo Vaca's ultimatum with an appeal to the 4th District Court of Civil appeals. The purpose of the appeal was to prevent the company from turning off the gas on the seventh. In the meantime Lo Vaca and city officials met to discuss the impasse. By this time the city was in arrears for $206,318.14. Lo Vaca asked the city to make an initial payment of $25,000 and issue a promissory note for $181,318.14. In addition, the company sought payment for future deliveries of natural gas within ten days of receipt of invoices. The proposed agreement also stipulated monthly installments of $10,073.23, with the first installment due and payable on or before December 5. The city rejected Lo Vaca's offer.[98]

While the city refused to pay Lo Vaca's adjusted rates, it continued to pay amounts based on the old contract rate. Attorney Ray Perez, representing the city, said that even the old rate was obsolete because Lo Vaca had announced that it had surplus natural gas. City officials in November were unsuccessful in their efforts to get Briscoe to intervene. Perez alleged that Briscoe was well aware of the brewing crisis.[99]

On March 17, 1976, the appellate court upheld Doughty's decision and ruled that Lo Vaca was entitled to cut gas service to the city if it failed to pay the nearly $300,000 that it owed. The city appealed to the Texas Supreme Court. In April the city affirmed its decision to pay Lo Vaca the old contract price of 36 cents. Attorney Perez reminded council members that if Lo Vaca declared bankruptcy, they would throwing the problem right into Briscoe's lap. On June 29 the Texas Supreme Court refused Cristal's application for a writ of error, noting no reversible error. The city lost another legal battle on July 20 when the Supreme Court denied its motion for a rehearing. Cristal city officials remained steadfast in their refusal to pay for gas delivered at the interim rate.

The gas situation did not become a crisis until late summer 1977. That August Lo Vaca president Greehey sent a letter to the people of Cristal attacking the city council for its intransigence. He informed them that the gas would be shut off on August 27 if the city did not pay Lo Vaca the amount of $720,765.77.[100] Cristal city officials countered Greehey's new ultimatum with an individual and class action suit. On August 15 five city residents filed suit in federal court in San Antonio. They requested a temporary restraining order preventing the gas cutoff. The suit asked that the Texas Railroad Commission intervene by holding a new hearing on the issue. By now the imbroglio was being seen as a war. The headline on the *San Antonio Light*'s July 30 story read, "Gas War Boils in Crystal City." And it certainly was a war: the city called for its police force to prevent Lo Vaca officials from coming in to shut off the gas supply. City Manager Raul Flores said, "We're going to place policemen at each valve station." Mayor Francisco Benavides declared, "We will not permit anybody—not even Gov. Dolph Briscoe's gendarmes—to come and cut us off."[101]

In August Cristal and Lo Vaca officials met again in another attempt to defuse the escalating crisis. On August 17 the city council agreed to pay the higher gas rate. It also agreed to turn over a thirty-three-acre parcel of city land to Lo Vaca for oil and gas exploration. In addition, it agreed to negotiate on the $720,765.77 debt to Lo Vaca. The city offered Lo Vaca payment of $100,000 if the company would agree to liquidate the balance. Lo Vaca rejected the city's offer and proceeded with its plans to cut off the gas.[102] U.S. Supreme Court Justice Louis Powell intervened in late August and ordered Lo Vaca officials not to turn off the gas. The petition for the restraining order was delivered to the Supreme Court by attorney Paul Rich, director of the Texas Rural Legal Aid Society office in Cristal.

But the restraining order was lifted within a few days. With the threat of the cut-off still pending, Zavala County Judge Gutiérrez issued his own temporary restraining order in early September. A hearing was scheduled for September 12, and Lo Vaca officials honored Gutiérrez's restraining order. Lo Vaca vice president Don Newquist explained, "Our position is that Judge Gutiérrez is without authority to issue such an order, but the company has elected to honor it for the time being."[103]

But the city lost. After a series of rulings from state appellate courts favoring Lo Vaca, the company made good on its threat on September 23, 1977, at 9:26 A.M. It cut off the gas. Rich immediately appealed to the Federal Power Commission in Washington, D.C., to restore the gas supply but had no success. The situation became even more tense. Cristal Police Chief Ramón Garza had predicted outbreaks of violence if Lo Vaca tried to shut off the gas. But that wasn't what happened. As the *Corpus Christi Caller* reported, "Several city and county officials had predicted the citizens of this town of 8,000 would 'strongly resist' attempts to cut off their gas. But most residents watched impassively from their front doors or yards as city crews went from house to house and shut off the gas."[104]

Gutiérrez was defiant. He warned that the matter was far from over and that the city could be put into receivership. He said, "Crystal City is Raza Unida. It is also Mexican American. This was a golden opportunity for the bigots and racists to say —— 'em. If this city is placed in receivership, I think all hell's going to break loose." The response of new guard city officials was much more subdued. Council member Rodolfo (Rudy) Espinosa Jr. met reporters outside city hall to notify them of the cut-off. Espinosa stressed that 67 percent of Cristal's population lived below the poverty level and that this cut-off would create extreme hardship. Asked why suppliers had refused to sell the city propane, another city official replied, "It's Briscoe's doing." The next day, infuriated with Lo Vaca's action, Espinosa said that the cut-off was "a concerted effort on behalf of the Texas judicial system, Lo Vaca, and the Railroad Commission to make an example of Crystal City. I truly believe it would not have happened if we hadn't alienated the Democratic Party in Texas."[105]

Mayor Benavides went to Washington to try to gain assistance from federal officials. In an interview with a reporter from the Washington, D.C., bureau of the Associated Press, he explained that the city did not expect miracles from the federal government. He said, "I don't know what we will do without gas and I don't know how long we will be without it. But this is America and if we can put a man on the moon, somehow we can find gas for a small Texas city."[106]

In Cristal people scrambled to buy electric ranges. Others flocked to stores to buy charcoal, butane, and firewood. Senator Edward Kennedy (D-Mass.) offered to help Cristal find federal assistance to pay off Lo Vaca and to have the gas turned on again. Shortly after the service was cut off, CSA gave the city a $310,000 grant as "crisis intervention funds." City officials used part of the money to buy propane tanks for every household and to run a meals program on Saturdays, Sundays, and Mondays. By the end of January 1978 Cristal residents had hooked up 960 electric stoves and had stockpiled five hundred cords of wood.[107] It was the beginning of a future without natural gas.

The situation only worsened in 1978. In its efforts to provide some relief to residents, the city installed propane tanks, but a serious problem developed. There were no propane suppliers close by. City officials soon learned that propane gas was more expensive than natural gas. So, although the city made propane gas available, many people could not afford it. In January Cristal's city manager reported that only three hundred tanks had been installed, and nearly five hundred families were on the waiting list. The twenty-five-gallon propane tanks were supposed to last a family thirty days, but the tanks ran out sooner because families were using the stoves to heat their homes.[108]

Although the community endured the increased hardships, the Lo Vaca crisis did not eradicate the fratricidal politics of Cristal. Between 1975 and 1977 the press alluded to the bickering among the warring factions over what approaches to use on Lo Vaca. The new guard in control of the council at times did not blame anyone. For example, schools superintendent Victor Lopez spoke to the *Corpus Christi Caller* about the conversion to propane. However, in trying to understand the community's willingness to endure the difficulties, the paper highlighted Cristal's leadership and the tendency for elected officials to hold several positions concurrently: "Lopez is a principal character. Besides serving as school superintendent, he also is a member of the city council trying to deal with an energy crisis. Also, on the city council is the assistant high school principal. The city chief of police serves on the school board."[109] But the white community was not so willing to trust in elected officials to resolve the crisis and endure hardship in the meantime. It was quite vocal in blaming the city's energy crisis on the city's mismanagement.

From 1978 to 1979 the issue of Lo Vaca remained in litigation and the people of Cristal remained without gas. In 1979 the city opposed the final settlement plan between Lo Vaca and the Coastal States Producing Co.

In early 1980, with people continuing to rely on propane and wood-burning stoves, the city began to experiment with solar conversion. The city implemented the Multi-City Solar Collector Demonstrating Project, which consisted of the installation of 120 solar heaters. That

year the city shut down its liquid gas (propane) plant, which had been
in operation since January 1978. By now the city owed Lo Vaca more
than $800,000. The city had been able to get into the propane gas busi-
ness with the assistance of a $310,000 grant from CSA. City Manager
Roberto Garcia explained the main reason for the plant closure: "When
the new city council went in April, it was evident to them that the
plant was not paying for itself."[110]

In late November 1980 the city council entertained the prospect of
getting the gas service reinstated. The council circulated questionnaires asking people whether they would be interested in reconverting
to natural gas. Lo Vaca was no longer the area's natural gas supplier.
A new company, Valero Transmission Co., a subsidiary of Coastal Producing Co. (which in turn was a subsidiary of Coastal States) and a
sister company to Lo Vaca, had taken over the franchise because Lo
Vaca no longer existed.[111] The arrangement would give the city regula-
tory power over the system and would grant a franchise to the new
supplier. The "gas shut-off crisis" was still up in the air when Gutiérrez
left Cristal in early 1981.

The failure to secure funding for ZCEDC, followed by the Lo Vaca
debacle, and the continued infighting among the various contentious
factions put an end to any hope of reviving RUP's economic empowerment agenda. Because of RUP's controversial past, the pervasiveness
of its fratricidal politics, and the acute energy crisis, Cristal became the
"politically untouchable city" of south Texas. Whatever city officials
did to attract industry was in vain. It was evident that by 1980 Cristal
still had no economic empowerment strategy. Thus it continued to be
dependent on the white elite and subordinate to internal colonialism.

10

Quest for Social Change

Equally important to RUP's peaceful revolution in Cristal was its commitment to social change. Through its political, educational, and economic struggles it fostered significant social change in Cristal's local government superstructures and policies, delivery of social services, establishment of new programs, Mexicano cultural awareness, organizational development, civic participation, and ultimately voting patterns. From the beginning of the peaceful revolution in 1970 to the political rupture in 1975, when it became moribund, the Cristal experiment in community control was also an experiment in social change. Control of local government structures, establishment of a Chicano third party, and community organization became the most important instruments for fostering social change. Next to politics and education, the peaceful revolution scored its greatest successes in the area of social change.

RUP's Struggle for Social Change

Community control of local government was crucial to RUP's efforts to bring about social change and begin the process of extricating Cristal from the clutches of internal colonialism.[1] Before the second revolt local governmental superstructures (e.g., the city council, school board, and county court of commissioners), all long controlled by whites, had not been instruments of social change but had been used to maintain control over the Mexicano majority. Furthermore, the white majority used government to promote infrastructure development and services and programs that benefited only the white minority. Cristal, like so many other south Texas towns, was like Charles Dickens's *Tale of Two Cities* with a racial twist. The white neighborhoods were essentially prosperous and represented the "best of times"—fairly nice modern homes, paved streets, street lights, utilities, few social problems, and numerous amenities courtesy of local government. Conversely, the barrios personified the "worst of times." The barrios were impoverished and featured dilapidated housing, unpaved streets, a myriad of social problems, and few services—some had no city water.

Having wrested political control from the minority gringo power holders, Mexicanos were now in a position to alter local public policy to meet the social welfare needs of the community. For five years RUP controlled the Cristal city council and held the reins in the county by 1974. During this time the peaceful revolution brought to Mexicanos the best of times. RUP was committed to improving Mexicanos' quality of life. Although local government became a servant of the majority, this did not happen at the expense of the white community; instead, the infrastructure development, services, and programs benefited everyone. Thus community control gave RUP the opportunity to bore from within to effect change.

During the next five years RUP city officials worked diligently to improve existing services and programs. To begin the process the city council moved aggressively to purge whites from the city's administration and commissions, and the city recruited Mexicanos to replace the city's administrators, technicians, and staff personnel. This enabled city officials to move expeditiously in bringing to improve Cristal's impoverished barrios—paving streets; installing curbs and gutters; laying sewer, gas, and water lines; and providing efficient trash collection. In addition, the city built hundreds of houses for low-income residents and renovated others. The city's poor got access to health care, mental health counseling, job training, and senior lunch programs.[2] Similar changes occurred at the county level when RUP won control of the county court of commissioners in 1974. Because both local governments were limited in their capacity to raise revenue, many programs were federally funded, making its approach to decolonization and social change paradoxical.

The peaceful revolution also sought to boost Mexicanos' civic participation, cultural adherence to "Chicanismo," and organizational development. RUP's social change agenda was predicated on involving residents in the decision-making process. Thus a form of participatory democracy under the aegis of Ciudadanos Unidos (CU) was integral to the success of the peaceful revolution.[3] Although CU evolved into a political machine, hundreds of families participated in various aspects of the Cristal experiment in community control. Existing organizations were strengthened and new ones formed. People who had never participated were encouraged to join organizations, attend local government meetings, serve on commissions and various committees, run for office, and especially to vote. Migrant workers, women, students, businesspersons, professionals, and teachers, among others, were all part of the peaceful revolution's participatory renaissance.

The city's effort to include the Mexicano populace in the process of community governance meant that officials conducted meetings in both Spanish and English and encouraged constituents to speak out with complaints or about problems. The council moved to revoke the jurisdiction of the state police and the Texas Rangers to prevent them from harassing people within the city's limits. Gringos had always used law enforcement to discourage the civic participation of Mexicanos. Now, to make the Mexicano community feel more at ease with the city's new police department, the all-Mexicano force was required to undergo a rigorous training program to increase its professionalism and efficiency.[4] The renaissance was also cultural. Pride in Mexicano culture, language, and heritage became pervasive and overt. Thus for five golden years Cristal was the epitome of a community determined to break socially from the yoke of internal colonialism.

Urban Renewal

In November 1970 the city council moved to purge the Urban Renewal Commission by filling two of the five terms. The seats targeted were held by old guard commissioners Del Harp and Carmen Contreras. Francisco Benavides, who was RUP mayor pro tem, recommended that Gutiérrez and Rodolfo Palomo be appointed. Mayor Paulino R. Mata was opposed to those appointments, but the RUP-controlled city council prevailed on a 3–2 vote. At the next city council meeting in December RUP's majority initiated a coup d'état against Mata. On a 3–0 vote the council removed Mata and named Benavides mayor. CU's political machinery quickly moved to justify the ouster. In an editorial in *La Verdad* Benavides explained: "The post of Mayor of Cristal is one which must be taken seriously. The Mayor is in the position to decide the direction of the influential commissions and via their power name people to these commissions. If those designated to those commissions do not have the general welfare of the community, then the decisions will not reflect the interests of the community of which they claim to serve."[5]

Before the final vote was taken, Mata and council member Santos Nieto walked out in protest. Mata was furious and argued that the charges against him "were out of line." He claimed that he had complied completely with the legal requirements when he refused to recognize the motion to nominate Gutiérrez and Palomo because such action was not on the agenda. Upon the resignation of old guard commissioner Alfonso Navarez on December 14, the RUP-controlled council appointed José Serna as his replacement.[6]

As a result of the removal of Mayor Mata and the appointments made by the council the U.S. Department of Housing and Urban Development (HUD) temporarily closed the Urban Renewal Agency in January 1971. The agency's executive director, Sam Anderson, objected to the appointments on the ground that the council had not followed HUD's guidelines in making them. With all the controversy, HUD officials ordered the agency closed until the question was settled. While the agency was closed, HUD kept threatening to withdraw its grants to the Urban Renewal Agency and the Housing Authority.[7]

Throughout January 1971 Cristal city officials met with HUD officials to work out the impasse, and by late February the agency had resumed full operation. All the restrictions that had been placed on it were removed, with the stipulation that all activities had to be carried out within the framework of HUD directives. HUD essentially sanctioned the council's action by not ruling on the legality of the two appointments. Finnis E. Jolly, area director of HUD, said in a letter to the council, "We wish to emphasize that by suggesting these procedures we are taking no positions as to who are and who are not the duly and legally appointed members of your Board of Commissioners."[8] HUD's guidelines included procedural directives for conducting the agency's meetings and business. RUP council members and commissioners continued to press for the removal of the agency's old guard personnel and two remaining two old guard board members.

The HUD ruling enhanced the efforts of RUP city officials to consolidate their control over the agency. Gutiérrez and the other RUP board members got into a tug-of-war with Anderson. Palomo resigned to take another position and was replaced by Virginia Musquiz. The conflict escalated to the point that Anderson threatened to resign, then withdrew his resignation. This was after the RUP-controlled board had informed Anderson at a meeting that he no longer had the power to hire and fire. When Anderson threatened to resign, Gutiérrez gave him a sheet of paper and invited him to write his resignation without delay.[9]

This series of events ended in July with Anderson's resignation and those of eleven of the thirteen members of the agency's staff. The only two employees who did not resign were Esmeralda Torres, receptionist, and Jesús Almarez, outside maintenance employee. In his letter of resignation Anderson wrote, "It appears that I no longer enjoy the confidence of the majority of commissioners which is imperative to the success of an operation of this kind." On a 3–1 vote the board voted to accept all resignations. The board subsequently named Juan E. Cotera of Mercedes as executive director.[10]

Upon taking over the agency, Cotera initiated a reorganization of administration, staff, and program priorities. With only two employees left from the previous administration, Cotera's first priority was to hire new staff. Rodolfo Palomo, a former urban renewal commissioner, was hired as deputy executive director. The other ten vacant positions were filled by loyal RUP supporters who had some college education. In contrast, few on Anderson's staff had even a high school education. The new staff members went through a HUD training program in San Antonio.[11]

For more than a month Cotera spent considerable time organizing the agency's filing system. He ascertained the status of projects, which revealed that the agency's four major projects were nearly bankrupt; people were afraid of and distrusted the agency; the agency was paying out small benefits to people displaced by the project's housing programs; Anderson's administration had done little to convince the Mexicano community of the benefits of the various projects; and most of the development, such as housing and street improvement, was occurring in the white parts of town.[12]

Between 1971 and 1973 the Urban Renewal Agency worked to fix these five problems. During this time another major task of the agency was getting HUD to refund its projects. Cotera made several trips to Washington, D.C., to meet with politicians and bureaucrats who had influence with HUD and submitted applications for additional funding. The agency was assured that HUD would come through. Meanwhile, RUP school officials initiated the $3 million school bond referendum, set for April 1972. An article in *La Verdad* explained the connection between the agency and bond effort: "The impact of the school bond on Urban Renewal is very great because ... the federal government gives three dollars for every dollar that the city spends [in a matching program] for the betterment of the community."[13]

In March 1972 Senator John Tower (R-Texas) informed the agency that it had been funded for $265,898. A month later the other three projects were funded, for a total of $5.5 million.[14] It had taken almost two years to resolve the agency's funding problems. This was accomplished in great part because Republicans in Washington were courting RUP for political support for the 1972 presidential elections.

For much of the next four years the Urban Renewal Agency made securing funding for its expanding projects a priority. Moreover, it continued to strengthen its educational and marketing campaign, which sought to win people's support as well as their confidence in its ability to provide services and programs. The agency bought radio spots and conducted interviews at the local radio station. It also ran ads and articles in RUP's *La Verdad*. Ciudadanos Unidos used its networks and meetings to distribute information about the agency's various projects. The campaign exhorted people to meet and talk with Cotera. According to Cotera, "Many of the people would just come in to see if I would really see them." He felt people were continually testing him. Whereas Anderson seldom sought feedback from the community, Cotera always did.[15]

In reinforcing the Urban Renewal Agency's community marketing efforts, *La Verdad* in almost every issue published stories and carried pictures of the homes built under the aegis of the agency (the Housing Commission, by contrast, was responsible solely for running low-income housing administered by the Housing Authority). Cotera's philosophy of "people involvement" did much to resolve the agency's past problems, especially the distrust. Cotera said that he worked with the following guidelines in mind:

1. Make different housing models available
2. Direct people's aspirations toward larger homes
3. Explain in detail the particulars of a contract for rental or title before the party signed it
4. Give families a choice of rebuilding on their lot or elsewhere in order to help them remain at their original home site
5. Give properties the highest reasonable appraisal
6. Ensure the availability of the agency's staff to assist people in whatever capacity they needed

From 1971 to the political rupture in 1975 the Urban Renewal Agency was zealous in its commitment to become an instrument of change and service for Mexicanos of Cristal. Unlike other urban renewal agencies, which at times were threatening to the poor, the agency in Cristal remained mindful of being people oriented. As Cotera said, the people in Cristal "know they have some power with us."[16]

Despite the agency's populist orientation, it was not immune from attack. In September 1971 Rafael Garcia, a Cristal citizen who was unhappy with an agency decision regarding his property, entered the agency's office and shot Cotera and agency employees Tom Cano and Mercedes Ruiz Casarez. Both Cotera and Cano were hospitalized, and Cotera lost two fingers on his left hand.[17]

The property dispute was a carryover from the Anderson administration. For about two years the agency had been unable to agree with Garcia and his mother on a price for property they owned in the agency's targeted redevelopment area. The agency offered the Garcia family $10,000 for their property, but the Garcias refused to sell, and the issue went into litigation. Anderson finally initiated condemnation proceedings. Garcia, armed, waited for the city to evict him. Months passed in stalemate. Finally, Garcia informed Anderson that he would take the city's offer. Anderson countered that Garcia was now entitled to only $400 because of liens that had been placed on the property. Throughout the two-year ordeal Garcia perceived the agency's action as a conspiracy against him and his mother.

When Cotera took charge of the Urban Renewal Agency, the matter still had not been resolved. For weeks Cotera sought to persuade Garcia to accept $2,500 for the property. On September 9 Garcia and his mother met with Cotera. At the meeting Cano informed them that Garcia was no longer eligible for the $2,500. According to Cotera, Garcia became enraged and declared, "This is not going to be solved until I kill one of them." Cotera and Cano were standing in the agency doorway, talking to Garcia's mother, when Garcia fired on them. Cotera explains: "As I reached for the door he shot me. He hit me in the hand. I looked at my hand and there was no finger. It was all jagged. When Tom heard the first shot, he just dropped to the ground. The gun was aimed at his leg and he was shot."[18] Both men were airlifted by helicopter to Santa Rosa Medical Center in San Antonio.

Garcia was indicted in October 1971 by a Zavala County grand jury on a charge of assault with intent to commit murder with malicious afterthought. He was subsequently found guilty. In June 1973 Cano sued the agency for $100,000, citing agency negligence, and claimed that he suffered severe and disabling injuries. Attorney Jesse Gamez, representing the city, filed a categorical denial of Cano's allegations.[19]

The Urban Renewal Agency's funding track record from 1970 to 1975 was impressive. The agency was in the vanguard of RUP's redevelopment efforts, and RUP agency officials succeeded in securing millions of dollars in federal funding for housing and city infrastructure improvements. The *Arkansas Gazette* wrote, "The big money has been federal Urban Renewal, a dormant program until La Raza Unida took over and put it to work for the Chicano."[20] Just a couple of months before the political rupture in 1975, Rodolfo Palomo, then executive director, reported on the agency's track record in housing: "Since 1971 the agency has built 166 new homes while the old administration built only 125 in a decade. Last year [1974] 56 new urban renewal houses valued at some $1 million went up and a 116-unit $1.9 million public housing project is going up."[21]

The RUP Urban Renewal Agency created a housing renaissance that liberated many poor families from substandard living conditions that had been created as a direct result of internal colonialism.

Housing Authority

RUP city officials also moved to consolidate their control over the city's Housing Authority. The closing of the Urban Renewal Agency in January 1971 affected their efforts to purge the Housing Authority. HUD's threats to cut funding to both entities forced the two new RUP appointees, Viviana Santiago and Elida Garza, to proceed prudently in consolidating RUP's control over the Housing Authority. In April 1971 Ramon "Monche" Mata was appointed to the Housing Commission, replacing José Talamantez, who had resigned upon being elected to the city council.[22]

As the Urban Renewal Agency's problems were being resolved, Santiago and others began organizing a tenants' union, Renteros Unidos, within the Housing Authority. Scores of tenants joined, and the union was incorporated. They elected officers and formulated three major goals: to remodel all housing-project buildings, to give tenant-occupants the jobs created by the remodeling project, and to make various new types of services available to the tenants. At several impassioned meetings Renteros Unidos pressured the housing director and commission to implement the three goals. Executive Director Elvira Galvan, a member of the old guard, resisted. She alleged that RUP was communist and that RUP commissioners only wanted to steal HUD's money.[23]

Nevertheless, by the May meeting HUD had recognized the legitimacy of RUP's housing commissioners. Renteros Unidos followed up by asking the commission to dismiss Galvan. With one commissioner absent, the board voted 3–1 to fire her and replace her with Eddie Treviño, a RUP school board member who had been fired from his job at Del Monte.[24] Treviño recounted how he got the job of executive director:

I didn't know anything. I didn't know how much the rent was for one of the houses nor how to go about collecting it. I didn't know anything about housing. The only thing I was told is that I was unemployed and that there was a job open, so I applied. They asked me if I knew anything about bookkeeping. I told them that the only knowledge I had on the subject was what I had learned in high school. That was it—that was all. They asked me, "Can you divide and multiply?" I said yes, I can. After three days they gave me the job.[25]

For the first two weeks he spent hours studying manuals on the different facets of running the housing project. In June he was sent to George Washington University in Washington, D.C., for an intense eight-week training course on public housing. According to Santiago, thanks to the efforts of Nacho Pérez, a MAYO leader, of San Antonio, Treviño received a $2,500 scholarship from the National Association of Housing Redevelopment.[26] While Treviño was in Washington, Santiago administered the Housing Authority.

By June 1971 RUP was in control of the Housing Authority's administration. An old guard commissioner, Epsie Bell Taylor, was ousted but not before she had hired a architect, Luke Galvan. He was contracted to develop plans for a low-rent public housing project for which HUD funding was anticipated. In May HUD approved $2.1 million for the project, and the agency fired Galvan. Santiago, who played a pivotal leadership role with the Housing Commission, explained why the architect was dismissed: "We saw the plans. They were awful. They were plans that he had done a long time ago. He used the same plans over and over again. We fired him, we gave him the three days' notice required by HUD. We refused to pay him. We immediately hired a new architect, Jorge Ozuna, on the basis that he was Mexicano."[27]

When Treviño returned from the training course in Washington, he initiated other changes. Treviño's administrative philosophy was to work with and for the benefit of the community and not to take their money. According to Treviño, Elvira Galvan had been a dictator. For example, rent was due on the fifth of every month. If a tenant was late with the rent, the Housing Authority turned off the utilities. Treviño abolished this policy and instituted new guidelines that included additional time to pay. Every case was handled according to the circumstances. The Housing Authority helped the elderly who resided in the housing project to maintain the lawns and gardens, and the agency assumed responsibility for painting the units. This reversed the earlier policy that required occupants to purchase the paint and paint the dwellings themselves. Renteros Unidos, acting in an advisory capacity, participated in the administration of the Housing Authority. Another important change was the lowering of monthly rents.[28]

During 1973 the Housing Authority continued to work on its two top priorities: construction of new units and upgrading existing dwellings. In 1970 the Housing Authority used a $356,712 HUD grant to build ten duplexes. The next year the agency landed the the $2.1 million HUD grant to build 125 units. The project was plagued by problems from the beginning. In 1971 Galvan, the architect, won his lawsuit and was awarded $24,000 in damages.[29] The agency ran into more problems when it tried to to get more money for relocating families displaced by the project as well as additional money to cover the costs of hiring the new architect.

After months of meetings HUD agreed to give the Housing Authority an additional $700,000. But the difficulties did not end there. HUD would not approve the plans prepared by Ozuna. According to Santiago, "The hassle with the plans was that HUD didn't want us to use so much land. They felt that twenty-nine acres was just too much." Ozuna managed to convince HUD officials that Mexicanos needed larger yards for vegetable and flower gardens. Then the Federal Aviation Administration, caretaker of the site, procrastinated in giving the city approval to use the land, again delaying construction.

In 1973 HUD awarded the Housing Authority nearly $300,000 to remodel units in the old housing project by enlarging kitchens and repainting both inside and out; providing new stoves and refrigerators; enlarging and replacing equipment in the community center; and constructing a new playground with a pool, barbeque pits, picnic tables and benches, and landscaping.[30]

In 1973 the Housing Commission also underwent a change in leadership. Because Viviana Santiago had been elected to the school board and was preoccupied with writing proposals, she resigned as both chairperson and member of the board. Juan Guerrero, a board member, was elected chair in her place. By early 1974 the Housing Commission consisted of Elida Garza, Santos Puente, Lupe Cortinas, and Pancho Rodriguez.[31] Their interests were in getting the $2.1 million project for 125 units off the ground and in securing additional funding.

It was not until August 1974 that the Housing Authority sought bids for construction of the 125 units. Treviño decided that twenty-five units would be designated for elderly housing and the remaining hundred would be family units. The project included construction of a community building that would house a day-care center, library, and meeting room.[32] Although the bidding process was open to all, most of the Housing Authority's construction and remodeling jobs went to Constructora Aztlán. These were contracts that had historically gone to white contractors. Thus the Housing Authority managed to stage its peaceful social revolution, putting Mexicano contractors to work building low-income housing for scores of poor families.

Zavala County Mental Health Outreach Program

In 1971 the city initiated efforts to provide mental health services for the community. Viviana Santiago again played a key role. She and others from Cristal attended a meeting on mental health called by the Hogg Foundation of Austin. After a series of discussions foundation officials and staff from the University of Texas Medical School at San Antonio agreed to give Cristal $26,556 to establish a city health department.[33] The staff and doctors at the medical school provided on-site instruction, supervision, coordination, and technical assistance.

The Hogg Foundation regarded the nine-month grant as seeding a project that had the potential to become a model for other areas with similar populations and health problems. The goals of the project were to eradicate all preventable disease through a combination of vaccinations, health education, and development of safer, more sanitary living conditions; establish facilities to serve all residents of Zavala County, regardless of economic status; develop mental health facilities and services geared to meet the specific cultural needs of Mexicanos; and eradicate alcohol and drug abuse. The project was designated the Zavala County Mental Health Outreach Program (ZCMHOP). The city council appointed Erasmo Andrade, the civil rights activist who had headed the school district's bilingual program, as the project's director, and he hired three field workers and a secretary-receptionist and recruited two community volunteers. A countywide citizens' advisory group, the Zavala County Health Committee, was formed to work with the staff to ensure the widest degree of participation by the community.[34]

In the early months of the program Andrade was able to hire additional personnel with funding from such sources as the Concentrated Employment Program of the U.S. Department of Labor. The new staff received in-service training on various aspects of mental health. While developing the mental health programs, Andrade initiated a weekend clean-up of the city that involved scores of volunteers. The goal was to beautify the city by cleaning up empty lots, sweeping sidewalks, picking up trash along the streets, and the like.[35]

In 1972 Andrade expanded the development of the new mental health programs. Working to meet the socioeconomic needs of the community, Andrade reasoned that "our job was to try to alleviate some of the social and economic problems of La Raza." This meant not only ensuring that people had adequate food, shelter, and employment but that they also had prenatal care, child care, family planning, nutrition, and other services vital to improving their quality of life. Andrade also sought to ensure that insensitive public agencies such as the Texas Department of Social Services, the surplus commodities program, and the county courts became more responsive to meeting the community's mental health needs.[36]

In June 1972 the the outreach program obtained a grant from the U.S. Department of Health, Education, and Welfare (HEW) to conduct an extensive study of the seven-county Winter Garden area. The project was known as the Winter Garden Research Project, and José Angel Gutiérrez was named its director. The project's three objectives were to determine the mental health needs and resources in the seven-county area; summarize or assess these findings in a report to enable the health clinic to develop an ideal mental health program; and create a training program.[37] The project, which began in June 1972 and concluded on June 1, 1973, provided valuable data about the pervasiveness of the poverty permeating the area, thus justifying the funding of health and mental health programs.

That same year Andrade succeeded in securing additional federal funding for a new social service program that would provide youth counseling, services to senior citizens, and home services. The program was administered through the the outreach program. Jeanette Lizcano, a former teacher in Cristal, administered the youth counseling service. Susana Elizondo was appointed to direct the senior citizens component and Beatrice Mata to run home services. In October a new multiservice community center opened in what was formerly the convent for the Sacred Heart Catholic Church. All the programs operated out of the center, which also offered guitar and painting classes, youth rap sessions, and other courses.[38]

By 1973 the outreach program was providing the community with badly needed services. It became an excellent medium for legitimizing and strengthening RUP's community control. Before the second revolt neither the city nor the county made much of an effort to provide the community with the services it needed so badly. Through Andrade's leadership the agency now had four components in place to alleviate social problems attributed to mental illness and antisocial behavior. The Home Maker component helped the elderly, ill, and incapacitated with cooking, housekeeping, shopping, and basic nursing care. The youth counseling program offered individual and group counseling services. Two areas of concern were drug abuse and vocational education. The third component was a variety of activities for the elderly, including arts and crafts, musical entertainment, gardening, and consumer education. The fourth component was direct mental health. It provided social counseling, psychiatric referrals, and consultation referrals to other public social service agencies, such as the Texas Department of Welfare, Social Security, and the Veterans Administration.[39] From 1973 until the political rupture in 1975 the city continued to promote mental health through a variety of services. In 1973 Andrade initiated a drug abuse prevention program in conjunction with the youth component of the outreach program and local migrant groups. In 1975 the outreach program was renamed the Zavala County Mental Health Center (ZCMHC). Its primary goals were to improve care and treatment for hospitalized patients, encourage the development of treatment centers in the community, improve services for mentally ill children, develop after-care and rehabilitative services, and to support programs aimed at preventing mental illness.[40]

Zavala County Health Corporation, Inc.

One of the greatest achievements of RUP's peaceful revolution was the establishment of a health clinic in Cristal. It has become a model in south Texas. Efforts to organize the clinic began in the summer of 1971 with the formation of an hoc committee of twenty-two RUP supporters. The committee's mission was to look into the possibilities of establishing a health clinic that would provide low-cost health care to the Mexicanos of the area, especially those who were migrants. The committee was impelled by a sense of urgency because of the limited health care available to poor Mexicanos. Few could afford to pay for the medical services offered by the area's few doctors and hospitals.

In August the ad hoc committee made a commitment to support establishment of a health center. That same month Tom Uridel, a representative from HEW, met with the committee to discuss feasibility and funding. Encouraged by Uridel's response, the ad hoc committee voted in February 1972 to apply for funding. In May the committee was incorporated as a nonprofit corporation, by-laws were drawn, a fifteen-member board of directors was selected, and the organization was renamed the Zavala County Health Association, Inc. (ZCHAI). Viviana Santiago, Erasmo Andrade, and Sally Andrade were instrumental in its formation.

That year, while Santiago was in Washington, D.C., attending a conference sponsored by the National Institute of Mental Health, she succeeded in securing funding for the city's mental health outreach program. While there she also met with officials from HEW and the Office of Economic Opportunity (OEO) about funding ZCHAI's proposed clinic. She convinced them to send personnel to Cristal to assist ZCHAI in developing a funding proposal.

On June 14, 1972, the OEO award ZCHAI $391,000 to establish a health facility that would provide a full-range of medical services— family medicine, dental services, and mental health counseling.[41] Luz Gutiérrez, wife of José Angel, became ZCHAI's first executive director in July. Until she left Cristal for Oregon in 1980, Luz Gutiérrez was the principal force behind the establishment of the successful health center.

From the grant ZCHAI allocated $277,000 for construction of a health center. The remainder was used to hire medical personnel for the clinic. In August Governor Preston Smith vetoed the local health plan, declaring, "The Zavala County Health Association's application does not adequately reflect that meaningful health services can be made available to the recipients within the near future." He was critical of ZCHC for supposedly failing to bring other agencies into the planning and coordinate with them.[42]

The governor's decision froze ZCHAI's funds. Luz Gutiérrez believed that Smith and others did not want to fund the project because ZCHC was a creation of RUP, which they saw as too militant and too radical. RUP countered by sending some ZCHC board members to Washington, D.C., in October to lobby Philip Sánchez, OEO's director. On September 19 Sánchez reinstated the grant over the governor's objections. ZCHC received a letter of credit for $140,000 to begin the preliminary work of providing health services to the poor of the area. In October it received $244,000 from HEW. The total funding for the project was more than $600,000.[43]

The reinstatement of the grant resulted in a firestorm of criticism from Democrats who alleged that RUP or, more specifically, José Angel Gutiérrez had cut a deal with the Nixon administration regarding the 1972 presidential election. In October Democratic presidential candidate George McGovern accused RUP of being on the Nixon payroll.[44] McGovern's anger was over the no-endorsement position taken by RUP at its El Paso national convention in September. According to the *Sentinel*, "The grant itself was termed 'a trick of the Republicans' to demonstrate President Nixon's commitment to the Spanish surnamed." This allegation was also made by Dr. Jorge Prieto, a physician who at the time was being considered to head the clinic. In a letter to Luz Gutiérrez he wrote: "You can scream that 'La Raza Unida' is not going to support either major party and that this is proof of your independence. But there is no way you can deny that the present administration is making you a gift of the clinic. . . . Divide and conquer, 'devide y ven-ceras,' has never been better applied than in your case. It will actually be a cheap price for Nixon to pay. Two or one million dollars to help him carry Texas."[45]

In an acrimonious reply to Prieto's letter, Luz Gutiérrez wrote:

You have proven by your actions that some weak members of La Raza, such as yourself, Dr. Prieto, are continuing to let themselves be used by the gringo in his political fights with each other. If you are truly concerned with reform of the American electoral and parties system, I suggest you look into your own local situation first. . . . Boss Daley's reputation is world-wide. Chicanos in Cristal have read your letter and have strongly voiced objections to being the object of your paranoia and senility."[46]

Joining Luz Gutiérrez and other RUP leaders in categorically re-jecting McGovern's allegation was Cristal's mayor, Francisco Benav-ides, who called McGovern a liar. Schools superintendent Angel Noe González sat for an interview with the *Sentinel* and conceded that RUP had no Democratic friends in Austin or Washington, D.C. He also called McGovern a liar for implying that the grant was a political trick. Throughout the presidential campaign Gutiérrez attacked McGovern and challenged Nixon to show the Mexicano community by action how badly he wanted their vote. More than twenty years later Gutiér-rez continued to maintain that neither he nor anyone else within RUP had cut a deal with the Nixon administration. Yet, according to Gonzá-lez, RUP in Cristal did rely heavily on Republicans in its acquisition of federal funding for its diverse programs; the Republicans' courting of Mexican-American voters, begun by the Nixon administration, is well documented.[47]

In November 1973 Jim Wood, reporter for the *San Antonio Express News*'s Washington bureau, wrote that, according to Watergate Com-mittee testimony, the Nixon administration overrode Governor Smith's objections to the health clinic grant in order to gain support from RUP for Nixon's reelection bid. Wood said that Senate Watergate files showed that Gutiérrez had in fact asked for "quiet" Republican help. According to Wood, a memorandum from Alex Almendaris—who was directing the Nixon reelection campaign's Mexicano activities—said that Gutiérrez had sought this help during the summer of 1972. The memo stated that Gutiérrez had approached Almendaris's office and requested a "quiet Republican contribution to La Raza Unida." The memo further stated that the money would be used to help Ramsey Muñiz, RUP's candidate for governor, and that in return RUP would condemn McGovern.

According to Wood, "It was never made clear if any covert contribution was ever made to the Raza Unida." He went on to say that according to the memos, the White House "was quite concerned with keeping them [RUP] neutralized." As the election drew nearer, Almendaris "asked a White House assistant for domestic affairs to try to shake loose some pending grants for Zavala County." Release of the health clinic grant, Armendaris said, would "help win, at least, the neutrality of Gutiérrez and he repeated his belief that the committee can't publicly support Raza Unida without angering Republicans and make Raza Unida appear it had sold out." Ramsey Muñiz said that RUP got no help from the Republicans, and he offered to testify before the Watergate Committee.[48]

This controversy continued to haunt Gutiérrez and RUP beyond the presidential election. However, according to Luz Gutiérrez, it was quickly overshadowed by various internal problems that were impeding the development of the health clinic. In November 1973 the OEO appointed a committee of Texas citizens to review the grant and to assist and advise on ways to make the clinic a viable entity for the area's poor. Another problem was recruiting a physician and trained medical personnel who were willing to live in a small rural town and work for low salaries. Luz Gutiérrez tried to recruit personnel in Mexico, but she was thwarted by the legal and professional restrictions.[49]

Then there were the concerted efforts of various people and groups that wanted to prevent the construction of the clinic. This opposition allowed OEO to procrastinate on signing the paperwork that would allow construction to begin. Cristal's two white physicians also opposed the clinic. According to Paul Rich, who ran the local legal aid agency, they were uncooperative because they owned the local hospital.[50]

Groundbreaking ceremonies for the clinic were held in July 1973. For RUP the building of a health clinic in Cristal was a major victory. About one thousand people attended the groundbreaking ceremony. The clinic was named El Centro de Salud [The Health Center]. RUP's leadership used construction of the clinic and reorganization of the health association to demonstrate the party's commitment to fostering real and concrete social change—by delivering health services and hiring Mexicanos through Constructora Aztlán to build the clinic.[51]

Between late 1973 and 1975 the the health association continued to provide and expand its delivery of health care services. In September 1973 Executive Director Luz Gutiérrez submitted a budget of $800,000 for the 1974 budget year. In 1974 Centro de Salud and another health care center were the only ones in Texas chosen by the U.S. Department of Agriculture to participate in the Special Supplemental Food Program for Women. Initially, the myriad services offered by Centro de Salud were provided from the Sacred Heart Church Parish Hall. These services included tuberculosis control, immunizations, venereal disease control, and family planning. Other more specific services involved diabetic screening, blood pressure testing, and pulmonary function tests for emphysema, chronic bronchitis, and other respiratory diseases. A mobile X-ray van equipped for diagnostic purposes was also made available.[52]

While Centro de Salud's health care services expanded in 1974, the clinic's construction became a problem. Initially, Constructora Aztlán was awarded the contract for $277,000 to build the clinic in 1973. However, as explained in Chapter 9, Constructora Aztlán was plagued by management and legal problems. Work on the clinic progressed for about a year, then was halted because of financial and legal difficulties. In August 1974 the health association board canceled the contract. However, in 1975, after negotiations with HEW, the health association was awarded an additional $925,000 to pay for ongoing services and to complete the clinic. The health association awarded a new construction contract for $291,818 to K&J Services of San Antonio.[53] Because of the delays the clinic had yet to be completed when the political rupture occurred in August 1975. However, Centro de Salud hired its first full-time physician and continued to provide health services without any serious disruptions.

Oficina de la Gente

In 1971 the city council moved to establish a legal aid agency. In an article in *La Verdad* Viviana Santiago described the city council's rationale:

For Chicanos in South Texas the law has traditionally been repressive and justice has been expensive—Texas Rangers (*los rinches*) have no Chicano blood in their veins but plenty on their boots. Too many Chicanos have died or been incarcerated without ever knowing "liberty" or "justice." The right of Chicanos to pursue happiness is neutralized by a desperate struggle to survive. Meanwhile, the law ignores usurious practices of merchants, ranchers, and elected officials that lock Chicanos into the unending cycle of poverty without recourse to the law. Chicanos may have been in the majority numerically, but they are consistently convicted by gringo juries and gringo judges.[54]

Santiago secured funding from various foundations in 1972 for the Legal Aid Association of Crystal City. The Akbar Foundation gave the city $20,000 as seed money. Other foundations sent $15,000 more. At first the city relied on weekly consultations from attorney Jesse Gamez to provide a semblance of legal services. When Paul Rich finished law school in 1973, he was hired as the agency's director.[55]

With Rich at the helm the agency's name was changed to the Oficina de la Gente [Office of the People]. An experienced administrator and proposal writer, Rich succeeded in securing additional foundation funding for the next two years. He explained that initial funding came solely from private foundations in the east that were interested not only because the program was unique but because it was in Crystal City, the heart of an alternative political situation in south Texas.[56] From 1973 to 1975 Rich expanded the agency's staff and operations. What began in 1972 as an office with a part-time attorney was by 1975 an operation with two full-time and two back-up attorneys, at least four law students, two full-time secretaries, and high school students who were used as paralegals. By 1975 there were six satellite offices in the surrounding communities run by law students from programs at Northeastern University and the University of California at Los Angeles. The role of the satellite offices was to distribute information about the legal services available to the community.[57]

The Oficina de la Gente's approach to providing legal services could be described as "have an injustice, will serve." According to Rich, the only restrictions the agency had were internal. Theoretically, he explained, the office was an autonomous agency free from local administrative controls. Initially, the office was involved in various types of litigation—divorces, deeds, wills, property disputes, and consumer fraud, to name a few. "Our case load is phenomenal," he commented in 1973. "I'm never bored. I never handle the same thing day in, day out. That's why the students come back."[58] During this time Rich was instrumental in assisting the workers at the local Del Monte plant in becoming unionized.

Rich and Gutiérrez were good friends. Writer Steve Thomas describes Rich's role in RUP's peaceful revolution in Cristal: "To the Chicanos, Gutiérrez has proven to be the political catalyst as Rich is the legal focal point. They prove also to work well together." Rich told Thomas, "Angel and I have an arrangement. He takes care of the politics, and I do the mechanics. He stays out of the Oficina, and I stay out of his office."[59] When the political rupture occurred in 1975, the Oficina de la Gente was thriving and expanding its legal services to various communities within the Winter Garden area; it survived the rupture.

Crystal City Credit Union

Work on establishing a credit union began in 1970. Cristal was home to seven flourishing loan companies, but none was owned by Mexicanos. The only bank in town had a reputation for being insensitive and uncooperative when Mexicanos needed loans. After discussing the matter, Ciudadanos Unidos decided to form a credit union that would be run under its direction. The credit union was named Obrero [Worker] Credit Union. Subsequently, the RUP-controlled school district decided to merge the local Teacher's Credit Union and Obrero Credit Union; the new entity was known as the Crystal City Credit Union (CCCU).[60]

The CCCU received its charter from the Texas Credit Union Commission in 1971 and began operating on a volunteer basis. From the beginning its goals were to provide a safe and convenient place that people could trust to save their money and earn them dividends; to provide low-rate financing so that people would not be at the mercy of local merchants and loan sharks; to initiate a strong consumer education and advocacy program; and to provide family financial counseling and budgeting assistance.[61]

Initial funding for the credit union came from the Catholic Church's Campaign for Human Development. Another source of capital was the membership itself. Members had to be approved by a member of the screening committee and had to purchase at least one $5 share and pay a 25-cent membership fee. In 1971 CCCU's membership was 125. By 1973 it had increased to 300. Credit union members were able to borrow up to $200 on their signature alone and more with collateral. The annual interest rate on loans was 1 percent of the unpaid balance. Members were also provided with life insurance. The family of a member who died would receive double the amount the deceased had invested in the credit union. Moreover, if a deceased member had an loan outstanding at death, the credit union canceled the debt.[62]

CCCU's life was brief. It had no resources to hire full-time staff, and administrative problems soon developed. Record keeping, collection of dues, loan transactions, correspondence, marketing, and general administration became impossible to carry out with volunteers. As Luz Gutiérrez explained, no one had realized that a credit union requires full-time administrators. "We soon realized that without staff it was doomed to fail," Santiago said. "Too few of us were responsible for too many other projects—we just didn't have the time and resources." There were other problems that impeded CCCU's development such as the practice of favoritism in the issuance of loans.[63] CCCU closed its doors in 1974.

Obreros Unidos Independientes

RUP's approach to creating social change included supporting existing labor struggles and forming unions, a reflection of Gutiérrez's commitment to using the organization to improve workers' quality of life. Gutiérrez and other RUP officials went out of their way to support Cesar Chávez's lettuce boycott, although Chávez had not yet voiced support for RUP as a third-party movement. That happened when Chávez visited Cristal in February 1971. Congratulating the crowd of about a thousand people, Chávez said, "You are the ones that are giving the examples that all of us are following. There is no other community so united with such a well-defined program." He went on to acknowledge Cristal as the cradle of liberty for Mexicanos in the United States. Chávez also addressed the Austin Chicano Huelga, a strike against the Economy Furniture Co. in Austin.[64] Pragmatically, RUP used Chávez's visit to further legitimize the peaceful revolution in Cristal, especially the party's embryonic efforts to organize the workers at Del Monte.

It was not until late 1970 that RUP moved to create its own union. As the RUP city council sought to annex the Del Monte plant into the city limits, CU moved to form a union at Del Monte. On October 23 CU met with RUP workers employed by Del Monte. They drafted a constitution and by-laws and elected officers: Antonio Ríos, president; Gilberto Sanchez, vice president; Alberto Sánchez, secretary; and Gregoria Delgado, treasurer. The employees named their union Obreros Unidos Independientes (OUI—Independent United Workers). Antonio Ríos a *La Verdad* reporter, explained that they chose the word *independent* to stress that they were not affiliated with another union, especially any that were white. Ríos said, " We have organized ourselves and we are the first union completely controlled and directed by Chicanos."[65]

The basic thrust of OUI was to displace the Teamsters local. RUP sought to control not only the local government, schools, and economy but also the workplace. RUP workers believed that the Teamsters were not responsive to or representative of their interests and reacted enthusiastically to the idea of creating a Mexicano-controlled union. Ríos tried to secure official recognition for OUI from the National Labor Relations Board (NLRB) but missed an important deadline. This error proved disastrous for the emerging OUI. Because of it the Teamsters were able to negotiate a three-year contract. It was not until 1973 that OUI once again began its organizing efforts to displace the Teamsters.[66]

When the Teamsters' contract with Del Monte expired in 1973, OUI swung into action. OUI held a meeting at which the workers decided to retain the same officers they had elected in 1970. Furthermore, they formulated a strategic plan to take Del Monte. This time around OUI organizers were more knowledgeable about securing NLRB recognition. They circulated a petition and obtained signatures from 30 percent of the workforce within thirty days, as the NLRB required. Rich, the new director of the Oficina de la Gente, provided legal assistance to the embryonic OUI in its dealings with the NLRB. From September through November OUI held meetings and rallies to galvanize support. Scores of RUP backers helped OUI pass out literature at the Del Monte cannery.

OUI's strategic plan entailed exerting pressure simultaneously on several fronts. The first was to get stockholders to pressure Del Monte. The second was to apply external political pressure through OUI and RUP. In late 1973 Gutiérrez and other RUP backers took the struggle to Del Monte's stockholders' meeting in San Francisco. RUP's plan was to educate the stockholders about OUI's struggles against Del Monte and thereby motivate them to pressure the company executives to settle with OUI. A few months earlier Gutiérrez and ten colleagues had bought Del Monte stock, which enabled them to attend and vote. At the meeting Gutiérrez was allowed to read a resolution containing specific demands, including that Del Monte

1. Draw up a contract with OUI
2. Close the labor camp at its farm east of Crystal City
3. Raise local wages to $5 an hour (it was paying $2 and $3 an hour)
4. Submit to annexation into the city limits or make a payment in lieu of taxes
5. Raise safety and health standards to bring the plant into compliance with state law
6. "Phase out" white employees or work out a plan to put more Chicanos in administrative positions
7. Do away with the present method of seniority and allow a grace period for seniority
8. Reinstate all employees who were fired or pressured to resign because of their political involvement or beliefs
9. Establish scholarships for children of all employees[67]

RUP applied pressure in other ways. As national chair of RUP, Gutiérrez became involved in the Food Action Campaign (FAC), a loosely organized coalition of groups and individuals who sought to break food trusts that contributed to the high cost of living. Gutiérrez toured the country with former Democratic senator Fred Harris of Oklahoma and spoke out against the targeted corporations. Harris named Del Monte as a principal target of the campaign. RUP and OUI applied pressure on the cannery in Cristal, holding rallies, meetings, and other social functions to explain the legal rights of workers seeking union representation and the procedures for voting.

On October 29, 1973, workers at the Del Monte plant voted to have

OUI represent them in collective bargaining; the vote (258 for OUI, 73 against, with 28 ballots challenging the election) ousted the Teamsters local. The Teamsters, which had represented the workers since 1956, had shown no interest in renewing the contract, which had expired in September. In November OUI formed a negotiations committee certified by the NLRB to negotiate a new contract. Its members included Gutiérrez, Antonio Ríos, Reverend Sherrill Smith, Olga Bonilla, Gregoria Delgado, and Paul Rich. OUI secured as a consultant one of Cesar Chávez's top negotiators, David Burciaga, to help the committee in negotiations, which were held from late November to January 1974.[68]

On January 17, 1974, OUI and Del Monte reached an agreement. The contract, approved by the workers, offered the establishment of a child-care center for preschool-age children; formation of a credit union; an additional holiday—Día de la Raza, October 12; a wage increase of 18 cents, bringing the minimum hourly wage to $2.30; medical insurance; a decrease in monthly union dues, which dropped from $6.50 to $5; discounts on purchases of certain goods such as automotive parts; and union-provided scholarships for workers' children. Rich represented OUI in ironing out the details of the contract.[69] OUI proved strong enough to survive the political rupture.

Warren Wagner Farm Strike

While organizing OUI, RUP supporters became involved in the Warren Wagner farm strike. On January 21, 1972, the Warren Wagner Co., which ran a packing shed in Cristal, unilaterally and with no notice cut wages from $1.60 an hour to $1.30. One hundred men and women walked off the job. That evening they held a rally and an all-night vigil. The next morning, fifty people were walking a picket line at the packing shed.

That morning Reverend Sherrill Smith and his long-time friend, Erasmo Andrade, the former union organizer now running the mental health outreach program, learned what was going on and immediately became involved (see Chapter 3). They became strong supporters of and advisers to strike leader Ismael Rivera. Indeed, Smith was the catalyst for the strike. Although he had just arrived in Cristal, the Catholic priest was no newcomer to social activism. He first drew public attention during the civil rights struggle of the 1960s when he joined Martin Luther King Jr. in several marches in Alabama. In the late sixties he became involved in the farmworkers movement. In 1967 he was arrested and jailed at a demonstration in Rio Grande City. In December 1971 he was assigned to the local parish in Cristal. He found Cristal so radicalized and polarized that it was a new experience for him.[70]

Smith's long history of activism made whites and some anti-Gutierristas apprehensive about his assignment to Cristal. According to Smith, "When the gringo knew that I was to come, they were up in arms. They thought that I was a political appointment—that I was going to be a political priest." He was greeted with the threat of a petition to have him replaced with another priest. From the outset he made it clear to his parishioners that he intended to be involved in the struggles for social justice and that his conscience would be his guide.[71]

CU and RUP also gave immediate support to the strike. *La Verdad* reported:

The 21st of January was a memorable day in Cristal. For the first time in Cristal's history, the Chicano agricultural workers united against the gringo foreman and struck. More important was the support given publicly by the city's Mayor Francisco Benavides as well as officials from other agencies, schoolteachers, administrators, and students of the school district. All who were at the picket listened to the speeches and showed their support for the strikers. This has never happened before. . . . The theme of the strike is "Todos diferentes, Todos unidos (All different, all united)."[72]

Numerous rallies and meetings were held in support of the Mexicano strikers. The central issue was the demand for wages of $2 per hour. From the pulpit Smith spoke of different facets of the strike, always trying to encourage unity and support for the workers' demands.[73] During the strike Andrade and Smith organized assistance for striking workers—information, free food, and, in cases of extreme need, financial assistance. *La Verdad* ran stories about the various types of assistance available from county welfare and other agencies.

Five people involved in the picketing, Smith, Rivera, Juan Duran, Pedro Vallejo, and Joséphine Rodriguez, were arrested on charges of obstructing a public highway. The arrests triggered a march of more than four hundred people that culminated in a rally at Cristal's city hall. The marchers proceeded to the courthouse where the five appeared before Justice of the Peace Frank Moreno Sr. RUP attorneys Ray Perez and Jesse Gamez signed bonds as sureties, and the five were released to join the marchers.[74]

The next day Juan Maldanado and Armando Treviño were arrested on charges of "using language directed to and in the presence of C. L. Sweeten, calculated to cause a breach of the peace." Maldanado and Treviño had been following a truck from Wagner Farms that was en route to Pearsall. A highway patrolman stopped their vehicle and ticketed them. Angry, the two men returned to Cristal, went to Sheriff

Sweeten's office, and demanded that charges be filed against the patrolman for conduct unbecoming to an officer. A heated verbal exchange ensued, and the sheriff had the two men arrested for disturbing
the peace. Within thirty minutes both men were released on a $300
bond set by County Judge Art Taylor. Treviño accused Sweeten of
badly twisting his arm.[75]

While the picketing continued, a workers' negotiating team comprised of Rivera and Duran met with Wagner Farm officials on January
27. Gamez acted as legal counsel for the negotiations, and Andrade
served as an adviser to the negotiating team. Mayor Benavides served
as a witness to the sessions. On January 29 the striking farmworkers
and packers signed an agreement with Warren Wagner Farms and
Warren Wagner, Inc., that included a raise to $1.65 per hour; a supply
of fresh drinking water and portable toilets in the fields; agreement
that Wagner Farm officials would act as mediators in any disputes
between the workers and truck drivers who took them to and from
work; and rehiring of all former employees without penalties or
retribution.[76]

The irony of the Wagner strike was that no one had anticipated it.
But the strike showed the wealthy white landowners that RUP in Cristal was resolute in its efforts to create major social change. The wage
increase of 5 cents per hour was no great gain. But the symbolic victory
provided an important psychological boost.

Civic Participation

The second revolt released an unprecedented current of civic participation. For the first five years of community control Cristal personified
participatory democracy, as reflected in CU's five-hundred-family
membership base; the high voter turnouts; the hundreds (if not thousands) who participated in rallies, marches, boycotts, and other political events; big attendance at school board and city council meetings;
and the many people who volunteered to serve on the various school
board, city council, and county commissions, boards, and committees.
This popular participation was an important aspect of RUP's peaceful
social revolution.

The widespread participation was a reflection of the radical attitudi-
nal change toward politics. RUP's decolonization strategy produced a
sense of empowerment, confidence, and purpose for most Mexicanos.
No longer subjugated by the despair they had felt, most were imbued
with a spirit of optimism and activism. No longer were they afraid or
humbled before the gringo or anyone else. Attitudes of submissiveness

and subordination were replaced with a sense of self-determination and equality.

A Mexicano cultural renaissance helped impel civic participation. Through RUP's intensive resocialization process the community felt a new pride in its Mexicano heritage and culture and felt inferior to no one. People were invigorated with a passion for their Mexicanismo. They displayed the Mexican flag, reveled in the playing of Mexicano marches by Cristal's high school marching band, and commemorated such events as Mexican Independence Day and Cinco de Mayo. RUP's peaceful revolution created a laboratory for civic participation and was stimulated by a rediscovery of Mexicanos' cultural roots.

Organization Participation

With the renaissance of civic participation came the development of Mexicano organizations. Foremost in power and influence was CU.[77] With its massive grassroots family membership, it was the catalyst for people's participation and empowerment. It was an organization of organizations. Such groups as the Sociedad Funeraria Miguel Hidalgo, Mexican Chamber of Commerce, MAYO, Educators in Action, G. I. Forum, IMAGE, and the Barrio Club were formally affiliated with CU, and cross-membership was common.

The organizations served a variety of purposes. The Sociedad Funeraria Miguel Hidalgo, a working-class organization, was the oldest. Its primary function was to provide its members with burial insurance, but it also sponsored cultural events such as the September 16 celebration of Mexican independence. The Mexican Chamber of Commerce was primarily made up of Mexicano businessmen and focused on business and economic development activities.

The MAYO chapter, which was organized after the school walkout, was the student advocacy organization that organized a number of protest activities. During the first five years of the peaceful revolution students were vital to RUP's mobilization capability. In 1971, 150 teachers in the Cristal school district formed Educators in Action and functioned as a support group for RUP's school administration and policies. In 1972 Cristaleños formed local chapters of the G. I. Forum, IMAGE, and the Barrio Club. Erasmo Andrade was the force behind the G. I. Forum chapter. It focused on issues and concerns pertinent to Mexicano war veterans. The general purpose of IMAGE (Involvement of Mexican Americans in Gainful Endeavors), headed by Elidio Lizcano, was was to bring more programs into Cristal and to aid in the creation of gainful employment for Mexicanos in Cristal. The Barrio Club also had its genesis in 1971.[78]

The Participation of Women

Women played a crucial role and indispensable in RUP's peaceful revolution from the second revolt to the departure of Gutiérrez in 1981. Luz Gutiérrez played a significant and prominent leadership role throughout the building of the peaceful revolution. Linda Richey, who was married to Bill Richey, played a key role in the development of RUP in Cotulla in 1969 and 1970. Of MAYO's thirty-nine school walkouts (see Chapter 1), Cristal's was by far the most successful, thanks largely to the efforts of Gutiérrez and three student leaders, Severita Lara, Mario Treviño, and Diana Palacios.[79] Earlier chapters have detailed the key roles played by Viviana Santiago, Virginia Musquiz, and other Mexicanas in orchestrating the second revolt.

The women's revolt within CU in 1970 (see Chapter 2) was indicative of their determination to break the exclusionary Mexicano "macho" machine. Although women were active in CU's various committees, they never served in the CU leadership during RUP's five years of community control. Although women often were CU's backbone when it came to work, no woman ever served as CU's president. It was not until 1973 that women began to serve on CU's board of directors.

In the political arena RUP's peaceful revolution was essentially all male. No woman served as council member, mayor, or city manager during the five years of community control. The city's commissions and committees were primarily male. However, Mexicanas fared much better on the school board. Viviana Santiago was the first Mexicana elected to the school board, in 1973. Mercedes "Chachi" Casarez was the second, elected in 1974. All school superintendents and school principals during those years were male. In county government Elena Díaz was the first Mexicana ever elected to Zavala County's commissioners court, in 1972.[80]

Four women were elected to county offices when RUP secured control of the county in 1974: Rosa Mata, district clerk; Virginia Musquiz, county clerk; Carmen Flores, county treasurer; and Irene Cuellar, justice of the peace in Precinct 3.[81] RUP's county apparatus also saw the leadership of women. Musquiz was elected RUP county chair in 1972. Because of her knowledge of the Texas Electoral Code, coupled with her practical experience in electoral politics, José Angel Gutiérrez relied heavily on Musquiz in building the RUP in Zavala County.

Thus, although RUP's peaceful revolution was essentially male dominated, José Angel Gutiérrez and CU would never have been able to develop and sustain community control for five years without the leadership and support of women.

The Decline of RUP's Social Change Revolution (1976–1980)

The first five years of community control were the golden years that brought about dynamic social change. Control of the city, schools, and the county enabled RUP administrators to bring in millions of dollars in federal and private foundation funding. This helped people get jobs for decent wages. They received better services. In fact, many of the services provided were entirely new. Unfortunately, with the political rupture in 1975 RUP's struggle for social change faltered. From late 1975 to 1977 most of RUP's social services, organizations, and civic participation gradually faded.

Implications of the Rupture for Social Change

By 1975 the emphasis was no longer on building for the greater good. Instead, it shifted to the relentless pursuit of power and profit for the governing faction. The politics of individuals and factions prevailed over the politics of community control. Most services, programs, and organizations were forced to take sides. Even the social arena became tainted by the devastating polarization caused by the rupture. Little or no time was spent combating the community's social problems. The paramount preoccupation was with which faction would control the allocation of patronage.

Inevitably the rupture had a devastating effect on people's willingness to mobilize politically. With all city commissions controlled by Mexicanos, the internal enemy was no longer the gringo. The paramount enemy of poor Mexicanos became essentially the middle-class Mexicanos who now held these positions. This was particularly true with the internecine battle for control of the powerful Urban Renewal and Housing Commissions. Control translated to resources and jobs. In 1978 Rodolfo Palomo, director of the Urban Renewal Agency, reported that 160 homes had been built with $5.7 million in federal funds. But that was also the year that the federal government replaced urban renewal programs with community development block grants directed by the states. "What happened was that the agency was phased out gradually, allowing the city to get rid of properties, so that by 1980 there was no more an urban renewal agency," José Luis Balderas recalled.[82] Without the funding, serving on the Housing Commission lost some of its political value.

The city's mental health agency became defunct because of lack of funding during the postrupture years. In 1976 Viviana Santiago left Cristal to go to the University of Houston's Bates College of Law. No one in Cristal filled the void. In 1980 the program failed to secure any federal or private funding, which brought it to a near halt. Thus the social services thrust of RUP's peaceful revolution virtually disappeared. According to Santiago, "Few people cared about what was good for the community. Everyone was caught in the game of advancing their own political agenda." Some services once provided by the mental health agency were absorbed and provided by the successful and expanding El Centro de Salud.[83]

During the postrupture years the health clinic became the success story of RUP's social revolution in Cristal. Functioning in a milieu of conflict and polarization, it nevertheless managed to survive RUP's politics of self-destruction. The Centro de Salud was completed and opened for business in March 1976, adding dental care to its broad range of medical services. By September the clinic had served 3,914 persons. In 1977 the health service expanded its budget, staff, and services, hiring two physicians, Abel Salas and Manuel J. Fausto, and adding emergency medical service on a twenty-four-hour basis. In December the Centro de Salud became Vida Y Salud Health Systems, Inc.[84]

Vida Y Salud Health Systems was not affected when the Gutierrista RUP alliance retook control of the city council and school board in 1978. That year the clinic expanded its services and health education programs to include emergency food assistance, prenatal care, tuberculosis diagnosis and treatment, nutrition, first aid, and hygiene. In early 1979 it opened a teen clinic to provide counseling and health education.[85] While José Angel Gutiérrez was busy confronting various political and legal problems in 1979, Luz Gutiérrez continued to build Viva Y Salud Health Systems.

Another success story was the Oficina de la Gente. From 1975 to 1977 Bill Richey adroitly maneuvered the legal aid clinic through Cristal's volatile politics. Richey continued to consolidate and expand the office's capability to provide the poor with legal assistance. According to Santiago, the delivery of legal services was not impeded by the pervasive infighting simply because the office was too busy litigating. In 1977 the Oficina was consolidated under the aegis of Texas Rural Legal Aid (TRLA). In addition to the office in Cristal, it had main offices in Westach and Edinburg and several outposts in Brownsville, Harlingen, Kingsville, and Rio Grande City.[86]

The Oficina's working relationship with OUI continued into 1980. Like the Oficina, OUI stayed out of the political wars and factionalism. OUI took a more neutral role, though it tended to be more friendly to the Gutiérrez faction. Under the leadership of Antonio Ríos, Gregoria Delgado, Alfonso Lozano, Maria Bonilla, and José Maria Flores, OUI continued to grow. In 1979 it successfully negotiated a contract with Southeastern Public Utility, an ice-making plant.[87] The self-destructiveness of the postrupture epoch did not impede OUI's development, for in 1980 it was still a strong and viable organization.

The "Viva Yo" Mind-Set

The bent toward social change that characterized RUP's peaceful revolution was a casualty of Cristal's self-destructive politics. After 1975 the *we* of RUP's first five years of community control was replaced with the "Viva Yo," or *I* mind-set. The pursuit of change and empowerment became individual and personal. It was no longer predicated on a sense of community but rather self-interest. This negative emphasis directly affected civic participation, which gradually gave way to a return of alienation, fatalism, and apathy. Only vestiges of Chicanismo remained. With people participating less, the lexicon that included "El Moviemento," "La Causa," and "Viva La Raza Unida" was replaced by a more conservative one in the Mexican-American community; the 1980s were the decade of the Hispanic.

The organizations suffered a severe decline in membership. With CU split into two groups, no central organization had the power or resources to command the once loyal and faithful RUP constituency. By 1980 CU was on the verge of disappearing, and the G. I. Forum, Educators in Action, and MAYO were among the other victims. The Sociedad Funeraria Miguel Hidalgo and the Mexican Chamber of Commerce were failing fast.

Women's Participation in Politics Increases

Reflecting what was happening nationally, women became even more politically active after 1975, the postrupture years. In the 1976 election Olivia Serna made an unsuccessful run for city council on the Gutierrista slate. She was elected in 1979 and became Cristal's mayor in 1980. Blanca Gomez won election to city council in 1977 on the new guard slate. By 1979 three women were serving on the school board: Esmeralda R. Torres (1978); Margarita Flores (1979); and Ninfa Moncada (appointed in 1979).[88] Valentina Mendez was elected to the school board in 1980.

In the county Elena Díaz was reelected as county commissioner and Gregoria Delgado as justice of the peace, Precinct 1, in the 1976 county elections. In 1978 Margarita Gonzalez was elected district clerk; Diana Palacios Garcia, county clerk; and Carmen Flores, county treasurer. But the election was contested, a judge ordered a special county election, and Garcia and Flores lost to two Mexicano Democrats.[89]

By the time Gutiérrez left Cristal in early 1981, little remained of

RUP's peaceful social revolution. The bottom line was that in 1980 Mexicanos still suffered an internal colonial status dependent on state and federal mechanisms, which were controlled by whites. The Mexicano community essentially was left to fend for itself. People were increasingly alienated, disorganized, and lacking leadership. Once again, they felt apathetic, frustrated, and hopeless.

Part Four

The Politics of Self-Destruction

11

Gutiérrez's Departure

The End of an Era

After nine years of political struggle RUP's peaceful revolution had all but disappeared by 1979. The destructive endogenous forces unleashed by the rupture in 1975, coupled with exogenous attacks on RUP's leadership and programs by state and federal politicians and officials, created a political climate that ultimately contributed to the demise of both RUP as a third-party movement and its peaceful revolution in Cristal. Despite the brief resurrection of RUP unity during the 1978 local elections, Cristal's politics for the next two years regressed to a self-destructive mode that resembled that of the transition years that proceeded the first revolt of 1965–1969. Although Mexicanos were still in power, their politics lacked a sense of ideological mission or "movimiento" thrust. The accommodationist and integrationist politics that perpetuated the Mexicanos's status as internally colonialized resumed. José Angel Gutiérrez's formal departure from Cristal ended the Cristal experiment.

The End to RUP's Peaceful Revolution

The 1979 local school board and city council elections would be the last in Cristal organized and won under the aegis of RUP. With the statewide party failing to secure the 2 percent vote necessary to field a candidate in the 1978 gubernatorial election, RUP was decertified as a political party. Ignacio Garcia explains that "by not receiving at least 2 percent of the vote, the party lost its ballot status and the state funds for its primary. More important, the dismal showing eliminated the party as an alternative to the Republicans and Democrats."[1] This proved to be the final undoing of RUP. It left Gutiérrez and the RUP coalition without an official political party from which to operate. Yet they had managed to retake control of both the school board and city council in 1978. The problem was how RUP could function as a political party if it had no legal certification. In addition, as the 1979 local elections approached, Gutiérrez found himself on the defensive. He was besieged by increasingly vociferous attacks from Democratic county commissioners and officials and the pending litigation contesting RUP's county victory in November. If that was not enough, Gutiérrez found himself trying to hold together a tenuous coalition made up of three competing power factions.

The Decline of RUP

As 1979 began, Gutiérrez realized that the party was over. Interviewed in 1995, he explained that even though RUP could have been maintained as an official party at the county level, people were no longer interested. "All the [leaders] had already rejected that option. Nobody wanted to be Raza Unida anymore." But the alliance decide to continue to run candidates under the RUP banner. Because the party no longer had legal status, this decision was made primarily for its symbolism. "It was the loyalty of the people who had struggled so hard and for so long for the changes we made. We felt we were making a difference, so there was no point in abandoning the RUP ship. It didn't matter if it wasn't official," Gutiérrez explained.[2]

By 1979 an exodus from RUP to the Democratic Party was underway. Gutiérrez explained, "All of a sudden our former members were joining the Democratic Party, finding open arms, and getting positions of power. Since our people were trained, they knew how to run elections. They started replacing whites as candidates and winning." The co-opting of RUP's leaders and adherents, lack of resources, burnout of some leaders, infighting, and changing attitudes were but a few of the factors that resulted in the end of RUP statewide.[3] Many former RUP activists found a new political home with the Mexican-American Democrats, an organization formed in late 1976.

The 1979 Cristal and County Elections

In January 1979 RUP moved to field its last slate of candidates for the school board and city council. This time the opposition was the Democrats. Despite RUP's loss of legal status, its opposition—disgruntled Mexicanos and whites—came together under the guise of the Democratic Party to take RUP on as if it were a recognized party. With the RUP alliance still in control of the schools and city and county government, the Democrats sought to end the third party's influence once and for all. They waged war with both ballot box and the courts.

In late January both contentious sides prepared for the electoral battle in April. RUP, through a debilitated Ciudadanos Unidos (CU), selected Margaret Flores, Pablo Puente, and Juan "Topper" Perez to run for the three-year school board terms and Ninfa Moncada to fill the unexpired term of Jesse Gamez, who had resigned a year short of term. The Democrats endorsed Fidel Benavides, Miguel "Mike" Delgado, and Francisco J. Martinez for the three-year terms and José R. "Chema" Mata to fill Gamez's seat.[4] For the city council RUP endorsed Rodolfo (Rudy) Espinosa Jr., Olivia Serna, and Juan E. Hernandez. The Democratic slate included Ramón "Monche" Mata; Juan Cornejo, who had been the mayor of the first revolt; and Cornejo's brother, Roberto. Although inconsequential as a political force, Jesús Salas ran as an independent.

As the 1979 political year began in January, all was not well for Gutiérrez or RUP at the county level. Despite a temporary restraining order issued on December 30 by 63d District Court Judge George M. Thurmond that prohibited Alejandro Perez from being sworn in as commissioner after winning in the November 1978 county election, Gutiérrez swore Perez in at a ceremony at 12:01 A.M. on January 1. This allowed Perez to participate as a member of the Zavala County Court of Commissioners. At the midnight ceremony notary public Marty Torres administered the oath to Gutiérrez as county judge. Gutiérrez then swore in Margarita Gonzalez as district clerk; Diana Palacios Garcia as county clerk; José L. Talamantez as commissioner of Precinct 2; and a host of others.[5]

At the next commission meeting on January 8 the RUP-controlled board approved some retaliatory policies. The board voted to fire Ramón "Monche" Mata, the county road administrator who was aligned with the Democrats, and all his employees in the road department. In Ramón Mata's place the commission hired José O. Mata. The board also rescinded a contract with attorney Rogelio Muñoz, who was representing Democratic commissioner Torres and others in a federal court suit brought against them by a former road department employee. Finally, the board decided to hold budget hearings and approved the hiring of attorney Alonzo Villareal to represent the county in another suit.

In response, Lupe Cortinas filed a motion of contempt of court against both Gutiérrez and Perez's attorney, Villareal. The petition contended that Villareal had advised Perez to take the oath while Gutiérrez administered it. Cortinas contended that Perez had been served with a temporary restraining order but refused to obey the court's order. Gutiérrez called Cortinas's contempt of court allegations silly.[6]

While Gutiérrez was under contempt of court charges in January, he struck back with his own charge of contempt against county attorney Pablo Avila. The charge stemmed from Avila's involvement and conduct in a drunken driving trial. Gutiérrez contended that Avila refused to let Gutiérrez examine an officer's offense report and Breathalyzer test during an arraignment. "As I approached the bench, the Judge grabbed the officer's report," said Avila. "I felt insulted and grabbed it back." Gutiérrez reacted by preparing an order of contempt of court and a writ of commitment that ordered Sheriff Elfego Martínez to confine Avila to jail for twenty-four hours, effective immediately, and levied a $25 fine. Gutiérrez also ordered Avila to make a public apology to the court in the presence of the sheriff upon Avila's release or be held an additional day in jail and fined another $25 for each day he refused to do so. Avila immediately filed for a writ of habeas corpus in the 38th District Court.[7]

In late January the RUP-controlled county commission moved to revise the budget. It met without Perez, who had been restrained by the district court from participating as a commissioner. The commission made several budgetary changes; the most political was to reduce county attorney Avila's salary from $13,700 to $8,700. It also made Avila's secretary a part-time employee. Commissioner Torres, the only Democrat sitting as commissioner, was livid. He opposed the budgetary changes, calling them irresponsible and discriminatory, and predicted that they would cause problems.[8]

Torres was right. In February the Texas Supreme Court overruled a motion by Gutiérrez that sought dismissal of a temporary restraining order against the Court of Commissioners that prevented spending monies in the revised budget. The order was first issued on February 1 by visiting district court judge Troy Williams. Williams's issuance of the order was a result of the vote by Perez, whose status on the board was being challenged. The application for the restraining order was made by Martha Cruz, Bea Bookout, and Jack Kingsberry as Zavala County taxpayers. They alleged that there was no statutory provision for the adoption of a new budget during January because the budget for 1979 had been adopted earlier, in July 1978.[9] An anonymous letter to the editor of the *Sentinel* severely criticized the actions of the RUP commissioners:

Once again the specter of the spoils system raises its ugly head in Zavala County. The Judge and his elected cronies have decided in their infinite wisdom to reward their lackeys who were instrumental in their election and to punish their opposition in the county's government. What is the most blatant way you can do this? The way the Judge and his cronies did it was to reduce the budget of all the county departments that were not a part of the Raza Unida and to increase the budget of his lackeys and hang-ons.[10]

County attorney Avila joined in the attack, calling the RUP commissioners' action illegal. In a letter to all the commissioners, the state controller, and to District Attorney Earle Caddel, Avila wrote, "The budget that you people adopted is illegal. Failure to comply with statutory requirements is a criminal offense."[11]

In February the political crisis worsened when the district court ruled McHazlett winner over Perez in the disputed commissioner's race after a recount of the vote. Judge Williams dismissed the suit for declaratory judgment brought by Perez. The recount gave McHazlett a four-vote margin of victory, whereas the original vote had gone to Perez by one ballot. The RUP-controlled commission voted to appeal the district court's decision. Democratic commissioner Torres voted nay. Gutiérrez justified the petition by saying that the board was not appealing the decision but that it wanted to see if the judge's ruling was valid. Dale Barker, the *Sentinel's* publisher, baited Gutiérrez in his column, writing, "Come on, judge—what's your strategy?"[12]

Meanwhile, Avila filed felony theft charges against RUP county treasurer Carmen Flores in a dispute over his salary. Avila had failed to pay an assessment made by the state bar, joining about nine hundred other Texas lawyers who were refusing to pay. Because Avila did not pay his assessment, the state bar temporarily suspended him. Then the RUP commissioners sought to have him ousted as county attorney. Avila then produced a telegram from the state bar that said Avila had paid the fee and had been reinstated. In his subsequent complaint Avila charged Flores with unlawfully exercising control over $420 belonging to him. The amount in question was his salary. When Avila initiated this action, he had just been released from custody following the contempt proceedings brought against him by Gutiérrez.

In February Judge Williams struck another legal blow to Gutiérrez and RUP. He declared the results of the November county elections

void and called a special county election for April 7, the same day as
Cristal's local elections.[13] He based his decision on evidence of election
irregularities and fraud. The ruling ordered that all persons holding
the contested offices as of December 28, 1978, should remain in office
until the April 7 elections. For Gutiérrez and RUP the decision meant
political disaster. At least until the special election the county commission would be in the Democrats' control. About eighty-five RUP supporters picketed the courthouse, carrying signs critical of Williams's
actions and those of the Democrats.[14]

In another related legal battle in February, at the order of the 4th
Court of Civil Appeals in San Antonio Judge Williams set a $15,000
supersedeas bond for Diana Palacios Garcia, whose election to county
clerk had been challenged. The bond prevented the recording of the
minutes of the four November and December commission meetings in
the official books until the appellate court heard Garcia's appeal. The
meetings were not attended by either Gutiérrez or RUP commissioner
Elena Díaz. A few days later Williams ruled that the meetings were
duly constituted and ordered the minutes entered into the record. Garcia appealed the judge's order.[15] In another critical ruling the Texas
Supreme Court overruled Gutiérrez's motion seeking dismissal of the
temporary restraining order that prevented spending monies in the
revised budget.

In yet another court action Judge Williams found RUP member Margarita Gonzalez in contempt of court for refusing to turn over her district clerk's post to Democrat Rosa Mata. But Williams also ruled that
neither Gutiérrez nor Talamantez should be held in contempt. He
ruled that they had acted in good faith, believing that Talamantez had
successfully posted a supersedeas bond, which would have allowed
him to stay in the commissioner's post until an appeal of the case. He
warned both Gutiérrez and Talamantez to adhere to the court's ruling
or they would be held in contempt.

In March, with RUP no longer in control of the county court of
commissioners, the polarization between the two bellicose political
forces became more acute. At a commissioners' meeting in early March
the only people present were Judge Gutiérrez and RUP commissioner
Díaz. According to the *Sentinel*, while Gutiérrez and Díaz waited for
other commissioners to arrive and provide a quorum, Gutiérrez declared, "For the record let's state that Matthew McHazlett and Frank
Guerrero are walking up and down the hall and don't want to come to
the meeting at this point." Apparently, he was using this tactic to give
Commissioner Torres time to arrive, which would have assured them

a quorum. McHazlett and Guerrero explained that they did not attend the meeting because RUP city clerk Diana Palacios Garcia had not been removed; their attendance would have been tantamount to officially recognizing her as the county clerk.[16]

With Democrats back in control in March Gutiérrez and RUP faced more attacks yet. Politically, they were on the defensive. Guerrero announced that he was personally investigating county spending records, targeting the county treasurer and the county clerk. Talamantez, who was opposing Guerrero in the April special election, saw Guerrero's action as political grandstanding designed to gain votes. In late March Judge Williams ruled that the Gutierrista-controlled commission's January resolution to transfer the voting registrar from the office of the county tax assessor–collector to the county clerk's office was void. He dissolved a temporary restraining order issued in a suit against the three Democratic commissioners filed by county clerk Virginia Musquiz and ousted county clerk Diana Palacios Garcia to stop the transfer.[17]

In another case Williams dissolved a temporary restraining order issued in a suit brought by José O. Mata against the three Democratic commissioners to prevent his ouster as county road supervisor. Mata's suit alleged that he had been fired without proper written notice and without a public hearing. Williams found that Ramón "Monche" Mata had been legally hired as the head of the road department on December 15, 1978. He also ruled that the commissioners did have the power to fire Mata on January 1, 1979, but that his firing was not effective until thirty days after he had been notified in writing. Representing the commission in the suit was former RUP leader and attorney Lupe Cortinas. Monche Mata was represented by Jesse Roy Botello.[18]

In another legal skirmish at about that the same time Gutiérrez was fined $100 for contempt of court following a hearing before Judge Williams. The judge charged Gutiérrez with "obstructionist contempt," or of being indirectly in contempt for swearing in Perez as commissioner of Precinct 4 back in January. This was in violation of a restraining order issued in late December preventing Perez from taking office. Williams found Gutiérrez not guilty of obstructionist contempt in the swearing-in of Perez but guilty of "constructive contempt" because Gutiérrez had allowed Perez to participate in a January commission meeting. Perez's attorney, Alonzo Villareal of Uvalde, was also found guilty of constructive contempt, whereas Perez was found in contempt. RUP supporters again picketed the courthouse carrying signs critical of Judge Williams, the Democrats, and the court's ruling. Gutiérrez responded that the earlier legal action recognizing McHazlett as the winner of the contested commissioner's race was an "opinion" rather than an order.[19]

Just before the special election in April another suit was filed in 38th District Court seeking the ouster of RUP member Carmen C. Flores as county treasurer. The plaintiffs were twenty-seven individuals who alleged that the county owed them money and that Treasurer Flores had refused to pay them. Among the plaintiffs were several former RUP Barrioista leaders like Lupe Cortinas and Arturo Gonzales.[20] Their involvement was indicative of the growing exodus of RUP leaders and supporters to the Democratic Party. Part of the irony was that several had become political allies of the local white power holders.

The Democratic-controlled court of commissioners continued to aim its political guns at Gutiérrez, and the question of who would control Zavala County's politics remained unanswered. Political forces on both sides sought to out-organize each other through grassroots campaigns. The RUP alliance formed in 1978 was led by Rodolfo Espinosa, José Mata, and José Talamantez. With Gutiérrez out of the area for a few weeks on a trip to Europe, Espinosa became RUP's chief strategist. The responsibility for mobilizing the Mexicano vote rested on the alliance of the three factions. José Mata led the Gutierristas. All closed ranks to organize the get-out-the-vote campaign. They canvassed door to door, held rallies, bought radio time, printed and distributed campaign literature, and ran sound trucks through the neighborhoods. Juan E. Hernandez, RUP candidate for the city council, was the only RUP candidate to advertise in the *Sentinel*. The Democrats too held rallies and used many of the same tactics deployed by RUP but made heavier use of newspaper advertising.[21] An inherent problem for both campaigns was that they were concurrently supporting candidates for three separate races.

On election day both political forces intensified their get-out-the-vote efforts. For Gutiérrez and RUP, control of the schools and city and county government was on the line. Politically, it was a do or die situation. With more than 3,700 voters going to the polls, the results of the county election proved a "die" for RUP: the Democrats won three of the five offices. Democrat Rosa Elva Mata won the district clerkship with 2,055 votes to RUP's Margarita P. Gonzalez with 1,908 votes. In the race for county commissioner of Precinct 2 Democrat Frank Guerrero Jr. won with 614 votes to 582 for RUP's José Talamantez. And for justice of the peace, Precinct 1, Democrat Bert Baxter won by 3 votes over RUP Alfredo G. Sanchez, 417–414. RUP's victories came in the races for county clerk and county treasurer. RUP's Diana Palacios Garcia got 1,981 votes to Democrat Rosaria T. Avila's 1,965 votes in the county clerk race. In the county treasurer race RUP's Carmen Flores received 2,022 to Democrat Margaret Williams's 1,914.

At both the city council and school board level the RUP alliance scored impressive victories. With three seats in contention for the city council, RUP candidate Olivia Serna was the top vote getter with 1,572. She was followed by Rodolfo Espinosa with 1,514 votes and Juan E. Hernandez with 1,443. The vote spread between the two slates was more than five hundred votes. Democrat Ramón "Monche" Mata got 1,005 votes. Former mayor Juan Cornejo received 963 and his brother, Roberto, got 970 votes. The same scenario occurred in the school board races. The three seats in contention were won handily by the RUP alliance. Margarita Flores was the top RUP vote getter with 1,577 votes. She was followed by Pablo Puente with 1,532 and Juan "Topper" Perez with 1,525 votes. Democrat Miguel Delgado received 1,260 votes. He was followed by Francisco J. Martinez with 1,126 and Fidel Benavides with 1,098 votes. Independent candidate Jesús Salas received 221 votes.

The RUP alliance's decisive victory was attributable to the reactivation of the grassroots get-out-the-vote machinery and the well-organized absentee ballot drive. There were 829 absentee ballots. RUP alliance candidates took the city council races on a five-hundred-vote margin. In the school board races the margin varied from three hundred to five hundred votes.[22]

For both Gutiérrez and RUP the election results were mixed. At the county level the victory by Democratic commissioner Guerrero signaled the end to Gutiérrez's reign. Guerrero's win meant an end to any hope that Gutiérrez and others had to rebuild RUP as a legal political party at least at the county level. In the city council and school board elections the RUP alliance won decisive and impressive victories. The election proved that although the embers of RUP's peaceful revolution were essentially out, they had sent out enough sparks before dying to enable RUP to win in Cristal.

Reemergence of the Politics of Self-Destruction

Despite the victories by the RUP alliance, it succumbed to a rekindling of the politics of self-destruction in 1979. With the debilitated CU and Gutiérrez under severe attack at the county level, the three factions that comprised RUP's coalition began bickering once again, renewing the power struggles and infighting that had become characteristic of Cristal's politics. Personal vendettas and agendas again became the major concerns of elected officials.

Even before the April elections serious schisms had begun to surface within the city council. In March council member Victor Lopez charged that Police Chief Ramón Garza and Assistant Police Chief Alfredo Menchaca had been involved in the distribution of confiscated drugs, possession of confiscated property, misappropriation of funds, solicitation and acceptance of kickbacks, selling of city property, acting as collection agents for wrecking services, violating prisoners' civil rights, releasing prisoners without proper authority, and a cover-up of transportation of undocumented workers.

The Texas Rangers investigated the allegations and cleared Garza and Menchaca of any wrongdoing after the elections. But the probe exacerbated already growing tensions and infighting. Discord among RUP council members again surfaced in late April. Mayor Rodolfo Espinosa remarked of the probe, "I feel it's Lopez's personal vendetta against Garza because he [Lopez] didn't get his contract extended." What Espinosa was referring to was Lopez's term as schools superintendent while Garza was a school board member. As a result of the investigation, Lopez lost the superintendency and was reassigned by the school board to a lesser administrative position. Meanwhile, Espinosa was named acting superintendent.

Once again, the problem was that the same people were holding several important positions simultaneously, a detrimental habit that had its genesis in the politics of community control but became especially commonplace after the political rupture. The 1979 election saw Rodolfo Espinosa reelected mayor of Cristal while he was acting superintendent of schools. Ninfa Moncada, newly elected to the school board, was chosen to serve as school board president; she was also acting city manager.[23]

Cristal's political turmoil intensified in August. The personal agendas of former RUP leaders had become so divisive and problematic that both Mayor Espinosa and school board president Moncada became casualties of the growing internecine conflict. Espinosa was replaced by Olivia Serna as mayor. The city council voted 4–1, with Espinosa abstaining, to replace Moncada with Roberto Garcia as executive director of the Zavala County Economic Development Corporation. Moncada remarked, "I didn't know the council was displeased with my work," and blamed her ouster on politics. Apparently, the move was retaliatory. Some council members had pressured her to fire a number of people who worked for the city. Moncada refused on the ground that she believed the firings to be political and unrelated to the individuals' ability to perform their duties.

Mayor Serna explained that Moncada was fired because she had been unable to form a viable working relationship with the council. According to Serna, Moncada had failed to keep the council informed. In turn, Espinosa, who had been demoted to assistant schools superintendent, alleged that his ouster was engineered by Gutiérrez and his factions. Serna was more specific. She believed that Espinosa was removed as mayor because he had opposed the hiring of Garcia as acting city manager. Serna saw the conflict between the two as detrimental to the council.[24] A week later the *Sentinel* quoted her as claiming that she had been misquoted and giving a new reason for Espinosa's removal. She explained that Espinosa's ouster was a result of his refusal to post a notice of a council meeting and not because of any conflict between Espinosa and City Manager Garcia. Dale Barker, in his editorial on the shake-up, wrote that it "brought an end to the coalition between at least the three groups which swept their candidates into office in the April and city and school elections." He alleged that Gutiérrez was behind the purges.[25]

That same week in August, while Serna was reclarifying her position, Moncada became the casualty of yet another coup when she was removed as school board president. In her place the board of trustees elected Juan "Topper" Perez. Another casualty of the coup was Espinosa, who was suspended indefinitely as assistant superintendent without being given a reason. After he was fired, Espinosa was charged with aggravated assault in connection with an incident involving Perez. The complaint against Espinosa alleged that he had threatened Perez with "imminent bodily injury by the use of a deadly weapon . . . a firearm." Perez claimed that he was shot at twice by Espinosa and that another shot was fired at Jesús Paz, an employee of the school district. Espinosa denied the charges and said that the incident was a "set-up deal." He was arrested and released on a $3,000 bond by Justice of the Peace Ron Carr. Reverend Sherrill Smith, hypercritical of the growing turmoil, wrote a letter to the editor of the *Sentinel* in defense of Moncada and Espinosa: "How do we keep count of the coups here? A new dimension has been added to the old law of control, not cooperation: if you can't control, then wipe out, destroy, humiliate. . . . Every community has to walk a fine line between political patronage and managerial competency, but in Crystal we are tormented by the task; for us it is a less-than-magnificent obsession."[26]

But words did not end the factionalism or power struggles. By November Espinosa had consolidated his forces. This became evident in the selection of a new police chief. City Manager Garcia recommended Ruben Gonzales for the job. Espinosa, supported by council members Victor Lopez and Luis Avila, refused to accept Garcia's recommendation of Gonzales because Espinosa had problems with Garcia's hiring and firing powers. Espinosa claimed that Garcia's duties as city manager did not include the power to hire Gonzales.

Instead, the new council majority, now led by Espinosa, passed a motion over Mayor Serna's objection that suspended the portion of the city charter that authorized the city manager to hire and fire. In the same motion Espinosa recommended Ruben Gonzales as Cristal's new police chief. The selection of the chief brought to the surface a festering power struggle.

Espinosa did not stop there. With his council majority he pushed for the ouster of Mayor Serna and City Manager Garcia. On a 3–1 vote, both were out. The new governing faction named former city manager Raul T. Flores as acting city manager and Espinosa as mayor. Council member Juan Hernandez called the council's action "completely outrageous." He accused council members of acting like "foolish babies by not getting along."[27]

The next political skirmish occurred at a school board meeting attended by about one hundred people. The so-called Gutiérrez faction eliminated the positions of truant officer, held by council member Luis Avila; migrant program director, held by Bonita Perez; and director of federal programs, held by José Talamantez. Avila was transferred to a teacher's aide position, Perez remained unemployed, and Talamantez was reappointed to head the combined migrant and federal directorships. The vote was 4–3, with Juan "Topper" Perez, now president of the board, José D. Cuevas, Mague Flores, and Pablo Puente voting to eliminate the positions. In opposition were Ninfa Moncada, Ramón Garza, and Esmeralda Torres. Felipe Flores, the district's business manager, also became a casualty. He was fired, allegedly because of a poor evaluation. Moncada accused Perez of recommending the firing of Flores for his own satisfaction, because Flores was the brother of newly hired city manager Raul T. Flores.[28]

In a letter to the editor published in the *Sentinel* in late November, fired city manager Roberto M. Garcia accused Espinosa of vendetta politics:

I can accept the fact that politics plays a big part of any city manager's job, but I cannot accept the unreasonableness that these gentlemen displayed. . . . After I terminated Esmeralda Torres from her job, Mr. Espinoza stormed into my office and demanded to know why I had fired her and not Juan "Topper" Perez or Teresa Flores since, in his opinion, they were not a qualified. He also stated that [if] I started using politics in my job he would "get me." . . . When I found it necessary to terminate Ramon Garza, or "Hot Checks" as he is known, as Chief of Police again, Mr. Espinoza alleged that I was playing politics. . . . Mr. Espinoza never did complain, however, about the fact that I fired his father. . . . It is obvious now that the primary reason that Mr. Espinoza pushed for my termination was the fact that I could not and refused to be controlled by him.[29]

By the end of 1979 Cristal's local politics had so deteriorated that the old racist stereotype of the Mexican crab—that Mexicanos were holding back the success of other Mexicanos—held an awful pincerful of truth.

County Politics: Gutiérrez Under Siege

After the special April 1979 election, Zavala County politics continued down the path of polarization and conflict. For Gutiérrez and the RUP minority in office, politics had so deteriorated that they felt they were under siege by the Democratic majority. Although he lacked the votes and was on the defensive, Gutiérrez did not give up. In May 1979 Gutiérrez took on the Democratic majority over budget amendments in a public letter to the *Sentinel:*

Serious violations of the law have occurred. Three commissioners . . . have seen fit to amend the county budget on three separate occasions. The public and taxpayers have not been notified, informed, or allowed in a public hearing to state their opinions on the budget amendments. Commissioners Torres, Guerrero, and McHazlett have overspent, hired extra employees, paid themselves and their political friends extra money, and dangerously depleted county revenues.[30]

The political sparring intensified during the weeks that followed. After the special election Rosaria Avila, the defeated Democratic candidate for county clerk, filed a suit alleging that persons not eligible to vote had participated in the election. She was represented by Luis M. Segura of San Antonio and Lupe Cortinas. After a recount in late May the court ruled that Diane Palacio Garcia had won by a margin of 4 votes.[31]

For Gutiérrez the first six months of 1979 were tortuous and filled with legal defeats, a living political nightmare. In a 1995 interview he spoke of his loss of power and control: "I was pissed and I tried to go after those guys . . . but it didn't do any good because I did not have the votes. They . . . called their own meetings . . . and under the rules, any three members of the commissioners court could post an agenda."[32]

While Gutiérrez was powerless to alter or stop the policies of the Democratic commissioners, he found time in August to hold a state conference in Cristal entitled Critical Issues Affecting Chicanos. The agenda focused on the progress of Mexicanos after ten years of the movement. Gutiérrez was the keynote speaker. Other participating speakers included Willie Velasquez, former MAYO cofounder and executive director of the Southwest Voter Registration and Education Project, and Antonio Orendain, president of the Texas Farm Workers Union. Although the conference was held in Cristal and drew hundreds of people, it received virtually no coverage from the *Sentinel* or the other media. That week the 4th Court of Civil Appeals upheld the right of Democrat Matthew McHazlett to retain the office of county commissioner over RUP candidate Alejandro Perez. Whatever hope Gutiérrez had of regaining control of the county commissioners court ended with this decision.

For Gutiérrez the political crisis worsened. In August the Democratic majority on the county board moved to cut his annual salary from $19,000 to $16,000. The board justified its action by saying it was part of budgetary cutbacks.[33] The salaries of RUP county clerk Diana Palacios Garcia and RUP county treasurer Carmen Flores were also reduced. Gutiérrez reacted to the salary cut by declaring, "I can't be expected to work full-time for that salary, so it will be a part-time job." In late August the commissioners again cut Gutiérrez's salary, from $16,000 to $11,000. Throughout the ordeal Gutiérrez vehemently attacked the board on budget issues, accusing the Democratic majority of so overspending that the county had a $500,000 deficit: "They (the majority) are going to bankrupt the county. They have no fiscal policies. I feel sorry for those who will have to take over this county in the future."[34]

The Democrats' anti-Gutiérrez crusade reached its apogee in September when Commissioner Guerrero called for Gutiérrez's resignation. In a letter to the *Sentinel* Guerrero attacked Gutiérrez's justification for reducing his work hours:

County Judge José Angel Gutiérrez has it backwards. . . . He is not adjusting his hours to his salary, his salary is being adjusted to his performance of his job. Judge Gutiérrez has neglected and refused to be present at several Commissioners' Court meetings, even while he is in the courthouse. It's a well-known fact that he has been delivering his beer two or three days a week, and along with that, he spends too much time traveling out of town. . . . The best thing the judge could do as a good service to the people of Zavala County is to resign—after all, the people did not vote for a part-time judge.[35]

In the same letter Guerrero conceded that because of the deficit the county would have to borrow $300,000 from the Zavala County Bank. But he blamed Gutiérrez and RUP for costing the county thousands of dollars in legal fees and costs for special elections.

Guerrero's letter precipitated an acrid written response from Gutiérrez in which he called Guerrero a liar. In a letter to the *Sentinel* Gutiérrez said to Guerrero, "Your blatant deceit is boundless to the point of being a walking fraud." Gutiérrez responded point by point to Guerrero and charged that the Democratic commissioners advocated terminating the Child Support Program, the Juvenile Probation Program, and the Meals for the Elders Program and opposed creation of a tax district for Zavala County. The letter concluded, "You do realize that your budget as adopted and its new rate of $1.30 is already in deficit for half a million."[36] In late 1979 the political situation for Gutiérrez became untenable, setting the stage for his departure from Cristal.

Gutiérrez's Self-Imposed Exile

Faced with increasing financial difficulties, Gutiérrez began his exodus from Cristal during the late months of 1979. For him and his family the situation became both politically and financially precarious. After ten years of struggle both MAYO and RUP were moribund; RUP's peaceful revolution had succumbed to its internal contradictions (endogenous antagonisms) as well as external (exogenous) antagonisms; and as county judge Gutiérrez was constantly being subjected to a flood of suits and investigations against him. By 1979 his leadership both in Cristal and at the national level had been neutralized. With RUP all but political history and the peaceful revolution over by 1979, Gutiérrez no longer had the leadership assets that had catapulted him to national prominence within the Chicano Movement, which itself was moribund, exacerbating the precariousness of Gutiérrez's position. Like MAYO and RUP, many other groups and leaders were disappearing from the activist arena. Chicano politics had become accommodationist, thanks to the "Viva Yo" generation's mind-set.

By this time Gutiérrez was hurting financially. With his income limited by the county commission's salary cuts, the primary wage earner was Luz, who continued as director of the health center. This difficult situation was aggravated by the scores of lawsuits filed by attorneys Lupe Cortinas, Louis Segura, and Jesse Gamez. "These suits," José Angel Gutiérrez declared, "are most threatening to the financial well being of my family."[37] The lawsuits against him clearly were part of a strategy to squeeze Gutiérrez financially. If he were fighting for his economic survival, he would have little energy left to threaten the political and economic interests of the white power holders and the new Mexicano politicos, both locally and statewide.

Facing a dismal political and financial situation, Gutiérrez decided in August to accept an offer to be a consultant on a census project in the northwest. The position involved working with David Hunter of the Stern Fund to provide groups in Oregon, Washington, Idaho, and Alaska with technical and organizational assistance in redistricting litigation and lobbying. For the next few months Gutiérrez found himself spending more of his time in the northwest and less time in Zavala County. He lived primarily in Tulatin, a small suburb of Portland. Meanwhile, his absence from Zavala County became an issue that continued to feed the vitriol of his Democratic adversaries on the county court of commissioners.

According to Gutiérrez, he and Luz decided to leave Cristal for good in 1979: "We knew we would not be able to find jobs in the state. . . . Activists and militants always find it hard to find employment. What is more important, allies and friends are afraid of hiring someone as political and vocal as we are for fear of not being able to control us." Believing that they had few viable alternatives, the Gutiérrezes decided to move to Oregon. Luz Gutiérrez was no stranger to the northwest. As director of the health clinic she had made many contacts there and was familiar with the region. She said she loved the beauty of the northwest. They kept their decision to move a secret and decided that Luz and the family would remain in Cristal until José Angel was settled.

From late 1979 through much of 1980 Gutiérrez shuttled back and forth between Cristal and Oregon. With Luz and most of the family still in Cristal, he found it difficult to be separated from his family as well as from the political struggle he had founded and led. He realized he was in quasi-exile, because he spent most of his time in the northwest. Yet officially, at least on paper, Gutiérrez was still Zavala County's judge. While in Oregon, he became involved as a volunteer with the Colegio César Chávez, a liberal arts Chicano college located in Mt. Angel. Gutiérrez was instrumental in helping the college's small corps of student volunteers to obtain a grant for bilingual education. Moreover, using his connections with the Mexican government, he initiated an international education course of study with Mexico at the college.[38] Thus, between his consulting and his volunteer work with the college, he was spending less and less time in Cristal.

In January 1980 Gutiérrez participated in an event that drew further criticism from his adversaries. Although RUP was no longer an official political party in Texas, Gutiérrez and a few other former RUP leaders and supporters celebrated the tenth anniversary of RUP by meeting with a delegation of fifty Mexicano political representatives from Mexico's Partido Socialista de Trabajadores (PST, the Socialist Workers' Party). The two delegations met in Laredo at the International Bridge,

which separates the United States and Mexico. After symbolically as-
sembling at the bridge, the speakers attacked U.S. imperialism with
shouts of "Raza Si, Yanqui No." The gathering was followed by a meeting at which Gutiérrez declared, "We have become an undocumented
person in our own land."[39]

Gutiérrez's absence from Cristal began to attract public notice in
February when Barker noted in his *Sentinel* column, "Zavala County
Judge José Angel Gutiérrez is on a leave of absence for six weeks. Attorney Joe Taylor was sworn in as County Court Judge for judicial
matters." In June the county commissioners denied Gutiérrez's request
for an academic leave of absence. Gutiérrez took the leave despite the
denial.[40] He was adamant in not acquiescing to their demands for his
resignation. For Gutiérrez it was an issue of principle. Politically, he
had nothing to lose. He and his family had already made the decision
to leave Cristal; this was his way of waging a psychological political
war against the Democratic commissioners.

Zavala County Politics of 1980

The 1980 county primary elections scheduled for May were essentially
noncombative. With RUP no longer on the ballot, the real challenge to
the Democrats came from within their own ranks. Four candidates ran
for the nomination for county sheriff, some of them former RUP office
holders who had reregistered as Democrats. In the weeks preceding
the primary approximately one thousand former RUP voters reregistered as Democrats. Some became active in the party's county politics.
On May 3 the former RUP adherents held a miniconvention in Cristal
and publicly endorsed a number of Democrats.[41]

The results of the Democratic primary were mixed for former RUP
adherents. Armando Rodriguez came in third in the county sheriff's
race, with 670 votes to Elfego "Fego" Martínez's 839 votes. On a positive note, incumbent commissioner Felipe Torres lost his reelection bid
to Hector Gomez, who won the Democratic nomination 312–244. In
the other race for commissioner the former RUP members lost. Their
endorsed candidate, Fidel Benavides, lost to David Garza, 235–176
votes. Paul Rich lost 1,095–991 to incumbent Abraham (Chick) Kazen.
But Mike V. Gonzalez won the nomination for state representative with
903 votes to Susan Gurley McBee's 794 votes, and Lucas Galvan took
the nomination for a seat on the state board of education with 720
votes over Bryan Crouch's 585. Rudy Esquivel won in his bid for re-
nomination to the Court of Civil Appeals.

The results reflected the transition that was rapidly giving the Democratic Party a monopoly. The endorsement of non-Mexicano candidates by former RUP supporters illustrated the resurgence of accommodation politics. What was left of CU endorsed the same candidates. Barker acknowledged the reason for a dramatic increase in the number of people who voted: "The increase was due to the large number of Raza Unida voters who took part in the Democratic Primary."[42]

That same month the Zavala County Democrats held their policy convention at which they would also select delegates to the state Democratic convention. The local convention turned into a competition between the delegations. The issue was which delegation would be recognized. In essence there were two delegations, the traditional Democrats and the RUP members who became reborn Democrats. The latter mounted a challenge for four of the county's six precincts. The Credentials Committee voted not to seat the challenging delegation. Because only two precincts were seated, Tim Miller, county Democratic chair, asked that the seated delegates place themselves on one side of the room and the challenging delegation on the other. The irony was that the challenging delegation was led by Luz Gutiérrez, who was committed to the nomination of Edward Kennedy as the party's presidential candidate. (José Angel Gutiérrez during this time was working in Oregon.) In demanding that the delegation be recognized, she said, "We are going to participate today."[43] Each delegation proceeded to elect four delegates and alternates to the state convention scheduled for June. Luz Gutiérrez was elected chair of the challenging delegation and Tim Miller of the other. As the convention adjourned, Luz Gutiérrez vociferously stated, "We are officially the people seated." She also accused Tim Miller of racism and of stealing convention documents.

The significance of this political skirmish was that the former RUP adherents had rejoined the Democratic Party and had sought to continue some aspects of their struggle by boring from within. The paradox was that after ten years of struggling against the proclaimed evils of the Democratic Party, their pragmatism had prevailed over their ideological zeal. In a 1995 interview José Angel Gutiérrez explained why they returned to the ranks of the Democratic Party: "We had no party. We had no labels so we all went back to being Democrats. We voted in the Democratic primary, and we became delegates to try to have some influence and leverage."[44]

The Politics of Transition (1980)

Gutiérrez spent most of 1980 in Oregon. In Cristal the politics of self-destruction continued. The unbridled divisiveness that reemerged in late 1979 went unchecked into 1980. Conflict continued to be based on what individual or faction would control the spoils system. In a 4–3 vote in late December 1979 the school board initiated another purge with the firing or reassignment of fifteen district employees, an action recommended by schools superintendent Armando Murrillo. Voting for the shake-up in personnel were board president Juan "Topper" Perez and trustees Margarita Flores, José D. Cuevas, and Pablo Puente. These board members were considered loyal to Gutiérrez. In opposition were trustees Ninfa Moncada, Esmeralda Torres, and Ramón Garza. A shouting match broke out among the crowded spectators, with some people demanding to know reasons for the board's action. Neither the board nor the superintendent provided answers.[45]

Within days the fired personnel filed contempt charges in U.S. District Court against the four Gutierrista trustees, Superintendent Murrillo, District Attorney Alonzo Villareal, and Judge Gutiérrez. Each plaintiff asked for damages exceeding $10,000. The Texas State Teacher's Association sent representatives to Cristal to investigate the matter. U.S. District Judge D. W. Suttle signed a temporary restraining order that reinstated the fifteen employees in their jobs.[46]

Rodolfo Espinosa Jr. and Benito Perez, who had been fired earlier by the same four-vote majority, joined the suit. They were not included in the temporary restraining order because they were working elsewhere. A few days later Espinosa won a motion for summary judgment following an administrative hearing on his firing before the Texas Education Agency's commissioner of education. The hearing officer ruled that it was evident that Espinosa had been denied due process of law at every level since his suspension without pay in August 1979. The officer sent the case back to the school district for resolution.[47]

While the school district was once again engulfed in political conflict and litigation, Cristal's local electoral season began. Even without the presence of Gutiérrez or RUP, the school board and city council elections continued to be a political game—the only question was which faction would control the spoils of patronage. Once again three factions that rose from RUP's ashes fielded candidates. The Gutiérrez faction ran Oscar Martinez and Alberto Sánchez for the city council and Valentina Mendez and Esequivel de la Fuente for the school board. The resurrected Barrio Club candidates for city council were Lupe Cortinas and Isaac Juárez. For the school board the Barrio Club backed David Cortinas and Victor Bonilla III. The Espinosa faction ran Victor Lopez and Henry Rivera for the city council and Ninfa Moncada and Felipe Flores for the school board. All three factions mounted campaigns but saw a declining number of volunteers. But Cristal's Mexicano community had lost its interest in politics. Political alienation had set in. *Sentinel* publisher Dale Barker commented on this political change: "I've said a couple of times during our political season that there doesn't seem to be as much excitement being generated by the city council and school trustee elections. Why, I've even heard some people say they aren't going to bother to vote. That's really switch! Time was when you couldn't keep anybody away from the polls."[48]

The results of the April elections were a major political victory for the Gutiérrez faction even though he had nothing to do with them. Gutierristas won decisively in both the school board and city council races. Top vote getters for the school board were Esequivel de la Fuente and Valentina Mendez with 1,090 and 1,040 votes, respectively. Ninfa Moncada received a mere 578 votes, while Felipe Flores, running on the same ticket, received a total of 626 votes. The Barrio Club's school board candidates, David Cortinas and Victor Bonilla, received 549 votes and 494 votes. The results of the election gave the Gutierrista faction a 6–1 majority on the school board. For the city council Gutierrista candidates Alberto Sánchez and Oscar Martinez garnered 1,031 and 1,023 votes, respectively. The Espinosa and Barrio Club faction candidates did poorly. Henry Rivera received 636 votes, while Victor Lopez, running on the same ticket, got 475 votes. Barrio Club candidates Lupe Cortinas and Isaac Juárez garnered 585 votes and 412 votes, respectively. Dale Barker editorialized on the results of the local elections: "There have been so many changes back and forth during the past couple of years—or has it been more than that?—that it's almost impossible to explain the goings on to anyone who knows nothing about Crystal City."[49]

The aftermath of Cristal's local elections produced still another purge. As had been the pattern, the victors—the Gutierrista faction—initiated a purge of the opposition's loyalist administrators. As a result of the shake-up, Chief of Police Ramón Garza resigned along with City Manager Raul T. Flores. With a majority on the city council the reenergized Gutierrista faction elected Olivia Serna, replacing Rodolfo Espinosa, as the city's new mayor. The Gutierristas also appointed Juan M. Perez as acting city manager. The purge was extended to some of the city's agencies. Five employees of the Center for Human Services were given the axe: Flor Macias, Maria Aguilar, Guadalupe Garza, Frank Rendon, and Mary O. Davila. The move for their dismissal came from Rudy Torres, the newly appointed acting director of the center who had replaced Alejandro Perez. Reaction to the firings was slow. Acting city manager Perez, who was also president of the school board, was out of town at a school board conference.[50] The purge included the Housing Commission, with the ouster of commissioner Jesús Rios. In addition, the city council appointed Ventura Gonzalez to the Housing Commission as a replacement for Alberto Sánchez, who had resigned upon his election to the city council.

In May the council hired Roberto Garcia as city manager. Garcia had served as city manager from August 7 to November 16, 1979, when he was fired after the faction to which he belonged lost control. The recirculation of leaders was still very much part of the political workings in 1980. When Garcia was fired, the school district hired him as its business manager. Before that he also had served as executive director of the Zavala County Economic Development Corporation.[51] The purges continued well into June and included the dismissal of ten employees of the city's Housing Authority.

On June 6 the U.S. District Court issued a preliminary injunction that blocked the firing of the Housing Authority employees. The ten had filed suit claiming that their firing was the result of their political opposition to or dissatisfaction with the leadership of the RUP faction. Named as defendants in the suit were the Housing Commission—José Serna, Ventura Gonzalez, and José Alvarado—both as commissioners and individually, and Gutiérrez, both as an individual and in his capacity as county judge. Gutiérrez was not included in the preliminary injunction; consequently, he was not served with the temporary restraining order and did not have to appear.[52]

With the Gutierrista faction firmly in control, the ensuing months of 1980 saw a lessening of infighting and power struggles among Cristal's factions. Careful content analysis of the *Sentinel* reveals few, if any, stories or editorials about the ongoing politics of self-destruction. The only issues to receive the attention of the press were the reorganization in July of the city's Public Works Department, the appointment of Pablo Puente as its new director, and the resignation of school board trustee José D. Cuevas in October. Other than that, Cristal's politics took on an unusually nonconfrontational and increasingly accommodationist posture. By the end of 1980 little remained of RUP's peaceful revolution. What survived were the memories, political wounds, and the continued relegation of the majority of Mexicanos in Cristal to an internal colonial status.

Gutiérrez's Resignation

Although the conflict lessened in Cristal's local politics, this was not the case with county politics. The efforts by the Democratic-controlled county board to get rid of Gutiérrez as county judge accelerated throughout most of 1980. During much of that year Gutiérrez spent most of his time in Oregon working on the redistricting project. After he had spent some time as a volunteer at the Colegio César Chávez in Oregon, the college president resigned, and Gutiérrez applied unsuccessfully for the position.[53] The job went to Irma Flores Gonzales. Determined to remain in Oregon, Gutiérrez secured a part-time teaching position in Monmouth at Western Oregon State College (later renamed Oregon College of Education). By this time efforts were in motion to force his resignation as county judge in Cristal.

The Democratic commissioners sought to keep the Gutiérrez issue quiet. Gutiérrez's absence did not appear to be of major concern until former RUP leaders and supporters decided to run a slate of independents against the Democrats for the various county positions. Lacking in formal structure and the leadership of Gutiérrez, the independientes ran a slate that included incumbent commissioner Elena Díaz for reelection; Victor Castillo for county sheriff; and Ofelia Juarez for commissioner of Precinct 1; and Ramón S. Lopez for tax assessor–collector, among others.[54]

As the independents waged their campaigns in October, the Democratic commissioners decided to hold off the electoral challenge by once again going after Gutiérrez, whom they perceived as the invisible organizing hand behind the challenge. They felt that by removing Gutiérrez from office once and for all, the threat to their control and power would be gone. Just before the November election in late October the commission split 3–2 on a vote to oust Gutiérrez as county judge, with commissioners Frank Guerrero Jr., Matthew McHazlett, and Felipe Torres voting yes and Gutiérrez, who had come back for a visit, and Elena Díaz voting no. The motion passed in the form of a resolution. In arguing in support of the resolution, McHazlett declared that Gutiérrez had missed twenty-two of the last twenty-eight commissioners' meetings. Gutiérrez countered that these were "dumb accusations" and reserved the right to answer all the accusations fully at the appropriate place and time.[55]

The exchange became caustic with both sides hurling charges and countercharges. Gutiérrez claimed that three Democratic commissioners had met and set the tax rate illegally and had voted to cut the Juvenile Board out of the budget just to retaliate against him. Guerrero countered that the budget cut was made because Gutiérrez was not available to handle the juvenile cases. Guerrero said that the Juvenile Board would be put back in the budget when a county judge was available to serve with the district judge on the board.

After making various charges connected to Gutiérrez's neglect of his judicial and administrative duties, the commission voted on the following resolution: "Therefore, be it resolved that the commissioner's Court of Zavala County petition the State Judicial Qualifications Commission to remove José Angel Gutiérrez because of willful and persistent conduct or neglect of official duties which is clearly inconsistent with the proper performance of his duties of which casts public discredit on the Judiciary or on the administration of Justice."[56] With the passage of the resolution, commissioners Guerrero and McHazlett went to Austin to present a formal complaint to the State Judicial Qualifications Commission requesting the removal of Gutiérrez.

While the campaign to oust Gutiérrez intensified, the November county elections brought defeat to most of the independent candidates. Democrat Ramón Garza won the race for sheriff by beating independiente Victor Castillo 2,056–1,595. In the tax assessor's race Democrat Martha P. Cruz won reelection by beating independent Ramón S. Lopez Jr. in a vote of 2,236–1,304. For the position of commissioner of Precinct 1, Democrat Hector Gomez won decisively with 432 votes to independiente Ofelia Juarez's 282 and write-in incumbent Democrat Felipe Torres's 215. The only major victory scored by the *independientes* was in the race for commissioner of Precinct 3, which Elena Díaz won by a mere 2-vote margin over Democratic challenger David Garza, 388–386. Except for Santa Castillo Guerrero, who won the race for constable in Precinct 3, the Democrats took the other three constable races.

A recount requested by David Garza proved detrimental to the independientes. With Rudy Palomo and Arturo Gonzales, now Democrats, on the Recount Committee, the final vote shifted the victory to Garza, with the latter receiving 402 votes to Díaz's 390. Díaz filed suit contesting the results of the count. The suit was filed by Abel Cavada, who represented the Texas Rural Legal Aid, Inc., of Kingsville.[57]

With no hope of retaking control of the county board Gutiérrez moved his family from Cristal to Oregon. The pressure to get him to resign continued. Right after the election Luz Gutiérrez resigned as executive director of El Centro de Salud. In her place José A. Rodriguez, a consultant from San Antonio, was hired as temporary executive director. By late November, with the Gutiérrez family now in Oregon, the movement to oust Gutiérrez grew became more intense. The Democratic-controlled county board approved an order declaring a vacancy in the office of county judge. The order read: "The Commissioners Court hereby declares a vacancy in the County Judge's Office of Judge José Angel Gutiérrez due to his total absence from Zavala

County, his lack of residency in the County and the County Judge's non-appearance in Commissioner's Court meetings or in county court sessions."[58]

The county treasurer was subsequently ordered to stop payment of the county judge's salary. Commissioner McHazlett commented on the action: "We're still knocking on the judge's door when we have meetings. I'd have to have arms long enough to knock on doors in Mexico City or Oregon if I wanted to reach the judge." Commissioner Guerrero considered Gutiérrez irresponsible and negligent and unqualified for the post because he no longer resided in Zavala County.[59]

The holidays and other events in the county impeded the Democratic commissioners' crusade to remove Gutiérrez. One such event was the death of Gutiérrez's nemesis, attorney Lupe Cortinas, on November 25. Cortinas was killed in an auto accident involving a tractor-trailer while en route to San Antonio. A second event was Elena Díaz's suit. In December Cavada, her lawyer, argued before the 38th District Court that twenty-five people had cast illegal ballots for David Garza. Cavada also argued that both Arturo Gonzales and Julian Rios were not qualified to serve on the Recount Committee because they were employees of the county. Garza's attorney, Peter Torres Jr. of San Antonio, made a motion asking that Cavada be disqualified from representing Díaz on the ground that he did not have the authority to file suit as an attorney for Texas Rural Aid. On another legal issue the 4th Court of Civil Appeals upheld the 38th District Court's decision to order Zavala County Clerk Diana Palacios Garcia to record the minutes of certain commissioners' court meetings held before January 1, 1979.[60]

The Democratic commission's efforts to oust Gutiérrez paid off early in 1981. After months of maneuvering and pressure by the commission, in late January Gutiérrez informed the board that he would resign, effective February 13, provided that the county pay him $9,000 in back pay.[61] Gutiérrez's offer to resign began with a telephone call to Ron Carr, justice of the peace, Precinct 1. Gutiérrez then was teaching at Colegio César Chávez in Oregon and informed Carr of his decision to resign because of his loss of interest in his position as Zavala County judge.

Gutiérrez, however, insisted that the county owed him $9,000 in back pay for services rendered. He also informed Carr that he would be returning to Cristal to attend the January 26 meeting of the commission, at which time he would inform the board of his decision and conditions. The *San Antonio Express* announced the decision in bold headlines on February 18, 1981, reporting that the "fiery" founder of La Raza, climaxing a yearlong feud with political enemies, had ended by saying "to h– with it," and had resigned as Zavala County judge. In explaining why he resigned, Gutiérrez said that the commissioners refused to pay him his salary, so he had to find other work. From his perspective it was a Catch-22. He concluded, "They finally got me."[62]

With Gutiérrez's resignation the Democratic-controlled county board moved quickly on two fronts. The commissioners accepted Gutiérrez's resignation in principle. Concomitantly, they appointed Ron Carr as his successor. The commissioners also agreed to pay Gutiérrez his back pay of $9,000. According to Barker, the meeting of January 26 was almost a complete disaster: "That meeting ended in a donnybrook, with Gutiérrez walking out, threatening to sue the commissioners."[63] At the heart of the conflict were Gutiérrez's conditions, namely, back pay.

It took the diplomacy and bargaining skills of Carr to resolve the impasse. He met with each commissioner. In executive session on February 12 the commissioners renewed their commitment to pay Gutiérrez the $9,000. Gutiérrez received payment five days later. Meanwhile, the Judicial Qualifications Commission had sent an investigator to Cristal to look into the matter. Asked years later why the commissioners had argued over reimbursement, Pablo Avila, who was county attorney, replied, "Even though they had the majority votes, they were afraid of him."[64]

Reaction to Gutiérrez's resignation and departure from Cristal was mixed. The *San Antonio Express* on February 18, 1981, concluded, "Gutiérrez's resignation apparently marks the end of La Raza Unida, the predominantly Mexican-American party born out of a tumultuous Cristal City school boycott in 1969 and 1970." The *Zavala County Sentinel* proclaimed in bold print, "The End of a Political Dynasty." In the accompanying editorial Barker observed: "In Crystal City on Wednesday morning, February 18, different points of view were expressed depending on what faction the person being interviewed belonged to. For those who had given him their confidence and faith in the mentor and leader of RUP, it was disillusionment and sadness; for others it was a climate of hope for those who had struggled for year after year to accommodate the community with common goals."[65]

The *Corpus Christi Caller Times*, which for years covered various aspects of the RUP's peaceful revolution, headlined its story "Gutiérrez Resignation Shows La Raza's Weaknesses at Home." Media throughout Texas made much of Gutiérrez's resignation. After all, no other Mexicano in contemporary Texas history had so audaciously challenged the gringo power holders and the Mexicanos' internal colonial status. Perhaps to some gringos as well as some conservative Mexicanos and his supporters Gutiérrez was the contemporary Juan "Cheno" Cortinas, who from 1859 to the 1870s had struggled as a guerrilla against gringo injustices along the Texas-Mexico border.

Mexicanos in Cristal also had a mixed reaction to the resignation. His supporters were sad, and some felt betrayed. County Clerk Diana Palacios Garcia noted, "When he [Gutiérrez] first came here, we weren't politically aware. No one was much on politics. One of the things [Gutiérrez pushed] was to make us politically aware. It succeeded too well perhaps, because now everybody is in it."[66] Severita Lara, who had been a key leader of the Cristal school walkout in 1969, later recalled, "I felt betrayed. A lot of people were loyal to him. We felt protected by José Angel. He was our *abogado* [lawyer] *sin titulo* [without a title]. When somebody would do us wrong, we would go to him. . . . We felt protected. When he left, we felt we were all alone. We felt he was running away from us."[67]

His adversaries were relieved. Zavala County Sheriff Ramón Garza said, "Angel hurt himself. He was the kind of guy that if you didn't do what he said, you were against him." City council member Rodolfo Espinosa told reporters, "Gutiérrez took the route of being a political boss instead of a political leader."[68] But years later Espinosa had mellowed somewhat: "About 40 percent who had experienced the suffering of gringo discrimination and who had been strong supporters of RUP felt bad about his resignation. Another 40 percent or so felt good about his resignation. They felt that they finally got rid of him. The other 20 percent didn't care if the devil himself were county judge."[69]

Barker wrote of Gutiérrez's resignation, "It was total frustration for him. The opposition was committed to getting him out of office any way they could." Jack Kingsberry recalled, "Those who opposed him were glad it had happened. They thought it was better for the county as a whole to see him leave." According to then-county attorney Pablo Avila, "A good number of people said good riddance."[70]

Upon his resignation Gutiérrez released a lengthy public letter entitled, «*Se Despide Gutiérrez*» [Gutiérrez Says Farewell], in which he explained the reasons for his resignation. The following are excerpts from the letter:

Dear Voter:

I forward to you my letter of resignation for the post of County Judge of Zavala County. I lament having to make this decision that offends my very being. I think that no matter how unpleasant this personal experience may be, it is a decision that is necessary for the well being of my family and the voters who in my various political campaigns supported me. My respect continues for all of you.

In the body of the letter Gutiérrez listed seven factors that contributed to his decision to resign: the consistent vote against his programs and projects by the Democratic-controlled county board in 1979 and 1980; the dramatic cuts to the salaries of RUP county officials; bankrupting of the county by the poor fiscal policies of the Democratic board; the Democrats' vote to increase taxes while not charging Uvalde Community College its share of taxes; the Democrats' decision to allow the county sheriff to illegally traffic in undocumented workers; the disastrous administration of the county ; and the attacks on many important projects and programs by ignorant people blind to the future. He concluded his letter by saying, "Thank you for the opportunity given me to work for and with you. I am not saying goodbye because in the short term I will be back."[71]

The departure of Gutiérrez and his family from Cristal in late 1980 and his resignation as county judge brought the Cristal experiment to an end. The experiment had sought to transform the powerless into the empowered by breaking the chains of internal colonialism with its stultifying dependency, racism, and subordination. The experiment's mission was predicated on fostering the decolonization of Cristal and that of the rest of south Texas. Its goal had been twofold: to establish community control over the schools and city and county governments; and to effectuate change in the political, educational, economic, and social arenas. Ultimately, the Cristal experiment succumbed to a myriad of endogenous and exogenous antagonisms. Endogenously, however, the power struggles and infighting were motivated by greed and destroyed the experiment. Exogenously, as was inevitable, it was unable to overcome the omnipotence of internal colonialism. Thus, with the departure of Gutiérrez from Cristal in 1981, a major chapter in the history of Texas came to a close.

Epilogue: The Unfinished Experiment

The Cristal experiment in community control was historic. After Mexicanos lost their political control to whites in 1836, Mexicanos in south Texas became powerless politically and otherwise. It was no different for Mexicanos in Cristal. For decades they were disenfranchised and governed locally by white patrones (bosses) who constituted a minority of the city's population. All this changed, however, with the two electoral revolts of 1963–1965 and 1970–1975. In both cases Mexicanos, tired of their powerlessness, infused with a passion for change, and impelled by rising expectations, successfully revolted against what they perceived as the tyranny of the white minority. Although the experiment in community control brought about numerous changes occurred, it ultimately failed. At the crux of its failure was its inability to overcome the insurmountable omnipresence of internal colonialism in south Texas and the workings of the liberal capitalist system. In the context of today both revolts suggest that the Cristal experiment remains unfinished.

The Cristal Experiment: The Findings

Both phases of the Cristal experiment produced positive and negative results. On the positive side the first revolt set a precedent for Mexicanos. Los Cinco scored a first in south Texas by fostering what was tantamount to the first successful political rebellion by Mexicanos against the entrenched white minority. Mexicanos sent the powerful message that they would no longer tolerate being disenfranchised. The white community feared that the revolt would spread throughout south Texas, creating many more Cristals. To the white elite Cristal represented a threat to the destabilization of the Mexicanos' internal colonial status in south Texas. The white elite was confronted with the lie of their ethnocentric perceptions of Mexicanos as inferior, servile, apolitical, and generally incapable of challenging white power. For these and other reasons the first revolt was historically significant.

344

Symbolically, the first revolt signified the political awakening of Mexicanos. For some Mexicanos in south Texas and the rest of the nation Cristal became a model for and an gauge of the emerging Chicano Movement. Throughout the southwest especially, the Cristal experiment helped raise Mexicanos' level of political consciousness and expectations. The phrase «si se puede» [yes, it is possible] began to replace negative attitudes marked by cynicism, skepticism, and fatalism toward politics, of some Mexicanos. Although the first revolt occurred many years after Arthur Rubel's study of Mexicanos in the lower Rio Grande Valley in the late 1950s, it gave lie to his postulate that Mexicanos were a "dormant mass" that did not want to cause trouble by voting and had little appetite for the formal organization of political behavior.[1]

As a result of the first revolt, some Mexicanos began to believe in themselves, becoming psychologically self-empowering. They believed that they had finally tasted the sweet fruit of democracy—political representation—and that it would no longer be denied to them. During those brief two years (1963–1965) Mexicanos controlled the politics of the community and brought about some positive changes in the city's delivery of services. Yet the first revolt did little to alter the poverty or the internal colonial status of the Mexicano community.

In fact, the first revolt quickly became contaminated and consumed by what I have described as the politics of self-destruction. Although the white elite contributed to the destabilization of the Teamster-PASSO alliance, the first revolt failed because of the pervasiveness of internecine warfare between Los Cinco, city administrators, and the PASSO-Teamster alliance. The first revolt succumbed to its contradictions. Nonetheless, the first revolt left a legacy that was not forgotten by those who led the second revolt—that some Mexicanos would no longer accept and tolerate their political oppression and powerlessness.

During Cristal's transitional political years (1965 to 1969) Mexicanos continued to control the city council. However, this period was characterized by a political coalition of conservative Mexicanos and white power holders. Despite the emergence of the Chicano Movement by 1965, none of Cristal's Mexicano factions espoused any form of progressive social change. They continued to practice an accommodationist politics that did not threaten the power of the local white elite. Factionalism among the competing Mexicano power bases continued, and voter and civic participation were low. For the overwhelming majority of Mexicanos, who were poor, these transitional years meant a continuation of the their internal colonial status. The only difference was that instead white politicians, the city was controlled by Mexi-canos who were essentially surrogates for the white economic power holders.

In 1970, at the apex of the epoch of protest, Cristal experienced a second electoral revolt. This time the experiment in community control occurred during a much more radicalized national political climate. The second revolt was much more controversial than the first, concen-trating as it did on the decolonization of the Mexicano community. Unlike the first revolt, the second revolt was guided by a plan of action, MAYO's Winter Garden Project, and was in the hands of an adroit and competent architect, José Angel Gutiérrez. He orchestrated the Cristal school walkouts, which acted as a catalyst for the formation of RUP and the second revolt itself.

What followed during the next five years (1970–1975) contributed substantially to the legacy of the Cristal experiment. The peaceful revo-lution engendered a period of unprecedented positive change in edu-cation, civic participation, delivery of social services, Mexicano entre-preneurship, employment, housing, formation of organizations, leadership development, and cultural reinforcement. Federal and pri-vate foundation monies financed many of RUP's change programs. The scope of RUP's peaceful revolution was so broad that some whites per-ceived it as a viable threat to their hegemony in south Texas. They saw Cristal as a mecca for radicals and subversives. Consequently, for nearly ten years the experiment was a thorn in the side of area's white power elites and the Democratic Party statewide.

On the other hand, to Chicano activists Cristal was the bastion of cultural nationalism, Chicano Power, and community control from 1970 to 1975. To some, Cristal meant that Aztlán was in the making. Cristal became famous to many Mexicanos and infamous to even more whites. Metaphorically, Cristal was an emerging island of Mexicano self-determination in the middle of a white sea of internal colonialism. No other small city in the nation could match Cristal, either in its uniqueness in putting into practice the politics of community control or in the breadth of the change realized and intended.

On the negative side is that by 1975 RUP's peaceful revolution had become riddled with internal schisms that led to the political rupture that brought about its demise. What ensued from 1975 to 1980 was in essence a replay of the first revolt—the politics of self-destruction. Driven by factional or individual avarice, the various factions vied for the prize of control of the allocation of patronage. The casualties of the politics of self-destruction were not only the peaceful revolution but the Mexicano community of Cristal, which relapsed into acceptance of the status quo.

Although the peaceful revolution ultimately failed, it left a powerful legacy. Because it attained community control and wrought many changes during its five golden years, Cristal was a beacon of hope and inspiration for the Chicanos. This small rural south Texas city personified the Chicano Movement's struggle for empowerment, community control, and, to some, self-determination. Mexicanos in Cristal succeeded in making the theory of community control a practical reality and participatory democracy more than a phrase in a textbook. Through RUP and CU, Mexicanos became so well organized that they helped make public policy. Scores of neophyte community activists became involved on the city's commissions and school committees and in county government. Their involvement in the decision-making process was especially evident within CU. Although CU was a political machine led by political boss Gutiérrez that ultimately evolved from a demosocratic to an elite power structure, the membership participated meaningfully within a quasi-democratic centralism form of a decision-making process. CU's grassroots membership of hundreds of families was a crucial to Gutiérrez's power and his success in moving RUP's peaceful revolution.

The allocation of patronage was basic to Gutiérrez's modus operandi—he used patronage to help redistribute wealth by awarding hundreds of jobs to those who were loyal to him, CU, and RUP. An important aspect of the legacy was that Gutiérrez built a powerful Mexicano political apparatus that was unequaled elsewhere. Unlike traditional political machines, CU was change oriented and quasi-ideological in its politics—it was committed to the decolonization of south Texas and espoused Chicanismo.

Thus in the end both phases of the Cristal experiment left a historical legacy that will not be forgotten: so long as Mexicanos and other oppressed peoples in the United States live under the specter of internal colonialism, they will revolt and struggle for their liberation from the political, economic, and social horrors and tribulations it creates.

Cristal Today: A Victim of Regressive Change

Cristal is worse off today than it was during the years of RUP's peaceful revolution. If anything, Cristal today is held more firmly in the clutches of internal colonialism. Cristal continues to have a depressed and underdeveloped economy. In the 1970s RUP's peaceful revolution

348 Epilogue

led to white flight. In the 1990s it suffers from brown flight, impelled by a acutely deteriorating economy. Mexicanos are migrating to Texas's urban areas—San Antonio, Austin, Houston, Dallas, and beyond—in search of employment. Cristal's population declined from 9,101 in 1960 to 8,263 in 1990; Mexicanos now are 90 percent of the population—a 5 percent increase since 1980. In a 1994 grant application Cristal reported that "with the diminishing agricultural growth due to . . . catastrophes came the added cost of pumping irrigation water for the crops and low paying markets for the products. The labor force began to migrate to other areas to find suitable employment and the factories and businesses began to follow them and are now becoming non-existent."[2]

As in many rural communities of south Texas, unemployment is chronic. In July 1996 Cristal's unemployment rate hit 28.3 percent. The median unemployment rate for the year (June 1996 to May 1997) was 23.2 percent.[3] The unemployment crisis of 1994 was exacerbated when Del Monte Foods—the area's second largest employer (the school district remains the biggest)—underwent a major downsizing of its workforce because of high freight costs and competitive product pricing. As a result, Del Monte began transferring its production lines to Wisconsin and other plants elsewhere.[4] According to *San Antonio Express* columnist Carlos Guerra, the scarcity of jobs in south Texas has been critical. He says the two industries producing the most jobs quickly are prisons and the U.S. Border Patrol. For example, in the early 1990s a detention center that houses 490 females inmates and employs 85 local residents was established in Cristal.

Zavala County today ranks as the second poorest county in Texas. Cristal's 1994 report underscores the severity of the economic crisis: "The per capita income in Zavala County is only 1/3 of the U.S. average. The current per capita income is $4,818 and the medium per capita is $11,822 while the state per capita income is $27,016. The poverty rate in the county is 50.14% and should increase with the Del Monte Foods mass lay off of its employees."

The Census Bureau reported in 1990 that 3,101 persons in Zavala County, or 25.5 percent, received cash public assistance. The state rate that year was 8 percent. In 1993, 9.3 percent of the national population received food stamps; 46 percent of Zavala County's population was on food stamps.[5]

A majority of the Mexicano population today still depends on the migrant stream. They toil for hours in the hot midwestern sun doing sometimes painful and excruciating work for low wages. Upon their return to Cristal they face unemployment and welfare. According to Dale Barker, who remains editor and publisher of the *Zavala County*

Sentinel, "They draw unemployment from the states where they were employed. The situation is bad. They are being displaced by automation and are becoming increasingly dependent on welfare. More then half of the town's population is on welfare and food stamps."[6]

Whereas the peaceful revolution of the early 1970s fostered hope and progress, the 1990s are imbued with a sense of hopelessness and fatalism. The city itself told a potential funding source that

> The Crystal City business district has become a necklace of deserted "for sale buildings," the once productive agricultural lands are now growing brush and cacti and being leased out for hunting, the railroad is almost non-existent, people are building colonies because of no code enforcement, dams are being closed along the Nueces River in order to provide irrigation waters to other communities up river. The residents no longer have a hospital, the industrial site is now brush, the cotton and grain mills are now closed and property market values have dropped due to abandoned and substandard housing.[7]

In 1990 the U.S. Census reported that housing conditions in Cristal were deplorable. In one of Cristal's barrios, Mexico Chico, families were living in extreme conditions that were not safe, sanitary, decent, or affordable. According to a city survey, 42 percent of the units lacked complete plumbing facilities and 70 percent of the units required reconstruction or substantial rehabilitation because of their extreme deterioration.[8] The vast majority are still dependent on expensive propane gas for their cooking and heating needs.

Nor has the peaceful revolution survived into the 1990s in Cristal's schools. RUP's prized bilingual-bicultural program is severely curtailed: bilingual instruction is once again transitional, focusing only on grades kindergarten through second grade. Chicano studies courses were eliminated. The emphasis now is on "American Studies" with some brief mention of the Chicano experience, yet Mexicanos account for 98 percent of the student population. Except for one Anglo, all school administrators are Mexicano, and 90 percent of the teachers are Mexicano.[9] Thus the spirit of Chicanismo that permeated the district's curriculum during the peaceful revolution has been replaced by a conservative quasi-cultural pluralism bent on mainstreaming students into the status quo of south Texas life.

Cristal's overall educational picture shows problems. For example, in 1994, 63.37 percent of all residents older than twenty-five had not completed high school. Only 4.21 percent held bachelor's degrees.[10] The quality of Cristal's schools is a matter of opinion. Mexicano administrators claim that the schools have continued to improve since RUP's peaceful revolution, but this is difficult to substantiate because they failed to provide me with the documentation I requested. Dale Barker, among others, disagrees with their assessment. In 1994 he told me, "The quality of education has not improved. The schools have grown in bureaucracy. They are an employment office. The schools are bad."[11] The 1991–1992 results of the Texas Assessment of Academic Skills [TAAS] test in Cristal schools found that "Grade 9 students scored below the state standard in all test taken (83 points below), Mathematics (77 points below), Writing (68 points), and Reading (66 points) on the TAAS test."[12]

With the majority of Cristal's Mexicanos still part of the migrant stream, the children pay a price. Migrant parents take their children on the road before school ends and bring them back after school starts. This means that children of migrant parents get only five to six months of schooling instead of the usual nine months. A city report concluded, "Once the student is retained in the same class all interest in the educational system is lost and that student joins the drop out statistics."[13]

The paradox of the Cristal crisis is that Mexicanos in the 1990s are in control politically but are powerless to change Mexicanos' quality of life socioeconomically. In 1994 all members of the school board, city council, and Zavala County Court of Commissioners were Mexicano. The stark reality, however, is that Mexicano politicians govern a community and a county worse off today than it was in the 1970s when RUP was in control. Plagued by a deteriorating economy, the local governments are experiencing serious erosion of the tax base and a high rate of tax delinquencies. This impedes their delivery of services and infrastructure development.

In Cristal political alienation permeates the body politic. Political participation has dropped dramatically. RUP's peaceful revolution was the result of hundreds of Mexicano votes cast and massive citizen participation. Today some local elections have been won with less than three hundred votes. The alienation of local citizens is evident in their conversation about Cristal's contemporary politics. Many express feelings of indifference and hopelessness. They feel that it makes no difference what faction is in power; nothing has changed. Interviews I conducted revealed that Cristal's politics today continue to be a competition of power factions, driven not by lofty ideals or "causas" but by control of patronage.

Today most Mexicanos in Cristal continue to be economically powerless and dependent. Much of the land and wealth in the Winter Garden area still remains in the hands of a small number of whites, many of whom are absentee landowners. It is commonplace for whites to own the banks and financial institutions; the farms and ranches that are thousands of acres in size; oil; and major businesses and industries. Benito Perez, the assistant superintendent of schools, buttresses my contention that economics remain at the crux of Cristal's problems. In a 1997 interview he told me, "What most people don't understand is that the basic problem is that while we control the politics, we don't control the economics. We are not the owners of the area's wealth. We are not the powerful."[14]

Cristal's Mexicano local elected officials and administrators have worked hard to improve the city's economy. Cristal has made many unsuccessful attempts since 1981 to attract new industries. And City Manager Miguel Delgado, for one, remains optimistic. "There is light at the end of the tunnel," he told me in 1997. "Within the next three to five years, we are going to turn things around. We expect to attract more job-producing businesses and industries due to the increased traffic diverted to our area due to NAFTA. The difference this time is that the city's administration is working in harmony with the mayor and city council."[15]

Yet many are wistful for the peaceful revolution. School Superintendent Rodolfo Espinosa Jr., who at various points was both friend and foe of Gutiérrez, told me in 1994, "There were times when I disagreed with Angel, and he would say to us, 'There is no room for too much discussion because this is a movement, this is a revolution.' But in retrospect we should have followed about 99 percent of what he wanted to do and how he wanted to do it. It was a revolution. The enemy was not us, it was the gringo."[16]

Lessons to Be Learned

I have developed twelve lessons or findings, based in great part on the Cristal experiment, that seek to bring an analytical light to the complex political, economic, and social aspects of why the peaceful revolution failed. They are products of three sources: this study's research, years of research on Chicano politics and political movements, and many years of personal political activism as a professional organizer and scholar-activist. Most are products of both revolts. However, they come much more from the second revolt because it is the primary focus of the study. Although there are others, these are the salient lessons to be learned. Theoretically, they provide a framework by which to better understand two cardinal political realities of local politics: the limitations and insurmountable obstacles inherent in the politics of community control; and the limits to fostering major change and political empowerment at the local level.

Lesson 1: Community control of local governmental structures is circumscribed in its capacity to effectuate major political, economic, and social change within the context of internal colonialism.

At the heart of this study is the contention that south Texas's pervasive internal colonialism was a major contributing factor to the failures of both phases of the Cristal experiment. Despite the various endogenous antagonisms that likewise contributed to their failures, it was internal colonialism as a manifestation of liberal capitalism that precluded the success of Cristal's first and second revolts.

For nearly 150 years of Mexicano subjugation and utter domination, Aztlán's capitalist economic development has relied on internal colonialism. Consequently, Mexicanos have been relegated to a status of powerlessness that has been political, economic, and social. Although capitalist economic development has brought about some degree of socioeconomic improvement for some Mexicanos, it has fostered what I call a "South African syndrome." Nowhere in the nation is this syndrome more apparent than south Texas, where Mexicanos in many counties have constituted a majority of the population but have been controlled and exploited by a minority of all-powerful gringos.

Only in the last two decades have Mexicanos made substantial progress in electoral representation. Today Texas has more Mexicano local elected officials than any other state.[17] But real political power and control rest with the state and federal governments, which are controlled by whites. José Angel Gutiérrez has described this situation as tantamount to having a white "racial dictatorship."[18]

The economic implications of internal colonialism have been devastating for Mexicanos. Whites have historically controlled most of south Texas's means of production and distribution (e.g., land, farms, ranches, banks, petroleum, service industries, and factories). Their insatiable demand for cheap labor has fostered a mutual economic dependency between the two ethnic groups, a key characteristic of internal colonialism. For many years this meant that Mexicanos were not to be educated or provided with adequate housing, social services, medical care, and the like. They were to be kept economically impoverished, socially oppressed, and politically suppressed and dependent in order to preserve an exploitable cheap labor pool that yielded huge profits for the white elite.

Moreover, under internal colonialism Mexicano culture has been incessantly under attack. Gringos have deprecated Mexicano culture and considered it inferior to white culture. Gringo racism and ethnocentrism have pervaded white-Mexicano relations in Texas. De jure and de facto segregation were the results of this racism. While gringos in Texas have demanded that Mexicanos abandon their culture, language, heritage, and embrace whites', gringos categorically—and paradoxically—oppose Mexicanos' assimilation. Thus, historically Mexicanos' progress as a people has been hamstrung by internal colonialism in south Texas and elsewhere.

Neither of the two phases of the Cristal experiment succeeded in fostering the decolonization of the city. The first revolt was essentially political in its objectives. It sought merely to win political control. But the leadership failed to consider both the macro- and microeconomic aspects of internal colonialism. This was not the case with the second revolt, however. Its leadership was cognizant of the consequences of internal colonialism and sought unsuccessfully to create a movement against it. In the end, both phases of the experiment failed in great part because of their inability to surmount the conditions and awesome white power relationships that are inherent to the maintenance of internal colonialism. More specifically, the Cristal experiment reveals that community control in an internal colonial setting is circumscribed in its capacity to effect change and empower the people. While Mexicanos controlled some aspect of Cristal's local superstructure in both revolts, they did not control its substructure.

Thus the Cristal experiment demonstrated that political power is subordinate to economic power. Those who wield the economic power are the truly powerful. In the end, the Cristal experiment reaffirmed the axiom that those who control economically control politically.

Lesson 2: The nature of the liberal capitalist system is such that power is concentrated in the hands of the few, which obviates the masses' empowerment and their ability to create change.

The Cristal experiment in community control was thwarted by the very nature of the liberal capitalist system. The nation's political system is based on liberalism, which is synonymous with a republican, or representative, form of democratic government predicated on the notion of popular sovereignty—the idea that the people are the all powerful and in control.

What appears in theory, however, is not what exists in practice. American adherence to liberal capitalism has yielded what political scientist Michael Parenti appropriately calls "democracy for the few."[19] The literature in both political science and sociology provides a plethora of studies that focus on the question of who governs. Most sociologists believe that power in the United States is concentrated in the hands of a relatively small, cohesive group—C. Wright Mills called them a "power elite," G. William Domhoff a "governing class," and Karl Marx a "ruling class." Conversely, many political scientists do not accept its basic tenets. They believe that the theory of a ruling elite exaggerates the concentration of power in the United States. Political scientist Robert Dahl describes U.S. political power as being widely dispersed among many separate and competing elites that are kept in check by divergent social, economic, and political forces.[20]

In theory, the U.S. political system is pluralist, but in practice it is elitist. Although power *appears* to be diffused in actuality, it is concentrated in the hands of an omnipotent elite.[21] The present trend suggests that the nation is evolving into a plutocracy in which the rich are getting richer and the poor poorer. Capitalism develops an interdependence among the various classes. Without the poor and middle class, there can be no rich. Yet people are conditioned through a process of socialization to believe that liberal capitalism is pluralist in nature. From the schools to the media this country celebrates the alleged virtues of liberalism as a political system and capitalism as an economic system.

The political reality that faces any one individual, organization, or party that seeks to create change is that if the change being proposed is not within the accepted liberal capitalist framework, it is next to impossible to achieve. To understand this statement one has only to refer to U.S. history. Once any political force that is not a purveyor of the status quo reaches the level where it is perceived as a threat, it is quickly neutralized through a variety of means, in some cases extralegal.

This lesson is clear in both phases of the Cristal experiment, even though both were reform oriented. The first revolt was essentially a struggle by Mexicanos to win political access. Los Cinco were not ideological architects for revamping Cristal's superstructure. They did not have a plan to empower the people or to alter the local social order. In fact, the opposition to the first revolt was in many respects simple anger on the part of the white elite at the audacity of Mexicanos. They were simply caught by surprise. They did not perceive PASSO's poll-tax rumblings as a threat until it was to late.

The white elite was forced to regroup. With Los Cinco succumbing to infighting and power struggles, the white elite used co-optation, economic intimidation, and harassment to manipulate the situation. Allying with some middle-class Mexicanos, the white elite retook control of Cristal's city council indirectly in 1965. Scholar Michael V. Miller describes what ensued: "From then [1965] until 1970, the [gringos] ran the city government through Mexican-American figure-heads. The Mexican-American community [was] given the illusionary appearance of representation, yet its ostensible representatives [were] beholden to [gringo] interests."[22]

Unlike the first revolt, the second revolt was a product of strong leadership, a third-party movement, grassroots organization, a defined plan of action, and a massive electoral mobilization throughout much of the tricounty Winter Garden area. This was, of course, a serious threat to the stability of south Texas's internal colonialism and liberal capitalist system. Gutiérrez's radical image and actions as a leader, the myriad changes brought by the peaceful revolution, the challenge of RUP to the Democratic Party, and RUP's relationships with Mexico and Cuba were the four main factors that activated powerful forces within Texas's powerful establishment to squelch and neutralize RUP's peaceful revolution.

Once RUP in Cristal moved to economically empower Mexicanos by establishing a cooperative farm and other business enterprises in 1975, white politicians exercised their power by successfully lobbying the federal government to pull the $1.5 million grant to RUP's Zavala County Economic Development Corporation. They were willing to tolerate Mexicanos' political control at the local level but not economic control. Once RUP in Cristal was on the threshold of achieving a semblance of the people's economic empowerment, the white elite mobilized its power and successfully stifled it. They were determined to not allow RUP to set up an economic beach head in south Texas. They saw Cristal as a Trojan horse, a thorn, a Mexicano little Cuba that needed to be stopped before it could propagate many more Cristals throughout the state, especially impoverished south Texas. Ultimately, the peaceful revolution's failure was in part attributable to its inability to overcome the pervasive power and control of the liberal capitalist system.

Thus, with its "militant integrationist" orientation the peaceful revolution was unsuccessful in its efforts to create a more equitable distribution of income and wealth. As a result, internal colonialism was not altered and continued to flourish.

Lesson 3: The Cristal Experiment showed that local governments are limited in their capacity to effectuate major change and raise revenue for the purpose of improving people's quality of life.

Under the current liberal capitalist system, community control is limited in the degree of change that can be realized. This is attributable to the legal and political fact that local governments are creatures of the state. The literature on local and state government reminds us that the formation of local governments is a function of the state legislature.[23] The legal position, or status, of local governments was well defined in 1872 by jurist and legal commentator John F. Dillon. His so-called Dillon's Rule essentially says that it is the state legislature that establishes the laws that determine how local governments are organized as well as the degree of their substantive powers.[24] The U.S. Constitution and the federalist system mandate the supremacy of the state over local governmental entities. The Tenth Amendment stipulates that the powers not "reserved" to the federal government belong to the states or people. The Constitution does not even mention local governments.

This means that the powers of local government are limited. Cities' powers are defined by their charter, which prescribes the basic governmental structure and its basic powers. There are essentially two forms of charters: home rule and general law. A home rule charter allows local governments to develop their own governmental structures and perform services as they see fit without obtaining the permission of the state legislature. General law charters are products of procedures developed by the state legislature to create cities. The general law charter is designed to provide uniform powers, privileges, and structures for every city in the state.

Robert S. Lorch explains that "no state can afford to give cities complete freedom. All cities continue to be instrumentalities of the state and are therefore obliged to do (or refrain from doing) what the state requests in matters wherein the state has paramount interest."[25] Hence, local governments may impose only those taxes that the state permits them to levy. This lawful relegation to a subordinate status profoundly limits local governments' capacity to promote major change.

In particular, local governments lack the fiscal capability to finance massive change. This in part stems from their limited capacity to raise revenue. Local governments may impose only those taxes that the state legislature permits them to levy. In most states local governments raise revenue from four main sources: taxes (mostly property), user charges and special benefit assessments, transfers from other governments, and borrowing. In the early 1970s the property tax was clearly the most important source of revenue for local governments. Despite a cooperative federal system that provided grants-in-aid, local governments provided about 70 percent of their own resources.

David C. Saffell concludes that a local government's capacity to raise revenue is determined "by the level of wealth and personal income within their boundaries. Unless they increase tax rates to unbearable levels, poor . . . communities simply cannot raise sufficient revenue to provide services comparable to those in more affluent areas."[26] Local governments do not possess the revenue-producing capability to address critical issues such as affordable housing and major infrastructure development. Their limitations become more evident in the area of program development for the creation of job training, health care, mental health services, economic development, gang prevention, substance abuse, and cultural programs. Small rural communities like Cristal, which have a limited revenue-producing capability, are lucky if they can provide minimal basic services.

Although this lesson comes from both phases of the experiment, it is much more the offspring of the second. Both proved unsuccessful in using their control of local governmental entities to dramatically improve the people's quality of life. They were overwhelmed by their inability to efficaciously address the plethora of problems plaguing the city. While political control rested with them, each one—the school board, city council, and county—found themselves circumscribed in their power to raise revenues and to address major concerns and issues, such as job training, health, mental health, housing, legal aid, or other badly needed services and programs. They quickly became cognizant that small rural communities generally stick to providing basic services. What rural voters want from their local governments are road maintenance, sewers, garbage disposal, education, public health, ambulance service, law enforcement, fire protection, libraries, agricultural extension services, and whatever administrative services, assessments, and tax collection are necessary.

Moreover, the first and second revolts' efforts to secure funding from federal and state sources at times were met with some resistance. This was a much more serious problem for RUP's peaceful revolution than it was for the first revolt. RUP was extremely successful in securing federal funding while the Republicans were in control of the White House. Gutiérrez established RUP's political threat to the Democrats in Texas. As a result, federal funding was secured from both the Nixon and Ford administrations for RUP's many social, educational, and economic development projects.

In the case of the state, however, politicians and agency bureaucrats, who were mostly Democrats, made it difficult for RUP to secure state funding or support from the state for federal funding. Numerous prominent anti-RUP politicians, such as Briscoe, exercised their power to personally thwart funding of RUP projects. Federal funding, followed by foundation money, became the peaceful revolution's primary funding sources. As long as there was a Republican administration in Washington, the financial spigot was turned on because Republicans felt it was good politics to position RUP to take votes away from the Democrats. Their other intent was to weaken Mexicanos' loyalty to the Democrats. However, once Democrat Jimmy Carter was elected president, Texas Democrats managed to get the federal spigot turned off.

What the Cristal experiment proved was that political control alone is not sufficient to bring about major social change. Furthermore, community control of local governments within the context of the nation's federal system is more symbolic than substantive. This applies to even local governments that have a rich tax base and have access to state and federal funding. Local government's subordination to state government limits the scope and nature of the change intended. In both revolts Mexicano local officials were impeded by this reality.

Thus, without a "macro" transformation of the liberal capitalist federalist system, local governments will continue to be relatively weak entities subordinated to the state's power. This limits the change capability of community control.

Lesson 4: The omnipotence of the liberal capitalist system and its two-party dictatorship makes it difficult if not almost impossible for a third-party movement to become a viable electoral contender for major social change and community control.

Ideologically, the nation's two-party system is zealously committed to liberal capitalism. The Republican and Democratic Parties are ideologically compatible. Chicano Movement leader Rodolfo "Corky" Gonzales appropriately described the nation's two-party system as one animal with two heads that eats from a single trough. While some subtle differences exist, generally their policies and programs are all oriented toward maintaining capitalism and its dictum of life, liberty, and the pursuit of property—wealth.

In essence, the nation's two-party system functions as a two-party monopoly. It can be appropriately described as a quasi-dictatorship that allows for symbolic and nonthreatening opposition from third parties. As political scientist Clinton Rossiter writes:

One of the most momentous facts about the pattern of American politics is that we live under a persistent, obdurate, one might say almost tyrannical, two party system. We have the Republicans and Democrats, and we have almost no one else. The extent of this tyranny of the two parties is almost dramatically revealed in the sorry conditions of third parties in the U.S. today.[27]

Both rely on a multiplicity of legal, political, and political cultural mechanisms to perpetuate its control. The fact is that the two-party system embodies an arrangement that has seldom been seriously challenged.

Historically, third parties have been effective voices of the elector-ate's discontent. They have contributed significantly to bringing about policy reforms to the liberal capitalist system. Women's suffrage, the graduated income tax, and the direct election of senators, to name a few, were all issues first proposed by third parties. The power of third parties has been in their capacity to affect the content and range of political discourse, and ultimately public policy, by raising issues and options that the two major parties have ignored.[28]

This lesson does not of course come to us from the first revolt be-cause it did not use a third party as its organizational weapon for community control. Rather, it relied on two interest groups: the Team-sters and PASSO. As interest groups, they sought not to control what political scientist David Easton describes as the "authoritative alloca-tion of values." Instead, they sought to influence public policy. As inter-est groups, they never developed the grassroots political machinery nor did they foster the people's massive civic participation.

The lesson, however, does come from the second revolt because it was an intrinsic part of a third-party movement. Third-party move-ments tend to be transitory and protest- and change-oriented phenom-ena.[29] This was true of RUP in Texas and throughout Aztlán. As a third-party movement RUP never really presented a serious threat to Demo-cratic Party control in Texas. Even though it had a large Mexicano con-stituency, particularly in south Texas, RUP failed to produce many more Cristals. This was attributable, in great part, to the Democratic Party's leadership and the powerful gringos who mobilized against RUP. From the outset of the second revolt in 1970 to Gutiérrez's depar-ture in early 1981, RUP was under attack, more from Democrats than Republicans. Ramsey Muñiz's gubernatorial elections of 1972 and 1974 were the high points of RUP's statewide efforts, whereas the period between 1970 and 1975 was the peak of RUP's power in Zavala County. Because the Democratic Party believed that RUP could become an elec-toral spoiler, in 1976 the state party encouraged the formation of Mexi-can American Democrats to counter RUP. Moreover, Texas enacted leg-islation that made it difficult for RUP to maintain its legal party status after 1974. During the next four years RUP went into a rapid spiral of decline throughout Texas. The decline of RUP in Texas after 1974 af-fected Cristal's peaceful revolution.

By 1975, when the political rupture occurred, all three RUP factions were voicing concern about RUP's stagnation as a third-party move-ment. When it failed to secure at least 2 percent of all votes cast for governor in the 1978 state elections, it was decertified as a party. This caused irreparable political damage to its peaceful revolution because county elections were partisan. It also signaled the end to CU. Without its partisan purpose CU was weakened and became ineffectual as a political organization. By 1980 some of RUP's partisans in Cristal, including most of the Gutierristas, had become born-again Democrats.

Why did RUP become moribund in Texas? The answer is complex. RUP's demise was a result of several endogenous and exogenous antagonisms. Endogenously, Cristal's political rupture, the arrest and conviction of former RUP gubernatorial candidate Ramsey Muñiz on drug charges, and divisions within its leadership and rank-and-file contributed to its decline. In addition, its statewide organizing efforts suffered from a chronic lack of financial resources, knowledgeable, and experienced full-time staff; lack of support from the majority of Mexicanos in the state; and the fervent commitment of many Mexicanos to the Democrat Party. All these became insurmountable obstacles. Consequently, even though RUP won several electoral victories in other communities, it found it almost impossible to replicate the breadth and scope of the changes enacted in Cristal.

The exogenous antagonism of Texas's Democratic monopoly over the state's laws and institutions, including the courts, further added to RUP's decline. Wary of Muñiz's two gubernatorial campaigns and a series of victories at the local level, the Democratic Party sought to fend off RUP's potential as a spoiler by making it more difficult for RUP and other third parties to be certified. Moreover, the Democratic Party sought to become more accessible to Mexicanos. All of a sudden, it encouraged Mexicanos to become involved as candidates and in the leadership of the party. By 1976 the Democratic Party's white leadership was encouraging former RUP leaders to form the Mexican-American Democrats to counter RUP. The result was an exodus of scores of former RUP leaders and supporters into the Democratic Party.

Without official party status, RUP after 1978 ceased to exist in Texas. This caused irreparable political damage to RUP in Cristal because county elections were partisan. This signaled the end of RUP's CU; without its partisan purpose it became further weakened. By 1980 some of RUP's most faithful supporters in Cristal, including most of the Gutierristas, had become born-again Democrats. As a result, Cristal returned to the old Texas one-party monopoly by Democrats.

A third-party movement may not be the vehicle to use in organizing a community control movement. One reason is that local elections in most states are nonpartisan. Therefore, without a power base at the state legislature, local third parties are powerless and at a disadvantage—they have no way to participate in or exercise control over the allocation of state resources. They are, in essence, at the mercy of Democrats or Republicans or both. It is important to note that RUP's community control was much more a product of CU than RUP because CU was not subject to state politics and control, as RUP was.

Thus, while a third party like RUP can be an effective instrument for change, a grassroots-based interest group is more appropriate for waging a struggle for community control than a political party because of the omnipotence of the two-party system.

Lesson 5: No community control or change-oriented movement can succeed if it is plagued by internal factionalism and power struggles.

The preceding lessons were cardinal exogenous antagonisms that contributed to the failure of both phases of the Cristal experiment. Endogenously, however, so did the prevalence of internal factionalism. It is not enough to put blame on the system or the gringo for the revolts' failure. Responsibility must also rest with Cristal's Mexicano community. In both cases internal schisms developed within the Mexicano community, especially its leadership. The unity of Los Cinco lasted for only a matter of weeks before they were at each others' throats. What ensued for the next two years was an extremely self-destructive mode of politics. Internecine conflict and power struggles permeated Cristal's city administration, especially between Cornejo and City Manager George Ozuna. The divisions fostered a volatile political climate that in 1965 witnessed a successful counterelectoral revolt against the debilitated PASSO by an alliance of whites and middle-class Mexicanos. These Mexicanos, who exercised community control, for the next five years did nothing to alter Cristal's internal colonial status. The greatest losers of the first revolt were the impoverished Mexicanos.

RUP's peaceful revolution also succumbed to internecine infighting and conflict. The difference was that there had been a five-year period of relative political calm, free from serious schisms. During the first five years of governance, RUP met every electoral challenge to its control of the schools and city and, by 1974–1975, the county government as well. Divisions or schisms were kept to manageable levels for a number of reasons: Gutiérrez's role as the indisputable boss; RUP's county infrastructure; CU's massive grassroots political machine; Gutiérrez's strategic manipulation and distribution of patronage; RUP's cultural nationalist perspective that encouraged unity of action; the polarization of politics to the point that every RUP adherent knew that the gringo was the enemy; and the presence of a national Chicano Movement.

By 1974, however, RUP had experienced a growing restiveness among some of its middle-class leaders, especially the new guard, because of unmet expectations. Schisms developed in 1974 and 1975 that by August 1975 precipitated a political rupture characterized by a self-destructive mode of politics reminiscent of the first revolt. Cristal's politics for the next five years was plagued by divisions and power struggles. The results were so devastating that it brought an end to RUP's peaceful revolution. What followed was a game of political musical chairs characterized by self-destructive politics until Gutiérrez's departure from Cristal in early 1981, with factions fighting relentlessly for control of the spoils. Cristal's body politic, from the city council and school board to the county, became contaminated with unbridled greed and power for power's sake. The lofty goals of RUP's peaceful revolution of community control, empowerment, and change were replaced by crass political movidas [maneuvers] for control of the patronage by RUP's recalcitrant competing factions. The factionalism became so acute that the factions adhered to a mind-set and lexicon that categorically rejected compromise and embraced intransigence. The leadership of the various factions failed to see that the many changes they had brought about and benefited from were products of the unity of action that had created the peaceful revolution and sustained it during its first five years. Regardless of ethnicity or race, factionalism and power struggles are an inherent vice of the pursuit and maintenance of power. Nonetheless, in both community control phases to the experiment the old dictum applied: "We have met the enemy and the enemy is us."

Thus, without discipline and unity of action, no struggle that seeks the decolonization of an oppressed community can afford to become engaged in an internal war. If it does, it will self-destruct, as it did in Cristal.

Lesson 6: No community control movement can succeed in meeting its goals if it does not have strong leadership and competent technicians.

Community control was realized in both the first and second revolts because of strong and committed leadership. A corps of competent and committed leaders is manifestly indispensable to any movement or struggle for community control. Leaders must be multifunctional: they are motivators of the people; visionaries who inspire hope and ideas; mechanics of organization; and strategists who plot and carry out the change. Sociologist Eric Hoffer identifies seven characteristics that any leader of a mass movement must have:

audacity and a joy in defiance; an iron will; a fanatical conviction that he has the one and only truth; faith in his destiny and luck; a cunning estimate of human nature; a delight in symbols (spectacles and ceremonials); unbounded brazenness which finds expression in a disregard of consistency and fairness; a recognition that the greatest craving of his followers is for communion and that there can ever be too much of it; a capacity for winning and holding the utmost loyalty of a group of able lieutenants.[30]

The first revolt was led by Juan Cornejo and the other four members of Los Cinco, PASSO state leader Albert Fuentes, and Teamster leader Ray Shafer. However, lacking a formal education, political knowledge, and especially experience, once in power and in control none of Los Cinco demonstrated the leadership qualities described by Hoffer. Yet Cornejo did act with audacity, a joy in defiance, and an iron will, but he demonstrably lacked the other qualities needed to give his struggle a mass movement or community-control orientation. This was evident in his failure to overcome the many internal and external problems that plagued his two years of leadership.

Ironically, although the political leadership fell short, on the technical side City Manager Ozuna was extremely competent. Some changes were the result of his administrative leadership. But he was not the policy maker. He was merely the city manager who carried out policy adopted by the often rambunctious Cornejo-led city council. The acute internal cleavages between Los Cinco and Cornejo and Ozuna became a salient antagonism to the political downfall of Los Cinco. The inability of Cornejo to surround himself with a cadre of able and committed lieutenants who were committed to him also contributed to the failure of the first phase of the Cristal experiment.

This was not the case with the second revolt. RUP's most valuable asset was its leader, José Angel Gutiérrez. If we follow Hoffer's typology of movement leadership, Gutiérrez embodied the roles of man of words, the fanatic, and the practical man of action. As a man of words, he agitated the community into challenging the local order; as the fanatic, he orchestrated the second revolt; and as the practical man of action, for at least for five years he consolidated the administration of the peaceful revolution.

Gutiérrez's leadership was indispensable to RUP's peaceful revolution. He was its architect, pilot, and navigator. This feeling was expressed in interviews by friends and foes. Gutiérrez's supporters described him as charismatic; courageous in his actions; intellectually bright; a superb organizer; adroit in the art of manipulating people, situations, and media; an eloquent and motivational speaker; endowed with boundless energy; and relentless and resolute in his convictions. A few described him as personifying Antonio Gramsci's "organic intellectual."

There were those, however, who believe Gutiérrez possessed some liabilities as a leader. They say he was dictatorial, Machiavellian, egotistical, too opinionated, and intransigent. Others describe him as being politically impulsive—shooting from the hip without seriously considering the ramifications of his controversial comments. They allude to Gutiérrez's trip to Cuba and the controversial comments he made upon his return. Others depict him as arrogant, hungry for power and publicity, and ruthlessly ambitious. They describe him as a man who wanted it all—power, wealth, and fame—and was willing to use whoever and whatever means to achieve his ends. Others refer to Gutiérrez's efforts to implement the CU's secretariat and the "little Cuba" statement as two situations he so miscalculated that they contributed to the discord that led up to the political rupture.

Beyond having strong leadership traits, Gutiérrez's emergence was in part a product of propitious timing. He was at the right place at the right time. Another factor that assisted his emergence as the leader of the peaceful revolution was the emphasis of Mexicano political culture on "personalism" (emphasis on the individual leader). Gutiérrez's charisma, audacity, courage, defiance of the gringo, eloquence in both English and Spanish, organizing prowess, and symbolic use of nationalism (i.e., Chicanismo) played extremely well with an overwhelming majority of Cristal's Mexicano population. The emphasis on Gutiérrez as a persona was what caused his followers to be called Gutierristas by friends and foes alike. All leaders of change movements are either loved or hated. The axiom that one person's liberator is another person's oppressor was true in regard to Gutiérrez.

No struggle for change is the product of only one person. The peaceful revolution was no exception. The changes that were made were products of Gutiérrez the leader and a few trained, competent, and committed lieutenants and technicians, buttressed by a powerful and well-organized base. His lieutenants wrote, lobbied, organized, and carried out the projects and programs of RUP's peaceful revolution. However, throughout the course of the five golden years of the peaceful revolution the recruitment of competent and committed technicians was a major problem. Gutiérrez and RUP officials were compelled to recruit technical and professional personnel from outside Cristal in their efforts to formulate, implement, and administer the numerous projects and programs and administer the city, schools, and later the county.

Thus, intrinsic to any mass movement or struggle for community control is the presence of strong leaders and technicians who are guided not by their own individual interests but by the collective interests of the people they serve.

Lesson 7: A cohesive ideology is a requisite to the building of any social movement that seeks either a reformation or revolutionary transformation of the social order; without one the movement sooner or later will succumb to internal power struggles and its own contradictions.

Every great movement is impelled by some great myth or set of beliefs or ideology. Like leadership, an ideology is indispensable to any movement and struggle for change. It delineates the movement's direction, symbolism, justification, and strategy. Its importance was underscored by Lenin, who argued, "There can be no revolutionary action, without a revolutionary theory."[31] Neither the Cristal experiment nor the parent Chicano Movement was ever predicated ideologically on a well-defined alternative to the existing liberal capitalist system.

This lesson comes from both phases of the Cristal experiment, which were reform oriented. In particular, the first revolt was "a-ideological." At no time was it impelled by the power of ideas or beliefs. The leadership was motivated by the simple notion that the time had come for Mexicanos to take control of their community. They succeeded by manipulating the Mexicanos' discontent and rising expectations. However, never during the course of the campaign did they articulate antagonism or bitterness or make disparaging attacks on the liberal capitalist system. In fact, the opposite was true. Some gringos perceived the first revolt's movement for community control as radical merely because Mexicanos wanted to be included in a local political system that historically had been off-limits to them. Without a set of alternative common beliefs, PASSO's politics of community control remained accommodation oriented. Nothing but raw self-interest held Los Cinco together, and after the election it transformed into ego trips, greed, and flagrant opportunism, which in turn nurtured the fatal politics of self-destruction.

The second revolt was also not a product of a "new" ideology. The adherence of RUP's leadership to Chicanismo, coupled with the usage of a "cooperative capitalism" approach, gave the peaceful revolution an eclectic and quasi-ideological thrust to its empowerment and change efforts. It was much more complex in its approach than the first revolt. At times its clashing ideas and strategies left it unable to develop a well-defined new ideology. In essence, the second revolt was militantly reformist and integrationist in its orientation. It became pragmatic, self-interest oriented, and accommodationist in its approach. An example was of this was in the political arena. Although RUP played by the local and state rules of the political game and operated within the confines of the liberal capitalist system, some of its leadership were hypercritical of the liberal capitalist system and identified more with Chicanismo and a watered-down form of socialism. Perhaps its eclectic approach impeded its success. Its leadership, especially Gutiérrez, had used nonmaterial inducements—La Causa, El Movimiento Chicano—to promote the peaceful revolution's agenda. In the end, individual self-interest prevailed over community self-interest.

Thus, without the presence of an alternative ideology to the liberal capitalist system, movements for community control offer no real alternative for creating change. In addition, without their own ideology, decolonization movements are overwhelmed and consumed by the pervasiveness of this nation's adherence to liberal capitalism as an ideology.

Lesson 8: Regardless of the ideological underpinnings of community control movements, all are subject to Robert Michels's "Iron Law of Oligarchy."

Both the first and second revolts proved the validity of Robert Michels's "Iron Law of Oligarchy." He posits the argument that all large organizations are oligarchies (meaning rule by the few), including radical political parties. In Michels's words, "He who says organization, says oligarchy."[32] Both phases of the Cristal experiment are examples of the omnipresence of elites in the local governments.

In the case of the first revolt, from the incipient organizing phase to the actual takeover, Los Cinco operated supposedly in a "pluralistic" milieu. However, once the new city council members took control, they became competing "power elites." They, especially Mayor Cornejo, sought control of the decision-making process and the benefits that came from their elected status. As elites, initially their power status merely denoted the influence and authority predicated on the elected positions they held. Their two years of governance were marked by destructive power struggles. With time the conflict spread to the city's administrative personnel and the leadership from within PASSO and Teamsters. During this time the community was largely alienated from the decision-making process. Most of Cristal's Mexicanos did not become involved in governance. The council never developed the requisite group cohesion to truly make Los Cinco an elite power structure. Consequently, they became political casualties of other better-organized and -financed white-supported Mexicano elites.

The situation was different during the second revolt. RUP's peaceful revolution produced a demosocratic elite. However, during the politics of community control CU developed into a full-fledged political machine, led by political boss José Angel Gutiérrez. This created an elite community power structure under the aegis of CU; power was much more concentrated and controlled than it was during the first revolt. CU initially had a sense of pluralism, but by the end of the politics of community control in 1975 power was being exercised by fewer and fewer elites.[33] With the political rupture in 1975 RUP's community power structure was shattered into multiple power factions, all competing for power. This rupture in essence fomented a self-destructive form of pluralism.

Thus RUP's peaceful revolution in practice was driven by a small power elite that practiced the dictum that political change is always a product of the few made in the name of the many.

Lesson 9: Although political machines are anomalies in contemporary local politics, RUP's peaceful revolution proved that political machines can be progressive instruments of change, but in the end they succumb to their inherent weaknesses.

Political machines were a phenomena of immigrant politics. Political bosses governed cities via the power of material and nonmaterial incentives. Immigrants hungry for opportunity and mobility became the machine's main constituents. Their vote was a commodity in the marketplace of boss-controlled politics. Yet, as the literature on political machines concludes, they were never entities for massive social change. In fact, they were purveyors of the existing liberal capitalist system.

The first revolt did not produce a political machine. The Teamster-PASSO coalition proved transitory. Neither possessed the leadership (boss) or the organizational infrastructure to control the vote. During the second revolt CU became the machine and José Angel Gutiérrez its boss. For five consecutive years CU proved relatively unbeatable as a political machine in Cristal's local politics. He relied on the use of both material and nonmaterial inducements to maintain his control. His foremost weapon was the use of material inducements in the form of patronage—jobs. To maintain control he also used nonmaterial inducements, such as Chicanismo and fear that the gringo power holders' would regain control. The omnipotence of CU's political machinery enabled it to institute a myriad of progressive changes in the schools, city, and county.

The second revolt revealed that in the end political machines are

not panaceas for effecting social change. By their nature political machines are creations of the liberal capitalist system. Their roles have
been ostensibly to work, adapt, and embrace the system's ideology and
structures, not to change them. This limited change capability became
apparent with CU. So long as Gutiérrez and CU were able to satisfy
the rising expectations or mobility and power wants of the machine's
beneficiaries, RUP's peaceful revolution was stable. It was relatively
free from schisms and power struggles. However, once the machine
could no longer satisfy its constituents' appetites, CU became plagued
with internecine divisions and conflict.

Thus, as long as a political machine has access to material inducements, it can be an agent for limited change. However, when the political machine has nothing more to offer than nonmaterial inducements,
it is less likely to survive.

*Lesson 10: Having Mexicano elected officials and administrators, especially
in a community control situation, does not necessarily translate to changes
in public policy.*

The election of Mexicanos to public office in most cases does not necessarily translate to an improvement in the people's quality of life, even
in a community control situation. This applies to all levels of government. For too many years Chicano politics has been driven by the idea
that the community needs to elect its own in order to expedite and
foster change. Yet in most cases the election of Mexicanos to public
office has failed to produce major policy change. Mexicanos replace
whites or others and the changes tend to be more symbolic than substantive. This stems from the omnipotent nature of the liberal capitalist
system—in particular in a internal colonial situation—to effectively
socialize, co-opt, and neutralize those that it perceives to be threats to
its stability.

Those few who do commit themselves to work for the advancement
of a Mexicano political agenda usually are not guided by any creative
new policies or ideas for reform. Some are elected and have no idea
of the workings of government or what needs to be done. Those who
do have some sort of agenda for change face the stark reality of often
not having the votes necessary to secure approval. Moreover, if their
agenda is perceived as being too radical, they become subject to attack,
ostracism, and isolation by their peers and especially the media. As a
result, those who serve in state legislatures or Congress can face loss
of support on other measures, important committee assignments, campaign contributions, and adequate office space and staff. Conformity

to the existing system is a requisite for a politician's reelection, mobility, and survival.

Thus most Mexicano politicians are ideological clones of the system. Their political beliefs, values, and general behavior are seldom different from those of most white politicians. Most are financially supported by the same competing special interests that lubricate the system's machinery via their political action committees. Under the guise of compromise, they become immersed with the mentality of cutting deals, of "you scratch my back, and I'll scratch yours." Many never become ardent advocates for the Mexicano community because, they say, they represent "all" the community. Unfortunately, this attitude prevails even in communities or districts where Mexicanos are the overwhelming majority of the population. These politicians seldom, if ever, become leaders or even direct participants of change-oriented social movements. Instead, they become disciples of the social order. Their paramount concern is getting reelected, maneuvering for higher office, or vying for an appointment.

Much of the same applies to bureaucrats, who are seldom change agents on their own. They tend to be conservative and are essentially the administrative mechanics for implementing public policy. Their organizational framework tends to be that of the prevailing superstructure. They go with the status quo.

Both phases of the Cristal experiment embody this lesson. The community control politics of the first revolt focused almost exclusively on the political aspects. Political control, not change, became the paramount focus of Los Cinco. Without a plan that spelled out a program of change and action, politics became a game of who or what faction was going to be in control of the city's spoils. Although Los Cinco made some changes that benefited the community, from a policy perspective they did nothing dramatically to alter Mexicanos' quality of life politically, economically, and socially. The few changes that were made were much more the result of the technical and administrative leadership of the city manager. With the exception of a brief increase in Mexicano civic participation, and their euphoria in winning control, Los Cinco as well as the administrators accomplished little in the struggle to extricate the Mexicano community from its wretched impoverishment.

On the other hand, during the five years of RUP's politics of community control its politicians and technicians played a significant role in ameliorating the community's quality of life. RUP politicians enacted many policy changes in the city council, school board, and county government that changed and improved people's living conditions to some extent. They provided better access to the decision-making process; better jobs and educational, social, and economic opportunities; and, equally important, a sense of hope and cultural pride. This was the result of the close collaboration between RUP's politicians and its technicians. Unlike the first revolt, organized power and Mexicano technical know-how activated RUP's peaceful revolution. All this ended, however, with the political rupture.

From late 1975 to 1980 the politics of self-destruction were so acute that the peaceful revolution became a casualty of infighting and power struggles. What transpired was similar to what occurred with the first revolt. Most politicians and technicians became embroiled in the self-interest aspect of politics. The idealism of the peaceful revolution for effectuating change was replaced with the pragmatism of winning and hanging on to the spoils of power. Although Mexicanos were still theoretically in control, both politicians and technicians—clearly without a mission greater than their own self-interest—returned to a politics of perpetuating the liberal capitalist status quo.

The premise that Mexicano political and administrative representation in local government translates to positive, tangible, and major change for Mexicanos in general was proved erroneous. They became what Franz Fanon and Albert Memmi describe as buffers and ideological zealots of the system.[34] For Mexicanos in south Texas this meant a continuation of internal colonialism. This became apparent by the 1980s when scores of Mexicanos were elected to local governments in south Texas. Significantly influenced by the second revolt, this trend merely reflected a strategic change in the modus operandi of the gringo power holders. Because they were a minority, they pragmatically became inclined to support those Mexicanos who were conservative or moderate in their politics and did not present a threat to their economic interests.

Thus, without Mexicanos and other Latinos developing an alternative ideology to the liberal capitalist system, Mexicano elected and appointed officials will dramatically increase in numbers but will have little effect on policy because they tend to be practitioners of the status quo. As a result, they will continue to perpetuate the very system that oppresses many of the people they represent.

Lesson 11: No movement for community control, empowerment, and change can expect to effectively function and survive if it is not fueled by the power of its own financial resources.

No struggle's machinery can expect to function and succeed if it is not lubricated by its own financial resources. Jesse Unruh, former speaker of the California Assembly, put it succinctly: "Money is the mother's milk of politics." My axiom—"Money is the lubricant for social change; no struggle can survive without it"—was true of Cristal. Carrying out the simplest tasks—printing flyers, sending mailers, using a telephone, putting gas in the car to go to meetings—requires money. This applies to both all-volunteer and organizations with full-time staffs. The latter require a budget for office space, hiring staff, telephone and fax service, purchasing office equipment, travel expenses, and resources for project development. This has been the Achilles heel of most social change–oriented organizations. Because few foundations fund efforts to bring about social justice, most such efforts depend on membership dues and constant fund-raising for their survival. Therefore, without some level of self-sufficiency, a mass movement or struggle for change will fail and become transient.

Both phases of the Cristal experiment illustrate this lesson. The organizing success of the first revolt was in part attributable to the external organizational and financial support that Cornejo was able to secure from both the Teamsters and PASSO. However, once both forces withdrew their political and financial support, Cornejo was unable to maintain his elected office and source of employment. For most of the two years that he served as mayor, he was unemployed. Cornejo's financial difficulties, as well as those of the rest of Los Cinco, made them extremely vulnerable to the white elite's tactics of economic intimidation. For Los Cinco, community control failed to produce financial and therefore political self-sufficiency.

Unlike PASSO, for at least the first five years RUP in Cristal succeeded in developing a semblance of financial solvency. From the beginning Gutiérrez and other RUP leaders were aware of the need to become financially self-sufficient. CU generated resources through a variety of fund-raisers, such as dances, dinners, and membership dues, and by 1975 a form of quasi-income-taxation of its members. However, because the great majority of RUP's supporters were poor, the amount of money raised was never enough to finance its political agenda or its economic development projects.

The fact that RUP controlled hundreds of jobs helped CU in its resource development. By manipulating federal and private foundation grants and control of the city, school, and county structures, RUP's peaceful revolution was able to develop a semblance of financial solvency but never self-sufficiency. I use the word *semblance* because financial self-sufficiency was largely dependent on external resources, primarily federal funds. With the political rupture and Governor Briscoe's crusade against RUP, the peaceful revolution lost much of its federal funding. Like so many other entities that grew out of the Chicano Movement, RUP in Cristal declined in part because of its inability to become financially self-sufficient.

Thus a movement's dependence on financial resources other than its own will in most cases lead to collapse. Without the financial solvency that ultimately brings self-sufficiency, no change struggle can expect to succeed or be able persevere against the system's powerful counterattacks.

Lesson 12: Mexicano change struggles in the United States should not depend on Mexico or any other nation to provide support for their agenda.

Some theorists and movement strategists propound that a struggle for change can be strengthened by developing a collaborative relationship with foreign nations that are supportive of its efforts. The rationale for such a relationship is the political, financial, or military support available from a foreign nation. The United States, the former Soviet Union, People's Republic of China, Cuba, Libya, Iran, and Israel, to name a few, have in contemporary history responded to calls from revolutionaries that complemented their so-called national interests. Conversely, reform-oriented movements in the United States have in most cases shied away from soliciting assistance from foreign nations. This is essentially because they are functioning within the system's existing structures and laws and want to merely reform the system and not radically transform it. But this nation's government and politics frown on domestic groups or leaders that seek support from foreign governments, especially if they are antithetical ideologically to U.S. interests.

This lesson comes more from the second revolt than from the first. Although the Mexican government took great interest in the politics of the first revolt, it never developed a formal relationship with either Los Cinco or PASSO. Los Cinco's politics were not driven by a desire to embrace Mexico. Conversely, RUP in Cristal, under the leadership of José Angel Gutiérrez, sought to foster a cooperative relationship between the Chicano Movement and the Mexican government. During the peaceful revolution RUP leaders met with Mexico's Presidents Luis Echeverría Alvarez and José Lopez Pórtillo as well as other Mexican government officials several times, in both the United States and in Mexico.

This strategy, devised by Gutiérrez, was more flamboyant than substantive. This was best illustrated by the rhetorical platitudes of solidarity of both the Echeverría Alvarez and Lopez Pórtillo administrations. Neither provided significant capital or assistance to promote and support the political, economic, educational, and social aspects of

RUP's peaceful revolution. Aside from some scholarships for Chicano students, a bust of Benito Juárez, books for the Cristal's library, a few cultural exchange events, and several meetings, RUP gained nothing but criticism for its overtures to Mexico from whites and even some Chicano activists who attacked Gutiérrez for allegedly collaborating with an oppressive regime.

The RUP delegation's trip to Cuba in 1975 also produced nothing tangible. Instead, it infuriated white power holders in Texas and subsequently those in Washington, D.C. They were so angry that they effectively went after the federal funding that was fueling Gutiérrez's power and RUP's peaceful revolution. Gutiérrez's statements praising Cuba, especially his comment that many more "little Cubas" were going to be created in south Texas, enraged the power holders, to the detriment of RUP's economic development efforts.

Although RUP's overtures to Mexico and Cuba received a great deal of notoriety and media attention, they realized no major political or economic return. Neither venture did anything to promote the overall RUP agenda. For a variety of reasons, especially the fear of offending the U.S. government by appearing to be engaged in meddling in the internal affairs of the United States, the Mexican government was extremely circumspect.

Thus, based on past experiences, Mexicanos in the United States should not expect to get substantive support from Mexico or any other country if their struggle is oriented toward confronting and changing the nation's liberal capitalist system.

What Was Learned?

What the Cristal experiment teaches is that community control is unattainable under the present liberal capitalist system, especially if it is oriented toward bringing about major social change. However, the second revolt suggests that a limited form of community control is attainable—one in which the people do not directly control the public policy process but instead influence it through their participation and their access to local elected officials. Moreover, the experiment made it evident that the locus of power for effectuating major social change is not at the local or state level but at the state and federal levels of government.

Both revolts highlighted the exploitative nature of capitalism. With its emphasis on private ownership of the means of production and distribution, the liberal capitalist system impedes any struggle for change, including community control. The maldistribution of wealth gives the rich an inordinate amount of power over all levels of government. Its Darwinist mind-set of "survival of the fittest" and emphasis on individualism fosters an unbridled and insatiable appetite for materialism and wealth. The result is a stratification of society into conflicting classes that require poverty for their survival. With most of the nation's wealth and power in the hands of the few, change struggles have yet to find a way to circumvent this frustrating reality. The middle class and poor have not been zealous supporters of community control. I say this because both classes are products of a socialization process that has conditioned them to accept as virtues the exploitative vices of capitalism.

I contend that the real problem behind the electoral crisis in this country is not liberalism per se but capitalism. Unless the capitalist system is reformed to provide for a more equitable distribution of goods, services, and power, representative democracy and community control will be unattainable and will remain illusionary and increasingly plutocratic. Thus the Cristal experiment remains the unfinished experiment in community control.

The Browning of America: Its Implications

The United States today is undergoing a demographic browning of its population. This will produce many more Cristals. Consequently, Mexicanos and other Latinos face a political dilemma. The empirical findings of the Cristal experiment lead to the clear conclusion that even if an ethnic group constitutes a majority and achieves community control of a city council, school board, or county, mere election to office does not resolve the many problems they face.

Many studies have concluded that if present demographic trends continue, whites will soon be a minority of the national population, particularly in the southwest. In California, for example, the state Department of Finance projected in 1994 that by the year 2010 the Latino student population (kindergarten through grade twelve) will comprise about 50 percent of the state's student population, whereas the white student population will decrease to 28 percent.[35] The Latino population growth is so rapid that by the 2020s Latinos could well be the state's new majority.

Radio personality Xavier Hermosillo commented in 1993, "We are not newcomers to this land. This land was originally ours. Wake up America and smell the refried beans. We are taking back Los Angeles house by house, block by block, and nobody is going to stop us."[36] The same demographic trend holds in New Mexico, Texas, Nevada, and

Florida, of course, as well as in New York, Illinois, New Jersey, Michigan, Colorado, Washington, Utah, and Kansas. This trend could accelerate interest in community control. This dramatic change in population will make it possible to create a transfer of power and control from the old predominately white majority to the new Latino majority, especially at the local level.

In the 1990s this demographic transformation has already contributed to a resurgence of nativism against Mexicanos and Latinos and a revival of neoconservatism. As a result, a reemergence of a political climate that is vehemently anti-Mexicano/Latino has occurred. The rampant immigrant bashing has been directed primarily at the Mexicano and Central American immigrant communities. Republican and Democratic politicians alike participate, pandering to the fears of the public and making Mexicanos and Latinos the scapegoat for many of California's and the nation's socioeconomic problems. This was evident with the passage in 1994 of Proposition 187 (the xenophobic initiative that would deny the children of undocumented parents an education and social welfare and health care benefits to undocumented workers). In 1996 voters approved Proposition 209, which ends the consideration of race and gender in school admissions and employment. And in 1997 some Californians are working to put on the 1998 ballot an initiative that would terminate bilingual education programs.

Among the essentially white groups active in propounding the nativist propaganda is Voices of Citizens Together, whose Web page tells visitors: "The evidence is clear, the United States is being invaded by Mexico. The intent is to retake the American Southwest and rename it Aztlán. Those who resist are called racist and will and are subject to attack. This is a clear act of aggression and those who aid in this endeavor are guilty of sedition."[37]

The nativist paranoia has been particularly evident along the U.S.–Mexico border. The Clinton administration has moved aggressively to militarize it, using regular military and National Guard troops to support "Operation Gatekeeper" in California and "Operation Rio Grande" in Texas; Congress chimed in, approving the use of ten thousand additional federal troops along the border.

At the same time, poverty among Latinos increased to 31 percent in 1994. Forty percent of the nation's poor children were Latino. In 1995 the median income rose for every ethnic or racial group, except the nation's Latinos, whose median income dropped 5.1 percent. Overall, the household income for Latinos has dropped 14 percent since 1989, from about $26,000 to less than $22,900, while rising slightly for blacks.[38]

As Mexicanos and Latinos enter the twenty-first century, their experience of internal colonialism continues to expand, not contract. Plagued by a multiplicity of social problems, such as high drop-out rates, unemployment, drug and alcohol abuse, lack of health care, malnutrition, lack of affordable housing, sexual abuse, crime, and gang violence, the barrios of some communities resemble impoverished war zones. It is, as Arturo Vargas, head of the National Association of Latino Elected Officials, said, "the American nightmare, not the American Dream."[39]

Unfortunately, as the situation deteriorates, no political movement is forming to ride to the rescue. Latinos have no recognized regional or national leaders. Although they have many organizations, most are not advocacy oriented, and those that are lack the numbers of people and dollars to reflect power. Although some protest activity appears from time to time, it tends to be sporadic and transient. Union activity has increased, but student activism has declined. Unlike the black and Jewish communities, Latinos have no "fear factor." I have described this lack of political clout as the "Rodney Dangerfield syndrome"—we get no respect from those in power.[40]

Yet even as the Latino community's quality of life has declined, its political representation, voter registration, civic participation, and citizenship have increased. The number of Latino elected officials is increasing every year. Driven by fears of what Proposition 187 will mean in California, Latino immigrants have become citizens and registered to vote in large numbers. Numerous articles point out that the Latino giant has awakened politically and that it is ready to take charge of its future. Only time and history will tell if it can realize its political potential in the twenty-first century.

One thing is certain: the browning of America will lead to Latino political takeovers of local governments. In many communities throughout Aztlán and beyond, Latinos already constitute majorities on city councils and school boards and in county government and special districts. This trend will become stronger in the twenty-first century. Latino control could very well include state legislatures and governorships, especially in Aztlán. At the local level "browns" are increasingly displacing whites, but the Latinos have few if any answers as to how to extricate impoverished barrios from internal colonialism. Thus an inherent problem to the growing numbers of Latino office holders is the absence of viable leadership, an organization, or a plan that directs change and empowerment to build a viable social movement.

The Building of a New Movement

If community control is to have a decolonization thrust, a new movement must emerge that will pick up where the Chicano Movement and the Cristal experiment left off.

The complexion of the nation is changing rapidly, and Latinos are a major force driving that change. The Cristal experiment was a product of the epoch of protest, which spawned a number of changes and empowerment movements such as the Chicano Movement. Gutiérrez, MAYO, the Winter Garden Project, RUP, and the peaceful revolution were all a result of the Chicano Movement.

In the 1990s no new movement appears to be in the making. If this vacuum continues, the Cristals of today and tomorrow are likely to be oriented to the status quo, lacking the leadership, organization, strategic and tactical plans, and the community's direct and massive participation. If we as a people are to prosper and progress collectively and put an end to our colonization in the twenty-first century, we must struggle to rekindle the spirit of the old Chicano Movement and create a new movement. To do this we must begin with what I call the three Rs: recommit ourselves to building a new movement; reorganize our communities; and remobilize to make major change and continue the struggle for our decolonization.[41]

The probability is great that a new movement will emerge. If a new movement that is oriented toward social change is to succeed, it must have the following six factors, or ingredients, which are intrinsic to its formation:

- a political climate permeated by chronic frustration and discontent caused by rising but thwarted expectations
- competent, knowledgeable, and committed leaders and a cadre of technicians
- a sophisticated grassroots organizational network to provide a powerful base
- formulation of an ideological vision for Latinos that seeks their decolonization and a reformation of the liberal capitalist system
- development of a strategic and tactical plan that complements the new vision and incorporates both the ballot box and direct action politics
- a power capability built on all the aforementioned factors and grounded in financial self-sufficiency

En conclusión, el futuro es nuestro, si nos preparamos y organisamos. Si no, estaremos relegados al abismo del síndrome de sur Africa—In conclusion, the future is ours if we prepare and organize. If not, we will be relegated to the abyss of a South African syndrome.

Notes

Index

Notes

Preface

1. Throughout the book I use the term *Mexicano* to identify those of Mexican ancestry who are born or reside in the United States. I feel that for the purposes of this book Mexicano is more appropriate than *Chicano, Mexican-American*, or any other term. The reasons are essentially two. In the course of my research I concluded that most Raza Unida Party supporters identified more as Mexicano than Chicano, whereas the leadership of both the Mexican American Youth Organization and the Raza Unida Party in Texas used both terms interchangeably to identify themselves. Also, I feel that in order to foster a greater sense of identity and community in the 1990s and the twenty-first century, using the term Mexicano is preferable, especially in the context of understanding the effect of the continuing exodus from Mexico. However, in some instances I do use Mexicano and Chicano interchangeably, because I and others see the terms as synonymous. Moreover, I will use the term *Latino* to generically describe all people with origins in Latin America and Spain.

2. *Gringo* is a term commonly used by Mexicanos and other Latinos to pejoratively describe whites who are racist, especially in regard to Mexicanos. Conversely, an *Anglo* is a white who tends to be supportive of Mexicanos. The distinction is clear and important for many Mexicanos. Similarly, *Merriam Webster's Collegiate Dictionary*, 10th ed., provides the following definition: "a foreigner in Spain or Latin America esp. when of English or American origin; *broadly:* a non-Hispanic person—often used disparagingly." The term's etymology is even more interesting: a Spanish alteration of the Greek *griego*, or stranger. Its earliest recorded date in English is 1849.

In addition, I use the term *white* to describe both gringos and Anglos without making distinctions about their politics.

"Gringo power holders" refers to those whites who are members of a community's elite power structure, which is comprised of elected officials, former elected officials, farmers, ranchers, businesspersons, and affluent society types. In the context of Cristal and south Texas, the phrase refers to those who are a minority yet wield an exorbitant amount of control and power in local politics.

3. See Armando Navarro, *Mexican American Youth Organization: Avant-Garde of the Chicano Movement in Texas* (Austin: University of Texas Press, 1995) for an examination of the exogenous and endogenous antagonisms instrumen-

tal in forging the Chicano Movement. *Exogenous* refers to the external and *endogenous* to the internal historical events, passage of laws, issues and problems, emergence of leaders and organizations, and so on that nurture a climate for change.

4. *Chicanismo* refers to a quasi-ideology predicated on cultural nationalism. It incorporates the word *Chicano*, which describes those Mexicanos who were born in the United States. The term came into vogue during the era of the Chicano Movement (1962–1974), popularized by activists who categorically repudiated their hyphenated status as Mexican-American and zealously embraced their "Mexicano-ness," meaning their Mexican heritage, culture, and language. It connoted a rediscovery of the "we," of a revitalized pride, or *orgullo*, in being Mexicano. For some activists it translated to either the formation of a separate Chicano nation called *Aztlán* or to a nation within a nation.

5. *Aztlán* refers to the southwestern part of the United States, the mythical homeland of the Aztecs. It refers also to the lands lost by Mexico to the United States during the U.S. War on Mexico (1846–1848). These lands included California, Nevada, Utah, Colorado, Arizona, New Mexico, Texas, and parts of others states contiguous to these.

6. The term *liberal capitalism* refers to the blending of traditional liberalism as a political belief system—the foundation of this nation's so-called democratic institutions—with capitalism as an economic system. In classical terms *liberalism* defined the relationship of the individual to society and government. It meant serving the needs of the individual and freeing the individual from restraints—most of which were assumed to have come from government. Traditional liberalism rests solidly on the following values: the right to individualism, right to private property, adherence to contracts and laws, guarantee of freedom, opportunity for equality, and—last and more important—democracy.

In contemporary usage some see liberalism as connoting government intervention in the nation's economy for purposes of promoting change for the disadvantaged. For others the term carries the negative connotation of big government that intrudes in people's everyday lives. Today most Democrats, and especially Republicans, adhere more to the more traditional form of liberalism and to a laissez-faire capitalist economic system.

Capitalism refers to an economic system within which the ownership of the means of production (land, factories, machinery, natural resources) is held by individuals and not the state. In its classical form capitalism embodies such beliefs as the sanctity of private property, the dynamics of the profit motive, the existence of a free market, and the presence of competition in the economic marketplace.

Introduction: Community Control as a Conceptual Framework

1. Integral to this book is the proposition that internal colonialism is a viable theoretical framework applicable to understanding the political, eco-

nomic, social, and cultural dimensions of the Cristal experiment. Specifically, I argue that the Cristal experiment in community control failed in great part because Mexicano communities in south Texas are victims of internal colonialism, which is a manifestation of liberal capitalism. Internal colonialism explains the immensity of the poverty, social problems, and racism against Mexicanos. For an in-depth examination of internal colonialism as it applies to Mexicanos in the United States, see Robert Blauner, *Racial Oppression in America* (New York: Harper & Row, 1972); Mario Barrera, Carlos Muñoz, and Carlos Ornelas, "The Barrio as an Internal Colony," *Urban Affairs Annual Reviews* 6 (1972): 465–98; Rodolfo Acuña, *Occupied America: The Chicano Struggle for Liberation* (New York: Canfield Press, 1972); Tomas Almaguer, "Toward the Study of Chicano Colonialism," *Aztlán: Chicano Journal of the Social Sciences and the Arts* (spring 1971): 7–21; Joan W. Moore, "Colonialism: The Case of the Mexican Americans," *Social Problems* (spring 1970): 463–72; and Alfredo Mirande, *The Chicano Experience: An Alternative Perspective* (Notre Dame, Ind.: University of Notre Dame Press, 1985).

2. John P. Diggins, *The American Left in the Twentieth Century* (New York: Harcourt Brace Jovanovich, 1973), 171.

3. The following are but a few examples of the many studies of the New Left that examine its embrace of participatory democracy: Terry H. Anderson, *The Movement and the Sixties: Protest in America from Greensboro to Wounded Knee* (New York: Oxford University Press, 1995); Stewart Burns, *Social Movements of the 1960s: Searching for Democracy* (Boston: Twayne, 1990); Daniel C. Kramer, *Participatory Democracy: Developing Ideals of the Political Left* (Cambridge, Mass.: Schenkman Publishing, 1972): Lyman Tower Sargent, *New Left Thought: An Introduction* (Homewood, Ill.: Dorsey Press, 1972).

4. Peter Collins and David Horowitz, *Deconstructing the New Left: From Vietnam to the Persian Gulf* (Lanham, Md.: Second Thoughts Books, 1991), 37.

5. For examinations of the New Left and the civil rights movement see Anderson, *The Movement and the Sixties,* and Robert Weisbrot, *Freedom Bound: A History of America's Civil Rights Movement* (New York: Plume, 1991), 253–56.

6. For an in-depth study of SDS see Kirkpatrick Sale, *SDS* (New York: Vintage, 1974)

7. Edward J. Bacciocco, *The New Left in America: Reform to Revolution* (Palo Alto, Calif.: Hoover Institution Press, 1974), 118–20; Paul Jacobs and Saul Landau, *The New Radicals: A Report with Documents* (New York: Vintage, 1966), 155.

8. James Miller, *Democracy Is in the Streets: From Port Huron to Chicago* (New York: Simon & Schuster, 1987), 143–44.

9. David Easton, *The Political System* (New York: Knopf, 1953), chap. 5.

10. Gabriel Almond and Sidney Verba, *The Civic Culture: Democracy in Five Nations* (Princeton, N.J.: Princeton University Press, 1963), 4.

11. National Advisory Commission on Civil Disorders (Kerner Commission), *National Advisory Commission on Civil Disorders Report* (New York: Bantam, 1968), 286. See also Mario Fantini, Marilyn Gittell, Richard Magut, *Community Control and the Urban School* (New York: Praeger, 1970), 10.

12. Martin Luther King Jr., *Where Do We Go from Here: Chosen Community*

(New York: Harper & Row, 1967), 112; Saul Alinsky, *Reveille to Radicals* (New York: Vintage, 1969) and *Rules for Radicals* (New York: Vintage, 1971).

13. Clarence N. Stone, Robert K. Whelan, and William J. Murin, *Urban Policy and Politics in a Bureaucratic Age* (Englewood Cliffs, N.J.: Prentice-Hall, 1986), 157. For an examination of Black Power ideologies see John T. McCarthy, *Black Power Ideologies: An Essay on African-American Thought* (Philadelphia: Temple University Press, 1992).

14. For good explanations of how CAP worked see Vincent Ostrom, Robert Bish, and Elinor Ostrom, *Local Government in the United States* (San Francisco: ICS Press, 1968), 54; and John J. Harrigan, *Political Change in the Metropolis* (Boston: Little, Brown, 1976), 154.

15. Bryan T. Downes, *Politics, Change, and the Urban Crisis* (North Scituate, Mass.: Duxbury Press, 1976), 210.

16. Harrigan, *Political Change*, 154–55.

17. Fantini, Gittell, and Magut, *Community Control*, 10–11.

18. For a succinct analysis of the origins of democracy see Douglas B. Klusmeyer, *Between Consent and Descent: Conceptions of Democratic Citizenship* (Washington, D.C.: Carnegie Endowment for Peace, 1996), 9–15.

19. Mostafa Rejai, ed., *Democracy: The Contemporary Theories* (New York: Atherton, 1967), 1–20.

20. Alan R. Gitelson, Robert Dudley, and Melvin J. Dubnick, *American Government* (Boston: Houghton Mifflin, 1991), 6.

21. David C. Minor and Scott Greer, eds., *The Concept of Community* (Chicago: Aldine, 1969), ix.

22. Harold W. PFautz, "The Black Community, the Community School, and the Socialization Process: Some Caveats," in *Community Control of Schools*, ed. Henry M. Leven (Washington, D.C.: Brookings Institution, 1970), 16–17.

23. Ibid.

24. V. O. Key, *Politics, Parties, and Pressure Groups* (New York: Knopf, 1960), 28; George E. G. Catlin, *A Study of the Principles of Politics* (New York: Macmillan, 1930), 68–69; Robert Lineberry and Ira Sharkansky, *Urban Politics and Public Policy* (New York: Harper & Row, 1974), 139.

25. Harrigan, *Political Change*, 156.

26. Alan Altshuler, *Community Control* (Indianapolis: Pegasus, 1970), 14–15; Milton Kotler, *Neighborhood Government* (Indianapolis: Bobbs-Merrill, 1969).

27. Joseph F. Zimmerman, *The Federated City: Community Control in Large Cities* (New York: Vintage, 1972), 81–82.

28. Kotler, *Neighborhood Government*, xii.

29. Advisory Commission on Intergovernmental Relations, *Fiscal Balance in the American Federal System*, vol. 2 (Washington, D.C.: Metropolitan Fiscal Disparities, 1967), 16.

30. National Advisory Commission on Civil Disorders (Kerner Commission), *Report*, 288–91.

31. National Commission on Urban Problems, *Building the American City* (Washington, D.C.: U.S. Government Printing Office, 1968), 349–50.

32. Harold H. Weissman, *Community Councils and Community Control* (Pittsburgh, Pa.: University of Pittsburgh Press, 1970), 168.

Chapter 1. The Electoral Revolt of 1963

1. John Staples Shockley, *Chicano Revolt in a Texas Town* (Notre Dame: University of Notre Dame Press, 1974), 15.

2. Zavala County Historical Commission, *Now and Then in Zavala County: A History of Zavala County, Texas* (Cristal, Texas: Shelton Press, 1986), 1–2.

3. Ibid., 1–2, 60.

4. Ibid., 61.

5. Shockley, *Chicano Revolt*, 2–7.

6. Carlos Velez-Ibanez, *Border Visions: Mexican Cultures of the Southwest United States* (Tucson: University of Arizona Press, 1996), 109.

7. Shockley, *Chicano Revolt*, 252.

8. Paul Schuster Taylor, *An American-Mexican Frontier, Nueces County, Texas* (Chapel Hill: University of North Carolina Press, 1934), 255.

9. R. Reynolds McKay, "Texas Mexican Repatriation During the Great Depression," doctoral dissertation, University of Oklahoma at Norman, 1982, 101–107, 270, 566–71; William McKinley Pridgen, "A Survey and Proposed Plan of Reorganization of the Public Schools in Zavala County," masters thesis, University of Texas, Austin, 1939, 7.

10. Shockley, *Chicano Revolt*, 11.

11. Interview, José Angel Gutiérrez, December 20, 1994.

12. Zavala County Historical Commission, *Now and Then*, 32.

13. Gutiérrez interview.

14. Carl Leiden and Karl M. Schmitt, *The Politics of Violence: Revolution in the Modern World* (Englewood Cliffs, N.J.: Prentice-Hall, 1968), 37.

15. Chalmers Johnson, *Revolutionary Change* (Boston: Little, Brown, 1966), 99–100; Harry Eckstein, "On the Etiology of Internal Wars," 124–59, in *Why Revolution?*, ed. Clifford T. Payton and Robert Blackey (New York: Free Press of Glencoe, 1964).

16. Julian Samora, Joe Bernal, and Albert Peña, *Gunpowder Justice: A Reassessment of the Texas Rangers* (Notre Dame, Ind.: University of Notre Dame Press, 1979), 90.

17. Ibid., 90–91

18. Shockley, *Chicano Revolt*, 16.

19. Robert A. Calvert and Arnoldo De León, *The History of Texas* (Arlington Heights, Ill.: Harlan Davidson, 1990), 375.

20. Shockley, *Chicano Revolt*, 18; Calvert and De León, *History of Texas*, 375.

21. *Zavala County Sentinel*, January 13, 1961; Shockley, *Chicano Revolt*, 19.

22. Shockley, *Chicano Revolt*, 255–56.

23. Ibid., 19.

24. This account of the López incident comes from Shockley, *Chicano Revolt*, 21–22.

25. Rodolfo Acuña, *Occupied America: A History of Chicanos*, 3d ed. (Cambridge, Mass.: Harper & Row, 1988), 313–14.

26. Shockley, *Chicano Revolt*, 21–22.

27. *National Observer*, April 22, 1963.

28. Shockley, *Chicano Revolt*, 24.

29. Interview, Juan Cornejo, September 21, 1994; Shockley, *Chicano Revolt*, 26; Roberto Cuellar, *A Social and Political History of the Mexican-American Population of Texas, 1929–1968* (San Francisco: R & E Research Associates, 1974), 56.

30. Cuellar, *Social Political History*, 43–45.

31. Ibid., 55; Samora, Bernal, and Peña, *Gunpowder Justice*, 94.

32. Cornejo interview; *San Antonio Express*, April 14, 1963.

33. Samora, Bernal, and Peña, *Gunpowder Justice*, 97; *San Antonio Express*, April 14, 1963.

34. Samora, Bernal, and Peña, *Gunpowder Justice*, 98.

35. Shockley, *Chicano Revolt*, 26.

36. José Angel Gutiérrez, *The Making of a Chicano Militant: Lessons from Cristal* (Madison: University of Wisconsin Press, 1998).

37. Shockley, *Chicano Revolt*, 27.

38. Cuellar, *Social Political History*, 57.

39. Samora, Bernal, and Peña, *Gunpowder Justice*, 103.

40. Ibid., 98–99.

41. Shockley, *Chicano Revolt*, 27.

42. Samora, Bernal, and Peña, *Gunpowder Justice*, 99–101; Charles Chandler, *The Mexican-American Protest Movement in Texas* (Ann Arbor, Mich.: Xerox University Microfilms, 1975), 176; *San Antonio Light*, April 1, 1963.

43. *Dallas Morning News*, July 28, 1965.

44. Cornejo interview.

45. Shockley, *Chicano Revolt*, 36.

46. Saul Alinsky, *Rules for Radicals* (New York: Random House, 1969), 126–31.

47. Gutiérrez, *Making of a Chicano Militant*.

48. *National Observer*, April 22, 1963.

49. Chandler, *Mexican-American Protest Movement*, 177–78.

50. Shockley, *Chicano Revolt*, 26.

51. Ibid., 29.

52. *National Observer*, April 22, 1963.

53. Samora, Bernal, and Peña, *Gunpowder Justice*, 101.

54. Ibid., 102.

55. Ibid., 106–107.

56. Cuellar, *Social Political History*, 59; *National Observer*, April 22, 1963.

57. Shockley, *Chicano Revolt*, 32–33.

58. Albert Peña, public letter to voters of Crystal City, March 25, 1963.

59. Samora, Bernal, and Peña, *Gunpowder Justice*, 108; David Montejano, *Anglos and Mexicanos in the Making of Texas, 1836–1986* (Austin: University of Texas Press, 1992), 282–84.

60. All three speakers are quoted in Shockley, *Chicano Revolt*, 37.

61. *San Antonio Express*, March 29, 1963.

62. Shockley, *Chicano Revolt*, 37; *Texas Observer*, April 22, 1963.

63. Shockley, *Chicano Revolt*, 258.

64. *Texas Observer*, April 18, 1963.

65. Samora, Bernal, and Peña, *Gunpowder Justice*, 112.

66. Larry Goodwyn, *Texas Observer*, April 18, 1963.

67. *Corpus Christi Caller Times*, May 19, 1963.

68. *San Antonio Express and News*, April 13, 1963.

69. *San Antonio Express*, April 4, 1993.

70. Larry Goodwyn, *Texas Observer*, April 18, 1963.

71. Shockley, *Chicano Revolt*, 45.

72. *San Antonio Express*, April 30, 1963.

73. Ibid.

74. Samora, Bernal, and Peña, *Gunpowder Justice*, 118.

75. Ibid., 117.

76. Shockley, *Chicano Revolt*, 55; *Zavala County Sentinel*, September 17, 1963.

77. Shockley, *Chicano Revolt*, 55.

78. *Zavala County Sentinel*, August 2, 1963.

79. Cornejo interview; Shockley, *Chicano Revolt*, 58.

80. The May election was a primary for county, state, and federal offices. At the county level, only the two highest vote getters were in the run-off in June. Whoever won in the run-off was declared winner of the Democratic primary. Because Republicans did not contest county offices, the run-off–winning Democrat secured the office. Had the Democrat had opposition, he would have had to run in the state general election in November.

81. *Zavala County Sentinel*, June 12, 1963.

82. Cuellar, *Social Political History*, 60,83; Shockley, *Chicano Revolt*, 59.

84. Ibid., 42.

85. Ibid., 47; *Zavala County Sentinel*, June 26, 1964.

86. *San Antonio Light*, September 12, 1964.

87. Shockley, *Chicano Revolt*, 46.

88. Samora, Bernal, and Peña, *Gunpowder Justice*, 119; *San Antonio Light*, December 9, 1964.

89. *San Antonio Express*, January 14, 1965; *Zavala County Sentinel*, January 15, 1965.

90. Cuellar, *Social Political History*, 61; Montejano, *Anglos and Mexicans*, 284.

91. Shockley, *Chicano Revolt*, 54.

92. *San Antonio Express*, August 14, 1964; *San Antonio News*, August 14, 1964; *San Antonio Light*, August 14, 1964; *Zavala County Sentinel*, August 21, 1964.

93. Cornejo interview; *Houston Chronicle*, February 21, 1965.

94. *Houston Chronicle*, April 14, 1965; Shockley, *Chicano Revolt*, 75.

95. *Houston Chronicle*, April 7, 1965; Shockley, *Chicano Revolt*, 74–75.

96. *Zavala County Sentinel*, April 9, 1965; Clarence L. La Roche, *Houston Chronicle*, April 7, 1965.

97. Shockley, *Chicano Revolt*, 77; Montejano, *Anglos and Society*, 284; Calvert and De León, *History of Texas*, 391.

98. *Houston Post*, February 26, 1965.

99. Shockley, *Chicano Revolt*, 98.

100. Ibid., 83–84.

101. Ibid., 90.

102. Ibid., 107.

103. Herbert Hirsch and Armando Gutiérrez, *Learning to Be Militant: Ethnic Identity and the Development of Political Militance in a Chicano Community* (San Francisco: R & E Research Associates, 1977), 17.

Chapter 2. The Second Electoral Revolt (1970)

1. Tony Castro, *Chicano Power* (New York: Saturday Review Press, 1974), 148.

2. See Eric Hoffer, *The True Believer* (New York: Harper & Row, 1951); James McGregor Burns, *Leadership* (New York: Harper & Row, 1978); Frances Fox Piven and Richard A. Cloward, *Poor People's Movements: Why They Succeed, How They Fail* (New York: Vintage Books, 1979); Crane Brinton, *The Anatomy of Revolution* (New York: Vintage, 1965). For a more detailed analysis of how Gutiérrez prepared the political ground for the emergence of the RUP in Crystal City, Texas, see Armando Navarro, *Mexican American Youth Organization: Avant-Garde of the Chicano Movement in Texas* (Austin: University of Texas Press, 1995).

3. Burns, *Leadership*, 18.

4. Gutiérrez unequivocally repudiates the great man theory. He calls it "too simplistic an analysis, equivocally male-centered, and imbued in social science fiction" (José Angel Gutiérrez, *The Making of a Chicano Militant: Lessons From Cristal* [Madison: University of Wisconsin Press, 1998]).

5. Hoffer, *True Believer*, 119–137.

6. Brinton, *Anatomy of Revolution*, 56–57; Thomas H. Greene, *Comparative Revolutionary Movements: Search for Theory and Justice* (Englewood Cliffs, NJ: Prentice-Hall, 1984), 5.

7. Matt S. Meier and Feliciano Rivera, *The Chicanos: A History of Mexican Americans* (New York: Hill and Wang, 1972), 257–80. For a thorough examination of MAYO see Navarro, *Mexican American Youth Organization*.

8. See Walter L. Adamson, *Hegemony and Revolution: A Study of Antonio Gramsci's Political and Cultural Theory* (Berkeley: University of California Press, 1980); Dante L. Germino, *Architect of a New Politics* (Baton Rouge: Louisiana State University Press, 1990); Paul Ransome, *Antonio Gramsci: A New Introduction* (New York: Harvester/Wheatsheaf, 1992).

9. Gutiérrez, *Making of a Chicano Militant*, 26; Richard Vara, *Houston Post*, June 12, 1977.

10. Vara, *Houston Post*, June 12, 1977; Gutiérrez, *Making of a Chicano Militant*.

11. Samuel Huntington, *Political Order in Changing Societies* (New Haven, Conn.: Yale University Press, 1968), 264.

12. For a comprehensive examination of the events that led up to the Crystal City school walkouts see Navarro, *Mexican American Youth Organization*, pp. 132–48, and for a detailed account and analysis of events and circumstances that gave rise to the second revolt and the genesis of RUP.

13. Interview, José Angel Gutiérrez, May 24, 1973.

14. Interview, Severita Lara, September 20, 1994.

15. Ignacio Garcia, *United We Win: The Rise and Fall of La Raza Unida Party* (Tucson, Ariz.: Mexican American Studies Research Center, 1989), 57.

16. Gutiérrez interview.

17. Interview, Viviana Santiago Cavada, May 28, 1993.

18. *Zavala County Sentinel*, January 29, 1970. Because RUP was not yet certified as a political party, it operated in Cristal at this time more as a political association, not unlike the Democratic and Republican clubs that operate in precincts throughout the country.

19. Gutiérrez interview; interview, Luz Gutiérrez, May 9, 1973.

20. J. A. Gutiérrez interview.

21. Interview, Mike Pérez, April 13, 1973; interview, Arturo Gonzales, May 22, 1973.

22. J. A. Gutiérrez interview.

23. *San Antonio Express*, March 23, 1970.

24. Interview, Dale Barker, April 17, 1973; John Staples Shockley, *Chicano Revolt in a Texas Town* (Notre Dame, Ind.: University of Notre Dame Press, 1974), 142–43.

25. Navarro, *Mexican American Youth Organization*, 171–74.

26. Pat McClurg, *Odessa American*, February 28, 1970, reprinted in the *Zavala County Sentinel*, April 2, 1970; Sam Kindrick, *San Antonio Express*, April 1970; Luz Gutiérrez interview.

27. *Zavala County Sentinel*, April 2, 1970.

28. John Staples Shockley, "Crystal City: La Raza Unida and the Second Revolt" in Renato Rosaldo, et al., eds., *Chicano: The Beginnings of Bronze Power* (New York: Morrow, 1974), 74–86.

29. Garcia, *United We Win*, 59.

30. Shockley, *Chicano Revolt*, 146–47.

31. Ibid., 142.

32. José Angel Gutiérrez, "Aztlán: Chicano Revolt in the Winter Garden," *La Raza*, vol. 1, no. 4 (1971): 34–35;

33. J. A. Gutiérrez interview.

34. *Zavala County Sentinel*, April 9, 1970.

35. *La Verdad*, February 1970; *San Antonio News*, April 8, 1970.

36. *San Antonio Light*, April 8, 1970; J. A. Gutiérrez interview.

37. José Garza, "La Raza Unida in Cristal City: A Study of a Chicano Third-Party Movement," master's thesis, Trinity University, San Antonio Texas, 1972.

38. Shockley, *Chicano Revolt*, 148.

39. *La Verdad,* April 1970.
40. *San Antonio News,* April 16, 1970; Garcia, *United We Win,* 59.
41. *Big Spring Herald,* April 5, 1970; *San Antonio Light,* April 8, 1970.
42. John R. Chavez, *The Lost Land* (Albuquerque: University of New Mexico Press, 1984), 145; David Montejano, *Anglos and Mexicans: In the Making of Texas, 1836–1986* (Austin: University of Texas Press, 1986), 285.
43. Matt S. Meier and Feliciano Rivera, *The Chicanos: A History of Mexican Americans* (New York: Hill and Wang, 1972), 278–79.
44. Interview, José Angel Gutiérrez, February 25, 1995.
45. Shockley, *Chicano Revolt,* 151.
46. 1995 J. A. Gutiérrez interview; Shockley, *Chicano Revolt,* 153.
47. Shockley, *Chicano Revolt,* 154.
48. 1995 J. A. Gutiérrez interview.
49. Ibid.
50. Ibid.
51. Ibid.
52. *San Antonio Light,* April 11, 1970.
53. *Zavala County Sentinel,* April 9, 1970.
54. Garcia, *United We Win,* 60.
55. Interview, Carlos Reyes, February 28, 1995.
56. 1973 J. A. Gutiérrez interview.
57. Luz Gutiérrez interview; 1973 J. A. Gutiérrez interview; see Chapter 10 for a more detailed explanation of the women's role within RUP's peaceful revolution as well as the five years of its decline.
58. Shockley, *Chicano Revolt,* 182.
59. *Zavala County Sentinel,* June 25, 1970. The resolution meant that the Highway Patrol would not issue tickets within the city limits and would not patrol in the neighborhoods unless asked to do so.
60. A. Y. Allee, Letter to the Editor, *Zavala County Sentinel,* June 25, 1970.
61. Shockley, *Chicano Revolt,* 175.
62. *Zavala County Sentinel,* September 10, 1970.
63. For accounts of the Mata ouster see *Zavala County Sentinel,* December 3, 1970, and *San Antonio Express,* December 3, 1970. Benavides was quoted in the *Express.*
64. Shockley, *Chicano Revolt,* 176.
65. For a much more detailed discussion of this issue, see Shockley, *Chicano Revolt,* 179–81.
66. Ibid., 156.
67. Ibid.; Gutiérrez, "Aztlán," 34–35.
68. Luz Gutiérrez interview.
69. *San Antonio Express,* October 12, 1970.
70. *Zavala County Sentinel,* October 1, 1970; *San Antonio Express,* October 9, 1970.
71. *Zavala County Sentinel,* October 8, 1970; *San Antonio Express,* October 12, 1970.
72. Shockley, *Chicano Revolt,* 159.
73. Luz Gutiérrez interview; *La Verdad,* October 30, 1970.

74. Shockley, *Chicano Revolt*, 159.
75. *La Verdad*, December 15, 1970; Shockley, *Chicano Revolt*, 159.
76. 1995 J. A. Gutiérrez interview.
77. Shockley, *Chicano Revolt*, 157.
78. Ibid., 158.
79. *Militant*, November 20, 1970. This is the official newspaper of the Socialist Workers' Party.
80. Ibid.
81. *Zavala County Sentinel*, November 5, 1970.
82. Luz Gutiérrez interview; *La Verdad*, November 20, 1970.
83. *San Antonio Express*, November 5, 1990.

Chapter 3. The Emergence of RUP's Machine Politics (1971–1972)

1. Eugene Lewis, *The Urban Political System* (Hinsdale, Ill.: Dryden Press, 1973), 42.
2. For a more historical analysis of the manifold social problems endemic to the urbanization of the United States that were conducive to the rise and maintenance of political machines, see Charles N. Glaab and Theodore A. Brown, *A History of Urban America* (New York: Macmillan, 1967), and Black McKelvey, *The Urbanization of America, 1860–1915* (New Brunswick, N.J.: Rutgers University Press, 1963).
3. Bryan T. Downes, *Politics, Change, and the Urban Crisis* (North Scituate, Mass.: Duxbury Press, 1976), 110. Harlan Hahn and Charles Levine, *Urban Politics: Past, Present, and Future* (New York: Longman, 1980), 78.
4. For an examination of how Mexicanos were subject to the control of gringo political machines in Texas see Rodolfo Acuña, *Occupied America: A History of Chicanos* (New York: Harper & Row, 1988), 33–37.
5. David Montejano, *Anglos and Mexicans in the Making of Texas* (Austin: University of Texas Press, 1994), 39–40.
6. Banfield and Wilson, *City Politics*, 115.
7. Robert K. Merton, *Social Theory and Social Structure* (New York: Free Press, 1957), esp. chap. 1, pp. 60–82.
8. Charles Adrain and Charles Press, *Governing Urban America* (New York: McGraw-Hill, 1968), 149.
9. Interview, José Angel Gutiérrez, February 25, 1995.
10. Ibid.
11. Armando Navarro, "El Partido de la Raza Unida in Crystal City," doctoral dissertation, Department of Political Science, University of California at Riverside, 1974, 368–77.
12. Gutiérrez interview, February 1995.
13. John Staples Shockley, *Chicano Revolt in a Texas Town* (Notre Dame, Ind.: University of Notre Dame Press, 1974), 182.
14. See Thomas P. Clifford, *The Political Machine: An American Institution* (New York: Vantage, 1975), 7, and Banfield and Wilson, *City Politics*, 116.
15. Gutiérrez interview, February 1995.

16. David Easton, *The Political System* (New York: Knopf, 1953), chap. 5.

17. Gutiérrez interview, February 1995.

18. Richard A. Schaffer, "Brown Power: Small City in Texas Is a Testing Ground for Chicano Movement," *Wall Street Journal*, September 5, 1975.

19. Ibid.

20. Interview, José Mata, September 20, 1994.

21. See Chapter 7 for a more detailed examination of CU's income tax.

22. Interview, Dale Barker, April 17, 1973.

23. Interview, Dr. Ronald Smith, April 16, 1973.

24. Barker interview.

25. Interviews with Gloria Bookout, March 30, 1973; Guin Casey, April 1, 1973; and Jack Kingsberry, May 8, 1973.

26. Ronald Smith and Casey interviews.

27. See William Madsen, *Mexican-Americans of South Texas* (New York: Holt, Rhinehart, and Winston, 1964); Arthur Rubel, *Across the Tracks* (Austin: University of Texas Press, 1966), and Julian Samora and James Watson, "Subordinate Leadership in a Bicultural Community: An Analysis," *American Sociological Review* 19 (August 1954): 413–21. All make reference to the difficulty in organizing and unifying Mexicanos in advocacy or political organization. See chap. 3 in Armando Navarro, *Mexican American Youth Organization: Avant-Garde of the Chicano Movement in Texas* (Austin: University of Texas Press, 1995) for an explanation of Alinskyism and its use by and influence on MAYO.

28. Shockley, *Chicano Revolt*, 183.

29. *La Verdad*, March 18, 1971.

30. Shockley, *Chicano Revolt*, 188.

31. *New Yorker*, April 17, 1971.

32. Navarro, "El Partido de la Raza Unida," 280–81.

33. Ibid.

34. Ann Ladner, Letter to the Editor, *Zavala County Sentinel*, April 1, 1971.

35. *Zavala County Sentinel*, April 2, 1973.

36. *Zavala County Sentinel*, March 25, 1971.

37. Navarro, "El Partido de la Raza Unida," 84, 203–4.

38. *Javelin Herald*, February 12, 1971.

39. Ibid.

40. *Zavala County Sentinel*, April 8, 1971. The presence of Peña and Bernal was significant because both were Democrats but not altogether surprising because both had strong records as civil rights advocates for Mexicanos. As a leader of PASSO during the early 1960s, Peña was a staunch supporter of the first revolt. Bernal carried state legislation that removed statues from the state code laws that provided for the segregation of schools in Texas.

41. *La Verdad*, September 1971.

42. *Zavala County Sentinel*, April 8 and April 18, 1971; *San Antonio Express*, April 7, 1971.

43. José Angel Gutiérrez, Production School lectures, "Fighting for Political Power," National Latino Communications Center and Galan Productions, Austin, September 10, 1995.

44. Gutiérrez lecture; *Zavala County Sentinel*, April 29, 1971.
45. *Zavala County Sentinel*, May 20, 1971.
46. *Zavala County Sentinel*, April 29 and June 10, 1971; Interview, J. A. Gutiérrez, March 27, 1995.
47. *Zavala County Sentinel*, April 15, 1971.
48. *Zavala County Sentinel*, June 17, 1971.
49. *Zavala County Sentinel*, August 12 and July 22, 1971.
50. *Zavala County Sentinel*, November 18, 1971.
51. Interview, Luz Gutiérrez, May 9, 1973.
52. Navarro, "El Partido de la Raza Unida," 293–94.
53. *Zavala County Sentinel*, March 2, 1972.
54. Ibid.
55. Ibid.
56. Interview, J. A. Gutiérrez, June 2, 1973.
57. *Zavala County Sentinel*, April 6, 1972.
58. Navarro, "El Partido de la Raza Unida," 297.
59. *Corpus Christi Caller-Times*, January 29, 1972; *San Antonio Express*, January 29, 1972; *Zavala County Sentinel*, February 3, 1972.
60. *San Antonio Express*, January 29, 1972; interview, Rev. Sherrill Smith, September 23, 1994.
61. *Zavala County Sentinel*, May 18, 1972.
62. Crystal City Independent School District, "Ten Years of Struggle: A Photographic Essay," 1979; *Corpus Christi Caller*, August 3, 1972.
63. Crystal City Independent School District, "Ten Years of Struggle."
64. Navarro, *Mexican American Youth Organization*, chap. 7.
65. *Zavala County Sentinel*, August 10, 1972.
66. Interview, Alberto Luera, former MAYO slate chairperson, April 4, 1973.
67. *Zavala County Sentinel*, May 4, 1972; *La Verdad*, May 10, 1972; Navarro, *Mexican American Youth Organization*, chap. 7.
68. Kingsberry interview; *Zavala County Sentinel*, May 4, 1972; Barker interview.
69. Kingsberry and Barker interviews.
70. *Zavala County Sentinel*, November 2, 1973.
71. For a full explanation of the transition, see Navarro, *Mexican American Youth Organization*, chap. 7; *San Antonio Express*, August 9, 1972.
72. Navarro, *Mexican American Youth Organization*, chap. 7.
73. Luera interview.
74. Interview, Ramsey Muñiz, May 15, 1973.
75. J. A. Gutiérrez interview, June 1973; Muñiz interview.
76. *San Antonio Express*, September 3, 1972; *Corpus Christi Caller*, September 5, 1972. For more information about the struggles of Gonzalez and Tijerina, see Acuña, *Occupied America*, 362–66.
77. Ignacio Garcia, *United We Win: The Rise and Fall of the Raza Unida Party* (Tucson, Ariz.: Mexican American Studies Research Center, 1989), 108.
78. Ibid.

79. Ibid., 111–12.
80. *Corpus Christi Caller,* September 15, 1972.
81. *El Paso Herald,* September 5, 1972.
82. *Los Angeles Times,* September 5, 1972.
83. Interview, Carlos Reyes, former Gutiérrez bodyguard and initially a member of Voluntarios de Aztlán, May 26, 1995.
84. *Zavala County Sentinel,* October 20, 1972.
85. Interview, Viviana Santiago Cavada, May 28, 1973.
86. Recorded speech, Mike Pérez, Radio Station KBEN, March 28, 1973.
87. Ibid.
88. *El Camino Recto,* Amistad newsletter, October, 1972.
89. *Zavala County Sentinel,* November 2, 1972.
90. Luz Gutiérrez interview.
91. *Zavala County Sentinel,* November 9, 1972.
92. John R. Fry, "Election Night in Crystal City," *Christianity and Crisis,* 32 (November 27, 1972): 254.
93. Ibid.
94. Ibid.
95. *Zavala County Sentinel,* November 9, 1972.
96. Fry, "Election Night in Crystal City."
97. *San Antonio Express,* November 12, 1972; Garcia, *United We Win,* 128.
98. *San Antonio Express,* November 10, 1972.
99. *Zavala County Sentinel,* December 7, 1972.
100. *Zavala County Sentinel,* December 14, 1972.
101. *Zavala County Sentinel,* December 28, 1972.

Chapter 4. The Calm Before the Political Storm (1973–1975)

1. *Zavala County Sentinel,* January 4, 1973.
2. *Zavala County Sentinel,* January 11, 1973.
3. Armando Trujillo, "Community Empowerment and Bilingual/Bicultural Education: A Study of the Movement in a South Texas Community," doctoral dissertation, University of Texas at Austin, August 1993.
4. *Zavala County Sentinel,* February 8 and January 25, 1973. See Chapter 8 for a more complete discussion of the twenty-two recommendations for bilingual education.
5. *Zavala County Sentinel,* January 25, 1973; Interview, Ponciano Hernández, April 18, 1973.
6. Ponciano Hernández interview.
7. Ibid.
8. *La Verdad,* February 11, 1973.
9. *La Verdad,* February 19, 1973.
10. *La Verdad,* March 13, 1973.
11. Interview, Luz Gutiérrez, May 9, 1973.
12. Armando Navarro, "El Partido de la Raza Unida in Crystal City: A

Peaceful Revolution," doctoral dissertation, Department of Political Science, University of California at Riverside, 1974, 321–44.
13. RUP radio spot, Ramon "Monche" Mata, KBEN radio station, April 1, 1973.
14. RUP radio spots, Richard Díaz and Viviana Santiago Cavada, KBEN radio station, April 1, 1973; Navarro, "El Partido de la Raza Unida," 328.
15. Navarro, "El Partido de la Raza Unida," 321–44.
16. Independent radio spot, Mike Pérez, KBEN radio station, April 1, 1973.
17. Ibid.; interview, Viviana Santiago Cavada, June 23, 1997.
18. Independent radio spot, KBEN radio station, April 1, 1973.
19. Interviews with Mike Pérez, April 12, 1973; Hernández; and José Mata, May 11, 1973.
20. Interview, Gloria Bookout, March 24, 1973.
21. Interviews with José Mata, Hernández, and Pérez.
22. *Zavala County Sentinel*, March 29, 1973.
23. Ibid.
24. *El Diaro*, March 30, 1973.
25. *La Mera Verdad*, no date.
26. *San Antonio Express*, April 7, 1973.
27. Navarro, "El Partido de la Raza Unida," 336–39.
28. *Zavala County Sentinel*, April 5, 1973.
29. *Zavala County Sentinel*, April 12, 1973; interview with Virginia Musquiz, April 13, 1973.
30. *Zavala County Sentinel*, May 10, 1973.
31. *La Verdad*, April 1973.
32. *Zavala County Sentinel*, February 22, 1973; interview, José Angel Gutiérrez, February 25, 1995.
33. 1995 J. A. Gutiérrez interview.
34. Ibid.
35. *Zavala County Sentinel*, February 14, 1974.
36. Ibid.
37. *Zavala County Sentinel*, February 28, 1974.
38. *San Antonio Express*, March 3, 1974.
39. *Zavala County Sentinel*, February 28, 1974.
40. *San Antonio Express*, March 3, 1974.
41. Ibid.
42. *Zavala County Sentinel*, March 21, 1974.
43. *Zavala County Sentinel*, March 28, 1974.
44. *Zavala County Sentinel*, April 11, 1974.
45. *Zavala County Sentinel*, April 4 and 11, 1974.
46. Cristal Independent School District, "Ten Years of Struggle: A Photographic Essay," 1979.
47. *Corpus Christi Caller*, June 23, 1975.
48. *Zavala County Sentinel*, March 14, June 13, and June 24, 1974.
49. *Zavala County Sentinel*, December 26, 1974.
50. *Zavala County Sentinel*, January 10, 1974.

51. *Zavala County Sentinel,* January 10 and May 2, 1974.
52. *Zavala County Sentinel,* May 9, 1974.
53. Ibid.
54. *Zavala County Sentinel,* May 16 and 30, 1974,
55. *Zavala County Sentinel,* February 14 and March 14, 1974,
56. *Zavala County Sentinel,* April 25, 1974.
57. *Militant,* December 28, 1973, and February 15, 1974; *San Antonio News,* February 5, 1974.
58. See chap. 7 in Armando Navarro, *Mexican American Youth Organization: Avant-Garde of the Chicano Movement in Texas* (Austin: University of Texas Press, 1995); *Zavala County Sentinel,* September 26, 1974.
59. *Zavala County Sentinel,* September 26, 1974.
60. *Zavala County Sentinel,* October 10 and 17, 1974.
61. *Zavala County Sentinel,* October 31, 1974.
62. Ibid.
63. *Zavala County Sentinel,* November 7, 1974; Ignacio Garcia, *United We Win: The Rise and Fall of La Raza Unida Party* (Tucson, Ariz.: Mexican American Studies Research Center, 1989), 189.
64. *Zavala County Sentinel,* November 14 and 21, 1974.
65. 1995 J. A. Gutiérrez interview.
66. Garcia, *United We Win,* 197.
67. For election results see *Zavala County Sentinel,* April 3 and 10, 1975.

Chapter 5. Schisms Emerge in Cristal's Power Structure (1972–1974)

1. Janet A. Hammang, *American Politics in a Changing World* (Pacific Grove, Calif.: Brooks/Cole, 1990), 140.
2. There are various schools of pluralist thought. For a look at two different views, both pluralist, see Robert Dahl, *Who Governs* (New Haven, Conn: Yale University Press, 1961), and Theodore S. Lowi, *The End of Liberalism* (New York: Norton, 1979), chap. 3. There is a plethora of literature on elite theory. For two perspectives on elitism, see C. Wright Mills, *The Power Elite* (New York: Oxford University Press, 1959), and William Domhoff, *Who Rules America Now? A View for the Eighties* (Englewood Cliffs, N.J.: Prentice-Hall, 1983).
3. Harold Lasswell and Abraham Kaplan, *Power and Society: A Framework for Political Inquiry* (New Haven, Conn.: Yale University Press, 1950).
4. Thomas Dye, *Who's Running America? The Bush Era* (Englewood Cliffs, N.J.: Prentice-Hall, 1990), 2; Vilfredo Pareto, *Mind and Society* (New York: Harcourt Brace Jovanovich, 1935); Gaetano Mosca, *The Ruling Class* (New York: McGraw-Hill, 1939); Robert Lynd, "Power and American Society," in Arthur Kornhauser, ed., *Problems of Power in American Society* (Detroit: Wayne State University Press, 1957); Harold Lasswell and Daniel Lerner, *The Comparative Study of Elites* (Palo Alto, Calif.: Stanford University Press, 1952); Robert Michels, *Political Parties: A Sociological Study of the Oligarchical Tendencies of Modern Democracy* (1915; reprint, New York: Free Press, 1962), 70.

5.   Interview, José Angel Gutiérrez, February 25, 1995.
6.   Crystal City Independent School District, "Ten Years of Struggle: A Photographic Essay," 1979.
7.   Interviews with J. A. Gutiérrez, May 1, 1995, and Virginia Musquiz, April 13, 1973.
8.   Gutiérrez interview, May 1, 1995.
9.   Ciudadanos Unidos, Articles of Incorporation and By-Laws, Article 3, sect. 4.
10. Gutiérrez interview, May 1, 1995; Ciudadanos Unidos, Articles and By-Laws, Article 6.
11. Floyd Hunter, *Community Power Structure* (Chapel Hill: University of North Carolina Press, 1953).
12. Ibid.; Robert Dahl, *Who Governs;* interview, J. A. Gutiérrez, June 2, 1973.
13. Arthur Vidich and Joseph Bensman, *Small Town in Mass Society* (Princeton, N.J.: Princeton University Press, 1958), 250–67.
14. Gutiérrez interview, June 1973.
15. Armando Navarro, questionnaire administered in Cristal May–June, 1973. Of the nineteen individuals interviewed, fifteen agreed to fill out the questionnaire. The four who refused were apprehensive about divulging information they considered private.
16. Gutiérrez interview, June 1973.
17. Peter Bachrach and Morton S. Baratz, *Power and Poverty* (New York: Oxford University Press, 1970), 43–46.
18. For an excellent analysis of the concept of circulation of elites, see chap. 7 in Kenneth Prewitt, *The Ruling Elites: Elite Theory, Power, and American Democracy* (New York: Harper & Row, 1973); Gutiérrez interview, June 1973.
19. Lasswell and Lerner, *Comparative Study of Elites,* 7.
20. V. O. Key, *Politics, Parties, and Pressure Groups* (New York: T. Y. Crowell, 1964), 3; interviews with J. A. Gutiérrez, May 20, 1995, and Lupe Cortinas, September 17, 1975.
21. For an in-depth examination of the concept of endogenous antagonisms, see Armando Navarro, *Mexican American Youth Organization: Avant-Garde of the Chicano Movement in Texas* (Austin: University of Texas Press, 1995).
22. Interview, J. A. Gutiérrez, February 25, 1995.
23. Armando Navarro, "El Partido de la Raza Unida in Crystal City: A Peaceful Revolution," doctoral dissertation, Department of Political Science, University of California, Riverside, 1974. See chaps. 7 and 8 for a broader analysis of Pérez's defection and leadership role.
24. Ibid., chap. 9.
25. Interview, Rudy Palomo, September 19, 1995.
26. *Arkansas Gazette,* June 16, 1974; *San Antonio Express,* March 3, 1974.
27. *Zavala County Sentinel,* February 28, 1974.
28. *Zavala County Sentinel,* April 11 and 18, 1974.
29. Interviews with Palomo, and Viviana Santiago Cavada, April 23, 1995.
30. Interviews with Cavada; J. A. Gutiérrez, February 25, 1995; and Luz Gutiérrez, April 27, 1995.

31. Interviews with Arturo Gonzales, September 15, 1994, and Luz Gutiérrez.

32. Gonzales and Palomo interviews.

33. Gonzales interview; *Wall Street Journal*, September 5, 1975.

34. Gutiérrez interview, February 1995; *Corpus Christi Caller-Times*, November 18, 1990; interview with Carlos Reyes, May 26, 1995.

35. *Wall Street Journal*, September 5, 1975; Gutiérrez interview, February 1995.

36. Interviews with Rodolfo (Rudy) Espinosa Jr., September 21, 1994, and Viviana Santiago Cavada, September 17, 1994.

37. Sally J. Andrade, *Chicano Mental Health: The Case of Cristal: An Evaluation of the Zavala County Mental Health Program* (Austin, Texas: Hogg Foundation for Mental Health, 1978).

38. Arnold L. Trujillo, "Community Empowerment and Bilingual/Bicultural Education: A Study of the Movimiento in a South Texas Community," doctoral dissertation, Department of Education, University of Texas, Austin, 1993, 105.

39. Reyes interview.

40. *Wall Street Journal*, September 5, 1975; *Corpus Christi Caller*, June 26, 1975.

41. *Wall Street Journal*, September 5, 1975.

42. Ibid.

43. *Texas Observer*, July 5, 1974.

44. Gutiérrez interview, February 1995.

45. Interviews with Cortinas, and Gutiérrez, February 1995.

Chapter 6. The Political Rupture (1975)

1. For an examination and explanation of both concepts, see Armando Navarro, *Mexican American Youth Organization: Avant-Garde of the Chicano Movement in Texas* (Austin: University of Texas Press, 1995).

2. Armando Navarro, "Impacto 2000 and Mexico: El Plan de Acercamiente," Institute for Social Justice, (San Bernardino, Calif., 1989. Paper presented to then-president Carlos Salinas de Gortari of Mexico at a meeting of Mexicano leaders in Tijuana.

3. Ibid. For an examination of the decline of the protest movements, including civil rights and black power, see Robert Weisbrot, *Freedom Bound: A History of America's Civil Rights Movement* (New York: Plume, 1991).

4. David Montejano, *Anglos and Mexicans in the Making of Texas, 1836–1986* (Austin: University of Texas Press, 1987), 289; Navarro, *Mexican American Youth Organization*, 241.

5. Armando Navarro, "The Chicano Community in a State of Siege," paper presented at the National Association of Chicano/Chicana Studies Conference, San Antonio, March 1992.

6. Juan Gomez-Quinonez, *Chicano Politics: Reality and Promise, 1940–1990* (Albuquerque: University of New Mexico Press, 1990), 118, 136.

7. David Sanchez, *Expedition Through Aztlán* (La Puente, Calif.: Perspective Publications, 1978), 190.

8. Carlos Muñoz, *Youth, Identity, Power* (New York: Verso, 1990), 84–97; Gomez-Quinonez, *Chicano Politics,* 141–53; Navarro, *Mexican American Youth Organization,* epilogue. See also Armando Navarro, "The Postmortem Politics of the Chicano Movement," *Perspectives in Mexican American Studies,* September 1997.

9. Ignacio Garcia, *United We Win: The Rise and Fall of La Raza Unida Party* (Tucson, Ariz.: Mexican American Studies Research Center, 1989), 197–216.

10. Muñoz, *Youth, Identity, Power,* 99–126.

11. Garcia, *United We Win,* 197.

12. Interview, Lupe Cortinas, September 17, 1975.

13. Interview, José Angel Gutiérrez, February 25, 1995.

14. I use the term *technocrat* to denote those who held leadership positions between 1975 and 1977, primarily within the schools and city government, who became anti-Gutierristas and were not members of the Barrio Club.

15. Cortinas interview.

16. Two excellent anthologies on the etiology of revolution are Clifford T. Payton and Robert Blackey, *Why Revolutions? Theories and Analysis* (Morristown, N.J.: Schenkman Publishing, 1971), and Mark N. Hagopian, *The Phenomenon of Revolution* (New York: Dodd, Meade, 1974).

17. Alexis de Tocqueville, *L'ancien régime et la revolucion* (Paris: Gallimand, 1967), 277.

18. Payton and Blackey, *Why Revolutions?,* 177–98.

19. Hagopian, *Phenomenon of Revolution,* 171.

20. Ted Robert Gurr, "Psychological Factors in Civil Violence," in Ivo K. Feierabend, Rosalind L. Feierabend, and Ted Robert Gurr, eds., *Anger, Violence, and Politics: Theories and Research* (Englewood Cliffs, N.J.: Prentice-Hall, 1972), 37–38.

21. Hogopian, *Phenomenon of Revolution,* 171–72.

22. The "new guard" was an anti-Gutierrista coalition comprised of the Barrio Club and technocrats. The party affiliation of both was RUP. Of the two, the Barrio Club was the more dominant and powerful until late 1977. For purposes of analysis *Barrioistas* describes those who were members of the Barrio Club.

23. For an examination of both concepts, see Chalmers Johnson, *Revolutionary Change* (Boston: Little, Brown, 1966), 27–33.

24. Harry Eckstein, ed., *Internal War: Problems and Approaches* (New York: Free Press, 1964), 1.

25. Interviews, Viviana Santiago Cavada, September 17, 1994, and Carlos Reyes, May 26, 1995.

26. *San Antonio Light,* January 9, 1975.

27. *Alicia-Echo Light,* January 16, 1975; *Zavala County Sentinel,* March 6, 1975.

28. Reyes interview.

29. *Zavala County Sentinel,* April 24, 1975.

30. *San Antonio News,* April 23, 1975.

31. Interview, Raul Ruiz, July 1, 1997.

32. *San Antonio Express*, May 5 and May 9, 1975.

33. *Alice-Echo News*, May 15, 1975.

34. *San Antonio Express*, May 9, 1975; *Corpus Christi Caller*, May 10, 1975; *Alice-Echo News*, May 15, 1975.

35. Interview, Ventura Gonzalez, September 20, 1994.

36. *Alice-Echo News*, May 15, 1975; interview, Jack Kingsberry, September 19, 1994; *Zavala County Sentinel*, June 5, 1975.

37. Interviews, Reverend Sherrill Smith, September 23, 1994; Moses Peña, September 15, 1994; José Mata, September 20, 1994.

38. Interview, Abel Cavada, September 17, 1994.

39. Interview, Arturo Gonzales, September 15, 1994; *Corpus Christi Caller-Times*, February 22, 1981.

40. Interviews, Rudy Polomo, September 19, 1994; José Luis Balderas, September 19, 1994.

41. Interview, Juan Cornejo, September 21, 1994; Sherrill Smith interview.

42. Balderas interview.

43. Gutiérrez interview.

44. Balderas interview.

45. Minutes, Ciudadanos Unidas, October 12, 1975.

46. Garcia, *United We Win*, 204.

47. Gutiérrez interview.

48. Ibid.

49. Lupe Cortinas and Balderas interviews.

50. *Corpus Christi Caller-Times*, February 22, 1981.

51. Interview, Amancio Cantu, September 14, 1975. The "oportunistas" [opportunists] were the technocrats who forged an alliance with the Barrioistas. Again, this new alliance was what I refer to as the new guard.

52. Ibid.

53. Gonzales interview.

54. Polomo and Balderas interviews.

55. *Alice-Echo News*, September 19, 1994.

56. Harry Eckstein, "On the Etiology of Internal Wars," in Feierabend et al., *Anger, Violence, and Politics* 9–30; *Zavala County Sentinel*, July 24, 1975.

57. *Zavala County Sentinel*, July 24, 1975.

58. Chalmers Johnson, *Revolutionary Changes* (Boston: Little, Brown, 1966), 32.

59. *Zavala County Sentinel*, August 14, 1975.

60. Peña interview.

61. Cortinas interview, September 17, 1975.

62. Gutiérrez interview.

63. Ibid.

64. Ibid.

65. Polomo interview.

66. *Zavala County Sentinel*, August 21, 1975.

67. *Complaint County vs. Crystal City Independent School District*, no date.

68. *Zavala County Sentinel*, September 11, 1975.

69. Gutiérrez interview; *Zavala County Sentinel,* September 25, 1975.
70. *Zavala County Sentinel,* September 4, 1975.
71. Gutiérrez interview.
72. *Zavala County Sentinel,* September 11, 1975.
73. *Zavala County Sentinel,* December 4, 1975.
74. *Zavala County Sentinel,* September 11, 1975; *Corpus Christi Caller,* September 11, 1975.
75. *Zavala County Sentinel,* September 18, 1975.
76. *Zavala County Sentinel,* September 25, 1975.
77. Balderas interview.
78. Minutes, Ciudadanos Unidos, September 25, 1975.
79. Minutes, Ciudadanos Unidos, October 12, 1975.
80. *Dallas Morning News,* September 26, 1975.
81. *Zavala County Sentinel,* September 25, 1975.
82. Ibid.
83. Minutes, Ciudadanos Unidos, September 28, 1975.
84. *Zavala County Sentinel,* October 2, 1975.
85. *Zavala County Sentinel,* October 9 and 16, 1975; Gutiérrez interview; *Alice-Echo News,* December 21, 1975; Minutes, Ciudadanos Unidos, October 12, 1975.
86. *San Antonio Express,* October 11, 1975; *Zavala County Sentinel,* October 16, 1975; *Alice-Echo News,* October 18, 1975; Gutiérrez interview.
87. *San Antonio Express,* December 21, 1975.
88. *Alice-Echo News,* October 19, 1975; *Zavala County Sentinel,* October 23, 1975.
89. *Zavala County Sentinel,* October 16, 1975.
90. *San Antonio Express,* October 22, 1975; *Dallas Morning News,* September 26, 1976.
91. *Zavala County Sentinel,* November 20, 1975.
92. *Zavala County Sentinel,* November 6, 1975; *San Antonio Express,* November 3, 1975.
93. *Zavala County Sentinel,* November 20, 1975.
94. Gonzales interview; *Corpus Christi Caller-Times,* November 18, 1990.
95. Interviews with Gutiérrez, September 11, 1975, and Cortinas.
96. *San Antonio Express,* October 1, 1975.
97. Garcia, *United We Win,* 205.
98. *Alice-Echo News,* December 21, 1975.
99. *San Antonio Express,* December 21, 1975.

Chapter 7. The Political Decline of the Peaceful Revolution (1976–1978)

1. Interview, Ventura Gonzalez, September 20, 1994.
2. *Corpus Christi Times,* November 18, 1990.
3. Interviews with Arturo Gonzales, September 15, 1994; José Mata, September 20, 1994; and Rodolfo (Rudy) Palomo, September 19, 1994.
4. *Corpus Christi Times,* November 18, 1990; Palomo interview.

5. Interview, Carlos Reyes, May 26, 1995.
6. Interviews with Lupe Cortinas, September 17, 1975, and José Angel Gutiérrez, February 25, 1995.
7. Palomo and Gutiérrez interviews.
8. Interviews with Moses Peña, September 15, 1994; and José Luis Balderas, September 19, 1994.
9. Gutiérrez interview.
10. Ibid.
11. Interviews with Arturo Gonzales; Severita Lara, September 20, 1994; and Peña.
12. Balderas interview.
13. *Zavala County Sentinel,* January 15, 1976.
14. *Zavala County Sentinel,* January 29, 1976.
15. Balderas interview.
16. Gutiérrez interview.
17. Ibid.; *Zavala County Sentinel,* January 29, 1976.
18. *Zavala County Sentinel,* March 4, 1976.
19. *Zavala County Sentinel,* March 18, 1976.
20. *Zavala County Sentinel,* February 5, 1976.
21. Ibid.
22. *Zavala County Sentinel,* January 29, 1976.
23. Reyes interview.
24. *Zavala County Sentinel,* April 1, 1976; Reyes interview.
25. *Zavala County Sentinel,* April 8, 1976.
26. Ibid.
27. Gutiérrez interview; *Zavala County Sentinel,* April 8, 1976.
28. Gutiérrez interview.
29. *Zavala County Sentinel,* April 15, 1976. The mayor pro tem, who is elected by the city council, presides over that body in the mayor's absence.
30. *Zavala County Sentinel,* April 22 and 29, 1976.
31. *Zavala County Sentinel,* April 29, 1976.
32. *Zavala County Sentinel,* May 6, 1976.
33. Ibid.
34. *Zavala County Sentinel,* May 13, 1976.
35. *Zavala County Sentinel,* June 17, 1976.
36. *Zavala County Sentinel,* September 23, 1976.
37. *Zavala County Sentinel,* November 4, 11, and 18, 1976.
38. *Zavala County Sentinel,* November 11 and 18, 1976.
39. *Zavala County Sentinel,* November 18 and 25, 1976.
40. *Zavala County Sentinel,* March 4, 1976.
41. *Zavala County Sentinel,* April 8, 1976, and interview with Alberto Luera, September 17, 1994.
42. *Zavala County Sentinel,* August 12 and November 25, 1976; *Corpus Christi Caller,* November 18, 1990.
43. Cristal Independent School District, "Ten Years of Struggle: A Photographic Essay," 1979.

44. *Zavala County Sentinel*, September 23 and 30, 1976.

45. *Zavala County Sentinel*, October 28 and December 30, 1976; Balderas interview.

46. *Zavala County Sentinel*, May 20, July 7, September 16, and 23, 1976.

47. *Zavala County Sentinel*, January 22, February 26, July 29, October 28, and November 4, 1976.

48. *Zavala County Sentinel*, February 17 and 24, 1977.

49. *Zavala County Sentinel*, February 24, 1977, and Cristal Independent School District, "Ten Years of Struggle."

50. *Zavala County Sentinel*, March 31, 1977.

51. *Zavala County Sentinel*, March 24, 1977.

52. *Zavala County Sentinel*, March 31, 1977.

53. Ibid.; *Zavala County Sentinel*, April 7, 1977.

54. Reyes interview.

55. *Zavala County Sentinel*, January 20, February 24, and March 10 and 17, 1977.

56. *Zavala County Sentinel*, April 21 and May 19, 1977.

57. *Zavala County Sentinel*, June 2, 1977.

58. *Zavala County Sentinel*, July 14, 1977.

59. *Zavala County Sentinel*, July 21and October 13, 1977.

60. *Zavala County Sentinel*, October 27, 1977.

61. *Zavala County Sentinel*, November 24 and December 22, 1977.

62. *Zavala County Sentinel*, February 17, June 9, and August 11, 1977.

63. *Zavala County Sentinel*, June 30, 1977.

64. Interview, Luz Gutiérrez, June 5, 1997.

65. *Zavala County Sentinel*, June 30, 1977.

66. *Zavala County Sentinel*, October 13, 1977.

67. *Zavala County Sentinel*, November 3 and October 13, 1977.

68. *Zavala County Sentinel*, February 23, 1978.

69. *Zavala County Sentinel*, March 2, 1978.

70. Jean Pierre Barricelli, *Niccolo Machiavelli* (Woodbury, N.Y.: Barron's Educational Press, 1975).

71. *Zavala County Sentinel*, March 2, 1978.

72. *Zavala County Sentinel*, March 30, 1978.

73. Palomo interview.

74. José Angel Gutiérrez, undated letter to Jorge Bustamonte, from the personal papers of José Angel Gutiérrez, University of Texas Library, Benson Latin American Collections, Austin; *Zavala County Sentinel* April 16, 1978.

75. Interviews with José Mata, Arturo Gonzales, and Palomo; *Zavala County Sentinel*, April 6, 1978.

76. *Zavala County Sentinel*, October 5 and October 12, 1978.

77. *Zavala County Sentinel*, January 19 and February 9, 1978; Gutiérrez interview.

78. Gutiérrez interview.

79. *Zavala County Sentinel*, February 9 and May 11, 1978.

80. Interview, Rodolfo (Rudy) Espinosa Jr., September 21, 1994.
81. *Zavala County Sentinel*, November 9, 1978.
82. *Zavala County Sentinel*, November 23 and November 30, 1978.
83. *Zavala County Sentinel*, November 23, 1978.
84. Ignacio Garcia, *United We Win: The Rise and Fall of La Raza Unida Party* 219.
85. *Zavala County Sentinel*, February 23, March 16, and April 6, 1978.
86. *Zavala County Sentinel*, April 20, 1978.
87. *Zavala County Sentinel*, May 25, July 20, and April 13, 1978.
88. *Zavala County Sentinel*, April 24 and May 11, 1978.
89. *Zavala County Sentinel*, June 8, 15, and 29, 1978.
90. *Zavala County Sentinel*, September 7 and November 23, 1978.
91. For an overview of RUP's acercamiento with Mexico Tatcho Mindiola and Max Martinez, eds., *Chicano-Mexicano Relations* (Houston: Mexican American Studies Program, 1986).
92. *Zavala County Sentinel*, November 23, 1978.
93. Ibid.

Chapter 8. Revolution Through Education

1. For a detailed examination of the Winter Garden Project, see Armando Navarro, *Mexican American Youth Organization: Avant-Garde of the Chicano Movement in Texas* (Austin: University of Texas Press, 1995), 190–97.
2. Edward Murguía, *Assimilation, Colonialism, and the Mexican-American People* (Austin, Texas: Center for Mexican-American Studies, 1975), 6.
3. Robert Blauner, *Racial Oppression In America* (New York: Haryoce Associates, 1964), chap. 3; Murguía, *Assimilation, Colonialism, and the Mexican-American People*, 78–79.
4. John Staples Shockley, *Chicano Revolt in a Texas Town* (Notre Dame, Ind.: University of Notre Dame Press, 1974), 117.
5. Ibid.
6. Ibid., 118.
7. Navarro, *Mexican American Youth Organization*, 132–48; interview, Severita Lara, September 20, 1994.
8. Lara interview; interview, José Angel Gutiérrez, February 25, 1995; Herbert Hirsch and Armando Gutiérrez, "Learning to be Militant: Ethnic Identity and the Development of Political Militancy in a Chicano Community," paper prepared for R & E Research Associates, San Francisco, 1977, 19.
9. Shockley, *Chicano Revolt*, 141; Joyce A. Langenegger, "The School as a Political Tool: A Case Study of Crystal City, Texas," master's thesis, Department of Education, Baylor University, Austin, Texas, December 1993, 4.
10. *San Antonio Light*, January 25, 1970; Gutiérrez interview.
11. Shockley, *Chicano Revolt*, 150.
12. Minutes, Crystal City Independent School District, April 12, 1970; Shockley, *Chicano Revolt*, 153.

13. *Militant* (newspaper of the Socialist Workers' Party), June 19, 1970.

14. *Zavala County Sentinel,* April 16, 1970.

15. Interview, Arturo Gonzales, May 22, 1973; interview, Luz Gutiérrez, May 9, 1973.

16. Antonio Camejo, *La Raza Unida Party in Texas* (New York: Pathfinder Press, 1970), 6; *Zavala County Sentinel,* May 14, 1970.

17. Paulo Freire, *Pedagogy of the Oppressed* (New York: Seabury Press, 1973), 82.

18. Langenegger, "School as a Political Tool," 4; *San Antonio Light,* April 28, 1970; *Laredo Times,* May 20, 1970; *Militant,* June 19, 1970.

19. *La Verdad,* April 1970.

20. *Laredo Times,* May 20, 1970; Shockley, *Chicano Revolt,* 166; *San Antonio Express,* August 28, and September 18, 1970.

21. *Corpus Christi Caller Times,* November 18, 1969; *Militant,* September 19, 1970.

22. *Militant,* June 19, 1970.

23. *Zavala County Sentinel,* June 11, 1970; Shockley, *Chicano Revolt,* 161. For more specific information on educational changes, see Shockley, *Chicano Revolt,* 161–74.

24. *San Antonio Express,* March 18, 1970; Shockley, *Chicano Revolt,* 143.

25. Armando Navarro, "El Partido de la Raza Unida in Crystal City," doctoral dissertation, Department of Political Science, University of California, Riverside, 1974, 487.

26. George L. Sanchez, "The Crystal City School Boycott," unpublished paper, 1969, Memorial Library, Cristal, 19.

27. *San Antonio Express,* September 16, 1970; Langenegger, "School as a Political Tool," 122.

28. *San Antonio Express,* September 10, 1970.

29. Luz Gutiérrez interview.

30. *San Antonio Express,* September 22, 1970; Langenegger, "School as a Political Tool," 125.

31. Langenegger, "School as a Political Tool," 125; *Zavala County Sentinel,* May 6, 1971.

32. Minutes, Crystal City Independent School District, May 10, 1971; Langenegger, "School as a Political Tool," 126.

33. *Zavala County Sentinel,* November 18, 1971.

34. Minutes, Crystal City Independent School District, August 16, 1970; Interview, Angel Noe González, May 25, 1973; *San Antonio Express,* August 22, 1970.

35. Langenegger, "School as a Political Tool," 138.

36. Ibid.

37. Shockley, *Chicano Revolt,* 162.

38. Gutiérrez interview; interview, Ventura Gonzalez, September 20, 1994.

39. Ignacio Garcia, *United We Win: The Rise and Fall of La Raza Unida Party* (Tucson, Ariz.: Mexican American Studies Research Center, 1989), 62. For a good synthesis of the literature on political socialization in the United States

as it applies to Mejicano youth, see Herbert Hirsch and Armando Gutiérrez, "Learning To Be Militant: Ethnic Identity and Development of Political Militance in a Chicano Community," paper prepared for R & E Research Associates, San Francisco, 1977.

40. Minutes, Crystal City Independent School District, July 13, 1970; *New Yorker*, April 17, 1971; Navarro, "El Partido de la Raza Unida," 487–90; Armando Trujillo, "Community Empowerment and Bilingual/Bicultural Education: A Study of the Movimiento in a South Texas Town," doctoral dissertation, University of Texas, Austin, August 1993, 68.

41. Shockley, *Chicano Revolt*, 185; Minutes, Crystal City Independent School District, October 5, 1970.

42. *Zavala County Sentinel*, October 8, 1970; Minutes, Crystal City Independent School District, October 5, 1970; Shockley, *Chicano Revolt*, 186.

43. Shockley, *Chicano Revolt*, 186.

44. Ibid., 187.

45. José Angel Gutiérrez, "Aztlán: Chicano Revolt in the Winter Garden Area," unpublished paper, Crystal City, 1970, 15–16, from the personal papers of José Angel Gutiérrez, University of Texas Library, Benson Latin American Collections, Austin; *Javelin-Herald* (student newspaper, Crystal City High School), February 12, 1971.

46. Angel Noe González interview, May 25, 1973.

47. Navarro, "El Partido de la Raza Unida," 490; Angel Noe Gonzalez, Letter to the Editor, *Zavala County Sentinel*, March 21, 1971.

48. Robert Hardgrave and Santiago Hinojosa, *The Politics of Bilingual Education: A Study of Four Southwest Texas Communities* (Manchaca, Texas: Sterling Swift Publishing, 1975); Ambrosio Melendrez, "A Rationale for Educational Change Through Political Action in a Predominantly Chicano School District," master's thesis, Department of Education, California State University, Sacramento, May 30, 1972; Walter Elwood Smith and Douglas Foley, *The Transition of Multiethnic Schooling in Model Town, Texas: 1930–1969*, prepared for the U.S. Office of Education, Report NIE Project No. R020825 and No. 3.3-4003, Washington D.C., 1972, 158.

49. Shockley, *Chicano Revolt*, 163.

50. Melendrez, "A Rationale for Educational Change."

51. *La Verdad*, September 16, 1970.

52. Interview, Roberto Fernandez, May 16, 1973; Shockley, *Chicano Revolt*, 164.

53. Shockley, *Chicano Revolt*, 164; *Zavala County Sentinel*, April 16, 1970.

54. Gutiérrez interview; Calvin Trillin, *New Yorker*, April 17, 1971; Shockley, *Chicano Revolt*, 165.

55. *San Antonio Light*, October 10, 1971. The clenched fist was a regular gesture among a variety of activists who were critical of the liberal capitalist system and sought its transformation either by reform or revolution. It was especially popular among Chicano and black power activists and became highly controversial when it was used by two black athletes as they stood on the medal platform at the 1968 Olympics in Mexico City.

56. Gutiérrez interview.

57. *Zavala County Sentinel*, March 25, 1971.

58. Interview, Angel Noe González, August 28, 1997; Garcia, *United We Win*, 63; Minutes, Crystal City Independent School District, February 8, 1971.

59. Minutes, Crystal City Independent School District, March 15, 1971; Langenegger, "School as a Political Tool," 133.

60. *Zavala County Sentinel*, March 25, April 1, May 25, and May 30, 1991; Gonzalez interview; *San Antonio Express*, May 20, 1971.

61. *San Antonio Express*, May 21, 1971; interview, Angel Noe González, August 18, 1997.

62. Crystal City Citizens Committee, Letter to the Editor, *Zavala County Sentinel*, July 15, 1971.

63. Shockley, *Chicano Revolt*, 172.

64. Langenegger, "School as a Political Tool," 136; interview, Amancio Cantu, September 14, 1975.

65. G. P. Bookout, Letter to the Editor, "Crystal City Coverage," *San Antonio Express*, July 21, 1971.

66. Interviews with Fernandez; Cantu; and Angel Noe González, May 1973.

67. Interviews with Fernandez; Guin Casey, April 1, 1973; and Cantu.

68. Amancio Cantu, Letter to the Editor, *Zavala County Sentinel*, July 1, 1971; *Corpus Christi Times*, August 23, 1971.

69. *Zavala County Sentinel*, July 22 and August 28, 1971; Langenegger, "School as a Political Tool," 197.

70. Interview, R. C. Tate, April 3, 1973; *Zavala County Sentinel*, September 2, 1971.

71. Tate interview; *Corpus Christi Times*, August 23, 1971.

72. *Zavala County Sentinel*, July 29 and August 19, 1971.

73. *Zavala County Sentinel*, September 2, September 9, and November 11, 1971.

74. *Zavala County Sentinel*, April 6 and April 20, 1972.

75. *Zavala County Sentinel*, January 13, February 3, and May 4, 1972.

76. *La Verdad*, September 1971; "Opportunities for Youth in Education," *O.E. Magazine*, 1972–1973, published by the U.S. Office of Economic Opportunity, Washington, D.C.

77. *La Verdad*, September 1971 and March 15, 1972.

78. Langenegger, "School as a Political Tool," 141; Fernandez interview.

79. Langenegger, "School as a Political Tool," 200.

80. *Zavala County Sentinel*, July 20, August 17, August 31, November 30, and December 7, 1972.

81. *Zavala County Sentinel*, December 21, 1972, and January 18 and March 22, 1973.

82. Armando L. Trujillo, "Community Empowerment," 69.

83. *Zavala County Sentinel*, February 1 and February 8, 1973.

84. Interviews with Cantu, and Angel Noe González, August 1997.

85. *Zavala County Sentinel*, April 6, 1973; *San Antonio Express*, April 6 and April 7, 1973.

86. Langenegger, "School as a Political Tool," 191; *Zavala County Sentinel*, April 5, 1973.

87. *Chicano Times*, April 26, 1973; Joan Moore and Harry Pachon, *Hispanics in the United States* (Englewood Cliff, N.J.: Prentice-Hall, 1985), 150.

88. *Corpus Christi Caller*, June 24, 1975; Gutiérrez interview; *Zavala County Sentinel*, October 4, 1973.

89. Cantu, graduation speech, May 31, 1973; *Zavala County Sentinel*, April 31 and April 26, 1973.

90. *Corpus Christi Caller*, June 23, 1975; *Zavala County Sentinel*, January 30, 1975, October 4, 1973, and September 5, 1974.

91. *Zavala County Sentinel*, September 5, 1974.

92. *Zavala County Sentinel*, October 25, 1973; *Corpus Christi Caller*, June 23, 1975; *Uvalde Leader News*, June 23, 1975.

93. *Uvalde Leader News*, June 23, 1975.

94. *Zavala County Sentinel*, January 30 and April 3, 1975.

95. *Zavala County Sentinel*, September 12, 1974, and December 6, 1973.

96. *Zavala County Sentinel*, August 29, 1974.

97. *Zavala County Sentinel*, January 1, 1975; *Corpus Christi Caller*, June 23, 1975.

98. *Zavala County Sentinel*, September 26, 1974; *Corpus Christi Caller*, June 24, 1975.

99. *Corpus Christi Caller*, June 24, 1975.

100. Langenegger, "School as a Political Tool," 241–42.

101. Brooks Peterson, "Crystal City Schools: Major Point of Change," *Corpus Christi Caller*, June 23, 1975.

102. *Corpus Christi Caller*, June 24, 1975.

103. *Zavala County Sentinel*, October, 16, October 23, and November, 13, 1975.

104. Trujillo, "Community Empowerment," 88.

105. Ibid.

106. *Zavala County Sentinel*, September 2, 1976, August 25, 1977, and August 28, 1980; interview, Viviana Santiago Cavada, September 17, 1994.

107. *Zavala County Sentinel*, November 16, and October 11, 1979; Trujillo, "Community Empowerment," 95.

108. *Zavala County Sentinel*, June 1 and August 10, 1978.

109. *Zavala County Sentinel*, November 29, 1979.

Chapter 9. Struggle for Economic Empowerment

1. For more information about Cristal's internal colonialism and internal colonialism in general, see Armando Navarro, *Mexican American Youth Organization: Avant-Garde of the Chicano Movement in Texas* (Austin: University of Texas Press, 1995), 190–97, for an analysis of MAYO and the Winter Garden Project;

Robert Blauner, *Racial Oppression in America* (New York: Harper & Row, 1972), 83, 190–97.

2. Navarro, *Mexican American Youth Organization*, 190–97.

3. Ibid.

4. Interview, José Angel Gutiérrez, June 23, 1973.

5. José Angel Gutiérrez, "Aztlán: Chicano Revolt in the Winter Garden," *La Raza* 1 (1971): 34–35.

6. Gutiérrez interview.

7. José Angel Gutiérrez, "How It Is in South Texas," *People and Land* 1 (Summer 1973).

8. Industrias Mejicanas, information booklet, September 15, 1972; Armando Navarro, "El Partido de la Raza Unida in Crystal City: A Peaceful Revolution," doctoral dissertation, Department of Political Science, University of California, Riverside, 1974, p. 403.

9. Industrias Mejicanas, Articles of Incorporation, January 1970; Interview, Viviana Santiago Cavada, May 28, 1973.

10. *Zavala County Sentinel*, January 29, 1970, and March 27, 1975.

11. Interview, J. A. Gutiérrez, July 21, 1995.

12. José Garza, "La Raza Unida in Crystal City: A study of a Chicano Third-Party Movement," master's thesis, Trinity University, San Antonio, Texas, 1972.

13. Antonio Camejo, "A Report from Aztlán: Texas Chicanos Forge Own Political Power," in Edward Simon, ed., *Pain and Promise: The Chicano Today* (New York: New American Library, 1972), 242.

14. Michael V. Miller and James D. Preston, "Vertical Ties and the Redistribution of Power in Crystal City," *Social Science Quarterly* 53 (March 1973): 772–84.

15. John Staples Shockley, *Chicano Revolt in a Texas Town* (Notre Dame, Ind.: University of Notre Dame Press, 1974), 140.

16. Camejo, "Report from Aztlán," p. 243; Interview, J. A. Gutiérrez, April 24, 1973.

17. *Zavala County Sentinel*, January 15, 1970.

18. Gutiérrez, "Aztlán: Chicano Revolt," p. 5.

19. Industrias Mejicanas, Inc., "Economic Development in Crystal City," undated proposal; *La Verdad*, February 1970.

20. Navarro, "El Partido de la Raza Unida," p. 407; interview, Viviana Santiago Cavada, September 17, 1994.

21. *La Verdad*, January 19, 1971.

22. 1994 Cavada interview.

23. Ibid.

24. *Zavala County Sentinel*, May 28, 1973.

25. *La Verdad*, October 29, 1971.

26. Navarro, "El Partido de la Raza Unida," p. 409; Industrias Mejicanas, Program Evaluation, September 15, 1972; Interview, José "Monche" Mata, May 11, 1973.

27. 1973 Cavada interview.

28. Mata interview.
29. 1994 Cavada interview; *Zavala County Sentinel*, January 29, 1970.
30. Interview, J. A. Gutiérrez, February 25, 1995.
31. *Zavala County Sentinel*, June 10, 1976; 1994 Cavada interview.
32. *Zavala County Sentinel*, October 2, 1975; Gutiérrez interview, February 25, 1995.
33. *Zavala County Sentinel*, December 12, 1973, and September 28, 1972; 1994 Cavada interview;
34. Proposal for Community Development Corporation by the Zavala County Economic Development Corporation, 1976, from the personal papers of José Angel Gutiérrez, University of Texas Library, Benson Latin American Collections, Austin.
35. Interview, Angel Noe González, June 26, 1995.
36. "After the Revolution in Crystal," *Texas Observer*, July 5, 1974.
37. Ibid.; Angel Noe González interview, July 26, 1995.
38. Angel Noe González interview, July 26, 1995.
39. Articles of Incorporation, De Zavala Businessmen's Association, Inc., 1971; Interviews with Gutiérrez, February 25, 1995, and Angel Noe González, July 26, 1995.
40. Proposal, "The Local Development Corporation: The Winter Garden Development Corporation," no date, Gutiérrez papers.
41. 1973 Cavada interview; Angel Noe González interview, July 26, 1995.
42. Personal letter from O. H. De Russy Jr. to Angel Noe González, February 6, 1974, Gutiérrez papers; Angel Noe González interview, July 26, 1995; *Zavala County Sentinel*, April 19, 1973.
43. Interview, Arturo Gonzales, September 15, 1994; Richard Schaffer, "Brown Power: Small City in Texas Is a Testing Ground of the Chicano Movement," *Wall Street Journal*, September 5, 1975; interview, Gutiérrez, July 26, 1995; *Arkansas Gazette*, June 16, 1974.
44. *Wall Street Journal*, September 5, 1975.
45. *Arkansas Gazette*, June 16, 1974.
46. Angel Noe González interview, July 26, 1995.
47. *Zavala County Sentinel*, March 3, 1977; Rick Casey, "Crystal City Misconduct Trial, Justice Undone," *Texas Observer*, March 25, 1977.
48. Interview, Angel Noe González, August 18, 1997.
49. Casey, "Crystal City Misconduct Trial."
50. Interview, Gutiérrez, February 25, 1995; *Alice-Echo News*, June 20, 1972.
51. *Zavala County Sentinel*, June 22, 1972; *Alice-Echo News*, June 20, 1972; *San Antonio Express*, June 27, 1972.
52. *Zavala County Sentinel*, July 6, 1972; *Corpus Christi Caller*, July 21, 1972.
53. Richard Beene, "Mexico Offers Aid to Crystal City," *Corpus Christi Caller*, July 21, 1972.
54. For an analysis of the Gutiérrez–Arturo Gonzales power struggles, see Ignacio Garcia, *United We Win: The Rise and Fall of La Raza Unida Party* (Tucson, Ariz.: Mexican American Studies Research Center, 1989): 91–116.

55. *La Verdad,* November 30, 1972; *Zavala County Sentinel,* November 23, 1972.
56. Angel Noe González interview, July 26, 1995.
57. Interview, Rudy Palomo, May 9, 1973.
58. *La Verdad,* November 30, 1972; interview, Eddie Treviño, April 20, 1973; interview, Lupe Cortinas, April 10, 1973; *Zavala County Sentinel,* February 15, 1973; Schaffer, "Brown Power."
59. Beene, "Mexico Offers Aid."
60. Schaffer, "Brown Power."
61. Gutiérrez interview.
62. Angel Noe González interview, July 26, 1995; 1994 Cavada interview; Luz Gutiérrez interview.
63. 1994 Cavada interview.
64. *Zavala County Sentinel,* September 9, 1976; John Muir, *Texas Observer,* October 15, 1976; Rough draft, proposal, ZCED Corporation, no date, Gutiérrez papers.
65. Rough draft, proposal, ZCED Corporation, no date, Gutiérrez papers; Lisa Spann, "Zavala County Co-op: Waylaid Again," *Texas Observer,* September 22, 1978; ZCEDC Annual Report (1976–1977).
66. Comments by the State of Texas Regarding the Proposed CSA Operational Grant of $1.5 million to ZCEDC, January 7, 1977, sent to José Angel Gutiérrez by the Office of the Governor, Gutiérrez papers; *San Antonio Express,* August 14, 1975.
67. Schaffer, "Brown Power."
68. ZCEDC Annual Report, no date, 4, Gutiérrez papers.
69. ZCEDC Annual Report (1976–1977), 6, Gutiérrez papers.
70. *Texas Observer,* October 15, 1976.
71. Letter from Louis Ramirez to José Angel Gutiérrez, October 18, 1976, Gutiérrez papers; Letter from Ramirez to Gutiérrez, Gutiérrez papers.
72. *Dallas Morning News,* December 29, 1976; *Militant,* February 26, 1977; *Zavala County Sentinel,* September 9, 1976; Letter from OMB to Governor Briscoe, August 25, 1976.
73. Letter from Governor Briscoe to President Ford, September 1, 1976.
74. *Daily Texan,* October 1, 1976; *San Antonio Express,* September 25, 1976.
75. RUP resolution, RUP State Convention, September 19, 1976; *Texas Observer,* October 15, 1976; *Militant,* February 26, 1977.
76. *Texas Observer,* September 22, 1978.
77. *Militant,* January 28, 1977.
78. RUP resolution, RUP State Convention, September 1976; *Texas Observer,* October 15, 1976; Lisa Spann, "Zavala County Co-op"; John Muir, *Texas Observer,* October 15, 1976.
79. *Zavala County Sentinel,* October 7, November 4, November 25, and December 23, 1976; *Dallas Morning News,* December 29, 1976; *Zavala County Sentinel,* January 13, 1977.
80. *Militant,* February 26, 1977.

81. *Texas Observer,* March 11, 1978; Angel Noe González interview, July 26, 1995.

82. *Texas Observer,* September 22, 1978.

83. Ibid.; *Journal of Commerce,* March 17, 1978.

84. Letter from Eduardo Gutiérrez to José Angel Gutiérrez, July 1, 1977, Gutiérrez papers.

85. Letter from José Angel Gutiérrez to Mexican president José Lopez Pórtillo, September 27, 1978, Gutiérrez papers; *San Antonio Express,* October 23, 1977.

86. ZCEDC board minutes, November 1, 1977, Gutiérrez papers.

87. Ibid.

88. *Texas Observer,* September 22, 1978; *Corpus Christi Caller,* June 16, 1978.

89. *Texas Observer,* September 22, 1978.

90. *Corpus Christi Caller,* April 8, 1978; *San Antonio Light,* April 8, 1970; *Corpus Christi Caller,* June 17, 1978.

91. *Corpus Christi Caller,* June 17, 1978; *Zavala County Sentinel,* June 22, and September 21, 1978.

92. *Dallas Morning News,* November 12, 1978; *Zavala County Sentinel,* January 4, 1979.

93. Annual Report, Community Agency for Self-Help, no date (apparently 1979), Gutiérrez papers.

94. *Zavala County Sentinel,* March 13 and March 20, 1975.

95. *Zavala County Sentinel,* March 20, March 27, June 12, and August 21, 1975.

96. *Zavala County Sentinel,* October 16, 1975; Letter from William E. Greehey to Crystal mayor Arturo Gonzales, October 1975.

97. *Zavala County Sentinel,* October 16, 1975; *San Antonio Express,* October 16 and 20, 1975.

98. *Zavala County Sentinel,* November 6 and November 13, 1975; *San Antonio Express,* November 13, 1975.

99. *Corpus Christi Caller,* November 6, 1975.

100. *Zavala County Sentinel,* March 25 and April 28, 1976, and August 4, 1977.

101. *Zavala County Sentinel,* August 18, 1977; *San Antonio Light,* July 30, 1977; *Corpus Christi Caller,* July 30, 1977.

102. *Zavala County Sentinel,* August 18 and August 25, 1977.

103. *Zavala County Sentinel,* September 8, 1977; *Corpus Christi Caller,* September 3, 1977.

104. *Alice-Echo News,* September 23, 1977; *Corpus Christi Caller,* September 24, 1977.

105. *Corpus Christi Caller,* September 24, 1977

106. Ibid.

107. *Corpus Christi Caller,* September 22, 1977; John Yemma, "Crystal City Survives the Gas Stoppage," no date, no source, Gutiérrez papers; *Zavala County Sentinel,* October 13, 1977.

108. *Corpus Christi Caller,* October 12, 1977, and January 7, 1978.

109. Yemma, "Crystal City Survives the Gas Stoppage"; *Corpus Christi Caller,* December 12, 1977.
110. *Zavala County Sentinel,* February 7 and June 29, 1980.
111. *Zavala County Sentinel,* November 20, 1980.

Chapter 10. Quest for Social Change

1. For an examination of internal colonialism's external administration, see Robert Blauner, *Racial Oppression in America* (New York: Harper & Row, 1972), chap. 3.
2. Interview, Viviana Santiago Cavada, September 17, 1994.
3. For a thorough analysis of the pivotal leadership role CU played in promoting and guiding RUP's peaceful revolution, see Armando Navarro, *Mexican American Youth Organization: Avant-Garde of the Chicano Movement in Texas* (Austin: University of Texas Press, 1995).
4. *Zavala County Sentinel,* July 16, 1970.
5. *Zavala County Sentinel,* November 26 and December 3, 1970; *La Verdad,* December 15, 1970.
6. *Zavala County Sentinel,* December 3 and December 24, 1970.
7. Interviews with Juan Cotera, April 23, 1973, and Viviana Santiago Cavada, April 28, 1971.
8. *Zavala County Sentinel,* February 25 and July 8, 1971.
9. *Zavala County Sentinel,* July 8, 1991; interview, Cavada, May 28, 1973.
10. *Zavala County Sentinel,* July 8, 1971.
11. Interview, Cotera, May 23, 1973; *Zavala County Sentinel,* July 22, 1973.
12. Interview, Cotera, May 23, 1973.
13. *La Verdad,* April 6, 1971, and March 1973.
14. Navarro, "El Partido de la Raza Unida," 444.
15. Interview, Cotera, May 23, 1973.
16. Ibid.
17. *Zavala County Sentinel,* September 16, 1971.
18. Interview, Cotera, May 23, 1973.
19. *Zavala County Sentinel,* September 16, 1971, and June 7, 1973.
20. *Arkansas Gazette,* June 16, 1974.
21. *Corpus Christi Caller,* June 22, 1975.
22. Navarro, "El Partido de la Raza Unida," 435.
23. Interview, Cavada, May 28, 1973.
24. *Zavala County Sentinel,* May 18, 1971.
25. Interview, Eddie Treviño, May 20, 1973.
26. Ibid.; interview, Cavada, May 28, 1973.
27. Interview, Cavada, May 28, 1973.
28. Interview, Treviño, May 20, 1973.
29. *Zavala County Sentinel,* April 21, 1970; interview, Cavada, May 28, 1973.
30. Interview, Cavada, May 28, 1973.
31. *Zavala County Sentinel,* January 3, 1974.

32. *Zavala County Sentinel*, August 8, 1974.

33. *Zavala County Sentinel*, October 14, 1971.

34. Zavala County Health Committee, summary report of collected data and a model mental health program for the seven-county Winter Garden area, submitted to the Mental Health Outreach Committee, May 31, 1973; *La Verdad*, September 1971.

35. *Zavala County Sentinel*, December 23, 1971, and October 28, 1971.

36. Interview, Erasmo Andrade, May 16, 1973; Zavala County Health Committee, summary report.

37. Interview, J. A. Gutiérrez, June 2, 1973.

38. *Zavala County Sentinel*, September 21, and October 19, 1972.

39. Zavala County Health Committee, summary report on the Winter Garden area, May 22, 1973.

40. *Zavala County Sentinel*, February 8, 1973, and May 22, 1975.

41. Interview, Luz Gutiérrez, May 9, 1973; "Vida y Salud Health Systems, Inc., Crystal City, Texas, 1972–1992, Twentieth Anniversary," brochure, presented at 1993 annual board meeting; interview, Cavada, May 28, 1973.

42. *Zavala County Sentinel*, August 10, 1972.

43. Luz Gutiérrez interview, May 9, 1973; *Zavala County Sentinel*, October 5, 1972.

44. *Militant*, October 27, 1972.

45. *Zavala County Sentinel*, November 2, 1972; letter from Dr. Jorge Prieto to Luz Gutiérrez, September 17, 1972, from the personal papers of José Angel Gutiérrez, University of Texas Library, Benson Latin American Collections, Austin.

46. Letter from Luz Gutiérrez to Dr. Jorge Prieto, September 17, 1972, Gutiérrez papers.

47. *Zavala County Sentinel*, November 2, 1972; *Militant*, October 13, 1972; interview, J. A. Gutiérrez, February 25, 1995; interview, Angel Noe González, July 26, 1995; David S. Broder, *The Changing of the Guard: Power and Leadership in America* (New York: Simon and Schuster, 1980), 297.

48. *Zavala County Sentinel*, November 22, 1973. The *Sentinel*'s story quoted from the Wood story in the *San Antonio Express News*, which appeared in that paper on November 18, 1973.

49. Interviews with Luz Gutiérrez, May 9, 1973, and Paul Rich, April 31, 1973.

50. Rich interview.

51. Vida y Salud twentieth anniversary brochure; *Zavala County Sentinel*, July 26, 1973.

52. *Zavala County Sentinel*, August 22 and May 9, 1974.

53. Vida y Salud twentieth anniversary brochure; *Zavala County Sentinel*, October 2, 1975.

54. *La Verdad*, September 1971.

55. Interview, Cavada, August 16, 1995.

56. Steve Thomas, "Rich for the Poor: How One Lawyer Helps Chicanos in Their Struggle to Survive Anglo Justice," *American Bar Association Journal*, 1975.

57. Interview, Paul Rich, May 31, 1973.

58. Ibid.

59. Thomas, "Rich for the Poor."

60. Navarro, "El Partido de la Raza Unida," 459; Information sheet, Crystal City Credit Union, no date.

61. *La Verdad*, September 1971.

62. Ibid.; Navarro, "El Partido de la Raza Unida," 459.

63. Interviews, Luz Gutiérrez, August 16, 1995; and Cavada, August 16, 1995.

64. *La Verdad*, February 18, 1971; *Zavala County Sentinel*, February 4, 1971.

65. Minutes, Obreros Unidos Independientes, October 23, 1970; *La Verdad*, November 1973.

66. Navarro, "El Partido de la Raza Unida," 466.

67. *Zavala County Sentinel*, October 11, 1973.

68. Ibid.; *Zavala County Sentinel*, November 1, 1973; Navarro, "El Partido de la Raza Unida," 469.

69. Navarro, "El Partido de la Raza Unida," 469–70; Thomas, "Rich for the Poor."

70. *Zavala County Sentinel*, December 9, 1971; interview, Reverend Sherrill Smith, September 23, 1994.

71. Sherrill Smith interviews, September 23, 1994 and April 4, 1973; *Zavala County Sentinel*, December 23, 1971.

72. *La Verdad*, January 24, 1972.

73. Interview, Smith, May 4, 1973.

74. *Zavala County Sentinel*, February 3, 1972; *San Antonio Express*, January 30, 1972.

75. *Zavala County Sentinel*, February 3, 1972.

76. Navarro, "El Partido de la Raza Unida," 464; *Zavala County Sentinel*, February 3, 1972; *San Antonio Express*, January 30, 1972.

77. Navarro, *Mexican American Youth Organization*, chap. 7.

78. *Zavala County Sentinel*, May 27, 1971, October 26 and November 23, 1972; interview, J. A. Gutiérrez, February 25, 1995.

79. Navarro, *Mexican American Youth Organization*, chap. 7; Diary, José Angel Gutiérrez, Gutiérrez papers; Navarro, *Mexican American Youth Organization*, chap. 4.

80. *Zavala County Sentinel*, April 12, 1973, and April 11, 1974; Navarro, "El Partido de la Raza," 319.

81. *Zavala County Sentinel*, November 7, 1974.

82. *Corpus Christi Caller*, November 18, 1990; interview, José Luis Balderas, November 22, 1995.

83. Interview, Cavada, May 22, 1995.

84. *Zavala County Sentinel*, September 2, 1976; January 6 and April 21, 1977; Vida y Salud twentieth anniversary brochure.

85. *Zavala County Sentinel*, January 25, 1979.

86. Interview, Cavada, August 16, 1995; *Zavala County Sentinel*, February 24, 1977.

87. Crystal City Independent School District, "Ten Years of Struggle."

88. *Zavala County Sentinel,* April 12, 1979.

89. *Zavala County Sentinel,* November 9, 1978, and April 12, 1979.

Chapter 11. Gutiérrez's Departure: The End of an Era

1. Ignacio Garcia, *United We Win: The Rise and Fall of La Raza Unida Party* (Tucson, Ariz.: Mexican American Studies Research Center, 1989), 219.

2. Interview, José Angel Gutiérrez, February 25, 1995.

3. Ibid.; Garcia, *United We Win,* 219–32.

4. *Zavala County Sentinel,* March 15 and March 22, 1979.

5. *Zavala County Sentinel,* January 11, 1979.

6. Ibid.; *San Antonio Express,* January 18, 1979.

7. *Zavala County Sentinel,* January 11, 1979.

8. *Zavala County Sentinel,* January 25, 1979.

9. *San Antonio Express,* February 25, 1979; *Zavala County Sentinel,* February 7, 1979.

10. Letter to the Editor, *Zavala County Sentinel,* February 1, 1979; where the letter writer's name would have appeared, the paper noted "name withheld on request," an unusual move for a newspaper.

11. Ibid.

12. *San Antonio Express,* February 25, 1979; *Zavala County Sentinel,* February 1, and February 8, 1979.

13. *Zavala County Sentinel,* February 8, 1979.

14. Ibid; *Zavala County Sentinel,* February 15, 1979.

15. *San Antonio Express,* February 25, 1979.

16. *Zavala County Sentinel,* March 1, 1979.

17. *Zavala County Sentinel,* March 8 and March 15, 1979.

18. *Zavala County Sentinel,* March 15, 1979.

19. *Zavala County Sentinel,* March 22, February 8, February 15, and March 22, 1979.

20. *Zavala County Sentinel,* April 5, 1979.

21. Interview, Rodolfo (Rudy) Espinosa Jr., September 23, 1994; *Zavala County Sentinel,* March 29, 1979.

22. *Zavala County Sentinel,* April 12, 1979.

23. *Zavala County Sentinel,* April 26, 1979.

24. *Zavala County Sentinel,* August 9, 1979.

25. *Zavala County Sentinel,* August 16, and August 9, 1979.

26. *Zavala County Sentinel,* August 9 and 16, 1979.

27. *Zavala County Sentinel,* November 8 and 22, 1979.

28. *Zavala County Sentinel,* November 22, 1979.

29. *Zavala County Sentinel,* November 29, 1979.

30. *Zavala County Sentinel,* May 10, 1979.

31. *Zavala County Sentinel,* May 24, 1979.

32. Gutiérrez interview.

33. *Zavala County Sentinel,* August 9 and 16, 1979; *San Antonio Express,* August 30, 1979.

34. *San Antonio Express,* August 30, 1979.

35. *Zavala County Sentinel,* September 6, 1979.

36. *Zavala County Sentinel,* September 6 and 20, 1979.

37. José Angel Gutiérrez, *The Making of a Chicano Militant: Lessons from Cristal* (Madison: University of Wisconsin Press, 1998).

38. Gutiérrez interview; Gutiérrez, *Making of a Chicano Militant.*

39. *Zavala County Sentinel,* January 24, 1980.

40. *Zavala County Sentinel,* February 7 and June 26, 1980.

41. *Zavala County Sentinel,* May 8, 1980.

42. Ibid.

43. *Zavala County Sentinel,,* May 15, 1980; Gutiérrez interview.

44. Gutiérrez interview.

45. *Zavala County Sentinel,* January 3, 1980.

46. *Zavala County Sentinel,* January 10, 1980.

47. *Zavala County Sentinel,* January 31, 1980.

48. *Zavala County Sentinel,* April 10 and April 3, 1980.

49. *Zavala County Sentinel,* April 10, 1980.

50. Ibid.; *Zavala County Sentinel,* April 17 and 24, 1980.

51. *Zavala County Sentinel,* April 24 and May 10, 1980.

52. *Zavala County Sentinel,* June 19, 1980.

53. Gutiérrez, *Making of a Chicano Militant.*

54. *Zavala County Sentinel,* November 6, 1980.

55. *Zavala County Sentinel,* October 30, 1980.

56. Ibid.

57. *Zavala County Sentinel,* November 6, November 20, and December 11, 1980.

58. *Zavala County Sentinel,* November 13 and 27, 1980.

59. *Zavala County Sentinel,* November 27, 1980.

60. *Zavala County Sentinel,* December 4 and 11, 1980.

61. *San Antonio Express,* February 14, 1981.

62. *Zavala County Sentinel,* February 19, 1981; *San Antonio Express,* February 18, 1981.

63. *San Antonio Express,* February 18, 1981, and *Zavala County Sentinel,* February 19, 1981.

64. *Zavala County Sentinel,* February 19, 1981; Interview, Pablo Avila, September 16, 1995.

65. *San Antonio Express,* February 18, 1981; *Zavala County Sentinel,* February 26, 1981.

66. *Corpus Christi Caller,* February 27, 1981

67. Interview, Severita Lara, September 20, 1994.

68. *Corpus Christi Caller,* February 22, 1981.

69. Interview, Rudy Espinosa, September 21, 1994.

70. Interview, Jack Kingsberry, September 19, 1994; Avila interview.

71. *Zavala County Sentinel,* March 15, 1981.

Epilogue: The Unfinished Experiment

1. Arthur J. Rubel, *Across the Tracks: Mexican Americans in a Texas City* (Austin: University of Texas Press, 1966), 119–39.

2. Proposal to Texas Rural Communities, Inc., prepared by Crystal City, Texas, July 26, 1994.

3. Interview, Victoria Contreras, employee of the Texas Work Force Commission, July 9, 1997.

4. Proposal to Texas Rural Communities, Inc.

5. *Zavala County Sentinel,* June 22 and July 6, 1994.

6. Interview, Dale Barker, July 30, 1997.

7. Proposal to Texas Rural Communities, Inc.

8. City of Cristal, Needs Assessment Survey, undated.

9. Interview, Benito Perez, assistant superintendent, Crystal City Independent School District, July 10, 1997.

10. "Zavala," booklet prepared by Zavala County, p. 271.

11. Interview, Dale Barker, September 16, 1994.

12. Crystal City Independent School District, "Student Performance Outcomes," follow-up accreditation report, undated but probably 1993.

13. Crystal City, "The Crystal City/Zavala County Vision Statement," 1994.

14. Perez interview.

15. Interview, Miguel Delgado, August, 19, 1997.

16. Interview, Rodolfo Espinosa Jr., September 21, 1994.

17. Armando Navarro, "The Postmortem Politics of the Chicano Movement," *Perspectives in Mexican American Studies,* vol. 6 (September 1997).

18. Interview, José Angel Gutiérrez, September, 13, 1997.

19. For a critical assessment of liberal capitalism see Michael Parenti, *Democracy for the Few,* 6th ed. (New York: St. Martin's, 1995).

20. Robert A. Dahl, *Preface to Democratic Theory* (Chicago: University of Chicago Press, 1950).

21. For an excellent overview of the elite/pluralist theory debate see Janet A. Flammang et al., *American Politics in a Changing World* (Pacific Grove, Calif.: Brooks/Cole, 1990), 138–69.

22. Michael V. Miller, "Chicano Community Control in South Texas: Problems and Prospects," *Journal of Ethnic Studies,* 3 (Fall 1975): 82.

23. Robert S. Lorch, *State and Local Politics: The Great Entanglement* (Englewood Cliffs, N.J.: Prentice-Hall, 1989, 254.

24. See Parenti, *Democracy for the Few.*

25. Lorch, *State and Local Politics,* 254.

26. David C. Saffell, *State and Local Government: Politics and Public Policies* (New York: McGraw-Hill, 1990), 216.

27. Clinton L. Rossiter, *Parties and Politics in America* (Ithaca, N.Y.: Cornell University Press, 1960), 3.

28. Steven J. Rosenstone, Roy L. Behr, and Edward H. Lazarus, *Third Par-*

ties in America: Citizen Failure to Major Party Failure (Princeton, N.J.: Princeton University Press, 1984), 8.

29. Eric Hoffer, *The True Believer* (New York: Harper & Row, 1951), 119–37.

30. Ibid., 105–6.

31. Quoted in E. H. Carr, *Studies in Revolution* (New York: Grosett & Dunlap, 1964), 149.

32. Robert Michels, *Political Parties: A Sociological Study of the Oligarchical Tendencies of Modern Democracy* (1915; reprint, New York: Free Press, 1962), 70.

33. For an examination on pluralism see Dahl, *Preface to Democratic Theory,* and for elite and class theory analysis see C. Wright Mills, *The Power Elite* (Oxford, England: Oxford University Press, 1956), or G. William Domhoff, *Who Rules America?* (Englewood Cliffs, N.J.: Prentice-Hall, 1967).

34. Franz Fanon, *The Wretched of the Earth* (New York: Grove Press, 1963), and Albert Memmi, *The Colonizer and the Colonized* (Boston: Beacon, 1965).

35. State of California, "K–12 Graded Public School Enrollment by Ethnicity: History and Projections," Department of Finance, Sacramento, October 1993.

36. Interview, Xavier Hermosillo, July 30, 1997.

37. Statement of Glenn Spencer, president, Voices of Citizens Together, July 30, 1996, World-Wide Web, *http://www.instanet.com:80/ñvct/navaro.htn.*

38. Carey Goldberg, "U.S. Hispanics Struggling Hardest to Make Ends Meet, *Riverside Press-Enterprise,* January 30, 1997.

39. Ibid.

40. Navarro, "Postmortem Politics."

41. Ibid.

Index

Acuña, Rodolfo "Rudy," xvii, 80, 87–88, 107, 231
Addison, H. M., 23
Aguilar, Maria, 336
Alaniz, John, 34
Alcozer, Santos, 41, 42
Alianza Federal de Mercedes, 159, 212
Alinsky, Saul, 6, 30, 62, 86, 96, 229
Allee, Capt. A. Y. (Texas Ranger), 32, 35, 37, 38, 77
Almarez, Jesús, 289
Almendaris, Alex, 299
Almond, Gabriel, 5
Altshuler, Alan A., 11
Alvarado, José, 337
Alvarado, Ray, 130
Amistad (anti-RUP organization): board of directors, 108; establishment of, 108–9; county elections (1972), 112–15, 157; Perez as leader of, 112–15, 151; supporting independents, 124. *See also* Los Catorce (The Fourteen)
Anderson, Sam, 288–89
Andrade, Erasmo, 225, 232, 295–97, 297, 306
Andrade, Sally, 297
Anglo, defined, 381*n*2
Aragon, Joseph, 277
Aragon, Juan, 107
Arcos, Luz, 40
Aristotle, 8–9
Arroyo, Richard C., 173, 191
Atzlán (Chicano nation), xi, 159, 382*n*5
Avila, Carlos, 40, 46, 49, 209
Avila, Luis R., 205, 206, 327, 328
Avila, Maria Balboa, 130, 132
Avila, Pablo (Paul), 187, 193, 208, 211, 320, 321, 342

Avila, Richard, 130, 140
Avila, Rosaria T., 325, 329

Baca, Herman, 110, 202
Bachrach, Peter, 147, 148
Baldenegro, Salomon, 110
Balderas, José Luis: county elections candidacy (1974), 134; school board elections (1975), 140, 141; on Cuba trip, 166; on opposition to Gutiérrez, 169, 175, 185, 186; on city and school board elections (1976), 187; as leader of CU, 197, 198; Housing Authority director, 200; Urban Renewal Commission chair, 201
Banack, Emerson Jr., 226
Banter, Bert, 138
Baratz, Morton S., 147, 148
Barker, Dale (editor of *Zavala County Sentinel*): CASAA board of directors member, 40; on Gutiérrez Odessa speech, 67; on migration from Cristal, 71; "The Barker" column by, 75; on CU as a political machine, 95; on Amistad, 108; RUP opposition, 113; on elections (1973), 118; on elections (1974), 130, 132, 133, 135, 138; on life in Cuba, 165; on RUP Cuban delegation trip, 165; on split in RUP, 170, 174; on elections (1976), 188; on RUP primary (1976), 189; on CU alliance (1978), 205; on community participation, 222; on white migration, 238; on baiting Gutiérrez, 321; on elections (1979), 327; on Gutiérrez's leave of absence, 333; on elections (1980), 336; on Gutiérrez resignation, 341, 342
Barmea, Armando G., 108, 115
Barnett, Warren, 63

420

Cantu, Amancio (*continued*)
ing of superintendent, 178–79, 191, 248;
on bilingual education program, 247;
on free meals program for students,
247; and De Zavala Businessmen's Association, Inc., 262
Cantu, Mario, 131
CAP. *See* Community Action Program
(CAP)
capitalism: criticism of, 4, 5, 9; cooperative capitalism, 252–54; liberal capitalism, 353–55, 382*n6;* defined, 382*n6;* and
internal colonialism, 382–83*n1*
Carbonell, Carlos D., 165
Cárdenas, Antonio: city council candi-
dacy, 29, 36; economic reprisals after
election, 37–38, 43; city manager dis-
cord, 43
Cardenas, Blandina, 107
Cardenas, José Angel, 107, 230
Career Opportunities Program (COP),
130, 186, 247
Carey, Guin, 95
Carlyle, Thomas, 59–60
Carmichael, Stokely, 6
Carnegie Foundation, School Administra-
tors Internship Program, 186, 247, 261
Carpenter, George Sr., 70
Carr, Ron, 327, 342
Carr, Waggoner, 39
Carrizo Springs, election results (1970),
70
CASAA. *See* Citizens Association Serving
All Americans (CASAA)
Casarez, Mercedes Ruiz "Chachi," 132,
133, 171, 172, 178, 189; shooting inci-
dent, 291
Casey, Guin, 237
Casey, Rick, 264
Castillo, Humberto, 46, 50
Castillo, Victor, 170, 172, 198, 199, 338,
339
Castro, Fidel, 165, 180
Castro, Tony, on analysis of Gutiérrez,
56–57
Catlin, George E. G., 10
Cavada, Abel, 164, 166, 339, 340
Cavazos, Marcela, 176
El Centro de Salud (The Health Center):
funding for, 107, 297–99; job appoint-
ments, 157; CU representative, 168;

Cuevas as director of, 205; construction
of, 260, 300–301; success story, 312; Luz
Gutiérriez as director, 339
Chacon, Ernest, 164
charter reform (1969), staggering council
terms, 64, 72
Chávez, César, 56, 58, 159, 228, 230, 304
Chavez, John, 71
Chicanismo: and Chicano studies in
schools, 249; defined, 382*n4*
Chicano Movement, xi, xvii, 3, 55, 56;
"four horsemen" of, 58; Gutiérrez as
leader of, 58; during early years, 72;
Cristal as symbol of, 100; leaders of,
131; end of, 159–60; of the future, 377
Chicano Revolt in a Texas Town (Shockley),
xiii
Child Support Program, 211, 331
Church Women United, 258
citizen/civic participation. *See* participatory democracy
Citizens Association Serving All Americans (CASAA): establishment of, 40;
women's auxiliary, 40; Zavala County
election (1964), 40–42; opposition to
Teamsters, 44; city council election
(1965), 45–48; city council slate of candidates (1965), 45–46; city council elections (1967–1969), 49; coalition politics,
50; anti-RUP strategies, 66–67, 157; city
council elections (1970), 66–68
Citizens Committee for Better Government, 28, 29, 33–34, 44
city council elections (1961), 25
city council elections (1963). *See* electoral
revolt of 1963
city council elections (1965): election results, 46 (table); overthrow of PASSO,
45–48
city council elections (1967), election
results, 50 (table)
city council elections (1970): election results, 69 (table); RUP candidates, 64–
65. *See also* electoral revolt of 1970
city council elections (1971), 96–101; election results, 100
city council elections (1972), 103–6;
results, 105
city council elections (1973), 117–28;
results, 127
city council elections (1974), 129–33

426

Index

electoral revolt of 1970 (*continued*)
64–65; RUP and Winter Garden Project
campaign activities, 65–69; CASAA's
anti-RUP strategies, 66–68; intimidation by white employers, 68; aftermath,
71–72, 72–85; newspaper coverage, 71;
RUP power consolidation, 72–85; city
officials resign, 74, 75; impact of, 346
elitism, 142, 143, 149–50, 354; demosocratic elite, 143; circulation of elites,
148; competing elites, 183; power elites,
366–67
Elizondo, Susana, 296
endogenous, defined, 382*n*3
epilogue of Cristal experiment, 344–77
epoch of protest (1955–1974), xi, 3
Erkfitz, Gordon, 229
Esequiel, Marcos, 157, 176
Espinosa, Beatrice (wife of Manuel Espinosa), 140, 141
Espinosa, Manuel Jr., opposing Gutiérrez
for county judge, 136–37, 152
Espinosa, Rodolfo "Rudy" Jr.: county
commissioner elections (1972), 115, 118;
on La Raza Libre, 130; county elections
(1974), 134, 136; on job competition,
154; as "new guard" member, 162, 176;
county commissioner elections (1976),
187, 191–92; city council candidacy
(1977), 199; city council member, 200,
201; and CU alliance, 205, 206, 208; on
firing city manager Flores, 210; and Lo
Vaca gas crisis, 282; city council candidacy (1979), 319, 325; RUP alliance, 324;
as mayor, 326; on Lopez-Garza vendetta, 326; as asst. superintendent of
schools, 327; firing of, 335; on Gutiérrez
as political boss, 342; on the peaceful
revolution, 351
Esquivel, Rudy, 333
Esquivel, Urbano, 256
exogenous, defined, 382*n*3

Falcón, Moses, 28, 42, 44, 50
Fannon, Franz, 370
Fanon, Frantz, 218
Fantini, Mario, 7
Fausto, Manuel J., 312
Fernandez, Roberto, 237
Flores, Carmen: county elections candi-

dacy (1970), 80, 84; county elections
candidacy (1974), 134, 138, 310; as RUP
Gutierrista leader, 192; county elections
candidacy, (1978), 209, 313, 325; law-
suits against, 321, 324; county treasurer
salary reduction, 330
Flores, Cornelio, 175
Flores, Felipe, 171, 328, 335, 336
Flores, Griselda, 189
Flores, Henry, 130, 140, 141, 262
Flores, José Maria, 312
Flores, Juan, Mental Health Outreach Pro-
gram director, 210
Flores, Juan Jr., Barrio Club member, 179
Flores, Mague, 328
Flores, Margarita "Margaret," 319, 325,
335
Flores, Noe, 277
Flores, Raul T.: school board candidacy
(1974), 132–33; school board president,
171, 172, 173, 191, 192; call for resigna-
tion, 178; and Serna investigation, 189;
as city manager, 201, 281, 328, 336; fir-
ing of city manager, 210; and Lo Vaca
gas crisis, 281
Flores, Salmon, 107
Flores, Teresa, 74, 279
Fohlis, Adolph, 40
Ford, Gerald, 277
form of government, 9
Fourier, François, 9
Franklin, Claude Jr., 70
Freire, Paulo, 222, 231
Fry, John, 114–15
Fuente, Ezequiel de la, 179, 205, 207, 335,
336
Fuente, José de la, 43, 45, 46
Fuente, Ramón de la, 51, 80, 84, 257
Fuentes, Alberto Jr., 27, 34, 363

Galvan, Elvira, 292, 293
Galvan, José Luis, 188, 190
Galvan, Lucas "Luke," 293, 333
·Galván, Salvador G., 25, 31, 36
Gamez, Blanca, 196, 197, 199, 210
Gamez, Jesse "Jesús": as school district at-
torney, 74, 221, 223, 239; as MALDEF at-
torney, 106, 116; as RUP attorney, 135;
excessive legal fees, 152–53; and Bud-
weiser beer distributorship, 153–54,